THE NATURE OF MELANCHOLY

THE NATURE OF MELANCHOLY

From Aristotle to Kristeva

Edited by
Jennifer Radden
•

OXFORD
UNIVERSITY PRESS

2000

OXFORD
UNIVERSITY PRESS

Oxford   New York

Athens   Auckland   Bangkok   Bogotá   Buenos Aires   Calcutta
Cape Town   Chennai   Dar es Salaam   Delhi   Florence   Hong Kong   Istanbul
Karachi   Kuala Lumpur   Madrid   Melbourne   Mexico City   Mumbai
Nairobi   Paris   São Paulo   Singapore   Taipei   Tokyo   Toronto   Warsaw

and associated companies in
Berlin   Ibadan

Copyright © 2000 by Oxford University Press, Inc.

Published by Oxford University Press, Inc.
198 Madison Avenue, New York, New York 10016

Oxford is a registered trademark of Oxford University Press.

Library of Congress Cataloging-in-Publication Data
The nature of melancholy : from Aristotle to Kristeva / edited by
Jennifer Radden.
p.   cm.
Includes bibliographical references and index.
ISBN 0-19-512962-8
1. Melancholy.   I. Radden, Jennifer.
BF575.M44N38   2000
152.4—dc21   99-16828

1 3 5 7 9 8 6 4 2

Printed in the United States of America
on acid-free paper

To my children,
Tristram,
Beatrice,
and
Patrick

•

Preface

For most of western European history, melancholy was a central cultural idea, focusing, explaining, and organizing the way people saw the world and one another and framing social, medical, and epistemological norms. Today, in contrast, it is an insignificant category, of little interest to medicine or psychology, and without explanatory or organizing vitality. In homage to its past, I have gathered here selections from some of the most influential sources on melancholy in the long tradition preceding Freud's 1917 "Mourning and Melancholia," an essay that ushers in a new type of theorizing and represents, in certain respects, the completion of this tradition. These texts on melancholic states form the centerpiece of the book. (The terms *melancholic state, melancholy,* and *melancholia* are not distinguished in the following discussion; nor were they, in any consistent way, in past writing.) But I have also included a small number of later twentieth-century discussion on clinical depression.

Writing about melancholy has customarily been broad, directed not only toward defining but also toward remedying melancholy dispositions, states, and conditions. Some of these prescriptions make for interesting reading, and others are closely related to the nature and causes of melancholy. However, I chose the excerpts and texts that follow to introduce conceptual questions about melancholy—what it is, rather than what to do about it. My emphasis is on the categorization, definition, origin (or etiology), and phenomenological qualities of these states. On another principle of selection, I preferred longer excerpts to wider representation. Thus, one excerpt often stands in for a whole tradition of writing (a tradition I have attempted to at least sketch in my remarks preceding each selection).

The texts are presented in the order they were written, although not always in the order they were printed, and in English translation. Represented are the humoral theories of the Greek physicians; Aristotelian speculation about melancholy and inspiraton; the early church fathers' writing on the sin of acedia, that state of despondency that seems to have shaped later medieval conceptions of melancholy; the Arabic doctors who preserved Greek learning and returned it to western Europe in the early Middle Ages; female saints of the early and late Middle Ages concerned with understanding melancholia among cloistered women; Renaissance thinkers such as Ficino, Bright, and Burton, who devoted whole treatises to melancholy; seventeenth-century speculations on melancholy, witchcraft, and demonic possession; eighteenth-century classifications of melancholic states; attempts to explain melancholy with the new, naturalistic science; illustrations of melancholy in Romantic, symbolist, and decadent literary traditions; some of the classics of early psychiatry from the end of the nineteenth century and the very beginning of the twentieth century; and, finally, a selection to illustrate twentieth-century models: loss theories, cultural causation theories, and biomedical theories.

By the twentieth century, when melancholy has lost its definitive and vital role, we ignore past discussion of melancholy at some cost. But these discussions have special interest for us at the end of the twentieth century for several more specific reasons. Most immediately, we now possess authoritative, recent English translations and editions of almost all of these works, some constituting the very first complete English versions, and others revising and reviving material long out of print.

The second reason is that we approach the writing collected here equipped with new methodology and theories of knowledge. Contemporary epistemologies encourage us to revisit what we once believed we knew and to reevalute that knowledge. We are impelled to question both what we supposed we found in a text and what we supposed the text discovered in the world.

This material has particular allure in contemporary times for a third reason. Current nonmedical writing about depression, and even melancholy, abounds. Moreover, contemporary discussions in philosophy, psychology, cultural and feminist studies, and the history of ideas all introduce distinctions and perspectives that require us to reconsider earlier writing about melancholic states.

We are uniquely positioned to reevaluate these texts for a fourth reason. The majority of the writing on melancholy predates the artificial divisions we know today as the academic disciplines. Thus a rigorous analysis of the type of writing included here, and the cultural conceptions of melancholy it illustrates, requires an approach that is thoroughly interdisciplinary. A shift toward interdisciplinary scholarship during the last quarter of the twentieth century, seen in thinkers such as Michel Foucault and Sander Gilman, and in new fields such as women's studies, has equipped us with a model for interdisciplinary inquiry and analysis. Nowhere is this model more necessary than in the study of the long cultural "obsession" with melancholic states evidenced in the material collected here.

The history of melancholy and melancholia told through the texts from Aristotle to Freud is particularly evocative and intriguing. Reading these sources we discover a kind of conversation, or dialogue, conducted across centuries—and continents—as their authors interpret and respond to the classical, Arabic, and Renaissance sources on melancholy. Each author reads, and variously understands, Hippocrates, Galen, and Aristotle. Later, in the Renaissance period, Robert Burton reads Ficino and Timothie Bright, and in turn is read by every thinker who follows him, through the eighteenth and nineteenth centuries.

This iterative effect is deeply and perhaps unexpectedly conservative. The conversation changes languages, going from Greek to Arabic and Syrian before it emerges in medieval Latin and finally in the French, English, and German of the modern period. It also changes cultures, taking place in Asia Minor as well as on the European and American continents. With such changes we would expect older theories, meanings, and associations to be superseded and eventually replaced by newer conceptions. We would expect new ideas and structures to overwhelm the old. Suprisingly, however, little is lost. Widely divergent and incompatible causal accounts are introduced together. (Melancholy is seen to result from earthly things—bile and dryness; astronomical movements [especially those of the planet Saturn]; and supernatural influences, the work of the Devil. Particularly since the modern period, it is also regarded as the result of social and psychological occurrences—too much creativity, idleness, or grief.) More puzzling: different and contrary meanings of melancholy and melancholia seem to accumulate and coexist, creating ambiguity and resonance as the centuries go by. Melancholy is both a normal disposition and a sign of mental disturbance; it is both a feeling and a way of behaving. It is a nebulous mood but also a set of self-accusing beliefs.

With increasingly scientific thinking and more exact clinical medicine, some of the ambiguities surrounding the issue of what melancholy is, which have gone strangely unremarked through many centuries, can be seen to come into sudden focus. A discernible tension and struggle ensue, whereupon melancholia and clinical depression begin to pull apart from the contradictory, multifaceted, amorphous, rich, and resonant melancholy of past times.

Of the many themes and recurrent assumptions revealed through this series of texts, the strangest one to contemporary readers is probably the appeal to humoral states. *Melancholy* comes from two Greek words, *melas* (black) and *khole* (bile). Greek science had taught that there were four elements (earth, air, fire, and water) and conceived of health as a balanced relationship between four humors, fluids or substances present in the human body: blood, phlegm, black bile, and yellow bile. Variations in these humors explained normal variation in temperament from one person to another, as well as states of disorder in a given person. Articulated first by the Greek physician Hippocrates writing in the century B.C.E., affirmed by Aristotle, Galen, and the Arabic physicians, and maintained in some form until well into the eighteenth century was the notion that, as is its name suggests, melancholy is a disorder, or a characteristic disposition, of the spleen or atrabiliary glands, the organ or organs supposed to produce the thick, acrid fluid known as black bile. Collecting the diverse forms of melancholy in its net, this humoral theory persisted even when seemingly alternative explanations or etiologies, natural and supernatural, were offered. With the advent of modern medicine and science, the link between melancholy and black bile in the European tradition gradually weakened. A series of alternative casual accounts finally left no room for humoral explanations.

The texts included in this volume represent a single tradition, the western European one. But the humoral medicine grounding that tradition, it should be noted, was not unique to the West. Both Indian and Chinese medical authorities adopted analogous theories in the centuries that saw the emergence of Greek and Arabic humoral medicine. In India the Ayurveda tradition (*Ayurveda* means "knowledge of longevity") from the first and second centuries B.C.E. had a theory of five elements (*bhuta*): earth, water, fire, air, and ether; and three humors (*dosha*): wind, bile, and phlegm, thus corresponding to two of three humoral substances employed in the Greek-Arabic humoral system.[1] Another concept that is central to Ayurvedic medicine and Indian philosophy is the theory of three inherent qualities or modes of nature (*Tri-guna*). These qualities include *sattva,* variously translated as "light," "purity," or "goodness"; *jajas* (action, passion, energy), and *tamas* (darkness or inertia). Theories of the three *gunas* describe many things, including personalities, food, and action. Thus the "Tamsik" person, in the *Bhagavad Gita,* is portrayed as dull, lazy, and indifferent. In Chinese medicine from the first and second centuries B.C.E. we find an emphasis on imbalance that is similarly evocative of the humoral theories of the Greek-Arabic tradition. Health is sustained by the flow of pneuma (*qi*) in the body, which alters as it accommodates to internal and external circumstances.[2]

Cultural influences presumably explain the similarities between these systems, for the medieval Arabic scholars knew not only Greek but also Indian and Chinese medicine. (Elements of Chinese lore were introduced to Galen's theories by Avicenna, for example.) But such speculation awaits an authoritative work of scholarship tracing the exact links in this intercultural chain.

The images of melancholy reproduced here require a special explanation. Because melancholy was for hundreds of years a central cultural idea, it spawned a long and distinguished pictorial tradition. Some of the more important of these works, such as one of Dürer's *Melencholia* series, are reproduced here. They provide, at times, critical support for my introductory claims. (For an explication of their full significance and the rich and elaborate iconography of melancholy, the reader is directed to Klibansky, Panofsky, and Saxl's authoritative *Sat-*

urn and Melancholy: Studies in the History of Natural Philosophy, History, and Art [1964] and to Maser's edition and translation of Cesare Ripa's *Iconologia* from 1758 to 1760 [Maser, 1977]).

Even in nineteenth-century artworks this tradition continued, as Delacroix's portrait of the melancholic Romantic poet Tasso in the asylum, illustrates. By the nineteenth century, however, another kind of portrait of melancholia was also common, that illustrating medical textbooks. Engravings, drawings, paintings, and finally photographs now sought to convey the melancholic patient in sharply realistic terms. Examples of these more clinical images are also included here, and they serve to illustrate and support my claims about the changes in conceptions of melancholy and melancholic states during the nineteenth century. (Again, to fully appreciate the cultural meaning of these clinical illustrations, the reader should consult such works as Gilman's *The Faces of Madness: Hugh W. Diamond and the Origin of Psychiatric Photography* [1976], *Seeing the Insane* [1982], *Disease and Representation* [1988], and *Picturing Health and Illness* [1995]).

From the host of writing about clinical depression since Freud published his watershed essay on mourning and melancholia in 1917, the narrow selection included here was designed merely to illustrate some of the types of theorizing to be found; it does not claim to be more widely representative. Regrettably, this limited focus excludes much that is important and influential in twentieth-century writing, especially among clinical and phenomenological accounts of depression and related disorders. (The reader interested in such accounts is directed to Sir Aubrey Lewis's methodical and sensitive work, for example [in Lewis, 1934].)

Clinical depression as it is understood today bears similarities to the melancholy and melancholic states of earlier times. But the addition of this later writing on clinical depression must not be taken to suggest any unproblematic continuity between these two bodies of writing, nor an unproblematic identity between these two similar but perhaps not equivalent conditions.

My curiosity over these mental states was piqued early by a mother who held that only the shallowest or most self-deceived people escape bouts of depression. It was a somber view, but thought-provoking. Much later, Frank Keefe extolled—and embodied—the charm of merrie melancholie, which led me to the Elizabethans and Burton. Friends, family members, and students who experienced melancholy and sometimes clinical depression have offered a continuing education for me, and I appreciate their candid revelation of their suffering.

Many friends and colleagues, and kind strangers, have contributed more immediately to this volume. First, Stanley Jackson gave my project his blessing, and welcomed me into the company of melancholiologists. Amélie Rorty and Roger Haydon guided and encouraged me through the early stages of the project, as did Jerry Kroll, Jim Phillips, John Sadler, Louis Sass, and other friends from the executive council of the Association for the Advancement of Philosophy and Psychiatry. Later, astute clinicians, theoreticians, and historians of psychiatry helped me with parts of my text, particularly Alex Bodkin, Nassir Ghaemi, Joan Radden Fordyce, Elizabeth Lunbeck, and participants in the Richardson History of Psychiatry Research Seminar at the New York Hospital–Cornell Medical Center. Members of PHAEDRA—Jane Roland Martin, Beatrice Kipp Nelson, Susan Fransoza, Janet Farrell Smith, Ann Diller, and Barbara Houston—played their indispensable part as resources, critics and supporters. Faculty colleagues trained in English and history—Bob Greene, Woodruff Smith, and Richard Lyons—offered advice and suggestions. Barbara Baum Pollans and Sue Miller have each borne with me through, and deeply enriched and informed, my ruminations about representations of melancholy in the visual arts.

Helpful librarians have also contributed to this enterprise, particularly at The Boston Athenaeum, Harvard's Countway Library, McLean Hospital, and the Healey Library at the University of Massachusetts at Boston.

My research assistant and friend, Kim Lienesch, provided wonderfully reliable support, moral and practical, during the last year of hard work on this anthology. Peter Ohlin at Oxford University Press proved an exemplary editor, enthusiastic from the start and insightful and attentive without being intrusive. Will Moore has supervised the copyediting and production with patience and intelligence.

My very special thanks are owed to Martin Eisner and Nina Seidenman for undertaking original translations of Avicenna and Baudelaire, respectively.

And finally, my family: Frank, Tristram, Beatrice, and Patrick have been unfailingly supportive over this project, and I am indebted to each of them. Frank has read, edited and commented on draft after draft. Each of them has kept me laughing and has as well offered suggestions, ideas, and encouragement.

Boston, Massachusetts   J. R.
August 1999

Contents

THE NATURE OF MELANCHOLY

Introduction

From Melancholic States to Clinical Depression

WAS THE MELANCHOLY of the Renaissance close enough to what the ancients referred to by the same name to be regarded as its equivalent? Or was melancholy as a normal part of the human condition distinguished, during the Renaissance and later, from melancholia, the disorder identified by the Greeks? How much do any descriptions of melancholia as a disorder foreshadow what later came to be known as clinical depression? Should we accept the identification between centuries-old descriptions of melancholy and melancholia, on the one hand, and twentieth-century accounts of depression, on the other, when the term *depression* was not even in common use until the last part of the nineteenth century?[1]

Contemporary opinion is at variance over these issues, although in much medical and psychiatric writing today, questions such as these either go unasked, or their answers are assumed. The mere presence of documented melancholic states is accepted as proof that melancholia was a constant condition, as observable and universal an affliction as gout or gallstones, that underwent little but a name change with more recent references to clinical depression. One discussion casually notes, for example, that "until the late nineteenth century, melancholia was the term usually used to refer to the depressive syndrome" (Andreason, 1982:24). Similarly, Stanley Jackson's work makes little effort to challenge the alignment between melancholia and depression—although it is a close, scholarly interpretive reading of the texts on melancholia and depression through which Jackson finds, as he says, "a remarkable *consistency*" between the earlier and later writing. (Jackson, 1986:27, my emphasis). In contrast to these perhaps overready equations, another analysis even denies commonality to early uses of *melancholy* and early descriptions of melancholic states. Berrios and Porter's recent *History of Clinical Psychiatry* asserts, implausibly I believe, that up to the period of the Napoleonic Wars, "melancholia was but a rag-bag of insanity states whose *only* common denominator was the presence of few (as opposed to many) delusions," while "sadness and low affect (which were no doubt present in some cases) were not considered as definitory symptoms" (Berrios and Porter, 1998:385, my emphasis).

Because of this notable interpretative disagreement over issues as fundamental as whether melancholy was one thing or many, and whether melancholia and depression are the same thing; and because melancholy and depression give evidence of being shaped or "constructed" by pervasive cultural assumptions, a careful reading of the long literature on melancholy, melancholic states, and depression requires us to entertain such questions.

Until the last decades of the nineteenth century and the beginning of the twentieth century, the term *melancholy* appears to cover several quite different things—at the very least: fleeting moods, mental disorders ranging from severe to very mild, normal reactions, and long-term character traits. The texts on melancholy written before the end of the nineteenth century seem to indicate that, for most of its history, what today seem to be distinct and incompatible senses of melancholy coexisted. They went undistinguished and apparently unremarked; at least their coexistence was without tension. Only with the writing that ushered in the birth of modern psychology and psychiatry do we find melancholy, with all its ambiguity and multiplicity, pulling apart from melancholia and the clinical categories of depression that are the concern of twentieth-century psychiatry.

Melancholy's meaning was sharpened, constrained, and significantly transformed in the late nineteenth century and the early twentieth century as a consequence of relatively new categories, contrasts, and emphases. Some structures—notably, the faculty psychological division between affective states and cognitive states—acquired salience only since the "modern" period of the sixteenth and seventeenth centuries. Others, such as the category of essentially subjective attributes, acquired prominence with late nineteenth-century psychology and psychiatry.

The essay that follows contains four parts. The first part concerns themes that recur in the readings to follow: (1) the variety of forms melancholia takes and the diverse connotations of the terms *melancholy* and *melancholia;* (2) fear and sadness without cause as the distressing subjectivity most central to melancholic states; (3) the association between melancholy genius and creative energy; and (4) the link between melancholy and states of idleness. The second part focuses on aspects of this set of texts informed by distinctions and stresses brought to light by the scholarship of the late twentieth century: the category of melancholic states as affective; melancholic complaints as subjective and private (in contrast to behavioral, and so more directly observable by others); ontological commitments about the nature of melancholy; melancholic states as mood states; gender issues; and, finally, the themes of narcissism and loss. In the third part I sketch a nineteenth-century shift whereby the hitherto encompassing category of melancholy divides, leaving a sharper distinction between the despondent moods and temperamental differences of normal experience, on the one hand, and, on the other, the clinical disorder of melancholia, which has come to be associated with the clinical depression of our own time. In the fourth part I note themes and developments in post-Freudian analyses of the condition known in the twentieth century as depression or clinical depression, identifying a typology of explanatory theories.

Four Themes in Writing on Melancholy

Melancholia: One Meaning or Many?
One Condition or Many?

> The Tower of Babel never yielded such confusion of tongues as this Chaos of Melancholy doth variety of symptoms.
>
> Robert Burton, *Anatomy of Melancholy*

The analysis offered earlier suggests that if different and sometimes contrary meanings attach to *melancholy* and *melancholia,* and these accumulate and coexist, then the terms may refer to diverse phenomena as well as connoting disparate ideas. Samuel Johnson's famous dictionary reveals that several such meanings or ideas were distinguished by the eighteenth century, two referring to forms of mental disorder, and a third to more common and normal states (Johnson, [1755] 1805).

First, melancholy suggested any disease resulting from an imbalance of black bile. In this most general sense (found, for example, in the writing of Galen and Avicenna), melancholia named a wide range of medical disorders, including epilepsy and apoplexy. Second, Johnson notes a connotation whereby melancholia was "a kind of madness with the mind always fixed on one object." This definition apparently captures what had come to be known in the eighteenth century as a partial insanity, characterized by delusional thinking about some limited subject matter.[2] Less than fully disabling and less severe than complete madness, this was the *tristimania* of Benjamin Rush, and is suggested by Hogarth's melancholic man, seated on the stairs, who is set apart from the more florid madness surrounding him in Bedlam; see fig. 1). Finally, Johnson notes, melancholy meant a gloomy, pensive "temper" or habitual disposition, such as we find in Samuel Butler's sketch of the melancholy "character."

Medieval illustrations of melancholy as one of the four humors typically blur such differences, as we might expect. The dejected central figure from the Augsburg Calender (fig. 2) might depict as much a normal man of sad and gloomy outlook as a victim of melancholic disorder. But it is unclear how sharply these several meanings were separated at all, at least before the eighteenth century. The notion of "adust," or burnt, melancholy—believed to result from a heating of the hypochondriacal organs, which sent smoky vapors to cloud and darken the brain and its functions—was sometimes used to identify abnormal as distinct from

Figure 1. William Hogarth, *A Rake's Progress,* plate 8, "Bedlam" (engraving, 1735). The Royal Collection, copyright © 1999, Her Majesty Queen Elizabeth II.

more normal states. (Robert Burton makes use of this concept, for example.) And attempts were sometimes made to divide the clinical forms of melancholia, although no authoritative division or consistent usage resulted. Whether a need for sharp divisions was even widely recognized remains doubtful, however. Reviewing the literary evidence of Elizabethan times, for example, one authority concludes that "there is no clear distinction in the layman's mind between the melancholy temperament and the melancholic disease. There is no clear knowledge of the differentia which mark the various melancholic disorders" (Babb, 1951:71).

Painted in 1532, Lucas Cranach's *Melancholia* (fig. 3) departs in several ways from the conventional iconography of melancholy from his period. Rather than dejected, the female figure here appears thoughtful, whittling at a stick as she follows the antics of children (or putti) playing nearby. In the distance above these figures is an unsettling scene: naked figures ride animals in a maniacal or, it has been speculated, *demoniacal* procession (Klibansky, Panofsky, and Saxl, 1964). Cranach's paintings on melancholy have resisted efforts at definitive in-

Figure 2. *Melancholicus* (1490), from the Augsburg Calender.

Figure 3. *Melancholy, An Allegory* (oil, 1532), by Lucas Cranach the Elder.

terpretation. Arguably, the apparently contradictory elements in this work are included precisely to convey the contradictory nature and elusive scope of melancholy. Certainly this mysterious image presents the array of associations made so evident in writing about melancholy: the reflective and intellectual, the playful, and the frankly delusional.

Again and again, writers on melancholy in the long tradition initiated by the Greek physicians and philosophers and ending in the nineteenth century seem to despair of capturing its disparate forms. That they are disparate is emphasized by Timothie Bright, author of the first full-length English work on melancholy, published in 1586. Bright's treatise, he announces, will discuss the "diverse manners of taking the name of melancholie, and whereto the name being one, is applied diverslie." Shakespeare's famous enumeration in *As You Like It* (iv. 1), while primarily jesting and ironic, also conveys the endless variety of melancholies:

> I have neither the scholar's melancholy, which is emulation;
> nor the musician's, which is fantastical; nor the courtier's,
> which is proud; nor the soldier's, which is ambitious; nor
> the lawyer's, which is politic; nor the lady's, which is nice;
> nor the lover's, which is all of these; but it is a melancholy
> of mine own, compounded of many simples, extracted
> from many objects.

That this diversity eluded attempts to find a shared form in a verbal definition was recognized as a problem. "Thou Proteus to abus'd Mankind," wrote Alexander Pope's courtly friend Anne of Winchilsea in the eighteenth century, "Who never yet thy real Cause cou'd find, Or fix thee to remain in one continued Shape." Burton's frustrations on this point a century earlier are particularly well known: Struggling to find coherence in the plethora of "symptoms" melancholy displayed, he compares his task to that of capturing a many-headed beast. The matter, as he puts it, is "diverse and confused" so that "I conclude of our melancholy species, as many Politicians do of their pure forms of Commonwealths, Monarchies, Aristocracies, Democracies, are most famous in contemplation, but in practice they are temperate and usually mixed" ([1621] 1989:1.170). Some authors sought to rein in melancholy by delineating its limits, what it was not. It was not that strange state of lycanthropy, in which one believed oneself a wolf, for example. Nor was it the suffering associated with a sense of sin. Bright, particularly, among the authors collected in this volume, explored the contrast between melancholy and forms of moral suffering to better capture the meaning of melancholy. The afflicted conscience is distinguishable from melancholy because it "taketh nothing of the body" or of the humor, but instead reflects a direct wound in the soul by an evil spirit sent by God. The sixteenth-century Spanish abbess Teresa of Avila carefully separates melancholy from other, divinely caused experiences of mental distress. The pain caused by God's "setting the soul on fire" is quite unlike the suffering of melancholy, which is the Devil's work, she explains.

Those who attempt to define and circumscribe in the long tradition of writing about melancholy seem at once convinced of the importance and centrality of the human category which is their subject matter, while doubtful they can recognize or capture its full span. Contemporary philosophical insights would allow us to say that even without a single encompassing definition for melancholy, this condition might usefully be regarded as one thing rather than many. But the question of one or many is also complicated by the humoral, astrological, and supernatural explanations of melancholy offered through the ages. From the Greeks to the Elizabethans, the humors, particularly, served to conjoin normal dispositions with more severe states of apparent disorder.

Humoral theories allowed variations in the black bile to determine causally the order and arrangement of dispositions, subjective experiences, and behavior, explaining many things: long-term tendencies in psychologically well-adjusted individuals, character traits in disturbed individuals, episodic but normal reactions to stressful circumstances, and episodic and florid mental disorder found, for instance, in "adust," or burnt, melancholy.

Not as long-lasting but almost as influential on the writers of the modern era were astrological explanations, particularly the link between melancholy and the planet Saturn. Most writers of the later Middle Ages and the Renaissance accepted that melancholy in each of its forms stood in some special relationship to Saturn, and that astrological movements played a causal role. Here, then, was another unifying feature. Like the alleged link between supernatural, particularly demonic, forces and melancholy, astrological theories provided a causal explanation that—while false—served to unify the disparate forms of melancholy in early modern conceptions of psychology.

In addition to causal theories that unified the seemingly disparate manifestations of melancholy, Michel Foucault and others have drawn attention to similarities between the *qualities* of coldness, blackness, dryness, and heaviness shared by the humor and by melancholy subjectivity, providing a "symbolic unity," as Foucault puts it.[3] The notion of a symbolic unity is introduced to explain how "scientific" analyses in the seventeenth century diverged from empirical canons, even when these were quite well understood. The ordinary notion of causality ("causality of substances") was replaced, at least during the seventeenth century, by a "movement" or "mechanics" of qualities, whereby one thing affects another merely because of the relationship between the qualities of each. And, "thus freed from a confining substantial basis," qualities—of heat, cold, dryness and moisture, colors—"would be able to play an organizing and integrating role in the notion of melancholia. . . . The morbid entity was not *defined* from observed signs nor from supposed causes; but somewhere between, and beyond both, it was *perceived* as a certain qualitative coherence, which had its own laws of transmission, of development, and of transformation" ([1961] 1973: 120). To summarize Foucault's thesis: Those states, traits, and responses sharing the title of melancholy did so in part because they shared the same "profile," not because they were believed to have a shared cause. (Symbolic unity may not have been limited to thinking about the qualities of the humors. Some authorities have also identified a shift in the medical conception of melancholy resting on changes in its associations, including changes derived from the mechanistic science of the seventeenth century. Notions of black bile and smoky vapors had engendered references to the patient as dark and gloomy in his melancholic state. Then, with the emergence of mechanical explanations, such references fade slightly from clinical accounts, to be replaced by "the idea of the *slowing of the patient's circulation* . . . associated with a slow and dejected state" [Jackson, 1986:130, my emphasis]).

When we reach Philippe Pinel's account of melancholia at the opening of the nineteenth century, all reference to bile and humors is gone. The observation of signs and symptoms alone, not obscure theorizing, can teach us about mental disorder, Pinel insists. And yet the heterogeneity of melancholia stubbornly remains, even in Pinel's analysis. Unified neither by symbolic unity nor by causes (he believed there was a multitude of these, ranging from "moral" effects like the horror of the French Revolution to cranial shape and menstruation), Pinel's notion of melancholia is as loose and uncentered as those of earlier authors. Despite a crisp definition (melancholia is "delirium exclusively upon one subject"), Pinel's enumeration of symptoms and characteristics still encompasses such variety that we struggle to find unity in his description.

Fear and Sadness ("Without Cause")

> . . . it seems correct that Hippocrates classified all [melancholic patients'] symptoms into two groups: fear and despondency.
>
> Galen, *On The Affected Parts*

From the earliest Hippocratic writing, melancholy is seen to involve states of fear and sadness, and this account of melancholic subjectivity varies little through the centuries. Galen affirms that although "each [melancholic] patient acts quite differently than the others, all of them exhibit fear or despondency." Bright, in 1586, states that for the most part the perturbations of melancholy "are sadde and fearefull, and such as rise of them as distrust, doubt, diffidence, or dispaire" (1596:99). Burton names sadness and fear without a cause as the true characters and inseparable companions of melancholy. By 1672, Thomas Willis is offering a more ostensibly "scientific" explanation of the fear and sadness of melancholia without challenging their centrality as symptoms. Melancholy is not only "a Distemper of the Brain and Spirits dwelling in it," he remarks, but "also of the Praecordia, and of the Blood therein inkindled, from thence sent into the whole Body: and as it produces there a Delirium or idle talking, so here *fear and sadness*" (Willis, 1672:191, my emphasis). Writing in the nineteenth century, the French authority Jean-Etienne-Dominique Esquirol defined melancholia, or *lypemania,* as he renamed it, as "a cerebral malady . . . sustained by *a passion of a sad, debilitating or oppressive character*" (Esquirol, 1845:203, my emphasis).

Subjective states of apprehension and sadness are also part of the pictorial tradition. The great Italian artist and illustrator Cesare Ripa added a commentary to explain his portrait *Melancholicus* (fig. 4). Behind the main figure of the melancholy scholar, a man is shown about to throw himself into the river to represent, Ripa notes, the melancholic man's "tendency to gloom and a sense of futility and despair" (Ripa, [1603] 1971:79).

Figure 4. *Melancholicus* (engraving, 1603), from Cesare Ripa's *Iconologia.*

This tradition of casting fear and sadness as vital to melancholy seems sufficient to call for a qualification on the remark by Berrios and Porter, quoted earlier, in which they deny that sadness and low affect were considered as "definitory symptoms" before the Napoleonic period (Berrios and Porter, 1995). Perhaps these feelings were something less than *defining* symptoms of melancholia. Indeed, as we have seen, for a diagnosis of melancholia they were sometimes separately sufficient rather than each necessary and together sufficient. Nonetheless, in contrast to twentieth-century theories of depression that sometimes allow diagnosis in the absence of *any* subjective distress, fear and sadness are conspicuously *central* features of melancholic states in the long tradition of writing about melancholy documented here.

With their origins in Greek allusions to the groundless despondency associated with melancholy, and prominent in later writers like Bright and Burton, this fear and sadness were frequently portrayed as without cause or without sufficient cause or occasion. Jackson has noted that emphasis on the groundless nature of the fear and sadness of melancholia declined in the eighteenth century. But it returned in nineteenth-century analyses such as Mercier's, in the influential *Dictionary of Psychological Medicine,* edited by Tuke, where melancholia is characterized by "a feeling of misery which is *in excess of what is justified by the circumstances*" (Mercier, 1892,2:787, my emphasis.) (A fuller discussion of this notion of fear and sadness without cause occurs in the second part of this essay.)

Melancholy, Genius, and Creative Energy.

> Why is it that all men who have become outstanding in philosophy, statesmanship, poetry or the arts are melancholic, or are infected by the diseases arising from black bile?
>
> Aristotle (or Follower of Aristotle), *Problems*

A third emphasis is on melancholy's alleged link with some kind of compensatory quality of brilliance, intellectual refinement, genius, or creative energy. The famous question from Aristotle's *Problems* sets the stage. This question is echoed throughout the centuries until the eighteenth, although with subtle shifts. From enabling agent, for example, melancholy becomes the noxious side effect of creativity and intellectual prowess—"spleen." By the nineteenth century, emphasis on the compensations of melancholy returns again; we see it forcefully conveyed in Delacroix's portrayal of the elevated suffering of the poet Tasso (fig. 5). But by the nineteenth century this theme emerges in several forms as melancholy itself pulls apart from melancholia, the clinical disease. Two of these transformations deserve particular attention: the link between melancholy and creative achievement that emerged with the Italian humanism of the Renaissance, and nineteenth-century

Figure 5. *Tasso in the House of the Insane* (oil, 1839), by Eugene Delacroix.

revivals of the idea that melancholy brings compensating moods of energy, creativity, and brilliance.

The earlier reawakening and transformation of this melancholic brilliance is documented by Raymond Klibansky, Erwin Panofsky, and Fritz Saxl (1964). The glorification of melancholy and the birth of the modern notion of genius can be traced to Florentine Neoplatonism, and particularly to the work of Marsilio Ficino, himself the author of a book devoted to the melancholy man of genius, and an important influence on English writers such as Burton. For Italian humanists like Ficino, melancholy was required to accommodate several new ideas. Absent from Aristotelian thinking had been Christian assumptions about the freedom of the will. Also new was the astrological emphasis of the day, which linked melancholy with those born under the sign of the planet Saturn (as Ficino had been). Finally, the old theme of the compensatory value of melancholy was sharpened with the introduction of the category of the man of genius, a category absent in earlier classical or medieval understanding (though certainly anticipated by Aristotle).

Italian humanists such as Ficino not only recognized the polarity in melancholy, observe Klibansky, Panofsky, and Saxl,

> they valued it because they saw in it the main feature of the newly discovered "genius." There was therefore a double renaissance: firstly, of the Neoplatonic notion of Saturn, according to which the highest of the planets embodied, and also bestowed, the highest and noblest faculties of the soul, reason and speculation; and secondly, of the "Aristotelian" doctrine of melancholy, according to which all great men were melancholics. (1964:274)[4]

The pictorial tradition of representing melancholia in works such as Dürer's series *Melencholia* (fig. 6) and Ripa's portraits *Melancholicus* (see

Figure 6. *Melencholia I* (engraving, 1514), by Albrecht Dürer.

fig. 4) faithfully captures these themes. The cheek resting on the hand, and the shadowed or darkened face in Dürer's work allude to the blackness of mood and countenance associated with melancholy from earlier traditions, but the geometer's tools indicate learned pursuits and inspiration. And of his own work, Ripa has written: "The open book represents the melancholic man's tendency to be a scholar, engrossed in all sorts of studies," ([1603] 1971:79).

The Aristotelian doctrine tying melancholy to more glamorous attributes was thus embellished and expanded with its revival in Renaissance Italy, and with the English writing on melancholy of the sixteenth and seventeen centuries, such as Bright's and Burton's. (The compensatory aspect of this equation is sharply etched by Milton at the very close of his poem "Il Penseroso," in which, after an enumeration of the intellectual and spiritual satisfactions he anticipates for his mature years, he concludes by striking a deal with their originator, Melancholy: "These pleasures, Melancholy, give, /And I with thee will choose to live."

The link with genius was also revived in the literary movement of the late eighteenth and early nineteenth centuries. Again the suffering of melancholy was associated with greatness; again it was idealized, as inherently valuable and even pleasurable, although dark and painful. The melancholy man was one who felt more deeply, saw more clearly, and came closer to the sublime than ordinary mortals. As we see in Keats's writing, exalted pleasures were reserved for those subject to the suffering of melancholy.[5]

At the same time as European Romanticism was glorifying melancholy and the man of sensibility subject to it, psychiatric classification was placing emphasis on the cyclical nature of affective complaints. Now even the depression and despair of mental disorder were followed by phases of enlivened mood, energy, and creativity. Earlier medical writing had from time to time noted the swings between melancholy and more elevated moods. But, in general, melancholia and mania had been classified as two unrelated disorders. (Indeed, in early classifications, melancholia and mania, together with the condition known as *phrenitis,* constituted the three broadest categories of mental disorder.) And even allusions to mania (or, as it was sometimes translated into English, "madness") as a part or aspect of melancholia are confusing because of the broad use by which melancholia sometimes covered every kind of mental disorder. When mania was identified with, or as an aspect of, melancholia, this broader usage may have been intended—a point ignored in some recent efforts to "discover" manic-depression in earlier eras.

The nineteenth century saw a renewed and more thoroughgoing development of the notion of cyclical conditions, however. Although for him melancholia and mania are distinct "species of mental derangement," Philippe Pinel, in 1806, asks whether melancholia of several years' standing may not degenerate into mania, and he describes a "thorough revolution of character" whereby those who were melancholic may eventually become "maniacs." In 1818 Johann Christian Heinroth interpreted Boerhaave to have held that mania was merely a more acute degree of melancholia, a position to which the French clinician Esquirol later subscribed. Along the lines of Pinel's earlier speculation, in contrast, Heinroth proposed that mania was apt to give way to melancholia when each were distinct and separate diseases. In 1854, two students of Esquirol, Jules Baillarger and Jean Pierre Falret, independently proposed a new disorder, distinct from both melancholia and mania but characterized by cyclical phases of melancholic and manic states: *la folie à double forme* (Baillarger) or *la folie circulaire* (Falret). This disorder category, known as *circular insanity* in England, was to have a central place in the psychiatric nosology of the second half of the nineteenth century.

Emil Kraepelin was at first slow to adopt this category. But by the sixth edition of his textbook in 1899, he had acknowledge a circular insanity and even acknowledged its centrality by grouping it, with other manic states and depressed states, under the rubric of "manic-depressive insanity." Not only the ostensibly bipolar and circular affective disorders but also unipolar conditions like depression and melancholia fell under this rubric.

The suggestion that all forms of mood disorder were actually or potentially circular and even bipolar expressed in this classificatory decision of Kraepelin's has not survived in later twentieth-century classification, at least not in the American Psychiatric Association's *Diagnostic and Statistical Manual* (*DSM*). Although ambiguity and uncertainty still surround the relationship between circularity and polarity in affective disorder, the cyclical bipolar disorder usually takes its place today alongside monophasic and unipolar depression and mania and under the more general category of affective or mood disorders.[6] Gone for the most part, along with the decline of the term *melancholia,* is the notion—so attuned to the Romantic ideas of its time—of a compensating energy and brilliance lurking behind *all* depressive disorder.

Interestingly, our present decade's renewed interest in bipolar disorder has again emphasized the compensatory aspect of the less extreme "hypomanic" and even manic phases undergone by those subject to cyclical mood disorders. Kay Redfield Jamison's writing on manic-depression and the artistic temperament suggests this connection, as does widespread interest in the frequency of bipolar disorder among those who have shown artistic brilliance (Jamison, 1993). If not a desirable feature of the vitality and creativity we all yearn for, depression may yet be an acceptable cost for those whose lives are blessed by genius. Far from the noxious by-product of the creative or sensitive character captured in the eighteenth-century conception of spleen, depressive mood states in the artistic temperament of today are honored in a manner reminiscent of Renaissance attitudes. Jamison speaks almost reverently of the occasionally "exhilarating and powerfully creative force" of manic-depressive illness, which "gives a touch of fire" to many of those who experience it.

Melancholy, Idleness, Labor, and Domination

> There is no greater cause of melancholy than idleness, no better cure than business.
>
> Robert Burton, *Anatomy of Melancholy*

Another of melancholy's associations is with the state of idleness, with aristocratic and courtly boredom, and with the curative value of action and labor. These themes have been explored by the contemporary German sociologist Wolf Lepenies, and they are identifiable at least as far back as Burton's famous observation that there is no greater cause of melancholy than idleness, no better cure than business. Lepenies is concerned to show that melancholy, or at least an enervating nostalgia and ennui, has been the fate of whole classes of people made idle by social, political, and economic arrangements. Melancholy was a bourgeois form of behavior abandoned by all but the intelligentsia with the advent of capitalism. Thus, "Reflection is defused in action, and with it the incentive to become melancholic; conversely action (labor) can counteract melancholy . . . labor . . . permitted the space of introversion to be left to those who could not or would not become economically active, namely the free-floating intelligentsia" (Lepenies, 1992:180).

Whether or not we adopt Lepenies's economic analysis, it remains true that early modern and later writing repeatedly proposed work as a palliative against melancholy. The danger of idleness recurs in the practical remedies of Benjamin Rush, who recommends "employment, or business of some kind," explaining that "man was made to be active" (Rush, 1812:117). Similarly, Samuel Smiles, writing in the middle of the nineteenth century, notes that the only remedy for the tendency toward "discontent, unhappiness, inaction and reverie" that he names "green sickness," which can be likened to melancholy, is "action, work, and bodily occupation of any sort" (Smiles, 1862:256). This conviction was expressed even by medical writers of the nineteenth century, such as Janet and Freud—although the so-called rest cure, recommended by Kraepelin, for example, in the treatment of involutional melancholia, and prescribed especially for middle- and upper-class women, also achieved popularity. Work was valuable primarily for men; for women it could be harmful.

An ironic comment on these attitudes toward melancholic tendencies and idleness comes from the early twentieth-century American author Charlotte Perkins Gilman. For many years, she has written, she suffered from a severe and continuous nervous breakdown "tending to melancholia—and beyond." Others have identified her disorder as "neurasthenia," although the distinction between the two categories of melancholia and neurasthenia was hardly clear, (see Gosling, 1987). During the third year of this trouble, "in devout faith and some faint stir of hope," she went to a noted specialist in nervous diseases. This was S. Weir Mitchell, whose famous cure requiring absolute rest in isolation and overfeeding is propounded in *Fat and Blood and How to Make Them* (Weir Mitchell, 1877). "This wise man," Gilman writes,

> put me to bed and applied the rest cure, to which a still-good physique responded so promptly that he concluded there was nothing much the matter with me, and sent me home with solemn advice to "live as domestic a life as possible," to "have but two hours' intellectual life a day," and "never to touch pen, brush, or pencil again" as long as I lived. This was in 1887. "I went home and obeyed those directions for some three months, and came so near the borderline of utter mental ruin that I could see over.
>
> Then, using the remnants of intelligence that remained, and helped by a wise friend, I cast the noted specialist's advice to the winds and went to work again—work, the normal life of every human being; work, in which is joy and growth and service, without which one is a pauper and a parasite—ultimately recovering some measure of power. (Gilman, [1913] 1980:19–20)

Gilman's description illustrates the emerging "gendering" of melancholia during the last decades of the nineteenth century and the first decade of the twentieth century. Increasingly, mental disorder in general and certain disorders in particular, including melancholia, were becoming women's complaints.

Cutting across the themes that link melancholia with idleness (although not perhaps boredom) is another association, as this passage reveals: the effect of meaningless labor and of oppression. In twentieth-century feminist writing, drudgery and domination are sometimes taken to explain women's depression. Thus we must qualify. Idleness may cause melancholy, as many have supposed, and work may cure it, as Gilman suggests. But it is meaningful work, and work outside of a system of domination and oppression to which we must look if work is to be a palliative against melancholy.

These four themes (the variety of forms melancholia takes and the broad meaning of the terms *melancholy* and *melancholia;* fear and sadness without cause as the distressing subjectivity most central to melancholic states; the association between melancholy genius and creative energy; and, finally, the link between melancholy and states of idleness) occur consistently in the writing about melancholic states collected here. What this means is another matter, however. And we should be particularly wary of regarding these recurrent themes as evidence of any unchanging disorder on the model of physical diseases like gout and gallstones. Until Kraepelin's writing, few of the descriptions excerpted here reflect anything approaching empirical and clinical "observation" as, however skeptically, we construe it today. Most were reached after close and careful reading of the accumulated writing on melancholy from past eras, with direct clinical observation, to a greater and lesser extent, forming their secondary source.

Melancholy through Our Contemporary Lens

Melancholy, Melancholia, and Depression as Affective States and Kraepelinian Diseases

Whatever their other associations, melancholy and depression are today viewed as states suffered, not sought—conditions beyond voluntary control. Our mental categories are framed by the faculty divisions only solidified in psychology and philosophy since the seventeenth and eighteenth centuries. (In faculty psychology, separable mental functions such a thinking, imagining, feeling, and willing were thought to be usefully conceptualized, if not explained, by positing mental faculties corresponding to each.) Other cultures and traditions and our own culture at earlier times can be shown to have employed different divisions, separating the soul and the person in other ways. Thus, examining the premodern texts collected here, we must be attentive to the "modernist" framing by which depression is today considered a mood or feeling and beyond the power of the will. And through a comparison of earlier with later writing we may identify the influence of these ways of constructing and dividing mental states and abilities.

As an illustration, consider the early medieval references to the monastic failing of despondency and inertia known as *acedia,* or *accidia,* and the related failing of the dejection, sadness, or sorrow known as *tristitia.* Scholars debate the exact relation between these failings and melancholy, but their closeness cannot be denied. Later, acedia was also allied to or identified with the sin of sloth, or *desidia* portrayed in Breughel's image of the sinful, slothful world (fig. 7). As Cassian's discussion makes clear, acedia was a fate to be resisted. The true Christian athlete "should hasten to expel this disease . . . and should strive against this most evil spirit." If acedia is regarded as a temptation and later a sin, then one might suppose it to be a state that is within our power to prevent. And if acedia were akin to melancholy, perhaps melancholy also once eluded the category of a state suffered passively.

May we conclude acedia was a state over which its sufferer exercised control? Not quite, apparently. Its later designation as a cardinal sin undoubtedly meant that there were moral injunctions against acedia. Yet one source for the answer we seek here is the handbooks of penance, or "penitentials," that became popular in the thirteenth century. Such handbooks frequently implied that confession was a form of

Figure 7. *Desidia* ("Sloth"; drawing, 1557), by Pieter Breughel. The accompanying Dutch text reads: "Sloth makes powerless and dries out the nerves (sinews) so that man is good for nothing."

healing and the sins of the penitent were afflictions for which, not literally, but employing a medical metaphor, the sufferer was to be treated and cured, rather than chastised. This suggests that acedia was never a state over which its sufferer was thought to exercise full control. Rather, it fell midway between a disease to which its victims haplessly succumbed and a bad habit (Jackson, 1986:70). It resists the modernist categories to which we are inclined to subject it.

Earlier faculty psychological divisions, such as that between thought and imagination, can sometimes be identified in works of classification from the eighteenth century like Kant's. But by the classifications of the following century the grid imposed by the cognitive and affective faculties is widely and consistently evident and acquires greater prominence. For example, it is found in aspects of the construction of melancholia or depression viewed as a clinical disorder that took place with the emergence of clinical psychiatry at the end of the nineteenth century. Thus, the category of affective faculties appears to have influenced a fundamental psychiatric division. Still found in the American Psychiatric Association's *DSM* and in the World Health Organization's *International Classification of Diseases* of the twentieth century, this is the division between disorders of mood or affect (of which depression is one) and other disorders.

The late nineteenth century saw the emergence of psychiatry as a distinct medical specialization, and with it a number of more or less authoritative psychiatric diagnostic classifications. Of these classificatory schemes, Kraepelin's system as it is developed through the editions of his famous *Textbook of Psychiatry* stands out as the most systematic and exhaustive, as the most influential in its time, and as the most clinically based.[7] Because of these and other factors, Kraepelin's scheme became the most obvious source for subsequent twentieth-century classifications such as those referred to earlier.

Kraepelin's ascendancy came at the end of a century of great change in thinking about every aspect of mental disorder. The growing medicalization of madness, the shift, documented by Foucault, from a conception of mental disorder as "unreason" to one in which it is a tamed, muted medical condition, has been widely portrayed. During the first half of the nineteenth century, the "birth of the asylum" (Foucault [1961] 1973) on the continent of Europe, and various English acts of Parliament, such as the Lunatics Act of 1845, reflected the "medical monopoly" (Scull, 1979) on madness. This gathering monopoly was based not on the success of medical treatments, historians have shown, so much as on the emerging power of institutionalized medicine, together with an increasingly confident materialism and physiological psychology that posited exact parallels between mental and physical disorders. Localized lesions of the brain, it had come to be held, must be the source of mental disorder.[8] While purely psychological "moral treatment" was not yet dismissed as worthless in curing the insane, only medical doctors understood the brain; doctors, then, became the rightful purveyors of care to the mentally afflicted.

Nowhere is this growing medicalization of madness as vividly conveyed as in the clinical illustrations that had now come to accompany medical works. The practice of illustration was itself a nineteenth-century innovation (Gilman, 1988). But now the conventions also had been transformed. From the careful engravings of Esquirol's atlas (figs. 8 and 9) to the photographs of Henri Dagonet (1823–1902) and Hugh Diamond (fig. 10), we see pictorial efforts directed at the detached, scientific view of the patient regarded as a clinical case. As psychiatry became a distinct subdiscipline of clinical medicine, with its own practices and subject matter, writing about mental disorder became more circumscribed. The distinction between melancholy moods, states, and dispositions attributable to most people, and melancholia as mental disorder—the distinction, that is, which remains blurred and unremarked in earlier writing about melancholy—has been emphasized, and serves to delineate the subject matter of such texts.

At the time of these broader changes, the relation between melancholia and depression also apparently underwent significant change. The term *melancholia* had hitherto served to indicate a range of conditions, some closer to today's delusional disorders, others closer to

Figure 8. *Lypemaniaque* ("Melancholia"; 1838), from the atlas of J. E. D. Esquirol's *Des maladies mentales*.

what we would distinguish as an affective or mood disorder. (One eighteenth-century usage cast melancholia as a form of delusional thinking about some limited subject matter, a partial insanity, for example, in line with the eighteenth-century tendency to classify all mental disturbance as forms of cognitive disorder.) The narrower and more recent term *depression* originally referred only to a quality or symptom of melancholia. Thus, writing in 1890, the English doctor Charles Mercier (1852–1918), noted: "The most marked and conscious feeling of the malady—the leading symptom—is the depression of spirits which always characterizes it." Again, writing of simple melancholia two years later in the *Dictionary of Psychological Medicine,* edited by Tuke, Mercier spoke of a condition in which "the depression of feeling is unattended by delusion" (Mercier 1892:789). By the time the term *depression* entered Kraepelin's writing, in contrast, it had come to be used for a syndrome or symptom cluster, rather than merely one symptom

Figure 9. *Lypemaniaque* ("Melancholia"; 1838), from the atlas of J. E. D. Esquirol's *Des maladies mentales.*

Figure 10. *Portrait of a Woman Suffering Suicidal Melancholy* (photograph, 1856), by Hugh Diamond.

of the broader category of melancholia. When, in 1886, Kraepelin revised his nosological scheme in line with the separation between more and less optimistic prognoses, he used the term *periodic psychoses* for the collection of affective conditions, which included mania, melancholia, and circular insanity. A year later, in the sixth edition of the *Textbook,* these became the *manic-depressive psychoses,* which included *depressed states.* By the time of the eighth edition excerpted here, published between 1909 and 1913, the depressive forms include five kinds of melancholia, divided primarily in terms of severity. *Depression* had taken its place beside—and would soon eclipse—"melancholia" as the name of a kind of symptom cluster or disease.

Kraepelin's era also saw increased confidence in the belief that mental disorder was analogous to brain disease and that specific, localized lesions in the brain would eventually be identified with psychiatric symptom clusters. In Germany this belief was known as *somatism*. The discovery of the relation between syphilis and the dementing symptoms that were its sequelae (known as *general paresis of the insane*) provided the model. It fostered the assumption that, like physical diseases, mental diseases were a class of natural kinds: discrete and uniform symptom clusters that afforded ready and reliable identification.

The analysis of diseases as syndromal entities and natural kinds was not of nineteenth-century origin. It is evident, for example, as early as the writing of Thomas Sydenham in England in the seventeenth century, who analogized diseases with the "determinate kinds" of botany. Nonetheless, it reached its high point in the historical era during which psychiatric classification came of age.

The influence of Wilhelm Griesinger, whose work is excepted here, and that of Rudolph Virchow, another important figure in the history of medicine, is reflected in these ideas. In 1845 Griesinger had published his somatist treatise, arguing, against the "moralism" of the time, that psychological diseases are brain diseases and that the pathological anatomy of the nervous system and brain would prove to be the source of all mental or psychical disorder. Virchow had established the principles of cellular pathology in 1858, insisting that all diseases are localized. This German somatism, while controversial, made a deep and lasting impression in America at the end of the nineteenth century. As the historian Elizabeth Lunbeck remarks, "However elusive the paradigm of general paresis would prove, the medical model of disease it underwrote attained a hegemonic position within psychiatric thought [allowing] practitioners to order their observations as if disease—with its attendant etiology, course, and outcome—underlay what they could see" (1994:117).

Two legacies from earlier eras acquired new significance when wedded to the nascent science of psychiatry, and together they encouraged a division of the brain and mental functioning into broad categories, including those concerned with cognition and those concerned with affection. One was *the legacy from faculty psychology* and later phrenology, in which functional divisions had been reified and concretized. Affection, or the affective faculty, corresponded to a localized part of the brain. Damage to or disease of that part of the brain accounted for diseases of the passions or the affective faculty. A second but related legacy was a strong set of *associations* growing out of the earlier, eighteenth-century distinction between reason and passion. These associations served to further polarize the mental functions of thinking or cognition, on the one hand, and feeling or affection, on the other.

The first of these legacies is well expressed in the division of mental diseases enunciated by Rufus Wyman, an American clinician of the first half of the nineteenth century. Wyman was the physician superintendent of McLean Asylum at Charlestown, a branch of the Massachusetts General Hospital, between 1818 and 1835. Writers on mental philosophy, Wyman remarks, "arrange the mental operations or states under two heads, one of which regards our knowledge, the other our feelings. The former includes the functions of the intellect. . . . The latter includes the affections, emotions or passions, or the pathetical powers or states. . . . This division of the mental states or functions has suggested a corresponding division of mental diseases of the intellect and diseases of the passions" (1830:810). Writing fifteen years later in Germany, Griesinger speaks in almost the same terms

> Observation leads to the conclusion that there are two grand groups . . . of mental anomalies, which represent the two most essential varieties of insanity. In the one, the insanity consists in the morbid production, governing, and persistence of *emotions* and *emotional states*. . . . In the other, the insanity consists in disorders of intellect and will, which . . . exhibit, without profound emotional excitement, an *independent,* tranquil, false mode of thought and of will. . . . ([1867] 1965:207)

This passage is particularly important because of its influence on the Kraepelinian classification to follow. In his belief that mood disorder was an entity per se, it has been asserted, Griesinger prepared the ground for the Kraepelinian view (Berrios and Beer, 1994:25).

Faculty psychology reflected functional divisions, as these passages from Wyman and Griesinger make clear. In addition, faculty psychology invited a reification of the functional units entitled faculties, suggesting that the intellect and the passions corresponded to parts of the brain, each separately subject to disease. The flourishing "science" of phrenology, which localized all functions and traits, probably hastened this tendency to suppose real parts of the brain corresponded to each functional category (Radden, 1996b). Nonetheless, not all who made use of faculty psychology to draw functional categories took the further reifying step. For instance, Henry Maudsley, an influential English psychiatrist of this period, succeeded in avoiding it, warning that "the different forms of insanity are *not actual pathological entities*" (Maudsley, 1867:323, my emphasis). This was because for him *all* insanity was inaugurated by a disturbance of the affective life.

The final division between disorders of affect (Kraepelin's manic-depressive diseases, which included melancholia) and disorders of the cognitive faculties (Kraepelin's dementia praecox) required a narrowing of the hitherto broader melancholia. Earlier than the nineteenth century, as we have seen, melancholia was often associated with fixed, false beliefs, or delusions, that is, with cognitive defects. But now the delusional features of mental disorder were increasingly separated from the affective ones. And, as this suggests, there was a growing emphasis during the first half of the nineteenth century on the affective symptoms of melancholia, together with a corresponding neglect of its more cognitive delusional features (Jackson, 1986).

Kraepelin attempted to model psychiatry on the natural sciences: the task of psychiatric classification involved discovering and naming the naturally occurring kinds of mental disorder. He was famous for the care with which he established his generalizations on the basis of the long-term case studies he accumulated. Yet intent on a process of what he took to be discovering natural kinds, convinced that the disease entities of psychiatry would present symptom clusters in the same way as organic diseases appeared to do, uncritical in his embrace of the division between cognition and affection, Kraepelin failed to recognize the possibility that the broad categories of affection and cognition were being imposed upon, rather than discovered in, his observation of the symptom clusters his patients suffered.

Interestingly, because of Maudsley's conviction that the course of every form of insanity included disorder of affectivity, he was not prey to Kraepelin's error. But more than that, Maudsley also seems to have anticipated that error, and he warns of it with spectacular clarity. There is in the human mind, he remarks, "a sufficiently strong propensity not only to make divisions in knowledge where there are none in nature, and then to impose the divisions upon nature, making the reality thus comfortable to the idea, but to go further, and to convert the generalizations made from observation into positive entities, permitting for the future these artificial creations to tyrannize over the understanding" (1867:323–24).

The second legacy from earlier eras inviting a division separating off disorders of affection was an entrenched set of *associations* clustering around cognition, reason, and thought, on the one side, and affection, passion, and feeling, on the other. With the appearance of modern scientific method in the sixteenth and seventeenth centuries had come an emphasis on the distinction between human subjectivity and value in contrast to the observable and measurable objects of scientific study (Lloyd, 1984). Reason alone was regarded as the means to discovering an objective and value-free reality; in this process reason's opposition to feeling and passion, which represented forces beyond their subject's control and eluding rational understanding, acquired greater stress. Later, additional associations gathered around each pole: reason represented maleness and the masculine; passion was identified with femaleness and the feminine. (In Hegel's writing in the nineteenth century, for instance, male and female roles were organized around this contrast. Reason was associated with the public realm, passion with the private and domestic.) The anthropologist Catherine Lutz has documented the full range of associations that came to attach to the notion of affective states in the European Enlightenment period. They include not only the feminine, the private, and the domestic but also estrangement, irrationality, unintended and uncontrolled action, danger and vulnerability, physicality, subjectivity, and value (Lutz, 1986). Such associations can be found to have made their way into medical writing from the period, moreover. By the midcentury, Thomas Laycock, professor medicine at Edinburgh University, is analogizing women to children in their "affectability" when he writes his book on the nervous diseases of women, and Brudenell Carter, a nineteenth-century authority on hysteria, speaks of a "natural conformation" that causes women to *feel,* under circumstances where men *think,* and builds on this allegedly natural division a proneness to hysteria in women and to hypochondria in men (Laycock, 1840:131; Carter, 1853:33). Out of this combination of ideas and assumptions of the late nineteenth century came the classificatory schema—still one of the most basic divisions in Western psychiatric nosological maps today—that separates disorders (or, as Kraepelin has it, "diseases") of affect from other conditions.[9]

The ascendancy of the distinction between affective and other disorders outlined here did not take place without a struggle. One alternative classificatory heuristic posited a single type of psychosis, inaugurated by a phase of melancholia. This unitary psychosis hypothesis had had its supporters even among eighteenth-century thinkers, although in a rather different guise, and was associated with several important figures in the nineteenth century, including the early Griesinger.[10] Moreover, although none achieved lasting influence, classifications employing alternative faculty psychology divisions were also proposed during the nineteenth-century period, positing diseases of the memory, will, personality, imagination, and moral faculties (see, for example, Ribot, 1881, 1893, 1885).

The influence of the mental faculties can also be found in early twentieth-century psychological accounts of emotion, such as the James-Lange theory, with their attempts to equate emotions with involuntary, noncognitive states of feeling and sensation. This view of emotion has been challenged both by cognitivists such as Aaron Beck and by "cognitivist" theories of emotion long maintained within philosophy in which emotions comprise cognitive and affective elements. Beck's analysis is causal. The mood states associated with depression are responses to distorted cognitive states. Therapy addresses and alters these cognitive distortions to alleviate despondent affective responses. In contrast, philosophical cognitivist theories of emotion elevate the cognitive states to the status not of causes but of "constituents," the essential features whose presence, either solely or together with affective features, serves to define the emotions in question. (Thus, for example, my response is identified as "regret" rather than "sadness" in part, or wholly, by the cognitive specification of its object as some past event for which I have some degree of responsibility.)[11]

Psychoanalytic thinking always and conspicuously avoided these mental faculty divisions between the cognitive and the affective, however. And nowhere is this better illustrated than in Freud's elaborate account of the mind afflicted with melancholia. The new, or at least sharpened, association of depression with loss and self-loathing that emerges from "Mourning and Melancholia" introduces a more closely formulated belief or cognitive element to the subjective states under discussion. Earlier accounts of a simple, almost moodlike subjectivity of nebulous fear and sorrow are at odds with the frame of mind of Freud's melancholiac. So Freud's innovative emphasis on the cognitive attitudes toward the self in melancholia introduces a further turn, new to any psychiatric thinking about melancholia and depression, and not consonant with the noncognitivist emphasis of the two decades of nonpsychoanalytic psychiatric thinking about melancholic states that preceded the publication of "Mourning and Melancholia" in 1917. (Further discussion of Freud's innovations is to be found later in this essay.)

Melancholy as an Essentially Subjective Condition

Several aspects of the subjectivity of melancholy and melancholia require attention. One concerns feelings of melancholy when these are construed as momentary, felt, affective *occurrences,* in contrast to *more habitual states.* Burton hints at something of this distinction when he speaks of "that transitory melancholy which goes and comes upon every small occasion of sorrow, need, sickness, trouble, fear, grief, passion or perturbation of the mind" ([1621] 1989:1.136). Burton's concern here, however, is to separate what he regards as normal, everyday subjective and behavioral manifestations of melancholy from more entrenched and more serious conditions. Thus, for Burton, melancholy is either "in disposition" or "in habit." The universal disposition from which no man living is free is ascribed when a man is "dull, sad, sour, lumpish, ill-disposed, solitary, any way moved or displeased." In contrast, this other kind of melancholy "is a habit, . . . a chronic or continuate disease, a settled humour . . . not errant, but fixed" ([1621] 1989:1.136).

Burton's division emphasizes the frequency and persistence of the subjective mood of melancholy. It is perhaps confusing to us in using the term *disposition* to name the state cast in contrast to the "habit" of melancholy, which is a more enduring trait—for nowadays the term *disposition* is allied to the habitual tendency. Moreover, the settled humor Burton describes as subject for treatment may merely manifest itself in more frequent occurrences of the "sad, sour, lumpish, solitary" feelings found, as he says, in all men.

Burton here reveals one distinction, that between transitory and more settled forms of melancholy. Another distinction, however, remains unemphasized. This is the division we would today mark between the subjective and the behavioral. The subjective captures what is able to be introspected, that which we alone know directly from our privileged and exclusive access to our own mental and psychological states. The behavioral is that which may be known from the detached

perspective of third-person observation, without the subject's coopera-
tion or verbal report. Like the modernist division between reason and
passion, the division between the subjective and the behavioral is a
product of a particular era, in this case the nineteenth century, and of a
particular set of purposes and practices, those of psychology.[12] As psychology separated from philosophy to become a distinct and distinctly
empirical discipline, the experimentalists and behaviorists did battle
with the introspectionists. These same contrasting sets of method and
assumption were to harden during the twentieth century into the division between experimental and phenomenological approaches. Burton
captures some of the subjectivity of melancholy in the *Anatomy,* but his
focus is not on this methodological distinction. To be sad at least, if not
to be sour, is to experience an essentially subjective condition determined, finally, from one's own subjective standpoint. In contrast,
lumpishness and solitary tendencies may be attributed to oneself by
others: "lumpish" and "solitary" are more behavioral terms.

The notion of melancholy as a subjective mood associated with literary work captures both the sense of a state that is transitory and passing
and the sense of an essentially subjective state. It was this notion that
gave rise to adjectival uses of *melancholy* such as Johnson notes in his
dictionary (quoted earlier). *Melancholy* as "a gloomy, pensive, discontented temper," yields the adjective *melancholy,* indicating "gloomy" or
"dismal," which is applied not only to persons but also to landscape and
events.

Klibansky, Panofsky, and Saxl identify in lyric writing, narrative
poetry, and prose romances of the postmedieval era a poetic sense of
melancholy as a passing subjective mood state. This poetic melancholy
contrasts with the notions of melancholy as both a disease and as a temperament. The poetic notion of melancholy as a temporary mood of
sadness and distress came partially to eclipse these earlier meanings. In
all modern European literature, these authors attempt to show, the
word *melancholy* lost the meaning of a quality and acquired instead the
meaning of a "mood" that could be transferred to inanimate objects.
Now we find references not only to melancholy attitudes but also to
melancholy scenes, miens, and states of affairs.

The importance of melancholy subjectivity seems to gather force
with the notion of Romantic melancholy that emerged at the end of the
eighteenth century. The man of melancholy in Romantic writing was,
like the suffering Werther, all feeling, all sensibility. At times exaggerated emphasis fell on feelings: feelings of solitude, darkness, grief, suffering, despair, longing, and elegiac sadness. Painters of the era, such as
Caspar David Friedrich, capture this range of responses and moods in
dark, haunting landscapes (fig. 11.). (This pictorial tradition is still to be
found; here it is illustrated in the brooding and plaintive *Melancholy* of
Edvard Munch [fig. 12] and in contemporary artist Sue Miller's uncompromising and stark tree [fig. 13]).

Figure 11. *The Monk by the Sea* (oil, 1809–1810), by C. D. Friedrich.

Figure 12. *Melancholy* ("Evening"; woodcut, 1896), by Edvard Munch.

Figure 13. *Tree* (oil, 1997), by Sue Miller.

Of the way the early modern poetic melancholy was transformed into late eighteenth-century Romantic sensibility, it has been observed that the pressure of the religious conflicts of the sixteenth century rendered melancholy "a merciless reality, before whom men trembled . . . and whom they tried in vain to banish by a thousand antidotes and consolatory treatises." Only later was it possible for the imagination to "transfigure [melancholy] into an ideal condition, inherently pleasurable, however painful—a condition which by the continually renewed tension between depression and exaltation, unhappiness and 'apartness,' horror of death and increased awareness of life, could impart a new vitality to drama, poetry and art" (Klibansky, Panofsky, and Saxl, 1964:233). And it was not until after the excesses of the Gothic Revival "graveyard school" of poetry, with its ruins, churchyards, cloisters, yews, and ghosts, and after writing about melancholy had become stale in the convention, that Romanticism's intensely personal and subjective utterance of "profound individual sorrow" was possible (238). (Only with the acuteness and vitality of early nineteenth-century writing such as Keats's, these authors believe, do we find writing on melancholy to match the Elizabethans').

Alongside this flowering of Romantic ideas of melancholy, with their emphasis on subjectivity, modern psychiatry was born. But in modern psychiatry's final and most definitive nineteenth-century analysis, that of Kraepelin's system of classification, the importance of melancholic subjectivity is diminished, and the behavioral and bodily are privileged over the subjective.

The distinction between subjective and behavioral is reflected in the contrast between a symptom-based and a sign-based diagnostic emphasis in clinical medicine. The *symptom* is a patient's complaint, a description of inner states; a *sign,* in contrast, is an outwardly observable feature of behavior or bodily condition. (A pain is a symptom, a rash a sign.) Maudsley's (1867) analysis of melancholia reproduced in this volume is psychological and symptom-based. Sixteen years later, Kraepelin's characterization of depression is more notably sign-based, de-emphasizing the subjective in favor of the behavioral.

The trend foreshadowed in this Kraepelinian emphasis on more behavioral aspects of clinical depression is understandable. Later psychiatric nosology had cause to diminish the importance of what is sometimes known as the mood factor in depression: against subjective symptoms like felt sadness, directly observable signs like sleeplessness and weight loss better fitted prevailing conceptions of scientific rigor. By the third edition of the American Psychiatric Association's *DSM* in 1980, clinical depression was characterized as much or more by certain behavioral manifestations, now sometimes known as *vegetative signs,* as by the moods and feelings it involved: by a slowing or agitation of movement, by fatigue, loss of appetite, and insomnia. Moreover, with this emphasis on behavioral and directly observable signs came refinement of the notion of depression. Now *agitated depression,* marked by restless overactivity, was distinguished from *retarded depression,* where activity was slowed down or inhibited. Nor has this trend diminished. For example, the fourth edition of the *Diagnostic Statistical Manual* has continued this behavioral emphasis, despite some resistance.[13] And a recent empirical study observes that psychomotor disturbance is "both the most consistently suggested and most discriminating feature, especially when measured as an observed sign," across *"all assessment approaches to melancholia"* (Parker and Hadzi-Pavlovic, 1996:25, my emphasis).

Perceived scientific rigor and a detached, objective, clinical gaze were also the goal of psychiatric photography. Proponents of this new field of illustration such as John Conolly, an influential mid-nineteenth-century English doctor and asylum keeper, noted that psychiatric photographs such as those produced by Henri Dagonet and Hugh Diamond (see fig. 9), surpassed the clinical engraving in earlier use due to their "singular fidelity" to the patients' physiognomy (Conolly, [1858] 1976, quoted by Gilman, 1976:168).

And the nineteenth-century emphasis was all on capturing the patient's facial features, whether through painting such as Géricault's searching portraits from the madhouse (fig. 14), engraving, or photography. It was presupposed that *the face held the key to the patient's psychological states,* and thus to the disorder (Gilman, 1988). On such a system of assumptions, the felt symptoms take a central place. Twentieth-century psychiatric photography, in contrast, often conceals the face (fig. 15). Such a shift in the conventions governing psychiatric photography might be explained by a recent respect for patient privacy. Yet this turn of attention from the full face seems to reflect, as it may also have hastened, the later era's elevation of the bodily and behavioral signs of depression over its subjective symptoms.

A theme in contemporary feminist writing on melancholy and depression emphasizes the contrast between loquacious male melancholy and the mute suffering (or, as Juliana Schiesari has it, the mourning) of women (Schiesari, 1992). Stress on women's loss of speech is to be found in the work of Julia Kristeva, Judith Butler, and Luce Irigaray, as well as in Lacanian ideas. Women's estrangement from language, in

Figure 14. *Insane Woman (Envy)* (oil, 1821–24), by Théodore Géricault.

Figure 15. "Darkness at noon" (commercial photograph, ca. 1980), *The Archives of General Psychiatry*.

turn, is explained by an estrangement from the self, associated with the inevitably masculine "author" of the "self-narrative." Without embarking here on an analysis of these complex ideas, I would note that a disorder increasingly understood in terms of its behavioral manifestations will also serve to "silence" its sufferers. As, and to the extent that, emphasis is placed on observable signs over subjective and voiced symptoms, so the silence of that mute suffering must be even more profound. Whether as its cause, or one of its effects, the trend toward a behavioral analysis of clinical depression would likely accompany the "silencing" of depression.

Ontological Commitments

What *is* a mental disorder such as depression? Recent writing in medical psychiatry often implies that depressive symptoms are at most the felt effects of an underlying dysfunctional state of the brain which has caused, and so causally explains, the felt symptoms and more readily observed signs. On an *etiological* Kraepelinian analysis, depression encompasses this total disease entity, an underlying brain state, together with a set of depressive signs and symptoms.

By contrast, a non-etiological analysis is said to be *descriptive*. Depression alludes to the symptoms—and perhaps signs—themselves, and nothing more. By privileging depressive subjectivity so that the symptoms of depression are necessary and sufficient conditions for an ascription of depression, some recent writing, for instance in cultural studies, embraces a descriptive analysis of depression. (I hasten to add that purely descriptive analyses do not deny the presence of underlying brain states. But on such analyses depressive symptoms are related to underlying brain states no differently from the way all psychological states are. [The nature of this relation is debated by philosophers, of course.])[14]

Significant issues in the epidemiology of depression rest on these differences in what is sometimes known as the ontology of mental disorder, the fundamental question of what mental disorder is. In the field of crosscultural psychiatry, pioneered by Arthur Kleinman, depression and related disorders are said to occur in China, but in a different cultural idiom: typically, in China at least, they are "somatized" appearing in the guise of bodily complaints such as headaches, inertia and dizziness. Adhering to a descriptive analysis of depression, we will be hard pressed to find between the disheartened states of Western depression and the headaches and dizziness of Chinese experience enough similarity to warrant identifying these two widely different symptom clusters. On an etiological analysis—which posits an antecedent, underlying state or condition in the brain of the depressed person—the evidence of a symptom cluster around headaches and dizziness in China confirms the view of depression as a universal condition, since the presence of depression might well result in symptoms varying according to the idiom of different cultures in which they occur and ranging from Chinese dizziness to Western despair.[15]

So-named masked depression provides a second example of what is at stake in choosing etiological over descriptive accounts. Studies of depression as gender-linked are sometimes challenged by the claim that men's depression finds expression in idioms of substance abuse, violence, and other antisocial behavior (Real, 1997). To hypothesize that due to differential socialization, the same underlying brain state causes one sort of symptom of depression in women and another in men, for example, implies that men's acting-out behavior is an expression of a different but parallel idiom to women's sadness and despair. (It may not: Arguably, men experience the same subjective distress that women do, albeit more fleetingly, and their differential socialization merely requires them to express their distress differently.) Only if depression is understood to preserve the subjective experience as necessary and sufficient will depression perhaps retain its strong gender link as a women's disorder. On an etiological and nondescriptive analysis of depression, there will be no difficulty allowing that men's depression compares with women's in extent and severity, regardless of whether men experience subjective distress comparable to women's.

These ontological considerations also enter into our discussion in a broader way. Is it useful to say that earlier accounts of melancholic states describe the same thing as today's descriptions of clinical depression? Part of the answer to this question rests on the degree of similarity between earlier and later descriptions. There are similarities between some of the mood states described throughout the centuries; indeed, there are also similarities between earlier humoral accounts and today's biochemical imbalance theorizing. On the other hand, there are also notable differences. Many people are struck by the similarities; yet like the glass which is at once half empty and half full, this range of similarities and differences might provoke a contrary response.

But the balance between similarities and differences is not all there is to this matter. At stake, in addition, are ontological decisions. Adherence to a descriptive analysis may discourage us from identifying early melancholy with clinical depression in light of the undeniable differences between them. Yet these same differences would be easily accommodated on an etiological account; leaving untroubled the identity claim that early melancholy was the same as clinical depression.

Melancholic States as Mood States

While familiar as central symptoms and subjective characteristics of melancholy and melancholia, fear and sadness without cause are states requiring analysis. In particular, the phrase "without cause" is ambiguous. We need to ask, without any cause, or without sufficient cause? It has been customary to read Burton and those who followed him to say the latter, yet a case can be made for emphasizing the former, in order to highlight that the subjective state so captured is a nebulous and pervasive mood rather than an affective state with sharper cognitive content. The contemporary philosophical distinction between moods and emotions frequently drawn by analytic philosophers is the one identified here.[16] If fear and sadness are *without sufficient cause,* they are directed toward or are over or about something which the sufferer understands to be so or to exist. They are accompanied, that is, by what are known as "intentional" objects. In this case (without sufficient cause), however, their objects do not appear to warrant the degree of feeling attributed to them. An example of fear and sadness without sufficient cause would be excessive fear over a clearly minimal danger, or excessive distress over a trifling event. In contrast, if melancholic fear and sadness are *entirely without* an identifiable cause (they have causes, of course, but not causes known to their subject, or are not felt to be what the mood is about), they are not over or about anything in particular. If so, then they are moods. By their nature such moods are elusive and unbounded, blurring into other states such as nostalgia and ennui and into bodily sensations. In a recent account of the features distinguishing moods, Gabriele Taylor explains,

> Moods are objectless in the sense that there is no specific thing, situation, or event which can be picked out and described independently of the mood itself and which the state is "about" . . . When in a mood-state . . . it is not a specific situation [a person] will see in a certain light . . . ; her mood will color everything in her perception. It is a constitutive feature of moods that they involve a way of seeing the world. They are distinguished from each other by the particular way in which the world is seen: in moods of elation everything is perceived as attractive and attainable, in moods of depression everything appears gloomy or irritating, the worthwhile out of one's reach (Taylor, 1996:165)

This distinction between emotions and moods reflects Brentano's theory of intentionality, which emerged only at the end of the nineteenth century. Nonetheless, it is a distinction that can be retrospectively applied. And such application suggests that Renaissance and later writing about melancholia concerns a much nebulous, pervasive, and nonintentional moods of fear and sadness (no cause) as it does fear and sadness in excess of their occasions (without sufficient cause). Medical accounts of the early modern period contain reference to fears and sorrows both "without cause" and "without apparent cause" (Jackson, 1986:107). This is readily illustrated through the copious casenotebooks of Richard Napier (1559–1634), presented and analyzed in contemporary times by McDonald (1981). Napier was a medical man and clergyman who saw many patients "troubled in mind" during the first thirty years of the seventeenth century. Napier's melancholic patients sometimes suffered what appear to have been delusions and hallucinations, although demonic possession may have complicated people's attitudes toward, and preparedness to acknowledge, these more severe symptoms (McDonald, 1981:155–66). But the majority complained of melancholy, mopishness (a kind of dullness and sour failure of interest commonly attributed during the seventeenth century), anxiety, fear, gloom, sadness, despair, heavyheartedness, inertia, and disinterest. (His patient was "solitary . . . and will do nothing," in Napier's words). Much here suggests moods (without cause) rather than more cognitive and belief-based states (without sufficient cause).

Although nebulous, moods of anxiety, fear, and apprehension form a cluster distinguishable from moods of despondency, despair, and sadness. And like earlier Greek and Renaissance symptom descriptions, early modern accounts such as Napier's give equal emphasis to each kind of feeling. With the more medical focus of the nineteenth century, however, descriptions of melancholia seem to place stronger emphasis on the second cluster. The "depressed" mood of early psychiatry is more of groundless sadness and despondency than of groundless fear and anxiety. Arguably, this narrowing is invited by new diagnostic categories. Neurasthenia and hysteria, and later obsessional and anxiety disorders, are more closely associated with groundless fears.

Gender: Depressive Subjectivity as Feminine

Reinforcing the isolation of diseases of the passions from other disease categories was a set of associations, of which one association was with the female and the feminine. This legacy directs us to the intriguing twentieth-century "gendering" of depression understood as a clinical and subclinical disorder.

Not only in epidemiological fact but also in cultural imagination, today's depression sufferer seems to be female. Yet in one identifiable pattern, beginning at least as early as medieval times and still evident in eighteenth-century writing, women were considered not more but less susceptible to melancholy than men. One of Galen's contemporaries in second-century Rome, Areteus of Cappadocia, believed that men are the more frequent sufferers of melancholy, as did the Arabic doctor Avicenna. So does Johann Weyer, writing in the sixteenth century (although by using women for case illustration more frequently than he does men, Weyer seems to belie his own generalization). Benjamin Rush notes that partial insanity, or *tristimania,* affects men more than women (1812:77). Sometimes a qualification is added: because of their nature, women are more severely affected when they experience melancholia.

This alignment between men and melancholic states is also to be found in eighteenth-century nonmedical writing, although it was not always accepted without objection. First, in a poem entitled "On a Certain Lady at Court" (1735), Alexander Pope identified "the thing that's most uncommon," a reasonable woman. Such an unusual woman, he remarks, would be

> Not warped by passion, awed by rumour,
> Not grave through pride, or gay through folly,
> An equal mixture of good humour,
> And sensible soft melancholy.

Sensible, soft melancholy, we may infer, is more common in men. Writing sixty years later than Pope's poem, that astute observer of cultural roles Mary Wollstonecraft identifies the same alignment between maleness and melancholy. She, however, protests the suggestion, which she attributes to an (unnamed) contemporary author, that "durable," steady, and *valuable* passions, like melancholy, are masculine traits, while women are subject only to fickle, changeable, and valueless passions (Wollstonecraft, [1792] 1988:34).

In apparent contradiction to this gender pattern linking melancholy with the masculine, iconic conventions between the early modern and the eighteenth-century period seem to favor the notion of "Dame Melancholy" and "Dame Tristesse" as a woman, Dürer's famous series on melancholia (see fig. 6) offering perhaps the best known, but by no means the only, example (fig. 16). However, experts on such images insist that these dames represented, at most, the "feminine" within man, and a metaphor of male sorrow (Klibansky, Panofsky, and Saxl, 1964:349–50; Schiesari, 1992; Benjamin, 1977); or the *cause* and *source* of male melancholy (Benjamin, 1977:151). (The latter is strongly suggested in figure 17, where, personified as a female, melancholy robs male reason of its powers.) Moreover, the link that reconnects melancholy with genius through the Italian humanist period inevitably represents melancholy in the *man* of genius and genius in the *man* of melancholy. The category of genius had no more place for women than had the category of melancholy.[17]

Drawing from the writing and iconic representation of the pre-nineteenth-century period to determine actual prevalence rates of melancholia in women and men must be speculative and imprecise. It does seem fairly widely accepted that sometime late in the nineteenth century, along with the emergence of melancholia as something close to today's depression, melancholic subjectivity becomes—or becomes increasingly and identifiably—feminine. This link between women, the feminine, and present-day depression has two aspects, distinguishable in principle but entwined in practice: the first is associative, the second, however, is epidemiological, concerning the actual prevalence of disorder in women and men.

The affective life of emotions, moods, and feelings was deemed unruly, unreliable, capricious, and beyond voluntary control; it was irrational and disordered, it was associated with the bodily, with subjectivity, and with the feminine. These associations, as we have seen, had been accruing since the eighteenth century. (Generalizations such as this oversimplify, of course; for example, eighteenth-century attitudes distinguished among the different passions. Nonetheless, this generalization is not a distortion. The more enduring passions, which were admired, were those associated with the masculine.)

Undeniably, the overall effect of this set of dualities was to identify the feminine and women with madness more generally. But some evi-

Figure 16. *Malinconia* ("Melancholy"; engraving, 1603), from Cesare Ripa's *Iconologia*.

Figure 17. *Melancholy and Reason* (drawing, 1565), by Alain Chartier.

dence, at least, encourages us to consider that melancholia and depression may have been gender-linked. For example, because of women's "constitutional" gentleness and the mobility of their sensations and desires," Esquirol remarks in 1845, as well as "by the little application which they make with reference to any matter," women seem at first sight to be less vulnerable to melancholy than men. And yet, he asks, are not "the extreme susceptibility and sedentary life of our women" the predisposing causes of this malady? "Are not women under the control of influences to which men are strangers; such as menstruation, pregnancy, confinement and nursing?" The amorous passions "so active in women," together with religion, "which is a veritable passion with many [women]," render girls, widows, and menopausal women prone to erotic and religious melancholy (Esquirol, 1845:211). Esquirol's discussion of the prevalence of women suffering melancholia, or what he termed *lypemania,* reveals a particularly explicit part of this evidence. Later in the century, however, customs of diagnostic classification obscured such straightforward correlations.

Although he offers case studies of both sexes in his essay on mourning and melancholia, Freud does not align melancholia in any clear way with the feminine. Indeed, a case can be made that his account of melancholic subjectivity was associated with the masculine rather than the feminine, just as earlier Renaissance traditions had been (Schiesari, 1992). Freud's contemporary Kraepelin, in contrast, while he aimed to be an empirical scientist through and through, reveals occasional glimpses of gender links connecting the affective with the feminine in his voluminous writing about manic-depression. Among ourselves, he remarks, referring to the patient population at his institution, "about 70% of the patients (suffering manic depressive insanity) belong to the female sex *with its greater emotional excitability"* (Kraepelin, 1920:174, my emphasis).

Lunbeck's discussion of the case materials of the Boston Psychopathic Hospital from this period illustrates the gender association a different way: she shows case descriptions of manic-depression that note the unmanly and effeminate traits of men who suffered this disorder (Lunbeck 1994:149–50). The cultural trope on which such judgments rest was a pervasive one. We see it in Samuel Smiles's revulsion over the degenerate, sickly, and *unmanly* excesses of feeling associated with "Wertherism" and "green sickness." This reaction to Romantic notions was influential, at least in America, and it allowed no place for manly men among the passive, helpless, unhappy subjects of melancholic states.

As early as Kraepelin's writing, the epidemiological identification between women and the affective disorder known as manic-depression had been established, as the preceding passage from Kraepelin illustrates. This is not to be confused, however, with the more general link between women and madness associated with the second half of the nineteenth century.

Concerning that more general link, a review of historical records from Victorian England concludes that this era saw insanity's "'feminization': . . . the mid–nineteenth century is the period when the predominance of women among the institutionalized insane first becomes a statistically verifiable phenomenon" (Showalter, 1985:52). The accuracy of such assertions has recently been challenged (Scull, 1998), but several factors seem to confirm a perceived, if not an actual, gender link in this period. The rising numbers of women believed diagnosed as suffering mental disorder were a source of concern on the part of reformers (Showalter, 1985). More significantly, attributions to the phases of female reproductive biology—puberty, pregnancy, childbirth, menopause—of women's proneness to mental disorder was now receiving emphasis in medical texts. Vulnerability to mental disorder had come to be seen as women's biological destiny.

This connection between the female reproductive system and the brain was believed to make women the victims of "periodicity." Thus, according to one medical authority of the time, women became insane during pregnancy, after parturition, during lactation, at the age when menses first appear, and at menopause; in fact, "The sympathetic connection existing between the brain and the uterus is plainly seen by the most casual observer" (Blandford, 1871:69). Most familiar to us today from the several maladies to which women's bodies made them prone, was a range of symptoms occurring after confinement and known as "puerperal" (childbirth) insanity or fever, of which at least some involved mild or severe depression leading to suicide and even infanticide. In puerperal insanity can be traced the sources of today's postpartum depression. Other authorities, including Maudsley, drew direct connections between women's reproductive cycles and melancholia in particular.

Despite Esquirol's bold insistence that melancholia was a women's disorder, late nineteenth-century historical data must be approached very cautiously. The more specific link between women and affective disorders such as melancholia or depression is not so easily discerned as the larger alignment between women and madness. The link between women and "manic-depressive illness" is supported in historical records and affirmed by present-day historians of psychiatry. Lunbeck, for example, speaking at least of North America, concludes that "from the start, manic-depressive insanity was interpreted as a peculiarly female malady" (1994:148).[18] But this Kraepelinian classification, which includes melancholia as one of several subdivisions of manic-depressive illness, does not permit us to keep track of a gender link with melancholia alone, for example. There is another difficulty, moreover. Women were identified with certain forms of madness, including hysteria and neurasthenia. But these appear to have been ill-defined and overlapping conditions, neither one clearly distinguished from melancholia (Gosling, 1987). Thus, diagnostic reliability seems doubtful at best.

Later observers continued to affirm women's particular proneness to depression into the twentieth century (see Chessler, 1972; Howell and Bayes, 1982; American Psychiatric Association, 1980, 1994); some continue to explain manic-depressive disorder in terms of problems peculiar to female reproductive organs (see Gibson, 1916; Howell and Bayes, 1981). These observations also must be approached critically. The extent of the sex link that makes women more likely sufferers of depression than men in today's culture has been challenged (Howell and Bayes, 1981; Corob, 1987; Busfield, 1996; Hartung and Widiger, 1998–99), as has the stability of the epidemiological profile. (Some studies suggest a shift, with fewer women relative to men suffering depression since the 1980s [Klerman and Weissman, 1989; Paykel, 1991]). And studies have pointed to obvious confounding factors, such as women's greater tendency to engage in help-seeking behavior, although certain research methods are believed to control for the distortion these factors introduce. Such reservations notwithstanding, most epidemiological assessments today continue to assert that depression is strongly gender-linked, a women's disorder.

Narcissism, Self-Loathing, and Loss

Freud portrays melancholia as a narcissistic disorder of loss intrinsically directed toward the self. In this respect he introduces a new kind of theory, not hitherto encountered in the range of imbalance theories found from Greek humoral theories to the biochemical models of present-day medicine.

Contemporary theorists point to an emphasis on self-identity and on loss in the language of male melancholy from the period predating Freud. As Lynn Enterline says of the early modern writing she examines, "melancholia . . . as a kind of grieving without end or sufficient cause, is a state that disrupts the *subject's identity* as a sexual and as a speaking being" (1995:8, my emphasis). For Schiesari, as well, the Renaissance *homo melancholicus* represents the "ego's warring over the object of loss, such that the loss itself becomes the dominant feature and not the lost object": (1992:11)—although for Schiesari the loss entailed in melancholy a is privileged form of male expression from which mourning women are precluded. And for Kristeva, depression is "the hidden face of Narcissus," so that "I discover the antecedents to my current breakdown in a loss, death, or grief over someone or something that I once loved." Again, Kristeva observes that we see "the shadow cast on the fragile self, hardly dissociated from the other, precisely by the loss of that essential other. The shadow of despair" (1989:5). Melancholy and melancholic states appear as disorders of self and self-identity and conditions of loss.

The emphasis on loss, on the one hand, and the link with the self, on the other, are separable. But in Freud's essay these two are firmly conjoined, and the conjunction has affected both diagnostic symptom description and literary themes for melancholia and depression until our day.

It seems widely agreed that the Renaissance ushered in a greater emphasis on the individual subject, or even that it saw the birth of the modern subject in the individualistic sense we understand today. Thus, the presence of narcissistic concerns in Renaissance literary writing on melancholy, which theorists like Schiesari and Enterline trace, is undoubtedly part of the tradition long before Freud. Also, the self is a theme given additional prominence during the Romantic movement. But melancholic states entail a greater emphasis on narcissistic concerns, loss, and themes of self-loathing *only after Freud's essay on mourning and melancholia.* Freud's writing on melancholia construes melancholy and melancholic states in significantly different terms. From a condition of imbalance and a mood of despondency and disquiet, melancholia becomes a frame of mind more centrally characterized by two things: a lack or want of something, or rather *someone,* that is, a loss, and, also, self-critical attitudes.

We can identify two stages in Freud's thinking about melancholia and loss and his development of the comparison between normal mourning, on the one hand, and states of melancholia, on the other. First, in letters written to Wilhelm Fliess in 1902, Freud identifies the loss as a lack of sexual excitement. Mourning is the longing for something lost; melancholia consists in mourning over a loss of libido. By the time of writing "Mourning and Melancholia," Freud has developed his notions of identification and introjection, and his understanding of narcissism. Now melancholia revolves around the early loss of and ambivalence over the "object," or mother. Self-accusation and self-hatred, which Freud describes as the central traits of the melancholic patient, reflect attitudes redirected toward the self as the incorporator of the lost object.

The parallel between the despondent frame of mind of melancholia and the frame of mind found in the normal mourning occasioned by the loss of loved ones was not Freud's invention, of course. We know that writing about melancholy had repeatedly drawn such parallels, at least since Elizabethan times. Yet the standard comparison likening the despondent mood and characteristic dispositions of lethargy, low energy, and low interest in normal mourning and melancholia was merely Freud's starting point. He went further, developing a more elaborate parallel: the mourner has lost something (someone, that is) and grieves his loss; thus, the melancholiac also must have suffered a loss.

Following these ideas, we sense the parallel with mourning, itself triggered by a long literary tradition on the subjective mood states of melancholy, directing Freud through a series of recognitions. First was the recognition that melancholia must be identified in terms of a lack, want, or absence; eventually came the recognition that it must be the loss of someone. Only then came the ideas of self-accusation and self-loathing.

Whether we look at casual comments or elaborate case records, clinical descriptions of melancholia from Freud's time fail to place the emphasis on self-loathing which Freud's essay does. Consider William James's intriguing observations on melancholic states in *The Varieties of Religious Experience.* He notes that the sense of sin is only one of three themes found in that melancholia which falls short of real insanity (James, 1902:158). And Kraepelin's generalizations concur with James's. At most, self-accusing states represent for Kraepelin one among several forms of melancholic subjectivity. (In speaking of the more severe *melancholia gravis,* Kraepelin notes that ideas of sin and self-reproach are more often present, but so also are ideas of persecution; while the less severe *melancholia simplex,* which seems to be closer to the cases Freud [and James] had in mind, is characterized as much by world loathing as by self-loathing: *"everything* has become disagreeable to him" [Kraepelin, 1920:76, my emphasis].)

This evidence from contemporary sources and authorities suggests that at least for the kinds of case Freud is concerned with, self-accusation was not a widely acknowledge feature of melancholia in Freud's own time. Despite their apparently "observational" status, then, Freud's remarks about his melancholiac's attitudes of self-loathing may have been invoked as much by his loss theory of melancholia as by his patients' complaints. Rather than clinical records, his cases serve as convenient illustrations of conceptual and theoretical necessities.

Interestingly, cross-cultural studies have also failed to reveal any emphasis on guilt and self-accusation in the symptom-idiom of other cultures (Kleinman and Good, 1985; A1-Issa, 1995). Nonetheless, in our own culture, self-loathing has from Freud's time on been accorded a central place in subjective accounts of both melancholia and clinical depression.[19]

In recent psychoanalytic writing Julia Kristeva has developed and expanded Freud's analysis on the element of loss in melancholia. Kristeva inherits Freud's model of "mourning" for the maternal object, but her analysis moves further in its insertion of gender into this experience of loss. We are all alike subject to the loss of the object, she suggests, and thus inclined, as Freud believed, to incorporate or "introject" the "other." But women's fate is different. As well as the introjection of the maternal body, the "spectacular identification" with the mother peculiar to the female infant is a source of women's particular proneness to depression (Kristeva, 1989:28). Here, then, is a theory that explains not only melancholic loss but also the particular affinity between melancholia and the feminine.

Discussions and theories that posit melancholia or depression as loss since Freud's "Mourning and Melancholia" have come in two identifiable strains. One, associated first with object-relations thinkers like Melanie Klein, W. R. D. Fairbairn, and Donald Winnicott as well as the attachment theory of Bowlby; and later with such thinkers as Kristeva, faithfully continues the ideas expressed by Freud in "Mourning and Melancholia," where *loss* is used in its more specific sense of a loss of a personified other, once possessed. (I would insist that *loss* does connote the more limited notion. We lose persons and things once possessed; we may lack almost anything at all, including qualities and things never possessed [like courage, and country houses].)

Another strain, associated less with the psychoanalytic traditions and more with mainstream psychology and psychiatry, and to be found in the work of several authors represented here, including Seligman and Beck, has seen a broadening and even a trivializing of the notion of depression as loss. Here *loss,* like *lack,* refers to any want of something desired or desirable, not necessarily something once possessed, not necessarily a personified other. We find reference to depression as a loss of self-esteem, loss of self, loss of relationships, loss of agency, loss of opportunity, and even, rendering such accounts entirely tautologous, a loss of hedonic mood states! (Noting this broad use of the concept of loss, Beck has drawn attention to its link with its slang cognate *loser.* A loser is someone *lacking* in every way: lacking opportunity, success, relationships, or happiness, for example.) While it pervades present-day writing about clinical depression, then, the legacy of Freud's loss theory often bears little resemblance to its source in "Mourning and Melancholia."

In this discussion I have tried to illustrate the far-reaching effects on conceptions of melancholia and melancholic states of faculty psychology divisions from the seventeenth and eighteenth centuries, and of the newer scientific categories of the nineteenth century. In addition, I have traced some of the themes we can identify in light of a late twentieth-century alertness to gender and to psychoanalytic loss theories. These several themes and categories pave the way for an understanding of the last years of the nineteenth century and the first years of the twentieth century as a watershed era for melancholy, melancholia, and depression, in which new theoretical models of melancholia became prominent.

From Melancholy to Melancholia and Depression

It has been proposed that the era between the Renaissance and our own times represents the historical boundaries of a "great age of melancholia," a tradition "inaugurated by the Renaissance, refined by the Enlightenment, flaunted by Romanticism, fetishized by the Decedents and theorized by Freud" before its current resurgence with postmodern writing on melancholy (Schiesari, 1992:3–4). This may be so. But another deep divide occurs at the end of the nineteenth century, as human, redeeming, ambiguous (and masculine) melancholy pulls apart from aberrant, barren, mute (and feminine) depression.

First, there is a slight shift in language, at least in English language patterns: *melancholy* becomes more firmly related to the normal conditions, *melancholia* to the abnormal. (In an exception to this trend, some feminist and literary writing during the last decade of the twentieth century, such as Judith Butler's, reblurs the distinction between normal and abnormal melancholic states and makes *melancholy* and *melancholia* again interchangeable [Butler, 1990, 1993, 1997]). In due time, the term *depression,* of more recent origin, and conveying another set of graphic and shaping metaphors, largely replaces *melancholia.* Now melancholy's different meanings produce a tension. Melancholy cannot mean all these things; it cannot connote these distinct and disparate states and conditions.

With the shift to regard melancholia as a mental disease have come reasons to diminish the importance of its intrinsically subjective symptoms in favor of a behavioral, sign-based analysis. Introspectionism was eclipsed by experimentalism and behaviorism in the emerging academic psychology of this era. In this light, the defeat of more subjective symptom-based analyses of mental diseases in favor of more behavioral sign-based analyses was inevitable. Moreover, with the strong disease model that influenced Kraepelin, there was no more reason to emphasize the subjective distress and suffering that had for so long characterized melancholic states.

But now we witness the divergence of melancholia from melancholy. Melancholia the disease comes increasingly to be regarded as behavior and bodily states. The subjective suffering associated with melancholy as a condition of poets, artists, and men, and as part of normal human experience, continues to be affirmed. While melancholy subjectivity is acknowledged, however, it is narrowed and limited to the cluster of moods associated with a sorrowful despondency and despair, rather than groundless fear and anxiety.

Freud's work on melancholia was at odds with the trends identified thus far. In "Mourning and Melancholia," a certain aspect of melancholic and depressive subjectivity, hitherto of little importance, becomes attenuated, elaborated, and changed. There is increased emphasis on melancholia (and later depression) as analogous to mourning in being subjective states of loss, and in being a condition associated not only with mood states but also with attitudes of self-loathing.

At the same time as this series of changes, melancholia has become associated with feminine gender. This derives in part from empirical observation—although today we want to question the science of such data collection—as well as from Freudian and more recent psychoanalytic theorizing. It may also come from deeper structures, as feminist theorists have suggested. Melancholy, with its loquacious male subject, leaves little room for the mute suffering of women. Women, instead, are victims of depression.

Since Freud: Clinical Depression

After Freud's 1917 essay, at least in the English-language tradition, melancholia becomes an increasingly rare disorder category, little more than a footnote to nosological schemes and, as the years go by, less and less frequently described in clinical case material. In its stead we find emphasis on the condition today known as *clinical depression*.[20] Now cast as a major mental disorder or disease, depression has been the subject of unceasing research and theorizing in both medical and non-medical fields of study since the first decades of the twentieth century.

The melancholic states of past eras bear no simple relation to today's clinical depression, as the preceding discussion has aimed to show. Even melancholic subjectivity, for so long "fear and sadness without cause," has become sadness without cause, loss and self-loathing. Nonetheless, earlier theories of melancholy and melancholia foreshadow, at least in broad form, most twentieth-century analyses of the disorder known as clinical depression.

Historically, it is possible to identify a few decisive trends. Within psychoanalysis, certain aspects of the theory inaugurated in Freud's essay were deepened and developed in the work of Melanie Klein. In turn, the Kleinian stress on early object relations gave its name to a vital and influential neo-Freudian school represented by thinkers like Fairbairn and Winnicott; it also spawned the "attachment" theory associated with Bowlby and others, which posits early severing of relational connection as the source of subsequent depression (and other disorders).

For several decades medical theorizing has been dominated by notions of what, if we allow the term *imbalance* the elasticity it enjoyed in humoral accounts, looks like biological imbalance. While no longer humoral, biomedical analyses depend on the presence of deficit, excess, or dysfunction in biological states to explain the presence and persistence of at least the more severe, intractable, "endogenous" depression without apparent psychological origins. Thus, depletion of biogenic amines, on one hypothesis, accounts for the symptoms of depression. As well as biological imbalance theories, recent years have seen accounts that propose structural changes in the brain as the source of clinical depression: in these we can see the heirs to the "brain lesion" hypotheses of the late nineteenth century.

These more biologically oriented theories have not gone unchallenged, even within medical psychiatry. As a result of the influence of thinkers like Karl Bonhoeffer in Europe and Adolf Meyer in America, some depression as a response to psychological trauma has been acknowledged. In the decades to follow their work, "reactive" or "exogenous" depression was often relegated to a lesser role, however. Severe, "endogenous" depression was widely maintained to be organically caused.[21]

Sometimes not only reactive depression but also the presence of more severe endogenous depressive states were explained by social and psychological factors. One such challenge to biological theories proposed that depression was "learned helplessness" (Seligman, 1975). On this account, the inertia characteristic of depression was a response to a sensed loss of efficacy: it was "giving up." Although it incorporates elements of loss theory as well, Seligman's hypothesis may be seen to illustrate a new kind for our taxonomy of theories, a cultural causation theory, as does the cognitivist theory of depression introduced by Beck in the 1960s. (Interestingly, Beck's theory also echoes earlier theorizing about melancholy. With its emphasis on distorted and disordered belief, it is reminiscent of eighteenth-century attempts, such as Boerhaave's and Kant's, to construe all mental disorder as forms of illogic, false belief, or delusion).

The explosion of feminist sensibility and scholarship in the late twentieth century was a remarkable catalyst for studies in melancholia and depression. Within the psychoanalytic tradition, it instigated further elaboration of loss theories and even a revival of interest in melancholy in work such as that of Irigaray, Kristeva, and Butler. Outside psychoanalytic traditions, it led to an expanded empirical and theoretical focus on cultural causation and also incorporated "loss" theory, more loosely understood, to develop explanations of depression acknowledging gender roles and women's socialization. (Jean Baker Miller's early and influential writing on women's psychology demonstrates this development.) It prompted research on the gender link between women and depression, research that today proceeds within each of the theoretical models distinguished here.

Our taxonomy of theories now contains three categories: imbalance and biological theories, loss theories, and cultural causation theories.[22] And today theorizing and empirical research emphasizing each theoretical model is burgeoning—both separately and in combination.

Complex multicausal accounts of depression posit an interaction between socially wrought trauma and biological, and even genetic, predispositions of the brain (see, for example Akiskal and McKinney, 1973; Kandel, 1998). Such trauma, moreover, is frequently construed as loss, using the broader, nonpsychoanalytic notion of loss that covers any lack. Sometimes regarded as permanent, the resultant biological changes, in turn, are believed to affect psychological states in a complex feedback system. (The sense of closure promoted by these multitheoretical studies is perhaps inflated. Even the fundamental distinction between organic correlates of subjective distress and organic etiology of such distress is ignored, or collapsed, in much theorizing.)

Attempts to evaluate different models and analyses of depression seem to lead us inevitably to a question for anthropology. Is depression a constant across cultures? If we only knew the answer to this question, it would seem, we could adjudicate between the different etiological accounts and emphases in the range of different and potentially incompatible models jostling in the field of depression studies today. Far from offering a quick remedy to this confusion of models and theories, however, the work of cultural anthropologists interested in the concept of depression has served to highlight the oversimplification and sketchy science implicit in such a question. To ask about a person's emotional functioning, whether in a remote culture or in our own, they have demonstrated, is to ask as many as six questions, not one (Shweder, 1985). What types of feelings are these? Which kinds of situations elicit these feelings? What do the feelings signify for those experiencing them? How are the feelings expressed? What rules of appropriateness guide the expression or display of these feelings? When they are not expressed or displayed, how are these feelings handled? Emotions have meanings. To understand a person's emotional life, it is necessary to engage in conceptual analysis. Moreover, causes and cures may be in some important ways secondary: "It is possible to understand what it implies to feel depressed without knowing what 'really' brought it on or how 'really' to get rid of it" (Shweder, 1985:199).

The cultural constructionism whose possibility is raised by these anthropological studies is orthogonal to the types of theory of depression outlined thus far. On radical constructionism, meanings constitute reality, making reality "independent of biology," in the words of Arthur Kleinman (Kleinman and Good, 1985:494). So to the more standard ontologies of the types of depression theory reviewed thus far, we must add another that privileges meanings above other entities.

Melancholic states always strained the lineaments in which medicine attempted to clothe and contain them, and, as the readings collected here illustrate, melancholia and allied states have from earliest times been the subject of intense theorizing and dispute. Even after a lifetime pursuing the nature of melancholy, Burton was left with an overabundance of theories, explanations, categories, and runaway observations. And the unflagging activity and theoretical disarray marking depression studies since Freud leave us similarly placed. About clinical depression we seem to have more questions than definitive or enlightening answers.

PART I

Aristotle to Freud

Brilliance and Melancholy

ARISTOTLE
(Or a Follower of Aristotle)

THE GREEK PHILOSOPHER Aristotle lived between 384 and 322
B.C.E. He studied under Plato at the Academy from the ages of
seventeen to thirty-seven, acting as tutor to Alexander the Great at the
Macedonian court during some of this time. When he was thirty-nine,
he started his own school in Athens at the Lyceum, where he attracted
many distinguished students from the Academy and gained great fame
for his lectures.

Aristotle's extant writings consist largely of student notes, edited in
the first century B.C.E. from his lectures at the Lyceum. Of these the
major writing consisted of six treatises *Physics; Metaphysics; De Anima;
Nicomachean Ethics* and *Eudemian Ethics; Politics* and *Rhetoric,* all
works whose influence on Western philosophy and even science has
been great. After the decline of Rome, Aristotle's work was lost in the
West; it survived as the result of Islamic and Jewish interest in Aris-
totelianism, an interest that was reintroduced to Europe at the beginning of the Middle Ages.

The authorship of the *Problems,* and its famous and influential discussion of melancholy, is in considerable doubt. Most authorities believe
it to be the work of one of Aristotle's followers, perhaps Theophrastus.
Nevertheless, its attribution to Aristotle in part accounts for its enormous influence, it is at least "Aristotelian," and it fits well with the rest of
Aristotle's work on biology and medicine.

The author of this Aristotelian discussion begins with a question:
Why is it that brilliance and achievement are associated with black bile
and the diseases of melancholy? Each element of this approach may be
challenged, not least its insufficiently supported assumption that brilliance and achievement are associated with melancholy. Yet because of
the authority of its alleged author and the boldness of its approach, subsequent thinkers, particularly during the Renaissance, which saw a revival of interest in Aristotelian writing on melancholy, accepted the
assumption without question and proceeded to the challenge of answering the question posed.

The connection drawn between inspiration and melancholia in this
discussion does seem to involve unwarranted assumptions: nonetheless,

the author offers an appeal to Homeric heroes as evidence of the link between brilliance and melancholia. Heracles, he says, Lysander of Sparta, and also the Homeric heroes Ajax and Bellerophon all showed evidence of diseases of the black bile. In introducing these examples, the author alludes to the connection derived from Plato between inspiration and the "sacred disease" of epilepsy (epilepsy is, after all, one of his forms of melancholy.) Some commentators have seen in these discussions a "secularization" of the spiritual Platonic notion of inspired madness or frenzy (Klibansky, Panofsky, and Saxl, 1964). (An explication of these ideas can be found in the work of Lilian Feder [1980].)

Writing in the fifth century B.C.E., the Greek physician Hippocrates had outlined a theory based on the four humors, and, although his work contains no systematic discussion of melancholia, he had identified melancholia (along with hemorrhoids, dysentary, and skin eruptions) as a disease caused by an excess of black bile. The Aristotelian passages quoted here illustrate how this humoral theory in Hippocratic writing shaped nonmedical as well as medical views of melancholy. The Aristotelian author assumes that excesses of black bile result in melancholia and more severe states of mental disorder, while a lesser and more stable imbalance of humors with additional black bile produces the melancholic temperament or disposition. (In the first case, there is disease, in the latter, "the temperament exists by nature" [163]. As he puts it, "those who have a small share of this temperament are normal, but those who have much are unlike the majority" [165].)

This development of humoral theory to explain normal temperamental variation appears to originate in the Aristotelian text. The connection with normal temperament becomes prominent in Galen's writing also, and Galenic discussions of normal temperament were in turn an important source for Renaissance and even eighteenth-century theories of character or temperament.

Like the Hippocratic writing on humors, this work accepts that there are four humors: blood, yellow bile, phlegm, and the black bile associated with melancholy, each linked to the qualities of heat, cold, moisture, and dryness. But unlike Hippocratic theory, which associated black bile with coldness and dryness only, Aristotelian writing allows that the black bile could be too hot or too cold. The different kinds of melancholic diseases resultant from an excess of black bile—epilepsy, apoplexy, despondency or fear, and overconfidence—the Aristotelian author believed came about according to "the mixture (of humors) and how it is related to cold and heat" (165).

Bile is not actually black. So why *black,* rather than blue, or pale, bile? Two answers to this question have been posited. Bennett Simon points to pre-Hippocratic associations of blackness, madness, and dejection, which he surmises may arise from inexplicable but common and perhaps universal subjective associations (Simon, 1978:235). Gilman, in contrast, emphasizes that "mythmaking" surrounds "fictive" or fictional signs and symptoms, serving as a means of representing an invisible state such as mental illness. Western cultural traditions assign to darkness a large collection of negative associations, he reminds us. Blackness signifies the other, the different, the abnormal and deficient (Gilman, 1988).

Finally, notice the author's remark that when the temperament is cold "beyond due measure," it produces "groundless" despondency, and his comment (165) that in those who are temperamentally melancholic these kinds of groundless affections "go deep." This introduces a theme that finds its way into Renaissance and later definitions emphasizing that the fear and sadness of melancholy are *without cause*. The account of melancholy in this passage probably traces to Hippocrates' comment that melancholia is signaled by prolonged (and thus, presumably, unwarranted or groundless) fear or sadness.

• ⌣ • ● • ⌣ •

From Aristotle (or a follower of Aristotle), "Problems
Connected with Thought, Intelligence, and Wisdom,"
in *Problems* (ca. 2nd century B.C.E.)

Why is it that all men who have become outstanding in philosophy, statesmanship, poetry or the arts are melancholic, and some to such an extent that they are infected by the diseases arising from black bile, as the story of Heracles among the heroes tells? For Heracles seems to have been of this character, so that the ancients called the disease of epilepsy the "Sacred disease" after him. This is proved by his frenzy towards his children and the eruption of sores which occurred before his disappearance on Mount Oeta; for this is a common affection among those who suffer from black bile. Similar sores also appeared on Lysander the Spartan before his death. The same is true of Ajax and Bellerophontes; the former went completely insane, and the latter craved for desert places, so that Homer wrote of him:

> But when he was hated of all the gods, then he wandered alone on the plain of Aleïum, eating out his heart, and avoiding the track of men.

And many other heroes seem to have suffered in the same way as these. In later times also there have been Empedocles, Plato, Socrates and many other well-known men. The same is true of most of those who have handled poetry. For many such men have suffered from diseases which arise from this mixture in the body, and in others their nature evidently inclines to troubles of this sort. In any case they are all, as has been said, naturally of this character.

But to revert to our former discussion, that such melancholic humour is already mixed in nature; for it is a mixture of hot and cold; for nature consists of these two elements. So black bile becomes both very hot and very cold. For the same thing can be naturally affected by both these conditions, as for instance water which is cold, but if it is sufficiently heated so as to reach boiling-point it is hotter than the flame itself, and stone and steel when heated in the flame become hotter than the coal, though by nature they are cold. There is a clearer discussion of this subject in the work on *Fire*. Now black bile, which is naturally cold and does not reside on the surface when it is in the condition described, if it is in excessive quantity in the body, produces apoplexy or torpor, or despondency or fear; but if it becomes overheated, it produces cheerfulness with song, and madness, and the breaking out of sores and so forth. In most cases, arising as it does from the daily food, it does not make men any different in character, but only produces a melancholic disease. But those with whom this temperament exists by nature, at once develop various types of character, differing according to their different temperaments; those for instance in whom the bile is considerable and cold become sluggish and stupid, while those with whom it is excessive and hot become mad, clever or amorous and easily moved to passion and desire, and some become more talkative. But many, because this heat is near to the seat of the mind, are affected by the diseases of madness or frenzy, which accounts for the Sibyls, soothsayers, and all inspired persons, when their condition is due not to disease but to a natural mixture. Maracus, the Syracusan, was an even better poet when he was mad. But those with whom the excessive heat has sunk to a moderate amount are melancholic, though more intelligent and less eccentric, but they are superior to the rest of the world in many ways, some in education, some in the arts and others again in statesmanship. This state produces considerable variations in the face of danger because many men are sometimes inconsistent in the face of fear. For they differ at different times according to the relation of their body to this mixture. The melancholic temperament is in itself variable, just as it has different effects on those who suffer from the diseases which it causes; for, like water, sometimes it is cold and sometimes hot. So that when some alarming news is brought, if it happens at a time when the mixture is cooler, it makes a man cowardly; for it has shown the way to fear, and fear has a chilling effect. Those who are terrified prove this; for they tremble. But if the bile is hot, fear reduces it to the normal and makes a man self-controlled and unmoved. So it is also with daily despondencies; for often we are in a condition of feeling grief, but we cannot say what we grieve about; and sometimes we are feeling cheerful, but it is not clear why. Such affections which are called superficial come to everyone to some extent, for some of the force which produces them is mingled in everyone; but those with whom they go deep are already of this character. For just as men differ in appearance not because they have faces, but because they have a certain type of face, some handsome, some ugly and some again having no outstanding characteristics (these are of normal character), so those who have a small share of this temperament are normal, but those who have much are unlike the majority. If the characteristic is very intense, such men are very melancholic, and if the mixture is of a certain kind, they are abnormal. But if they neglect it, they incline towards melancholic diseases, different people in different parts of the body; with some the symptoms are epileptic, with others apoplectic, others again are given to deep despondency or to fear, others are over-confident, as was the case with Archelaus, king of Macedonia. The cause of such force is the mixture, how it is related to cold and heat. For when it is colder than the occasion demands it produces unreasonable despondency; this accounts for the prevalence of suicide by hanging amongst the young and sometimes amongst older men too. But many commit suicide after a bout of drinking. Some melancholic persons continue to be despondent after drinking; for the heat of the wine quenches the natural heat. But heat in the region with which we think and hope makes us cheerful. This is why all are eager to drink up to the point of drunkenness, because much wine makes all men confident, just as youth does boys; for old age is despondent, but youth is full of hope. There are some few persons who are seized with despondency while drinking, for the same reason that some are so after drinking. Those upon whom despondency falls as the heat dies away are more inclined to hang themselves. This is why young men and old men are more liable to hang themselves; for old age causes the heat to die away, but in the young the cause is their condition which is natural. But when the heat is suddenly quenched is the time at which most men make away with themselves, so that everyone is amazed as they have given no sign of it before. Now when the mixture due to black bile becomes colder, it gives rise, as has been said, to all kinds of despair, but when it is hotter, to cheerfulness. This is why the young are more cheerful, and the old less so. For the former are hot and the latter cold; for old age is a form of chilling. But it may happen that the heat is suddenly quenched by extraneous causes, just as objects which are heated in the fire and cooled unnaturally, like coals when water is poured over them. This is why some men commit suicide after drinking; for the heat from the wine is a foreign element, and when it is quenched the affection occurs. After sexual intercourse most men are rather depressed, but those who emit much waste product with the semen are more cheerful; for they are relieved of waste product and of breath and of excessive heat. But the others are usually rather depressed; for they are chilled by sexual intercourse, because they are deprived of something important. This is proved by the fact that the quantity of semen emitted is small. To sum up what we have said, the melancholic are not equable in behaviour, because the power of the black bile is not even; for it is both very cold and very hot. But because it has an effect on character (for heat and cold are the greatest agents in our lives for the making of character), just like wine according as it is mixed in our body in greater or less quantity it makes our dispositions of a particular kind. Both wine and black bile are full of air. But since it is possible that even a varying state may be well attempered, and in a sense be a good condition, and since the condition may be warmer when necessary and then again cold, or conversely, owing to the presence of excess, all melancholic persons are abnormal, not owing to disease but by nature.

2

·

Diseases of the Black Bile

GALEN

COURT PHYSICIAN TO THE emperor Marcus Aurelius, Galen of Pergamum (or Pergamos) stands as one of the two most influential Greek physicians of the Roman era. (The other was Rufus of Ephesus, who lived during the time of Emperor Trajan [98–117].) Galen was born of Greek parents in Pergamum, in Asia Minor, and he is believed to have lived between the years 130 and 200. His father was a well-to-do architect of Pergamum, an ancient center of civilization containing a library second only in importance of that of Alexandria itself. Of the influence of his parents, Galen said:

> I have had the great good fortune to have as a father a highly amiable, just, good, and benevolent man. My mother, on the other hand, possessed a very bad temper; she used sometimes to bite her serving maids, and she was perpetually shouting at my father and quarrelling with him—worse than Xanthippe with Socrates. When, therefore, I compared the excellence of my father's disposition with the disgraceful passions of my mother, I resolved to embrace and love the former qualities, and avoid and hate the latter. (Quoted in Galen, 1916: Introduction, xvi)

Galen was schooled in all the psychological systems of the day—Platonic, Aristotelian, Stoic, and Epicurean—and then sent abroad to study medicine in Greece, Smyrna, and Alexandria. Returning to Pergamum, he served briefly as a physician to the school for gladiators before settling in Rome, where he lived, on and off, from the age of thirty-two until his death in his seventies. In Rome he had a large practice and wrote on medical and philosophical topics. He wrote prolifically (he is credited with some 500 treatises); and although many have been lost, at least 83 of his works on medicine remain, representing an unequaled influence on medieval and Renaissance medicine. Galen consolidated and systematized past medical writing, to which he added his own empirical findings from experimentation and the dissection of animals, and his own theories, with their emphasis on purposive creation. Until the sixteenth century his treatises were regarded as medical orthodoxy, and, despite his own indisputable contributions, especially

61

in anatomy and physiology, his work served to discourage original investigation and scientific progress. Summing up the importance of Galen in the history of medicine, one commentator has remarked that if the work of Hippocrates, writing some 600 years earlier, is the foundation upon which the edifice of historical Greek medicine was raised, then Galen must be looked upon as the summit or apex of the same edifice. For "it is essentially in the form of Galenism that Greek medicine was transmitted to after ages" (Brock, 1916:ix).

Galen's *On the Affected Parts,* whose third book is devoted to the function and diseases of the brain and spinal cord, contains a chapter on melancholia, and it is from that chapter that the following passages are drawn. In order to place Galen's particular views on melancholia, it is necessary to understand the prevailing humoral theory, also found in the work of earlier authorities such as Hippocrates, Aristotle, Praxagoras, and Rufus of Ephesus, whose ideas Galen accepted. With the four elements of earth, air, fire, and water were associated qualities: fire was associated with heat, air with cold, water with moisture, and earth with dryness. The four humors of blood, yellow bile, phlegm, and black bile were also attached to these elements and qualities. Thus black bile was cold and dry, yellow bile warm and dry, phlegm cold and moist, and blood warm and moist. It was this emphasis on the four qualities of warm, cold, dry, and moist that marked Galen's own contribution to humoral theory. This emphasis is summed up in a passage from another Galenic work, *On the Natural Faculties;* all the observed facts agree, Galen remarks, that

> when the nutriment becomes altered in the veins by the innate heat, blood is produced when it is in moderation, and the other humors when it is not in proper proportion. . . . Thus, those articles of food, which are by nature warmer are more productive of bile, while those which are colder produce more phlegm. Similarly of the periods of life, those which are naturally warmer tend more to bile, and the colder more to phlegm. Of occupations also, localities and seasons, and, above all, of natures themselves, the colder are more phlegmatic, and the warmer more bilious. (*On the Natural Faculties,* II, viii, pp. 184–85)

Humoral theory was regarded as empirically supported; these substances were believed in the body, as indeed phlegm and blood were. In excess, they resulted in disease, according to Galen: acute disease for blood or yellow bile, and chronic disease for phlegm or black bile. The spleen or the atrabiliary glands were the organs associated with black bile as the agent of disease (*melancholia* was the Greek term; *atrabilia* the Latin). As Aristotle had, Galen also noted less extreme imbalances than those excesses resulting in diseases. The balance of qualities (warmth, cold, dryness, and moisture) determined individual variation in "temperament," long-term traits or dispositions, such as a tendency toward melancholy or phlegmatic or choleric nature.

In the preceding chapter of this work, Galen has announced his preference for the terms *atrabilious humor* or *atrabilious blood* rather than *black bile*. Atrabilious blood or humor may occur in different parts of the body, on his account, and is not restricted to the area of the spleen. Galen's classification of melancholia into three kinds rests on the location in the body of the source of affection: whether in the brain, throughout the bloodstream, or in the stomach.

Following Hippocrates, Aristotle, and other authorities who preceded him, Galen emphasizes the subjective states of fear and despondency attending melancholia. He also reiterates and develops two distinct associations with darkness: the color of the humor, which for him means the sooty or smokelike vapor resulting from the overheated, atrabilious blood "clouding" the activities of the brain, and the coloring of those likely to suffer from melancholia ("lean persons with a darker complexion").

An interesting comparison with Galenic descriptions of melancholia is to be found in the writing of a contemporary of Galen's, also Greek, and believed to have practiced medicine in Rome at the same time. Aretaeus of Cappadocia (ca. A.D. 150–200) speaks of patients suffering melancholia and mania as "dull or stern; dejected or unreasonably torpid, without any manifest cause." Those affected with melancholy "are not every one of them affected according to one particular form; but they are either suspicious of poisoning, or flee to the desert from misanthropy, or turn superstitious, or contract a hatred of life." Unreasonable fears seize them, and "they are prone to change their mind readily, to become base, mean-spirited, and illiberal." If the illness becomes more urgent, moreover, hatred, avoidance of the haunts of men, and vain lamentations are seen: "They complain of life and desire to die; in many the understanding so leads to insensibility and fatuousness that they become ignorant of all things and forget of themselves and live the life of inferior animals" (Aretaeus, *On the Causes and Symptoms of Chronic Diseases,*" 299–300).

·⌣ ● ⌣·

From Galen, "Function of Diseases of Brain and Spinal
Cord," in *Diseases of the Black Bile,*
from *On the Affected Parts* (ca. 165 C.E.)

Considerable differences exist among the sympathetic diseases of the head and those which originate there primarily. The thick humors which collect in the substance of the brain damage it in its functions as an organ or its uniform composition. The brain is damaged as an instrumental ["organic"] part of the body by obstruction of its channels, but as a homogeneous organ by alteration of its humoral mixture. Therefore, the following statement is written at the end of [*Hippocrates'*] sixth book *On epidemic diseases:*

> Those affected by black bile [literally: melancholics] become, as a rule, epileptics after a long [delay] and the epileptics suffer from black bile [literally: become melancholics]. Each of these [conditions] occurs by preference, if weakness befalls one or the other: if weakness [affects] the body, people become epileptics: if it [affects] the mind they become melancholic.

In his lecture *Hippocrates* indicated that frequently though not always one affection is transformed into another. Although epilepsy is not produced by the black bile only but also by a phlegmatic humor, a condition provoked by the black bile sometimes turns into melancholy, whereas one caused by phlegm can turn into other types of which I will speak later, since it does not produce melancholy.

Secondly, *Hippocrates* expressed an important viewpoint in this passage. Since the soul is either the mixture of the active qualities [especially warm and dry] or is altered by the mixture of these qualities, *Hippocrates* declared that the bile inflicts damage to the brain as an instrument, since it is diverted to the substance of the brain as happens through obstruction [of the channels of the pneuma]. However, when the bile damages only the homogeneous mixture of the brain it affects the intellect. But it seems to me that the former point has to be defined, since the physicians have neglected it.

Sometimes the same [humoral] mixture appears in all visible parts of the body, for instance in jaundice and the so-called *elephantiasis* and dropsy, and further in cachexia and during discoloration [of the skin] in diseases of the liver and spleen; sometimes when a single part [of the body] receives the humor or bitter bile, phlegm or black bile, it changes its local composition. In the same manner it is occasionally possible, when the entire blood in the vessels has become melancholic [turned into black bile], that the brain itself has undergone such damage according to the general rule of this illness.

But in another manner, when the blood of the whole body of a patient has remained unaffected, only the blood in the brain is being changed. This happens in two ways; the [change] entered the brain from somewhere else or the atrabilious humor developed in this place. This [black bile] is produced by intense local heat which burns the yellow bile *(xanthe chole)* or the thicker and darker blood.

This distinction is of considerable importance for the therapy. If the entire body contains atrabilious blood, it is customary to start the treatment with a phlebotomy. If only the brain is involved, the patient does not need bloodletting for this diathesis, though in another [condition] this still might be helpful. You have now to base your decision [*diagnosis*] on the following [considerations]: whether the whole body carries atrabilious humor or whether this humor has accumulated only in the brain.

I judge that you first have to observe the quality of the somatic type of the patient, remembering that thin, pale and fat persons harbor a minimum of atrabilious humor, but that lean persons with a darker complexion, much hair and large veins are more apt to produce this type of humor. It also happens that a person with a very red complexion suddenly changes to an atrabilious constitution.

Besides these types are those of a fair complexion especially when they happen to be exposed to sleeplessness, to much pain, lots of worry and a meager diet. The [therapeutic] indications are of the same kind: suppression either of blood loss from piles or of some other customary form of elimination of blood or of menstrual bleeding in women. In addition, we should know which foodstuffs were used and whether these produced atrabilious blood or its opposite.

I can tell you that atrabilious blood is generated by eating the meat of goats and oxen, and still more of he-goats and bulls; even worse is the meat of asses and camels, since quite a few people eat these as well as the meat of foxes and dogs. Above all, consumption of hares creates the same kind of blood, and more so the flesh of wild boars. [Spiral] snails produce atrabilious blood in a person who indulges in them, and so do all kinds of pickled meat of terrestrial animals, and of the beasts living in water, it is the tuna fish, the whale, the seal, dolphins, the dog shark and all the cetaceous species [related to the whale].

Of the vegetables, cabbage usually produces this type of blood, as do sprouts prepared in brine or in a combination of vinegar and brine. I also mention [the shoots of] mastich, terebinth and bramble, and the white rose. Of the pulses, the lentil is an intensely atrabilious nutrient; and so are all the so-called wheatbreads which are made from bran; and bread made from the one-grained wheat and those [made] of spoiled seeds which some of the tribes use instead of regular wheat. But these were analyzed in my treatise *On the effects of the foodstuffs*.

Also heavy and dark wine is very much inclined to produce an atrabilious humor if people consume it in large quantities while remaining in very hot surroundings. Also aged cheeses readily produce this humor, when by chance their body gets overheated.

If a person remained on a diet of this kind before getting ill, one can draw additional conclusions. If he kept a well-balanced diet, one should inquire whether he performed exercises, had worries [or suffered from] sleeplessness and anxiety. Some persons acquire the atrabilious humor through febrile disease, as previously mentioned. Quite helpful for a better founded diagnosis is a knowledge of the time of the year and of the past and present conditions [*katastasis,* climate and environment], of the particular location and the age of the patient.

When after previous consideration of all these [factors] you still expect that all veins of the body contain atrabilious blood, then you shall confirm this diagnosis by performing a phlebotomy at the elbow. It is better to cut the medially located vein, because it is connected with the so-called humero-cephalic and the basilic vein which runs through the armpit to the hands. However, if the outflowing blood does not appear to be atrabilious, then stop [drawing blood] at once. But if the blood seems to be of this kind, then withdraw as much as you deem sufficient in view of the constitution of the patient.

There also exists a third type of *melancholia* which, as in epilepsy, has its origin in the gastric cavity. Some physicians call this condition a hypochondriac or gassy disease. It is sufficient for me to quote here the related symptoms which *Diocles* described in the book *Disease, cause and cure* where he wrote in exactly these words:

> Another disease arises in the cavity of the stomach, unlike those previously mentioned; some [physicians] call it melancholic (*atra-bilious*), others gassy. After meals, and especially after food which is difficult to digest and feels hot, this condition is accompanied by much watery spitting, sour eructations, gas and heartburn [literally: burning in the hypochondria], also by splashing noises [in the abdomen] which do not occur instantly but after some delay. Sometimes there are severe pains of the [gastric] cavity which in a few persons extend toward the broad of the back. These pains abate by [the use of] well-cooked food but return when the same [heavy] food is eaten again. The pain often becomes annoying during fasting and after the principal meal. Those who suffer from vomiting bring up undigested food and mucus which is not very bitter but hot and so acid that even the teeth become bloody. This befalls mostly young people and quite suddenly. But in whatever form it may start, it can persist in all cases.

Right after this introduction *Diocles* added [a remark about] the etiology; he wrote:

> One should assume that the so-called flatulent persons have more heat than customary in those veins which receive the nutrients from the stomach and that the blood of these patients becomes thick. This shows that these veins are obstructed, since the body does not receive the nutrients which remain in the stomach, whereas prior to this condition first these pores had absorbed, then discharged most food-stuffs into the lower abdominal organs. Therefore, on the next day these patients vomited foodstuff which was not absorbed into the body. One can well understand that there is more than natural heat because of the fever from which they suffer and of the type of their nourishment. But they seem to obtain relief from cold food which cools this type of heat and quenches the [innate fire].

Continuing this chapter *Diocles* wrote as follows:

> Some people say that in similar affections the [lower] opening of the stomach which leads to the intestines is inflamed and that because of

the inflammation this opening is obstructed and blocked so that transfer of food to the bowels cannot take place during the allotted time. Since under these circumstances the food has to remain in the stomach for a longer period, it provokes swelling, heat and the other [symptoms] already mentioned.

This was described by *Diocles;* but he omitted from this list the most essential symptoms which characterize melancholy and the flatulent and hypochondriac affection. It appears to me that *Diocles* did not include these because the term of the disease is evidently self-explanatory, as *Hippocrates* taught us:

Fear or a depressive mood (*dysthamia*) which last for a long time render [patients] melancholic [i.e., atrabilious].

Why did *Diocles* write in his explanation of the causes of other symptoms, but failed to discuss that it is worthwhile to investigate [the conditions] which cause a damage to the intellect? This question is worth asking. He omitted explaining why melancholic symptoms arise when the heat in the gastric veins is excessive, or when the parts around the pylorus are inflamed. It is evident that when the stomach is filled with gassy pneuma the patients are relieved by belching and, above all, by vomiting, as *Diocles* himself mentioned. But it was difficult to describe the characteristic symptoms of melancholy together with the above-mentioned affection of the stomach. Let us now supplement this which a clear explanation of the diathesis of the stomach in these affections.

For it seems that there is an inflammation in the stomach and that the blood contained in the inflamed part is thicker and more atrabilious. As some kind of sooty and smoke-like evaporation or some sort of heavy vapors are carried up from the stomach to the eyes, equally and for the same reason the symptoms of suffusion occur, when an atrabilious evaporation produces melancholic symptoms of the mind by ascending to the brain like a sooty substance or a smoky vapor.

We certainly observe that headaches most frequently arise from yellow bile contained in the stomach, just as they instantly subside when the bile is eliminated by vomiting. Some pains of this type are biting and corrosive, others are heavy or accompanied by tension or sinking spells.

The best physicians agree that not only these [pains] but also epilepsy start in the stomach but then affect the head. Fear generally befalls the melancholic patients, but the same type of abnormal sensory images do not always present themselves. As for instance, one patient believes that he has been turned into a kind of snail and therefore runs away from everyone he meets lest [its shell] should get crushed; or when another patient sees some crowing cocks flapping their wings to their song, he beats his own arms against his ribs and imitates the voice of the animals. Again, another patient is afraid that Atlas who supports the world will become tired and throw it away and he and all of us will be crushed and pushed together. And there are a thousand other imaginary ideas.

Although each melancholic patient acts quite differently than the others, all of them exhibit fear or despondency. They find fault with life and hate people; but not all want to die. For some the fear of death is of principal concern during melancholy. Others again will appear to you quite bizarre because they dread death and desire to die at the same time.

Therefore, it seems correct that *Hippocrates* classified all their symptoms into two groups: fear and despondency. Because of this despondency patients hate everyone whom they see, are constantly sullen and appear terrified, like children or uneducated adults in deepest darkness. As external darkness renders almost all persons fearful, with the exception of a few naturally audacious ones or those who were specially trained, thus the color of the black humor induces fear when its darkness throws a shadow over the area of thought [in the brain].

All of the best physicians and philosophers agree that the humors and actually the whole constitution of the body change the activity of the soul. I demonstrated this in a single commentary, *Why the faculties of the soul correspond to the humoral composition of the body.* Therefore, those who were ignorant of the activity of the humors, like for instance the followers of *Erasistratus,* did not dare to write anything about melancholy.

It is worthwhile here to question the common notions of people and many other beliefs [of *Erasistratus*] of which quite a few philosophers and physicians are ignorant. All persons call this affection *melancholia,* indicating by this term the humor responsible for it. If the first symptoms which appear in the stomach become more severe, they are followed by a melancholic affection. When the patient is relieved through bowel movements, vomiting, expulsion of flatus and belching, then we should rather call this illness hypochondriac and flatulent and define despondency and fear as its symptoms.

If, however, the symptoms of melancholy become serious but the [gastric] cavity is hardly involved, then we should consider this disease as a primary affection of the brain due to an accumulation of black bile in this organ.

Based on these symptoms one has to distinguish whether this humor is confined only to the brain or [distributed] throughout the entire body, as was mentioned a short time ago. I want to remind you that my pupils saw me achieve a perfect cure of melancholy by [recommending] frequent bathing; a well-balanced and fluid regimen, without other remedies if the damaging humor did not resist evacuation for any length of time. When, however, the illness had become chronic, it required stronger methods of treatment than those previously mentioned. This type of melancholy follows a preceding hot condition of the head which can arise from a burning fever, an inflammatory affection of the head, or phrenitis. It also comes from worry and grief combined with sleeplessness. But this should be enough [discussion] about melancholy.

3

Accidie

Cassian was raised in a Christian monastery in Bethlehem during the second half of the fourth century, and although not much is known about his early life, he is one of the most influential figures in the history of the early Christian church. This is because he provided the Christian West with information on the life led by the "desert fathers," or "cenobites," early monk who lived alone or in small groups in Egypt seeking lives of simplicity and asceticism. After many years in Egypt studying the desert fathers on long journeys undertaken between 390 and 400 C.E. Cassian founded two monasteries in Marseilles, one for men and one for women, based on the cenobitic model. He also contributed extensive writing about the organization and way of life he had observed in the desert. His first work, written around 416 at the request of the bishop of Apt, Saint Castor, set out rules for the monastic life, describing the details of the monastic regimen in dress, prayer, and daily routine. This was entitled *The Foundations of the Cenobitic Life and the Eight Capital Sins,* and it is from this text that the following excerpts are taken. These passages concern the sin of acedia, that peculiar state of despondency, apparently common in the lives of the desert fathers. Cassian's later writing included *Collationes (Conversations),* in which he reported on conversations or interviews with the monks in Egypt, exploring their inner states, including, again, acedia. Because Cassian experienced the cenobitic life at first hand but wrote in Europe, he stands as a key figure linking the early church in the East with its later development in the West.

The notion of acedia or accidia is an obscure one that requires further explanation. (The earlier spelling was *acedia;* later it came to be *accidia.) Acedia* is from a Greek word that means "noncaring state." It was referred to as the midday demon, as Cassian observes, because of the state described in Psalm 91: "Thou shalt not be afraid of the terror by night; nor of the arrow that flieth by day; nor the pestilence that walketh in darkness; nor of the destruction that wasteth at noonday." Regarded as a sin, acedia was a mental state of despondency, lethargy, and discouragement that distracted a solitary monk from his duties. Because it involved dejection and despondency, it is sometimes identified with melancholia. It was also identified during the Middle Ages with the sin of sloth (the desidia portrayed in Breughel's drawing from 1557 [see fig. 6]). Yet, associated as it was both with sorrow and dejection and with inertia and lassitude, acedia seems to be reducible to neither. It is perhaps best seen as a distinct category, capturing a state that arose with the unique cultural conditions associated with the desert fathers. The state and the category disappeared, or were transformed, after those cultural conditions ceased. Those unique conditions? Isolation, a burning sun and dry climate, stringent regimens of fasting, work, and prayer, and a profession whose object, as Cassian puts it, is "nothing but meditation and contemplation of that divine purity which . . . can only be gained by silence and continually remaining in the cell."

Some of Cassian's ideas about acedia were derived from an earlier authority, also one of the desert fathers, Evagrius Ponticus (C.E. 345–399). Evagrius listed eight temptations to which the monks were subject, including exhaustion, listlessness, and sadness or dejection. The monks must serve Christ with joy, not sadness; this was particularly emphasized in writing by the desert fathers. Following Evagrius, Cassian understood acedia to result from temptation by demons. These temptations were later construed as the eight vices or sins important in the medieval church: vainglory, anger, dejection, acedia, pride, covetousness, gluttony, and fornication, out of which, after Pope Gregory (540–604), emerged the seven deadly sins of vainglory, anger, envy, dejection, covetousness, gluttony, and fornication).

Acedia, however, was a special sin. It had a redemptive aspect for Evagrius because the victory over acedia brought joy, the highest of all the virtues, and the state associated with mystical union with God.

Cassian's writing about acedia makes use of medical metaphors, but it is important to recognize that they are metaphors. In emphasizing the link with noontime, he likens acedia to a fever that seizes a person at the same time each day. Later he speaks of this condition as a "disease." Yet these are not a literally medical interpretation such as we find in later writing about states of despondency. Moreover, in quoting the psalmist David, whose condition he recognizes ("My soul slept from weariness"), Cassian makes clear that acedia is a disorder not of the body but of the soul.

The term *acedia* continued in use until the end of the Middle Ages but underwent shifts in meaning. Of these shifts, and of its complex and contested relation to melancholy, Jackson has noted:

> Some modern authors have viewed acedia as little more than a medieval term for what we would call depressive states or as a synonym for melancholia in its own time. Others have thought of it as merely a term for sloth or laziness. These are clearly misleading simplifications. This troublesome state was not merely dejection or sorrow.

Nevertheless, from its beginnings it was associated with tristitia (dejection, sadness, sorrow), and this connection continued; there were frequent references to desperatio (despair) in writings about acedia; and it was intermittently brought into association with melancholia in the late Middle Ages. Similarly, despite having come to be referred to as "the sin of sloth" in the later medieval period and subsequently, acedia was not merely sloth. Nevertheless, lassitude, weariness, inaction, carelessness, and neglect were all aspects of acedia to varying degrees in various instances. (Jackson, 1986:66)

One of the most famous later accounts of acedia comes from the Italian Renaissance poet Petrarch, who speaks of an infliction that "clings to and tortures me for whole days and nights together." In such times, he describes being plunged into hell itself, while yet feeding upon his tears and sufferings "with a morbid attraction" (Petrarch, [1342] 1911:84–85).

•⌐ ● ⌐•

From John Cassian, *Of the Spirit of Accidie,* in *The Foundations of the Cenobitic Life and the Eight Capital Sins* (ca. 416 C.E.)

How our sixth combat is against the spirit of accidie, and what its character is.

Our sixth combat is with what the Greeks call ἀκηδία, which we may term weariness or distress of heart. This is akin to dejection, and is especially trying to solitaries, and a dangerous and frequent foe to dwellers in the desert; and especially disturbing to a monk about the sixth hour, like some fever which seizes him at stated times, bringing the burning heat of its attacks on the sick man at usual and regular hours. Lastly, there are some of the elders who declare that this is the "midday demon" spoken of in the ninetieth Psalm.

•⌐ ● ⌐•

A description of accidie, and the way in which it creeps over the heart of a monk, and the injury it inflicts on the soul.

And when this has taken possession of some unhappy soul, it produces dislike of the place, disgust with the cell, and disdain and contempt of the brethren who dwell with him or at a little distance, as if they were careless or unspiritual. It also makes the man lazy and sluggish about all manner of work which has to be done within the enclosure of his dormitory. It does not suffer him to stay in his cell, or to take any pains about reading, and he often groans because he can do no good while he stays there, and complains and sighs because he can bear no spiritual fruit so long as he is joined to that society; and he complains that he is cut off from spiritual gain, and is of no use in the place, as if he were one who, though he could govern others and be useful to a great number of people, yet was edifying none, nor profiting any one by his teaching and doctrine. He cries up distant monasteries and those which are a long way off, and describes such places as more profitable and better suited for salvation; and besides this he paints the intercourse with the brethren there as sweet and full of spiritual life. On the other hand, he says that everything about him is rough, and not only that there is nothing edifying among the brethren who are stopping there, but also that even food for the body cannot be procured without great difficulty. Lastly he fancies that he will never be well while he stays in that place, unless he leaves his cell (in which he is sure to die if he stops in it any longer) and takes himself off from thence as quickly as possible. Then the fifth or sixth hour brings him such bodily weariness and longing for food that he seems to himself worn out and wearied as if with a long journey, or some very heavy work, or as if he had put off taking food during a fast of two or three days. Then besides this he looks about anxiously this way and that, and signs that none of the brethren come to see him, and often goes in and out of his cell, and frequently gazes up at the sun, as if it was too slow in setting, and so a kind of unreasonable confusion of mind takes possession of him like some foul darkness, and makes him idle and useless for every spiritual work so that he imagines that no cure for so terrible an attack can be found in anything except visiting some one of the brethren, or in the solace of sleep alone. Then the disease suggests that he ought to show courteous and friendly hospitalities to the brethren, and pay visits to the sick, whether near at hand or far off. He talks too about some dutiful and religious offices; that those kinsfolk ought to be inquired after, and that he ought to go and see them oftener: that it would be a real work of piety to go more frequently to visit that religious woman, devoted to the service of God, who is deprived of all support of kindred: and that it would be a most excellent thing to get what is needful for her who is neglected and despised by her own kinsfolk; and that he ought piously to devote his time to these things instead of staying uselessly and with no profit in his cell.

Or the different ways in which accidie overcomes a monk.

And so the wretched soul, embarrassed by such contrivances of the enemy, is disturbed, until, worn out by the spirit of accidie, as by some strong battering ram, it either learns to sink into slumber, or, driven out from the confinement of its cell, accustoms itself to seek for consolation under these attacks in visiting some brother, only to be afterwards weakened the more by this remedy which it seeks for the present. For more frequently and more severely will the enemy attack one who, when the battle is joined, will as he well knows immediately turn his back, and whom he sees to look for safety neither in victory nor in fighting but in flight: until little by little he is drawn away from his cell, and begins to forget the object of his profession, which is nothing but mediation and contemplation of that divine purity which excels all things, and which can only be gained by silence and continually remaining in the cell, and by meditation, and so the soldier of Christ becomes a runaway from His service, and a deserter, and "entangles himself in secular business," without at all pleasing Him to whom he engaged himself.

How accidie hinders the mind from all contemplation of the virtues.

All the inconveniences of this disease are admirably expressed by David in a single verse, where he says, "My soul slept from weariness," that is, from accidie. Quite rightly does he say, not that his body, but that his soul slept. For in truth the soul which is wounded by the shaft of this passion does sleep, as regards all contemplation of the virtues and insight of the spiritual senses.

How the attack of accidie is twofold.

And so the true Christian athlete who desires to strive lawfully in the lists of perfection, should hasten to expel this disease also from the recesses of his soul; and should strive against this most evil spirit of accidie in both directions, so that he may neither fall stricken through by the shaft of slumber, nor be driven out from the monastic cloister, even though under some pious excuse or pretext, and depart as a runaway.

How injurious are the effects of accidie.

And whenever it begins in any degree to overcome any one, it either makes him stay in his cell idle and lazy, without making any spiritual progress, or it drives him out from thence and makes him restless and a wanderer, and indolent in the matter of all kinds of work, and it makes him continually go round the cells of the brethren and the monasteries, with an eye to nothing but this; viz., where or with what excuse he can presently procure some refreshment. For the mind of an idler cannot think of anything but food and the belly, until the society of some man or woman, equally cold and indifferent, is secured, and it loses itself in their affairs and business, and is thus little by little ensnared by dangerous occupations, so that, just as if it were bound up in the coils of a serpent, it can never disentangle itself again and return to the perfection of its former profession.

4
•

Black Bile and Melancholia

AVICENNA

*A*vicenna is the Latinized form of the Arabic *Ibn Sina,* an abbreviation of Abu Ali al Husain ibn Abd, Allah ib Sina. Avicenna lived between 980 and 1037. He was born near Bukhara and was of Persian origin. As a child he was precocious: at the age of ten he is said to have been a perfect master of the Koran, general literature, dogmatic theology, arithmetic, and algebra. Of his medical studies, undertaken while still a youth, Avicenna writes in his autobiography: "Medicine is not a difficult subject and, in a short space of time, I excelled in it so that the master of Physic came to read with me and I began to visit the sick. . . . Consequently there were opened the doors to various kinds of treatment which I learnt by experience (or experiment). I was then about sixteen years of age" (quoted by Shah, 1966:440). A philosopher as well as a physician, Avicenna is widely judged the most important philosopher of medieval Islam, as well as one of the most important medical writers of the era between 1000 and 1500. Avicenna's masterpiece, written in Arabic, was the four-volume *Canon of Medicine.*

The writing on melancholy in the *Canon* illustrates the way humoral theory and the symptom descriptions of melancholia traveled between ancient and medieval (western European) medicine by way of Arabic medicine. Arabic medical authorities such as Avicenna and his immediate influences Ishaq ibn Imran and Haly Abbas knew Greek medical lore, and, although there were also more direct sources through the Latin translations of the Greek works, were to a significant extent responsible for its return to western Europe to influence medieval medicine.

So thoroughgoing was the first step of this series of cultural displacements that the notion of "Arabic" medicine requires qualification. Arabic medical authorities wrote in Arabic, but they were often Christians or Jews; nor were they all Arabs, but also Syrians, Persians, and even Spaniards. And they propounded a medicine that was primarily Galenic and Hippocratic, and is more accurately entitled Greco-Arabic. Their knowledge of Greek traditions was derived from translations of Greek medical writing thought to have been the work of Christian groups driven out of the Byzantine empire, and in these the influence of Galenism predominated.

The second step of this exchange whereby Greco-Arabic medical ideas made their way back to western Europe, enriched by Arabic interpretation and interpolation, is attributable to figures like Constantinus Africanus and Gerard of Cremona. Constantinus was a Muslim who in the eleventh century traveled to Italy from the East, became a convert to Christianity and a Benedictine monk, and translated Arabic medical texts into Latin. Working in Spain in the twelfth century, Gerard of Cremona undertook a similar task, translating into Latin many of the works of Arabic medicine.

One of the works translated by Gerard of Cremona was Avicenna's *Canon of Medicine*. Here, echoing Greek humoral theory, Avicenna proposed that there were four primary fluids or humors whose disposition explained temperament as well as states of health and disease. These were blood, phlegm, (yellow) bile, and black bile, or *sauda,* which is literally "black" or "blackness" in Arabic (Shah, 1966). Normal black bile is defined as the sediment, or heavier constituents, of blood. It is necessary for health. All abnormalities of the black bile, such as those that account for the disease of melancholia, result from combustion and a process of sedimentation allowing overheated vapors to interfere with bodily and brain functioning. Avicenna appears to derive his ideas from earlier thinkers in this Greco-Arabic tradition in positing three types of melancholia, only one of which immediately affects the brain. (The others are centered in the stomach and abdomen or "hypochondriacal" region, on the one hand, and diffused throughout the body, on the other.) Whether more or less directly, however, all psychological effects—delusions, confusions, moods, and fears—stem from overheated black bile in damaging combination with other elements such as phlegm.

Having identified melancholia with the presence of abnormal black bile rendered harmful by a process of overheating and sedimentation, Avicenna lists symptoms, described in the following passages, which also echo those familiar from Greek writing. There are a host of bodily discomforts, such as flatulence, tingling, and sleeplessness. Unreasonable fears and apprehensions predominate, and melancholia is represented primarily as a disorder of imagination, although, as he says, "these signs are truly indefinite," and include an array of false beliefs and distorted perceptions impossible to easily sum up. (Some patients love death, "others abhor it," for example.) The sufferer is downcast and alienated, and demonstrates the darkness of coloring and thickness of hair which the Greeks associated with melancholia.

From Avicenna, "On the Signs of Melancholy's
Appearance," in *On Black Bile and Melancholy,*
from *Canon of Medicine* (ca. 1170–87 C.E.)

The first signs of melancholy are bad judgment, fear without cause,
quick anger, delight in solitude, shaking, vertigo, inner clamor, tingling, especially in the abdomen. When, moreover, fear is confirmed, as
well as badness of judgment, there are anxiety, abandonment of conversation and craving for coitus due to a multitude of flatulence; and
the appearance of fear of things which do or do not exist; and a greatness of fear of things which are not customarily feared. But these appearances certainly are indefinite. For certain bodies fear that the sky
will fall on them, while others fear that the earth may devour them.
Others fear robbers. Others still fear lest a wolf approach them. The
following five things especially they fancy: they imagine themselves
made kings or wolves or demons or birds or artificial instruments. Further, there are certain melancholiacs who laugh whenever they imagine
something that pleases and delights them, especially those whose
melancholy is pure melancholy. There are certain ones who love death.
Others abhor it. Melancholy's signs, which are in the brain, are especially an overflowing of thought and a constant melancholic anxiety,
and a constant looking at only one thing, and at the earth. Melancholiacs show the same color of the head, face, and eyes and the same blackness and thickness of hair and head. There is also an antecedent sleeplessness, meditation, sluggishness in the sun and such things similar to
these, like antecedent sickness of the brain. . . .

The signs of melancholy, however, which are common to the whole
body are the body's blackness, its dryness, its retention of that which is
emptied out of the spleen and stomach and that which is cleaned out
with the periods of the year and months, the multitude of body hair, its
powerful blackness, the preceding intake of bad and melancholic foods
and such things as we teach in the second book. The sicknesses that
melancholy follows are thus temporary and disordered fevers.

The signs of melancholy which are derived from the spleen, are a
multitude of cravings because of the effusion of black bile to the stomach, a scarcity of digestion because of the coldness of the melancholic
condition, a multitude of wrinkles on the left side, and a swelling of the
spleen. . . .

The signs of melancholy that are from the stomach . . . are an increase of sickness with dry nauseousness and a feeling of uncomfortable fullness accompanying digestion. Very many times pains are felt
in the stomach, and these pains continually spread. Then they rest
near the digestive tract. If it is hot, however, this leads to inflammation

and dryness in the abdomen and consequently the spleen has more melancholy.

The signs of melancholy which are in the phlegmatic humor are a heaviness of the phlegm, its attraction to the upper parts of the body, constant nausea, a sickness of the spirit, the disruption of digestion, sour vomit, wet spit, wrinkles, the expulsion of flatulence, swelling, pain in the stomach or pain between both shoulder blades, and the pain spreading especially after eating. He vomits phlegmatic bile. And sour phlegm congeals his teeth. And these things happen due to intake of food, or soon thereafter. The phlegmatic bile will be carried away and alleviated on account of the goodness in food eaten, and increased by the decrease of good foods. . . . Great trembling may be discovered in the abdomen at certain hours. The sickness, however, is increased with the dryness of the nausea and the speed of digestion.

We say above that the black bile makes the disease of melancholy. When black bile is mixed with blood, there is happiness and laughter, and strong sadness does not share in it. If however it is mixed in with phlegm, there is laziness, intertia, and rest. And if it is mixed with or from yellow bile, there are agitation, lesions, some demonic influences, and similar manias. And if it were pure black bile, then there would be a great deal of deliberating, and a reduction of agitation or frenzy; unless it was stirred and upset, or unless there were emnities which could not be forgotten.

5

Melancholia in Men and Women

HILDEGARD OF BINGEN

ONE OF THE MOST TALENTED, eclectic, and interesting personalities of the German Middle Ages, Hildegard lived between 1098 and 1179. She was born the tenth and last child in a noble family at Bingen, which was in the area of Rhenish Hesse, and was as a small girl consecrated to God and entrusted to a woman hermit Jutta of Spanheim (or Sponheim), who lived at the Benedictine monastery of Disibodenberg. From Jutta, Hildegard learned the "Rule of Saint Benedict," the liturgy, the Psalms, and the Bible; later a monk, Volmar, introduced her to the writing of the church fathers. But Hildegard received no training in the classical languages, grammar, logic, mathematics, astronomy, or music, and would later refer to herself as *indocta* (unlearned), which, by the standards of education of her time, she was.

As a young woman Hildegard became a nun, and after Jutta's death she was elected to direct the small convent attached to the Benedictine monastery at Disibodenberg. Later this convent was relocated to Rupertsberg, near Bingen, where Hildegard undertook the planning and construction of a monastery for her nuns, eventually also establishing a daughter house at Eibingen on the Rhine above Rudesheim. In recognition of her work, Emperor Frederick had issued an edict in 1163 granting Hildegard the status of abbess and providing her monastery at Rupertsberg the protection of the imperial realm. Although she suffered much ill health, Hildegard undertook not only the duties associated with her role as abbess, which included looking after the sick in her care, but also traveling and preaching duties. Between 1158 and 1171 she journeyed widely around Germany, offering sermons that had a profound impact on her listeners' lives.

In addition to these religious duties, Hildegard composed music, wrote poetry, invented a language, wrote extensively on religious and spiritual matters and on matters of medical and scientific interest (she is known as the first published woman physician), and kept up an extensive correspondence with influential ecclesiastical and secular leaders—popes, cardinals, archbishops, priests, abbots, and abbesses, as well as monks and nuns. Hildegard was a visionary (by her own testimony she had been favored with visions since she was a small child), and much of her spiritual writing was based on her visions, such as the first major work *Scivas seu visionum ac revelationum libri III* (*Know the Ways of the Lord or Three Books of Visions and Revelations*), written between 1141 and 1151. On the basis of this work Pope Eugene III certified her charisma as a visionary and encouraged her to continue writing. Between 1151 and 1158 she completed two works of more scientific interest, *Physica* (also called *A Study of Nature*) and *Causae et curae*, or *Of Causes and Cures* (a standard abbreviation for what was originally entitled *Liber compositae medicinae* [*Book of Holistic Healing*]), from which the remarks on melancholy that follow are taken.

Of Causes and Cures contains information and suggestions about matters of illness and healing. It reflects a knowledge of the popular and monastic medical practices of its day, as well as Hildegard's own personal experience not only as a sufferer but also as one who herself attended and healed the sick. Because medical teaching and thinking at the time were imbued with spiritual explanation, this is also a book about the theological place of illness. Hildegard treated illness and disorder more as a trial from God than as a punishment for sin, and in this she differed from the "monastic medicine" often practiced in her time. But she also believed that original sin must ultimately explain the presence of suffering, as of sin. In addition, she accepted the doctrine of the four humors known from Greek medicine. Hildegard's overarching ideas have been summarized and simplified by Palmquist and Kulas in the following way: "The interaction and exchange of cosmic matter or energy makes life on this planet possible and gives it shape; this is particularly true of human life. With winds functioning as agents, cosmic forces are introduced into the human being's system of humors. These determine good and bad health as well as moral behavior" (Hildegard, 1994:xviii). Thus mental disorders such as melancholy reflect instability in the person's system of humors, but ultimately that instability is attributable to original sin. Hildegard's writing on melancholy includes the supposition that melancholy afflicted Adam after his sin, and that such melancholy was a type likely to cause illness and disease; indeed, it is possible to read her passage about Adam's state so as to *identify* melancholy with original sin, thus rendering melancholy part of the human condition.

Melancholy takes different forms in men and women for Hildegard. (This aspect of her analysis has earned praise from contemporary thinkers: what is unprecedented in Hildegard, Juliana Schiesari remarks, is that there *are* melancholic women *as a matter of course,* and "these women, in fact, are not the dread icons of male paranoia but *subjectivities* in need of both care and understanding, an attitude that makes Hildegard's text, anachronistically or not, a feminist or protofeminist one" [1992:143].) Hildegard's account of melancholy men is far from flattering: they are embittered, suspicious, resentful, dissolute in their passions, and "as unregulated in their interaction with women as a donkey." Women who are prone to melancholy are also unstable, irresponsible, and dissolute, but their disorder is primarily of sexual function, and they can apparently flourish in a celibate life (such as that of the cloister). They are "more healthy, more powerful, and happier without a mate than with one because they become sick from relations with a husband." (Interestingly, Burton also distinguished male from female forms of melancholy, although in doing so he reveals a predictable misogyny.)

Hildegard's discussion stresses the sense of melancholy as a character trait rather than a mental disorder. However, she does recognize as melancholic disorders—conditions that "come from the bile"—headache, migraine, and dizziness, and it is a combination of these occurring simultaneously that result in madness, a condition of derangement robbing the person of proper understanding. Moreover, there is one reference in this text to melancholy as an acute state. For a person overcome by melancholy, Hildegard recommends "he should quickly heat some wine on the fire, mix it with cold water, and drink it" so that the vapors from his bile will be suppressed.

•⌣ • ⌢•

From Hildegard of Bingen, *Book of Holistic Healing*
(ca. 1151–58 C.E.)

The Melancholic. There are other people who are dour, nervous, and changeable in their mood so that in their case there is no single constant disposition. They are like a strong wind that does harm to all plants and fruits. That is, a phlegm grows in them that is neither moist nor thick, but lukewarm. It is like a slime that is sticky and can be stretched to various lengths. It causes bile that came into being at the very beginning out of Adam's semen through the breath of the serpent since Adam followed his advice about eating the apple.

Melancholy as a Disease. Bile is black, bitter, and releases every evil, sometimes even a brain sickness. It causes the veins in the heart to overflow; it causes depression and doubt in every consolation so that the person can find no joy in heavenly life and no consolation in his earthly existence. This melancholy is due to the first attack by the devil on the nature of man since man disobeyed God's command by eating the apple.

From this meal, this melancholy developed in Adam and in all his posterity; and it is the cause of all serious disease in humans. Because the above-mentioned phlegm is lukewarm, it cannot overcome the power of the melancholy as the other two above-mentioned phlegms can do. These two—the one on the basis of its moisture and the other on the basis of its thickness and bitterness—have so great a power that they can withstand the melancholy like a kettle that hangs over the fire and holds the fire down so that it does not blaze up. People with such a disposition are often angry and—which is a good thing—show reverence before God and men. Some of them live a long time because the strong influence of the above-mentioned phlegm is such that it neither completely kills nor fully empowers, just as happens to a prisoner who is neither killed nor set free. So man lives, as we said above, from the four humors just as the world rests on the four elements.

The Humors. There are four humors. The two dominating ones are named phlegm, and the two that come after them are named slime. Each of the dominating humors is covered with a quarter of the one coming after and a half of the third. The weaker humor regulates the two parts and the remaining part of the third, to make sure it doesn't exceed its limits. In this manner, the first humor dominates the second. These two are called phlegm. The second humor dominates the third, and the third the fourth. These last two, that is the third and the fourth humors, are called slime. The stronger humors surpass the weaker because of their excess, and the weaker humors have a moderating influence on this excess by their weakness. A person in such a state finds himself in peace. However, whenever any humor increases beyond its proper amount, the person is in danger. Whenever either of the above-mentioned slimes exceeds its proper amount, it does not have enough power to take control of the humors lying on top of it, whether it be aroused by an inferior slime to be the preeminent humor, or whether it is an inferior humor supported by a superior one. If such a slime spreads out excessively in a person, his remaining humors cannot remain in peace unless we are dealing with people in whom the grace of God has been poured out—either as strength as with Samson, wisdom as with Solomon, prophecy as with Jeremias, or as with certain pagans, for example Plato and people like him. When the above-mentioned people are not healthy, the grace of God sometimes moves them to change so that they are first sick, then healthy; now anxious, then strong; sometimes sad, then happy. God brings them back to order; that is, he makes them healthy when they are sick, strong when they are anxious, and happy when they are sad. If the dry humor is stronger in a certain person than the moist, or the moist humor than the foamy and the lukewarm, then the dry phlegm is like a lady and the moist like a servant, and the foamy and the lukewarm ones are like two smaller slimy servants standing in the background. For these last two are, corresponding to their powers, the slime of the first two. Such a person is naturally clever, angry, and stormy in everything that he does. He does not have patience, for the dryness consumes these humors and then easily lifts itself again. He is healthy and lives a long time although he will not reach advanced age because he does not receive adequate support from the moist phlegm, and as a result his flesh becomes dried out by the fire.

Madness. If ever the foamy or the lukewarm humors that were drawn together as slime behind the before-mentioned phlegm—that is, of the dry and the moist, which should maintain themselves peacefully—have exceeded their proper amount, like a wave in the water that becomes too big, they change themselves into a poison. A tempest arises out of them in such a way that no humor can be balanced with any other, and they no longer carry out their tasks. These above-mentioned humors fight so strongly against the two harmonizing ones that all four fall into conflict.

Any person who suffers this opposition and contradiction in his body will become mad. For when the inner humors rebel against one another, the person turns violent and fights himself if he is not bound with ropes. This lasts until the above-mentioned foamy and lukewarm humors have weakened and returned to their proper order. Such a person will not live long. However, if the moist humor is stronger than the dry and the dry stronger than the foamy and the lukewarm, which then constitute the slime following after them, such a person is naturally clever and constant, remains so, is sound of body, and will live a long time.

Raving. If one humor overcomes the others in a person and does not observe its proper limits, that man becomes sick and weak. However, if two such humors arise simultaneously against the order in a person, he cannot endure it; he will then be destroyed either physically or mentally, now that the proper proportion is missing. If three such humors spread out simultaneously and excessively, the person will become sick and soon die. If all four humors rise up against the proper order, that person will quickly, in an instant, be killed by them on that very spot. At no time can he endure such a conflict, but will experience a complete breakdown. In such a manner all things will be smashed on the Last Day as the four elements fight among themselves.

Why There are Only Four Humors. Man cannot maintain himself using one, two, or even three humors; he requires four so that they can regulate one another. In the same way, the earth consists of four elements that harmonize with one another.

The Melancholic Man. There are men whose brain is fat. Their scalp and blood vessels are entangled. They have a pale facial color. Even their eyes have something fiery and snake-like about them. These man have hard, strong veins that conduct dark, thick blood; large, firm flesh; and large bones that contain but little marrow. However, this burns so strongly that their behavior with women is as improper and undisciplined as animals and snakes. The wind in their loins comes out in three forms: fiery, windy, and mixed with the smoke of bile. For that reason they really love no one; rather they are embittered, suspicious, resentful, dissolute in their passion, and as unregulated in their interaction with women as a donkey. If they ever refrain from their desire, they easily become sick in the head so that they become crazy. If they satisfy their desire for women, they suffer no spiritual sickness. However, their cohabitation with women which they should maintain in a proper way, is difficult, contradictory, and as deadly as with vicious wolves. Some of them traffic enthusiastically—in the male way—with women because they have strong blood vessels and marrow that burns mightily in them; however, afterwards they hate these women. Others can avoid the female gender because they do not care for women and do not wish to have them, but in their hearts they are as wild as lions and conduct themselves like bears. In practical matters, however, they are handy and skillful, and they enjoy working. The storm of desire that invades the two receptacles of these men comes as unmastered and suddenly as the wind that shakes the entire house mightily, and it lifts the stem up so powerfully that the stem, that should stand in full blossom, curves in the disgusting manner of a viper and in the evil way that a death and decay-bringing viper passes on its malignity to its offspring. The influence of the devil rages so powerfully in the passion of these men that they would kill the woman with whom they are having sexual relations if they could. For there is nothing of love or affection in them. For this reason the sons or daughters that they beget usually have a devilish craziness in their perversity and in their characters because they were begotten without love. Their offspring are often unhappy, impenetrable, and devious in all their conduct. For that reason, also, they cannot be loved by people, and they themselves are not happy in the company of people because they are plagued by many hallucinations. Moreover, if they stay with people, they become envious, resentful, and bitter, and they have no satisfaction with them. However, once in a while some of their children become clever and useful. However, in spite of this usefulness, their evil and contradictory behavior is so manifest that people still cannot love or respect them. They are like ordinary stones that lie around without any shine, as if randomly scattered. Because of that, they cannot be prized among the brilliant stones, for they have no attractive gleam.

The Melancholic Woman. [Some] women have thin flesh, thick blood vessels, moderately strong bones, and blood that is more viscous than bloody. Their complexion is as though mixed with a dark grey color. These women are heedless and dissolute in their thoughts and of evil disposition if they are grieved by any irritation. Since they are unstable and irresponsible, on occasion they also suffer from melancholy. During the monthly menses they lose much blood, and they are infertile because they have a weak, fragile womb. For that reason, they can neither receive, retain, nor warm the male seed. For that reason they are more healthy, more powerful, and happier without a mate than with one because they become sick from relations with a husband. However, men avoid them because they do not speak in a friendly manner to men and because men love them only a little. If ever they feel a desire of the flesh, it goes away again quickly. Some of them still bring at least one child into the world if they have a powerful, full-blooded husband, even when they have attained a mature age, for example, fifty years old. If, however, their husbands are of a weaker nature, they do not conceive by them but remain unfruitful. If their monthly menses ever stops earlier than corresponds to the womanly nature, they get arthritis, swollen legs, or headaches that cause melancholy. They may have back or kidney pains, or their body may swell up a short time because the contradictory impurity, that should be expelled from their body through the monthly menses, remains closed up within. If they receive no help and are not freed from their sufferings by God's help or through a medicine, they will soon die.

6
•

Learned People and Melancholy

FICINO

SON OF A DOCTOR, Marsilio Ficino was born in Italy in 1433 and died in 1499. He lived to be a renowned figure of the Italian Renaissance, a Neoplatonist humanist, a translator of Greek philosophical writing, and the most influential exponent of Platonism in Italy in the fifteenth century.

Ficino received most of his formal education at the university in Florence, where the learned professor Niccolo Tignosi of Foligno taught him philosophy and medicine. It is known that he was attached to a hospital and practiced medicine, although he probably did so without completing a medical degree.

Pursuing his philosophical interests, Ficino worked under the patronage of Cosimo de Medici, who appointed him to head a new Platonic Academy in Florence. He translated many works from classical Greek, including the philosophy of Plotinus. His most important work was *Platonic Theology* (1482), which reflects his Christian and humanistic Platonism.

Three Books on Life, from which the following passages are taken, is a work not on philosophy but on health, in particular the health hazards associated with the intellectual life. Here Ficino offers the learned causes, cures, and particular warnings concerning their health and well-being. This work was immensely popular in Ficino's day. It was read by Robert Burton in the seventeenth century, we know, because Burton lists "Ficinus" as a model for a treatise on melancholy and makes frequent allusions to *Three Books on Life* throughout his work.

Three Books on Life is an arresting and, in several respects, a unique work. It was the first book to single out the health of the intelligent and learned for special attention. It was the first Renaissance work to revive the Aristotelian link between brilliance and melancholy, a link that, due to Ficino's influence, was to become a resounding theme throughout Renaissance and later writing on melancholy. Finally, *Three Books on Life* was distinctive in developing the astrological significance of melancholy, particularly its relation to the planet Saturn.

The personal nature of each of these aspects of the work is revealed in Ficino's own life. He was an intellectual and a brilliant man, a man of ge-

nius. He also suffered melancholy. And he had been born under the in-
auspicious sign of Saturn. Believing as he did that his character was fore-
ordained by his horoscope, Ficino developed the Aristotelian (and, he
insists, even Platonic) connection between melanchonic states and intellectual brilliance. To this he added the accepted astrological link between Saturn and the contemplative and intellectual life, to advance the
idea of genius as the compensating virtue of states of melancholy.

The passages that follow are from the very beginning of this set of
three books. Here Ficino draws the link between the black bile of
melancholy and the inspiration and exalted moods and achievements
of genius. In the second book, the black bile is not presented in such a
positive light, and various nostrums and remedies are proposed to
lessen and diminish its effects. In the third and last book, Ficino develops astrological explanations for melancholy, linking the melancholic
states of Saturnine intellectuals to their horoscopes.

As well as his emphasis on the particular tie between melancholy
and genius, Ficino's remarks in these passages reveal many Galenic and
Aristotelian themes. The dryness and coldness of the humor, the associations of darkness and blackness, and the reference to burnt, or
"adust," black bile and to dusky vapors all find their way into his account. So, also, do the subjective states earlier associated with the
humor. Suffering melancholy, he says, "we hope for nothing, we fear
everything," and "it is weariness to look at the dome of the sky"; the
thick, dense, dusky vapors make the soul "sad and fearful," since "interior darkness much more than exterior overcomes the soul with sadness and terrifies it." Ficino's debt to thinkers of the past, medical and
philosophical, is paid openly. Hippocrates, Aristotle, Galen, Avicenna,
and most of all Plato he acknowledges lavishly.

•‿ • ‿•

From Marsillo Ficino, *Three Books of Life* (1482)

On Caring for the Health of Those Who Devote
Themselves to Literary Studies

Marsilio Ficino the Florentine sends greetings to Giorgio Antonio
Vespucci and Biovanni-Battista Buoninsegni, men who excel in probity
and learning. We have talked much with you recently, strolling like
Peripatetics, about caring for the health of those who devote themselves
fulltime to literary studies. These matters, condensed in a brief compendium, I decided to entrust to you above all. Nor will I myself approve this little piece before I either ascertain that you approve it—you
whom I have put to a more thorough proof than any, both as men and
as friends—or else permit it to undergo the refined judgment of our
dear Lorenzo de' Medici, whose good health indeed is my special con-

cern if ever there is need. For one will hardly be taking any care at all of the intellectuals of today, especially those of our own city, if he does not first take care of their patron, their Maecenas. Read carefully, then, and take care of your health still more carefully. For if health suffers, we either never even reach the high doors of the Muses or at least knock at them in vain—unless God who is omnipotent lead us and open them by miraculous power. We intend this medical disquisition of ours to have in view particularly as a theme, that if for the attainment of wisdom, health of body is so greatly to be sought, much more so is health of mind, by which alone wisdom can be comprehended; if it is not, they will seek knowledge but ignorantly who undertake to grasp wisdom with an unsound mind. Hippocrates promises health of body, Socrates, of soul. But the true health of both is furnished only by Him who cries: "Come unto me, all ye that labor and are heavy-laden, and I will refresh you. I am the way, the truth, and the life."

Learned People Are Subject to Phlegm and Black Bile

Not only should learned people take very diligent care of those members and of the powers and of the spirits, but also they are told always scrupulously to avoid phlegm and black bile, even as sailors do Scylla and Charybdis. For just as they are inactive in the rest of the body, so they are busy in the brain and the mind. From the former circumstance they are compelled to secrete pituita, which the Greeks call phlegm, and from the latter, black bile, which they call melancholy. Phlegm dulls and suffocates the intelligence, while melancholy, if it is too abundant or vehement, vexes the mind with continual care and frequent absurdities and unsettles the judgment. Hence it can justly be said that learned people would even be unusually healthy, were they not burdened by phlegm, and the happiest and wisest of mortals, were they not driven by the bad effects of black bile to depression and even sometimes to folly.

How Many Things Cause Learned People Either to Be Melancholy or to Eventually Become So

In the main, three kinds of causes make learned people melancholics. The first is celestial, the second natural, and the third human. The celestial: because both Mercury, who invites us to investigate doctrines, and Saturn, who makes us persevere in investigating doctrines and retain them when discovered, are said by astronomers to be somewhat cold and dry (or if it should happen to be true that Mercury is not cold, he is nonetheless often very dry by virtue of his nearness to the Sun), just like the melancholic nature, according to physicians. And this same nature Mercury and Saturn impart from birth to their followers, learned people, and preserve and augment it day by day.

The natural cause seems to be that for the pursuit of the sciences, especially the difficult ones, the soul must draw in upon itself from external things to internal as from the circumference to the center, and while it speculates, it must stay immovably at the very center (as I might say) of man. Now to collect oneself from the circumference to the center, and to be fixed in the center, is above all the property of the Earth itself, to which black bile is analogous. Therefore black bile continually incites the soul both to collect itself together into one and to dwell on itself and to contemplate itself. And being analogous to the world's center, it forces the investigation to the center of individual subjects, and it carries one to the contemplation of whatever is highest, since, indeed, it is most congruent with Saturn, the highest of planets. Contemplation itself, in its turn, by a continual recollection and compression, as it were, brings on a nature similar to black bile.

The human cause, that which comes from ourselves, is as follows: Because frequent agitation of the mind greatly dries up the brain, therefore, when the moisture has been mostly consumed—moisture being the support of the natural heat—the heat also is usually extinguished; and from this chain of events, the nature of the brain becomes dry and cold, which is known as the earthy and melancholic quality. Moreover, on account of the repeated movements of inquiry, the spirits continually move and get dispersed. But when the spirits are dispersed, they have to be restored out of the more subtle blood. And hence, when the more subtle and clear parts of the blood frequently get used up, the rest of the blood is necessarily rendered dense, dry and black. On top of this, nature in contemplation is directed wholly to the brain and heart and deserts the stomach and liver. For this reason foods, especially the more fatty or harsh foods, are poorly digested, and as a result the blood is rendered cold, thick, and black. Finally, with too little physical exercise, superfluities are not carried off and the thick, dense, clinging, dusky vapors do not exhale. All these things characteristically make the spirit melancholy and the soul sad and fearful—since, indeed, interior darkness much more than exterior overcomes the soul with sadness and terrifies it. But of all learned people, those especially are oppressed by black bile, who, being sedulously devoted to the study of philosophy, recall their mind from the body and corporeal things and apply it to incorporeal things. The cause is, first, that the more difficult the work, the greater concentration of mind it requires; and second, that the more they apply their mind to incorporeal truth, the more they are compelled to disjoin it from the body. Hence their body is often rendered as if it were half-alive and often melancholic. My author Plato signified this in the *Timaeus;* he said that the soul contemplating divine things assiduously and intently grows up so much on food of this kind and becomes so powerful, that it overreaches its body above what the corporeal nature can endure; and sometimes in its too vehement agitation, it either in a way flies out of it or sometimes seems as if to disintegrate it.

Why Melancholics Are Intelligent, and Which Melancholics Are So and Which Are Not

So far, let it suffice that we have shown why the priests of the Muses either are from the beginning or are made by study into melancholics, owing to causes first celestial, second natural, and third human. This Aristotle confirms in his book of *Problems,* saying that all those who are renowned in whatever faculty you please have been melancholics. In this he has confirmed that Platonic notion expressed in the book *De scientia,* that most intelligent people are prone to excitability and madness. Democritus too says no one can ever be intellectually outstanding except those who are deeply excited by some sort of madness. My author Plato in the *Phaedrus* seems to approve this, saying that without madness one knocks at the doors of poetry in vain. Even if he perhaps intends divine madness to be understood here, nevertheless, according to the physicians, madness of this kind is never incited in anyone else but melancholics.

After this, reasons must be assigned why Democritus, Plato and Aristotle assert that not a few melancholics sometimes so excel everyone in intelligence that they seem to be not human but rather divine. Democritus, Plato, and Aristotle affirm it unhesitatingly, but they do not seem to give a sufficient explanation for so important a fact. One must have the courage, however, God showing the way, to search out causes. Melancholy or black bile is of two kinds: the one is called natural by doctors, the other comes about by adustion. The natural is soothing but a more dense and dry part of the blood. The adust, however, is divided into four kinds. it originates from the combustion either of natural melancholy, or of the purer blood [as opposed to the more dense . . . part of the blood], or of bile [meaning yellow or red bile, better known as choler], or of salty phlegm. Any melancholy which arises from adustion, harms the wisdom and the judgment, because when that humor is kindled and burns, it characteristically makes people excited and frenzied, which melancholy the Greeks call mania and we madness. But as soon as it is extinguished, when the more subtle and clearer parts have been dispersed and only a foul black soot remains, it makes people stolid and stupid; they properly call this disposition melancholy and also being out of one's wits and senselessness.

Only that black bile which we call natural, therefore, leads us to judgment and wisdom—but not always. If it is alone, it beclouds the spirit with a mass that is black and dense, terrifies the soul, and dulls the intelligence. Moreover if it is mixed simply with phlegm, when cold blood stands in the way around the heart it brings on sluggishness and torpor by its heavy frigidity; and as is the nature of any very dense material, when melancholy of this kind gets cold, it gets cold in the extreme. When we are in this state, we hope for nothing, we fear everything, and it is weariness to look at the dome of the sky. If black bile—either simple or mixed—putrefies, it produces quartan fever, swellings of the spleen, and many infirmities of the same kind. When it is too abundant, whether alone or joined with phlegm, it makes the spirits heavier and colder, afflicts the mind continually with weariness, dulls the sharpness of the intellect, and keeps the blood from leaping around the Arcadian's heart. But the black bile should not be so small in quantity, that blood, bile, and spirit, as it were, lack a rein, from which will arise an unstable wit and a short memory; it should not be so great in quantity that, burdened with too much weight, we seem to sleep and to need spurs. Therefore it must be every bit as subtle as its nature allows; for if it were rarefied very greatly, to the extent of its nature, perhaps there could even be much of it without harm, and even so much that it should seem to equal the [yellow] bile, at least in weight.

Therefore let black bile abound, but very rarefied; make sure it has the moisture of the more subtle phlegm surrounding it, so that it doesn't become hard and completely dried up. But let it not be mixed only with phlegm, especially the more frigid sort, or much of it, lest it get cold. But let it be so mixed with bile and with blood, that one body is made of the three humors, compounded in a double proportion of blood to the [sum of the] two others; where there are eight parts blood let there be two portions bile and two again of black bile. Let the black bile be kindled a bit from these two others, and having been kindled let it shine, but not burn, lest, as harder material characteristically does, when it boils too strongly, it should burn too intensely and become agitated, but when it cools off, it similarly should become cold in the extreme. For black bile is like iron; when it starts to get cold, it gets cold in the extreme; and on the contrary, once it tends towards hot, it gets hot in the extreme. Nor should it seem surprising that black bile can be kindled easily and when kindled burn with great intensity, for we see something similar in lime, in that when sprinkled with water it begins at once to boil and burn. Melancholy has a similarly great tendency towards either extreme, in the unity of its fixed and stable nature. This extremism does not occur in the other humors. Extremely hot, it produces the extremest boldness, even to ferocity; extremely cold, however, fear and extreme cowardice. Variously imbued with the intermediate grades between cold and heat, however, it produces various dispositions, just as wine, especially strong wine, characteristically induces various dispositions in those who have imbibed to the point of drunkenness, or even just a little too freely.

Therefore it behooves you to temper black bile in an appropriate manner. When it is moderated as we specified and mixed with bile and blood, because it is dry by nature and in a condition rarefied insofar as its nature admits, it is easily kindled by them; because it is solid and tenacious, once kindled, it burns longer; because it is very powerful in the concentration of its very tenacious dryness, it burns vehemently. Like wood in straw when both are kindled, it burns and shines more and longer. But certainly by means of long-lasting and vehement heat, there arises huge radiance and vehement and long-lasting motion. This is what Heraclitus meant when he said, A dry light, a soul most wise.

7

Melancholia, Witches, and Deceiving Demons

WEYER

JOHANN WEYER (spelled Wier in his native Dutch) was a physician practicing in the Low Countries (on the border of present-day Belgium and Holland) in the sixteenth century. Although his language and culture were Dutch, he was born in Graves, in Belgium, in 1515. Weyer's medical education was received in France, at a time when Renaissance interest in classical Greek culture would have exposed him to the writing of the Greek physicians. He later practiced medicine in his home country, serving from 1550 to 1578 as a court physician for Duke William V of Cleve. Weyer's first and most important work, written between 1561 and 1562, was *De praestigiis daemonum* (*Of Deceiving Demons*), from which the following excerpts are taken. In this work, sometimes thought of as the first textbook of psychiatry, he covers the topic of witchcraft from four different viewpoints, theological, psychological, medical, and legal. Weyer lived in a time of intellectual awakening, of religious fervor, as Protestantism emerged to challenge Catholic practices, and of intense social focus around witchcraft and demonology. Discussions of the relation between mental abnormality, witchcraft, and *lamiae* (literally, witches) may be said to have been one of his enduring contributions to early medicine. Another was his emphasis on careful clinical examination and description.

Weyer's view of the atmosphere of fear and accusation concerning witches and witchcraft is conveyed in the following passage from a letter to his patron: "Witches can harm no one through the most malicious will or the ugliest exorcism, . . . rather their imagination—inflamed by the demons in a way not understandable to us—and the torture of melancholy make them only fancy that they have caused all sorts of evil" (quoted by Weber, 1991:viii). Thus, for Weyer, the seeming presence of supernatural power associated with witchcraft is better understood as a disturbance of the imagination.

Melancholia was a condition identified with the bodily humors, on Weyer's view; in this respect his thinking accords with that of earlier sources. Weyer is remembered in part for his notably humane attitudes toward the treatment of the victims of mental disorder, particularly those whose disturbed imaginations created the delusions misinterpreted as sorcery. As this suggests, Weyer seems to have understood melancholia as more than a mood state: rather, it was a disorder whose central feature was delusions.

While more enlightened and humane than the views of many in his time, Weyer's writing still appears to countenance a demonic source for melancholic states, and it still conveys an unmistakable misogyny. However, Weyer's true views on demonic influence are a matter of controversy. Some historians believe his introduction of a demonic element in his account may have been a device to avoid persecution by the Inquisition. His position is complex: Melancholia made people vulnerable to the disordered imagination mistakenly believed (by themselves and others) to grant supernatural powers. But they were in actuality powerless. (As he says, if these demented old women could do what they confess to doing, the crops would scarcely survive in sufficient amount to sustain mankind!) Thus, victims of these states should not be punished or blamed for their disordered imaginations. Melancholic people were more susceptible to the Devil's influence ("The Devil loves to insinuate himself into the melancholic humor"), albeit the Devil merely created disturbances of their imaginations.

That Weyer could accept any role for demonic influence while at the same time adopting a humane attitude toward those affected still places him at a far remove from the prevailing attitudes of his times. Throughout the fifteenth and sixteenth centuries in Europe, influenced by the notorious *Malleus Maleficarum* written for Pope Innocent VIII in 1485, an equation was widely made between sin, mental disorder, witchcraft, and demonic influence (Sprenger and Kramer, [1487] 1928).

Weyer was primarily a physician, and from all accounts a remarkable one. This makes his work one of the more reliable sources on the balance of men to women suffering melancholia. However, his ideas on this matter are also slightly confusing, even inconsistent. He asserts that men are more often subject to melancholia than women (although he believes that women are more severely affected by it: "melancholia being more opposed to [women's] temperament, it removes them further from their natural constitution"). But he also notes that women are more vulnerable to demonic influence than men, because of a temperament "inconstant, credulous, wicked, uncontrolled in spirit, and . . . melancholic." Thus, we must suppose a humoral imbalance combined with grief over a loss, for example, results in melancholia in men by making them vulnerable to the demons' arts and illusions; while it is perhaps more their dispositional traits that place women at risk. The source of Weyer's inconsistency here seems apparent from his negative portrayals of women, particularly of old women. In an era of witchcraft, the category of eccentric old woman was one that was highlighted. And the women Weyer describes are repeatedly portrayed in terms associated with witches: "stupid," "worn-out," "unstable," "not in the possession of their faculties," and "foolish."

•⤳ ● ⤳•

From Johann Weyer, *Of Deceiving Demons* (1562)

Which Persons Are More Vulnerable to the Demons' Arts and Illusions

On this same subject, the sort of person most likely to be attacked is one who possesses such a temperament or who is so moved by external or internal causes [e.g., if he is attacked by a demon-specter or tempted by a demon's suggestions] that as a result of specious inducements he will readily present himself as a suitable instrument of the demon's will. Melancholics are of this sort, as are persons distressed because of loss or for any other reason, as Chrysostom says: "The magnitude of their grief is more potent for harm than all the activities of the Devil, because all whom a demon overcomes, he overcomes through grief." There are also the people without faith in God, the impious, the illicitly curious, the people wrongly trained in the Christian religion, the envious, those who cannot restrain their hatred, the malicious, old women not in possession of their faculties, and similarly foolish women of noted malice or slippery and wavering faith [for he who believes easily goes back on his belief easily]. These persons [as being fitting instruments] the Devil waylays however he can, in his own time and place. He approaches, follows, and entices such in some special manner, since he knows from sure indications the interests and feelings of every heart. He may assume some attractive form, or variously agitate and corrupt the thoughts and the imagination, until finally these people agree to his proposals, give way to his persuasion, and believe whatever he puts into their minds, as though bound by treaty—depending upon his will and obeying him. They think that everything that he suggests is true, and they are devoutly confident that all the forms imposed by him upon their powers of imagination and fantasy exist truly and "substantially" [in the theological sense] (if I may use this word). Indeed, they cannot do otherwise, since from the time of their first assent he has corrupted their mind with empty images, lulling or stirring to this task the bodily humors and spirits, so that in this way he introduces certain specious appearances into the appropriate organs, just as if they were occurring truly and externally; and he does this not only when people sleep, but also when they are awake. In this manner, certain things are thought to exist or to take place outside of the individual which in face are not real and do not take place, and often do not even exist in the natural world. Such is the almost incomprehensible subtlety of these unclean spirits, and their indefatigable [pursuit of] fraud, deceiving the senses of men. St. Peter, in the writings of Clement, informs us that the demon also besieged the senses of the ancient Egyptians in this way.

Concerning the Credulity and Frailty of the Female Sex

Most often, however, that crafty schemer the Devil thus influences the female sex, that sex which by reason of temperament is inconstant, credulous, wicked, uncontrolled in spirit, and (because of its feelings and affections, which it governs only with difficulty) melancholic; he especially seduces stupid, worn-out, unstable old women.

The Distorted Imagination of Melancholics

Now, lest you regard it as quite absurd that the organs of the imaginative powers should become corrupted in this manner in the case of these poor women, and that their eyes should be blinded (as I have shown above), consider the thoughts, words, sight, and actions of melancholics, and you will understand how in these persons all the senses are often distorted when the melancholic humor seizes control of the brain and alters the mind. Indeed, some of these melancholics think that they are dumb animals, and they imitate the cries and bodily movements of these animals. Some suppose that they are earthen vessels, and for that reason they yield to all who meet them, lest they be "broken." Others fear death, and yet sometimes they choose death by committing suicide. Many imagine that they are guilty of a crime, and they tremble and shudder when they see anyone approaching them, for fear that the person may lay hands upon them and lead them off as prisoners and haul them before the tribunals to be punished. A certain noble-born old man would sometimes suddenly leap from his chair thinking that he was being attacked by enemies; laying hold of them, he would at once stuff them into the oven (at least in his own mind). Another man used to be afraid that Atlas was growing tired of supporting the whole world on his shoulders, and that in his weariness he was going to shake off his burden, and everyone would be crushed by the great collapse. Also, I have learned that three men in Friesland not far from Groningen were so carried away with religious enthusiasm that they believed that they were God the Father, God the Son, and God the Holy Spirit, and that the barn in which they were standing was Noah's ark; and many similarly afflicted persons came streaming to this "ark" for safety. And I know of a melancholic Italian who believed that he was monarch and emperor of the whole world and that the title pertained to him alone. In other respects he was well off, a skilled speaker, and suffering from no other malady. Meanwhile, he took great pleasure in composing his Italian verses about the state of Christianity and religious disputes and the wars that had arisen in France and Belgium, as though these verses were divine proclamations. And he spread his title abroad everywhere by means of the letters R. R. D. D. M. M.—that is, *Rex Regum, Dominus Dominatium, Monarcha Mundi* [King of Kings, Lord of Lords, Monarch of the World]. . . .

But as for . . . the peasant from our own country who vomited glass and hair and nails and heard the sound of glass breaking in his belly and felt the striking of the hours in his heart—the things which these persons convinced themselves that they saw or heard are partly true and partly false, in my opinion. Actually, to see something truly, and to continue in the state of seeing, is quite absurd unless there exists something that may be seen. And yet, they do see certain things and hear certain things; and this is caused by the black bile which comes partly from food and drink, from the air, from grief, from the fear of poverty, partly from the constitution of the sky and climate, and partly from associations with other delirious persons.

I once had a friend whose misfortune it was to be compelled to live in one of these "valleys" for eighteen months. When he returned to me, he told many incredible stories about these phenomena, although he was scarcely ignorant of philosophy; and I admonished him to speak no further of such things unless he wished to be considered a fool and to be put in jeopardy of his life. And so he involved himself in hard work; and by changing his manner of life, he recovered, while enjoying the association of others. Also, for many individuals, retention of seed and of menses causes this disease to arise or increase. In general, the delusion comes from three sources: from the images presented by the black bile, from the steadfastness of the persons impaired by this illness, and from the deceit of the judges. For it was once permitted that the very persons to whom the goods of the condemned would accrue were the ones who accused and condemned them. And so, lest they seem to condemn these unfortunates most unjustly, they added many details to the fables. But in the examination of these people and in their confessions, there was never found anything that was not inane or false or inconsistent or unimportant, except for the despising of religion. Certain women did in fact deny Christ, and others would sew the Host into their clothing, and others used to spit upon the images of the Saints and do other things of the like.

. . . But to return to my point, the former group sometimes persuaded themselves that they saw and heard certain things, then afterwards, in keeping with their own frivolity, they expanded the material with lies, and because of their mutual conversations "a gnat gave birth to an elephant" (as they say). Most people occasionally see and hear some unusual things; but they make little of them and show sound judgment by rejecting and disregarding them. . . .

Narratives of this sort were included among historical accounts by many writers. Because of their inexperience and their excessive gullibility, they convinced themselves (from the "examples" of times past) that whatever is said or discussed by the crowd or whatever is handed down by others not only could have happened but actually did happen. Although these "examples" are wrapped in fable, with these writers they attain to the credibility of history. . . .

Tired of fables, I shall include a true story, quite charming and relevant, about a worn-out old woman given to imagining things. Persons who stray from common sense are sometimes popularly said to be "imagining things," and their distortion of understanding or reasoning or thought is termed their "imagination." This poor woman used to make up medications and forecast the future in Waldassen around the year 1555. She was therefore summoned for questioning by the administrator of those domains. Wishing to deceive him, she responded to his questions by reproaching the folly of those who followed her. But when she was pressed harder, with threats of torture, she said she belonged to a group called "vagabond spirits" by the Germans, and that four times a year she left her body behind as though lifeless and wandered far abroad in the spirit—to solemn assemblies and feasts and dances, at which the emperor was also present. She said that on the authority of an Imperial letter of privilege bestowed upon her she was allowed to make curses, predict the future, and frequent those assemblies, with her spirit flying forth. Upon being ordered to show the letter of privilege, she produced a letter in Latin, pertaining to the ordination of so-and-so, Imperial chaplain, now a bishop, which had been lost at Eger in the expedition against Saxony. She also produced the papers of a certain vagabond wherein he extolled his unguents and his skill in cutting out the stone [a stone in the head], and other things of the sort. Relying on these pieces of evidence, and no doubt deluded by the demon, if she said these things seriously, the irresponsible old woman confessed that she had unlimited powers in administering medications and performing divination. But she was warned to desist and repent, and she was punished with exile. In the meantime, nevertheless, she greatly desired the return of the Imperial letter (without which she was probably convinced that no good result could come from her customary arts). And when some persons asserted that her apparently lifeless body had been seen, the former administrator of Waldsassen, Master Henricus Wessius (a most learned Doctor of Law, now Chancellor of Cleves, who reported this whole story to me as it happened) prudently advised that if they should see it again they should hold a fire to it. He had perhaps read in the *Book of Conformities* about Brother Rodicosanus who was sleeping by the hearth when the demon moved a burning coal next to his hand; awakening at once, the brother snatched the coal from the Devil's hand in order to strike him with it, if he had not disappeared.

That the Air Can in No Way Be Disturbed by Lamiae and How They Are Led by the Devil to This Belief in their Own Power Also, That Crops Are Not Enchanted

As regards the stirring up of the air, these poor old women are *singularly* deluded by the Devil. As soon as he foresees from the movement of the elements and the course of nature that the air will change and there will be storms (which he sees more quickly and easily than men can), or as soon as he realizes that a plague is to be visited upon someone in keeping with the hidden will of God and that the task of bringing it about will be his, he agitates the minds of these poor women and fills them with various images and suggestions, as though they are going to disturb the air and rouse tempests and call forth the hail because of jealousy against a neighbor or for revenge against an enemy. He therefore instructs them in such a way that sometimes they throw pebbles behind their back toward the west, sometimes they throw sand from a rushing stream into the air, and frequently they dip a broom into water and sprinkle it toward the sky, or they make a little ditch and pour in urine or water which they stir with their finger. Occasionally they boil boars' bristles in a pot, and sometimes they set tree trunks or logs crosswise on a river bank, and perform other nonsensical actions of the sort. To draw his noose tighter, Satan fixes in advance the day and the hour (known to him in the way already described). And when these women behold the outcome, all the desired disturbances in the air, they are confirmed all the more [in their beliefs], as though this result follows upon their activities (which could not even call forth a drop of water). No person of sound mind should believe that the elements obey the futile actions of poor crazy women and that at their pleasure the natural order of things, instituted by God, is impeded or inverted. But this would assuredly be the case if tempest, rains, hail, and lightning served the will of these women, so as to appear whenever and however they command. So, too, divine power would be surpassed and overcome by human will, "as though reduced to servitude," as Hippocrates has so effectively put it. Seneca's verdict will therefore be correct: "Antiquity, still lacking in education, believed that rains were attracted and repelled by charms; but it is so obvious that none of this is possible that we need not repair to the school of some philosopher in order to appreciate the fact." If, however, they have gotten it into their minds that they can accomplish some great result by some evil curse or the muttering of certain words, I would say (along with Socrates) that enchantments and incantations are *words* that deceive human souls because of the way that they are interpreted, or because of the fear that they strike into the hearer, or because of the despair that they engender. I definitely feel that no value whatever should be attributed to these words, since they can produce no effect truly and naturally, and for that reason cannot change health to sickness—

although old women falsely believe that they can do this by use of these words. However, diseases of this sort are often brought about and inflicted by the Devil, with God's permission because of men's lack of faith and their ill-founded belief in the power of witches. I would like to say the same about the crops, which can in no way be damaged by words of enchantment or by curses, though if God allows, they can be damaged by the demon, to be sure, or by poisoning. Far less can they be transferred to another place, although the ancients were nursed upon another quite different belief at the breasts of the poets, a belief which has also come down to us. Hence, this well-known law of the *Twelve Tables:* "Let him who has enchanted the fruits of the field pay the penalty. Do not by charms attract another's crop. Do not enchant or rob the field of its fruit."

But Gaius Furius Cresinus shows us the true "charms and poisons" by which crops are attracted and transferred into a field. Freed from slavery, he was reaping much larger harvests from this very tiny little field than his neighbors were from their huge fields, and he began to be greatly resented as though he were attracting the crops of others by *maleficium* or evil-doing. Therefore, on the day appointed by the magistrate Spurious Albinus, when the matter was to come to a vote of the tribe, in fear of condemnation, he brought all his farm equipment along with him into the forum and also brought his daughter, who was strong and (as Piso says) well nourished and well clad, and his skillfully made iron implements, stout mattocks, heavy ploughshares, and well-fed oxen. Then he said "These are my 'evil-doings,' my fellow citizens; I cannot show you or bring into the forum my nightly toil, my wakefulness, and my sweat." And so he was acquitted by unanimous vote.

Because of its unusual nature, I will here include, in passing, another story, not so commendable, of attracting crops and wealth, though scarcely by magical charms. It concerns a certain citizen of a prominent town in the district of Overijssel, who personally explained the tale to a man renowned for his learning and virtue, and added that he had truly experienced wondrous good fortune. At first endowed with modest wealth and living at home from his own table, he remained unmarried. Every Saturday he would purchase cheaply as much whey as would last him as food for a whole week; crumbling rye bread into it, he would allow it to sour for seven days before eating of it, less he be overly influenced by the delicious taste of a fresher product and consume too much thereof. With this preparation of curds, he would allay not only hunger but also his thirst, and he would thereby refresh himself, since the preparation filled the place of both food and drink. But whenever he was moved by some festive occasion or by a gladdened spirit to cheer and spoil himself with a more generous feast, he would add to this first course a second—of an egg or two (For this purpose he nourished a hen, on the "splendid" fodder of her own dung.) And with singular dexterity he fortified himself against any ill effects of the cold by carrying the few pieces of firewood that he had once purchased up to the top floor of the house and back down again until he became warm. In this way, it was ever the case that "the closed kitchen was cold, with bare hearth." He had no need for lights, save those of the heavens—the sun and the moon, that is—since he knew how to obey the season and adapt himself to it, no less than the swallow, the stork, or any other creature which thus conceals itself. All year long, when the sun set, he too would retire, and when it arose, he too would appear; he availed himself of the moon less frequently. Furthermore, he washed his linens from time to time no less frugally, scrubbing them with hen droppings in place of soap. By this wealth of foresight he supported and sustained his house without any expenses and so satisfied his wishes that whatever came in annually from his properties was put out at interest. So finally this "Euclio" [the proverbial miser] attained to wealth—if a man owned by his own possessions can be called wealthy. Although it is with kindly intentions that I have revealed this technique for attracting wealth, I would hope that there is no need to point out that no one should wish to imitate it. But what actually came of all this?—that which the comic writer has described well and truly: "The frugal man is just looking for a prodigal." Scarcely had the fellow drawn his last breath, when (at the funeral) his heirs mourned his passing in a manner quite new to the house and with drink of a different sort, and in such a way that they did not forbear to slander him for the shamelessness of his unequal greed, boasting that they would keep accounts differently, and so they did. Whatever had been amassed over the many years by his pursuit of frugality was more quickly squandered, and with less effort. But let us return to our subject.

For the above reasons, I am understandably compelled to wonder greatly, and regret deeply, that in years past, in those parts of the Empire and neighboring regions where the voice of the Gospel is believed to ring out more clearly, when a vineyard has been ruined by storm or a harvest already in blade has been scattered, the magistrates have not turned their minds; eyes to the hand of a testing or punishing God; rather have they neglected the hand of God and looked to the large number of poor, raving, mentally unstable women, and had them hauled off to filthy jails (the hospices of demons) and dreadful torture-chambers, where they are forced to confess to raising storms and bringing damage to property; and then they are solemnly consigned to Vulcan's fires. But there is no doubt that they were deluded in mind by the Devil, who corrupted their imagination with tricks and illusions so that they confessed to things that they could not have done, just as possessed persons are wont to confess, and also melancholics and persons suffering from incubus, and "wolf-men," and "dog-men," and demented persons, and fools, and children. It has been abundantly demonstrated that a just and most merciful God has not subjected the air or the elements to the will and power of a malicious woman, or of some other evil individual, so that they can cause harm by commanding them. If the Devil has "power over the air," it is only God's permission that he awaits and longs for, ever desirous of causing harm; and so I will say frankly that it is an absurd error if anyone believes that the Devil is subjected to the power of a crazy evil-doing old woman. In fact, the woman is so subject to him that in thought word and deed she complies with his will, whereas he certainly cannot choose to do her bidding, even if they both seek the same end, because he is compelled to obey always the edit of God and sometimes that of God's faithful ministers. In corrupting things by violent disturbances of the air or in any other way, the spirit of storms awaits the consent and approval of God alone, when He has decided to test or punish His faithful; but His true ministers will sometimes be able to expel a demon in Christ's name. Accordingly, those who think that their eyes are penetrated by the light and rays of truth [the clergy] should alter the opinions of the magistrate and the common people; trying diligently, with authoritative discourse, to call their hearers back from the crime of idolatry, they should also explain this most unspeakable form of idolatry whereas people attribute to *Lamiae* that which pertains to the Divine Majesty alone—the voluntary stirring of storms and inciting of hail. Also [they might add], the human spirit is sometimes so downcast in time of affliction that it can scarce believe that there still exists a God Who can bring assistance.

If these demented old women could do what they confess to doing, the crops would scarcely survive in sufficient amount to sustain humankind; in fact, nothing in all nature would remain incorrupt and not even man himself would endure. . . .

Many Persons Beset by Melancholia Are Thought to Be Possessed, and Vice Versa

The depraved imagination of melancholics and their subsequent foolish and deranged behavior, and also the occasional serious, grievous, and frightful things that they do, have been discussed above at sufficient length and there is little need for repetition. As a result of these actions, such persons are often judged to be either stupid or possessed by demons—just as possessed persons in turn are often called melancholic. And so there is need for careful judgment here, to distinguish between the two afflictions (which are even found together in many instances). As I have remarked previously, the Devil loves to insinuate himself into the melancholic humor, as being a material well suited for his mocking deceptions; St. Jerome has therefore most appropriately termed melancholia "the Devil's bath." Nevertheless, not all melancholics are driven by demons. On the other hand, it usually happens that all possessed persons are rendered melancholic because of their bitter torments and grievous afflictions. A woman of Büderich was troubled every year by such melancholia (or rather, mania), so that for weeks on end she lingered by night about the tombs in the cemeteries. Sometimes, too, she would run out into the streets, breaking down one person's doors or smashing another's windows; and occasionally she would run away to more remote and wooded places. Because these attacks came on especially around the feast of Easter—that is, in the springtime (which is appropriate for this malady, because of the mixture of humors)—it was popularly supposed at the time that she was being harassed by an evil spirit.

How Lamiae—Afflicted with Mental Error by the Devil and harmful to No One—Are to Be Brought Back to the Faith, and What Penalty Should Be Decreed for Them Also, an Argument That Not Every Intention Is to Be Punished

Let it be recognized, therefore, that these *Lamiae* have been deluded by error and fantasy and seduced by Satan's perverse teaching. Let it be known with certainty that no harm has come to anyone from them in reality but only in their imagination. They should be informed with sounder doctrine, so that they may repudiate the demon's illusions and pledge allegiance once more to Christ, and so that, like limbs disjointed from their bodily connections, they may by repenting be restored to place with the suitable binding. . . .

But if anyone should argue contentiously that the will or intent should be punished more severely, let him first distinguish between the fully-formed will of a sane person, which has truly begun to be directed toward action, and the feelings of an impaired mind or (if you prefer) the corrupt will of a mentally defective person. With this "will" the Devil mockingly cooperates, as though his activities were those of the other party; no other effect follows upon the foolish wishing of such a person. This impairment of the will might also be imputed to melancholics, fools, and children, who are easily induced to imagine falsely and confess that they have perpetrated this or that evil. And yet God, Who searches the heart and the reins, does not allow them to be punished equally with those of sound mind; far less should they be so punished by mere men.

8

•

Melancholy Nuns

TERESA OF AVILA

A CARMELITE NUN who lived in Spain between 1515 and 1582, Saint Teresa (or Theresa) of Avila was one of the most remarkable women of her time. Coming from a wealthy family of Jewish "converso" origins (they had been required to adopt Christianity at the end of the previous century), she entered the Carmelite order in her teens. Here, after a period of spiritual aridity and a "second conversion" in 1555, she experienced mystical states and visions, and came to yearn for a simpler, humbler cloistered life. Teresa possessed several rarely combined talents. She was a mystic and contemplative of great spirituality; she has been named Doctor of the Church for her work on prayer and contemplation, which is judged some of the very finest in the tradition of Christian mystical writing. She was also a reformer. Sometimes at odds with the church and the Inquisition (the papal nuncio Felipe Sega referred to her as a "restless gadabout" in 1577), she founded the separate "Discalced" (barefoot) Carmelites whose more spiritual and ascetic rule was to influence the Catholic Reformation not only in Spain but also throughout Europe. Finally, she was a practical organizer and a brilliant and sensitive leader of her groups of nuns in the several convents where she served as abbess.

Saint Teresa wrote in Castilian, which was closer to common speech than the more formal ecclesiastical Latin. Her longer works include her *Life,* written between 1562 and 1565; *The Foundations* (1573–82), describing the beginnings of her order; *The Way of Perfection;* and *The Interior Castle.* The passages excerpted here are from *The Foundations* and *The Interior Castle.*

Teresa acknowledges the standard theological explanation of melancholy in terms of demonic influence, yet she seems loath to press this explanation or to burden the suffering person with it. While melancholy is caused by the Devil, in *The Interior Castle* she counsels against telling the melancholics so when their condition produces what Teresa calls "locutions," or inner voices. One should not disturb these persons by telling them their locutions come from the Devil; instead, "one must listen to them as to sick persons." Nonetheless, as the passages from the *Foundations* illustrate, Teresa believed that particularly firm treatment was required for nuns suffering lesser forms of melancholy who retained some self-control. ("If words do not suffice, use punishment; if light punishment is not enough, try heavy" [135–36].) These differences between severe affliction and even madness as the result of melancholy, and less severe melancholic states are also carefully distinguished by Teresa. The reason is "darkened" in the severely disordered, and they must not be punished. The condition should be called a serious illness, in these cases, she insists, and be cared for as such (137). But those maintaining some self-control should be forced to control themselves. This last group impose a special burden, because one is obliged to "consider someone a rational person and deal with her even though she isn't" (134).

Written in 1577, during a time of conflicts in Madrid and Rome over her work and writing, and of personal and perhaps physical suffering (of that period, Teresa reported "great noise and weakness in my head"), *The Interior Castle* is a book solely about the inner life. Devoted to a discussion of prayer and contemplation, it uses the extended architectural metaphor of a castle with its interior chambers. The outer wall of the castle, the body, is ordinary, but the interior contains levels of spirituality or "dwelling places" found through spiritual searching, at the center of which is to be found communion with God or, in Teresa's expression "spiritual betrothal."

It is in her long discussion of the sixth dwelling place of the inward journey that Teresa again speaks of melancholy, a condition of which, she asserts, the world is full. In this later discussion, she seems to adopt a softer attitude toward those who suffer from melancholia. She is concerned over confessors not sensitive to the difference between the suffering and delusion produced by melancholy and the struggle and pain we undergo in spiritual quest. Melancholy places its sufferer beyond religious consolation or ministration: "There is no remedy in this tempest," she remarks, and at best, those undergoing these afflictions should be encouraged to engage in external works of charity and to hope for the mercy of God.

Inexperienced confessors can confuse spiritual suffering and the pain caused by God's "setting the soul on fire" with the suffering of melancholy, which is the Devil's work, so Teresa describes how those states may be distinguished. The quality of the "delightful pain" we experience in closeness to God is never permanent or continuous: it comes and goes; it leaves our senses and faculties unaffected; it is accompanied by spiritual quiet and delight of the soul; it brings the determination to suffer for God and to withdraw from earthly satisfactions. The experience of those who are melancholic have none of these characteristics, Teresa insists.

Throughout her discussions on melancholia, Teresa reveals her concern and her ability to distinguish melancholic from related states, and her compassionate yet practical treatment of melancholic experience.

From Teresa of Avila, *The Foundations* (1573–82)

How one must deal with the nuns who have melancholy.
This chapter is necessary for prioresses.

These Sisters of mine at St. Joseph's in Salamanca, where I am staying while writing this, have repeatedly asked me to say something about how one must deal with the nuns who have that bodily humor called melancholy. For however much we strive not to accept those who have it, it is subtle and feigns death when it needs to, and thus we do not recognize it until the matter cannot be remedied. It seems to me that in a little book I said something about this; I don't remember. Little is lost in saying something here, if the Lord be pleased that I succeed in doing so. It could be that I said something about this already, at another time; I would mention it another hundred times if I thought I could say something pertinent about the matter. So many are the contrivances that this humor seeks in order to do its own will that there is a need to search them out in order to know how to bear with those who have it and govern them so that no harm is done to the other nuns.

It must be pointed out that not all of those who have this humor are so troublesome, for those who are humble and goodnatured, even though they are disturbed within themselves, do not hurt others, especially if they possess sound intelligence. And also there are greater and lesser degrees of this humor. Certainly, I believe the devil takes melancholy as a means for trying to win over some persons. And if they do not walk with great care, he will do so. For since this humor can subdue reason, what won't our passions do once reason is darkened? It seems that if reason is wanting, madness results, and so it does. But in those of whom we are now speaking, the melancholy doesn't reach the point of madness, which would be much less harmful. But to have to consider someone a rational person and deal with her as such even though she isn't is an unbearable burden. Those who are totally afflicted with this illness are to be pitied, but they do no harm, and if there is a means for bringing them under control, it is to put fear into them.

With those in whom this very harmful affliction has just begun, even though it is not so strong, the same remedy is necessary if other attempts prove insufficient. The affliction, in sum, springs from the humor or root and stems from that stock. And it is necessary that the prioress make use of the penances of the order and strive to bring these persons into submission in such a way as to make them understand they will obtain neither all nor part of what they want. For if they come to think that sometimes their cries, and the furies the devil speaks through them in order to bring them to ruin if he can, are sufficient for them to get what they want, they will be lost. And one such person is enough to disrupt the quiet of a monastery. Since the poor little thing has no one to help her defend herself from the things the devil puts before her, it is necessary for the prioress to proceed with the greatest care in governing her not only in exterior but also in interior matters. For since reason is obscured in the sick person, it must be clear in the prioress so that the devil doesn't begin to bring that soul under his control, taking that affliction as a means. Only at intervals does this humor afflict so much as to subdue reason. And then the person is not at fault, just as insane people are not at fault for the foolish things they do. But those who are not insane, whose reason is weak and at other times well, still have some fault. Thus it is a dangerous thing if during the times in which they are ill they begin to take liberties, which is a terrible artifice of the devil. It's necessary that they do not do so; otherwise, they will not be masters of themselves when they are well. If we consider the matter, that which interests these melancholic persons most is getting their own way, saying everything that comes to their lips, looking at the faults of others with which they hide their own, and finding rest in what gives them pleasure; in sum, they are like a person who cannot bear anyone who resists him. Well, if the passions go unmortified, and each passion seeks to get what it wants, what would happen if no one resisted them?

I repeat, as one who has seen and dealt with many persons having this affliction, that there is no other remedy for it than to make these persons submit in all the ways and means possible. If words do not suffice, use punishment; if light punishment is not enough, try heavy; if one month in the prison cell is not enough, try four months; no greater good can be done for their souls. For as I have said and I repeat (and it is important for the afflicted themselves to understand this, even though at times they may be unable to help themselves), since the affliction is not confirmed madness of the kind that excuses one from any fault—although sometimes it may be, but it is not always so—the soul remains in much danger. . . .

There is another very great harm, leaving aside the danger that was mentioned: Since the afflicted nun appears to be good and the force the illness exercises interiorly is not understood, our nature is so miserable that each one will think that she herself is melancholic and that thus others must bear with her. And, in point of fact, the devil will cause the matter to be thus understood, and he will bring about such havoc that when one comes to recognize the fact there will be difficulty in providing a remedy. This matter is so important that no negligence whatsoever should be allowed. But if the melancholic nun should resist the prelate, who is the superior, she should pay for it in the same way as the healthy nun and should not be pardoned for anything. If she should utter an insulting word to her Sister, the same holds true. So likewise in all similar things.

It seems to be unjust to punish a sick person, who can't help it, just as one would a healthy person. Therefore, it would also be unjust to bind and whip the insane, and the just thing would be to allow them to kill everyone. Believe me, I have tried and, in my opinion, attempted many remedies, and I find no other. It absolutely must not be tolerated that the prioress out of pity allow such nuns to begin taking liberties, for when she gets down to remedying the situation much harm will have already been done to others. If the insane are bound and chastised so that they will not kill others, and this is right and even seems to be a very compassionate thing to do since they cannot control themselves, how much more must one be careful not to allow these melancholic persons liberties by which they could harm souls. And I truly believe that this affliction is often, as I have said, found in those whose dispositions are unrestrained, lacking in humility, and poorly disciplined; and the humor doesn't have as much strength as in the insane. I mean that "in some" the humor doesn't have as much strength, for I have seen that when there is someone to fear they do control themselves and they can. Well, why can't they do so for God? I fear that the devil, under the guise of this humor, as I have said, wants to gain many souls.

Nowadays the term is used more than usual, and it happens that all self-will and freedom go by the name melancholy. Thus I have thought that in these houses and in all Religious houses, this term should not be uttered. For the term seems to bring along with it freedom from any control. Rather, the condition should be called a serious illness—and how truly it is one—and be cared for as such. For sometimes it is very necessary to reduce the humor by means of medicine in order that it be endured; and the nun must remain in the infirmary and understand that when she comes out and returns to the community she must be humble like all and obey as do all. And she must understand that when she does not do so she may not use the humor as her defense. For the reasons that I have mentioned, and more could be said, this procedure is fitting. The prioress must, without letting these nuns realize it, lead them with much compassion, like a true mother, and seek whatever means she can to provide a remedy.

It seems that I am contradicting myself because up to now I said that these nuns must be dealt with strictly. So I repeat that they must not think they can come out and do what they want, nor should they be allowed out except under the condition that they must obey. For the harm lies in their thinking that they will be free to do whatever they want. But the prioress can refrain from ordering them to do what she sees they will be unable to do because of their not having the strength within themselves. She should lead them with all the skill and love necessary so that if possible they submit out of love, which would be much better, and usually happens. She should show that she greatly loves them and make this known through words and deeds. And she must note that the greatest remedy she has is to keep them much occupied with duties so that they do not have the opportunity to be imagining things, for herein lies all their trouble. And even though they may not perform these duties so well, she should suffer some defects so as not to have to suffer other greater ones that will arise if the melancholy over-powers them. I know that this is the most suitable remedy you can pro-vide. And strive that they do not have long periods of prayer, not even those established in the constitutions, because, for the greater part, their imaginations are weak and the long prayer will do them much harm. Otherwise, they will fancy things that neither they nor anyone who hears them will ever understand. Let her take care that they eat fish only rarely; and also during the fasts, they ought not fast as much as do the others.

It seems excessive to give so much advice for this affliction and not for any other, there being so many serious ones in our miserable life, es-pecially when considering the weakness of women. It is for two reasons that I do so: First, it seems these nuns are well, for they don't want to know that they have this affliction. Since it doesn't force them to stay in bed, because they do not have a fever, or to call the doctor, it's necessary for the prioress to be their doctor; for it is a sickness more prejudicial to all perfection than that of those who are in bed and in danger of death. Second, in the case of other illnesses it happens that either one is cured or one dies; with this illness, very seldom are the afflicted cured, nor do they die from it but they come to lose their minds completely—which is a death capable of killing all the nuns. They suffer more than death in themselves through afflictions, fantasies, and scruples, all of which they call temptations, and so they will have a great deal of merit. If they could come to understand that the illness is the cause of these, they would find much relief provided they paid no attention to them.

Indeed, I have great compassion for them, and it is also right that all those living with them have it. These latter should reflect that the Lord can give this compassion, and they should bear up with them, without letting this be known as I have said. Please the Lord I may have suc-ceeded in pointing out the proper thing to do in regard to so serious an illness.

•◡ ● ◠•

From Teresa of Avila, *The Interior Castle* (1577)

The Lord is wont also to send it [the soul] the severest illnesses. This is a much greater trial, especially when the pains are acute. For in some way, if these pains are severe, the trial is, it seems to me, the greatest on earth—I mean the greatest exterior trial, however many the other pains. I say "if the pains are severe," because they then afflict the soul interiorly and exteriorly in such a way that it doesn't know what to do with itself. It would willingly accept at once any martyrdom rather than these sharp pains; although they do not last long in this extreme form. After all, God gives no more than what can be endured; and His Majesty gives patience first. But other great sufferings and illnesses of many kinds are the usual thing.

I know a person who cannot truthfully say that from the time the Lord began forty years ago to grant the favor that was mentioned she spent even one day without pains and other kinds of suffering (from lack of bodily health, I mean) and other great trials. It's true that she had been very wretched and that everything seemed small to her in comparison with the hell she deserved. Others, who have not offended our Lord so much, will be led by another path. But I would always choose the path of suffering, if only to imitate our Lord Jesus Christ if there were no other gain; especially, since there are always so many other benefits.

Oh, were we to treat of interior sufferings these others would seem small if the interior ones could be clearly explained; but it is impossible to explain the way in which they come to pass.

Let us begin with the torment one meets with from a confessor who is so discreet and has so little experience that there is nothing he is sure of: he fears everything and finds in everything something to doubt because he sees these unusual experiences. He becomes especially doubtful if he notices some imperfection in a soul that has them, for it seems to such confessors that the ones to whom God grants these favors must be angels—but that is impossible as long as they are in this body. Everything is immediately condemned as from the devil or melancholy. And the world is so full of this melancholy that I am not surprised. There is so much of it now in the world, and the devil causes so many evils through this means, that confessors are very right in fearing it and considering it carefully. But the poor soul that walks with the same fear and goes to its confessor as to its judge, and is condemned by him, cannot help but be deeply tormented and disturbed. Only the one who has passed through this will understand what a great torment it is. For this is another one of the terrible trials these souls suffer, especially if they have lived wretched lives; thinking that because of their sins God will allow them to be deceived. Even though they feel secure and cannot believe that the favor when granted by His Majesty, is from any other spirit than from God, the torment returns immediately since the favor is something that passes quickly, and the remembrance of sins is always present, and the soul sees faults in itself, which are never lacking. When the confessor assures it, the soul grows calm, although the disturbance will return. But when the confessor contributes to the torment with more fear, the trial becomes something almost unbearable—especially when some dryness comes between the times of these favors. It then seems to the soul that it has never been mindful of God and never will be; and when it hears His Majesty spoken of, it seems to it as though it were hearing about a person far away.

All this would amount to nothing if it were not for the fact that in addition comes the feeling that it is incapable of explaining things to its confessors, that it has deceived them. And even though it thinks and sees that it tells its confessors about every stirring, even the first ones, this doesn't help. The soul's understanding is so darkened that it becomes incapable of seeing the truth and believes whatever the imagination represents things the devil wants to represent. The Lord, it seems, gives the devil license so that the soul might be tried and even be made to think it is rejected by God. Many are the things that war against it with an interior oppression so keen and unbearable that I don't know what to compare this experience to if not to the oppression of those that suffer in hell, for no consolation is allowed in the midst of this tempest. If they desire to be consoled by their confessor, it seems the devils assist him to torment it more. Thus, when a confessor was dealing with a person after she had suffered this torment (for it seems a dangerous affliction since there are so many things involved in it), he told her to let him know when she was in this state; but the torment was always so bad that he came to realize there was nothing he could do about it. Well, then, if a person in this state who knows how to read well takes up a book in the vernacular, he will find that he understands no more of it than if he didn't know how to read even one of the letters, for the intellect is incapable of understanding.

In sum, there is no remedy in this tempest but to wait for the mercy of God.

O my powerful God, how sublime are your secrets, and how different spiritual things are from all that is visible and understandable here below. There is nothing that serves to explain this favor, even though the favor is a very small one when compared to the very great ones You work in souls.

This action of love is so powerful that the soul dissolves with desire, and yet it doesn't know what to ask for since clearly it thinks that its God is with it.

You will ask me: Well, if it knows this, what does it desire or what pains it? What greater good does it want? I don't know. I do know that it seems this pain reaches to the soul's very depths and that when He who wounds it draws out the arrow, it indeed seems, in accord with the deep love the soul feels, that God is drawing these very depths after Him. I was thinking now that it's as though, from this fire enkindled in the brazier that is my God, a spark leapt forth and so struck the soul that the flaming fire was felt by it. And since the spark was not enough to set the soul on fire, and the fire is so delightful, the soul is left with that pain; but the spark merely by touching the soul produces that effect. It seems to me this is the best comparison I have come up with. This delightful pain—and it is not pain—is not continuous, although sometimes it lasts a long while; at other times it goes away quickly. This depends on the way the Lord wishes to communicate it, for it is not something that can be procured in any human way. But even though it sometimes lasts for a long while, it comes and goes. To sum up, it is never permanent. For this reason it doesn't set the soul on fire; but just as the fire is about to start, the spark goes out and the soul is left with the desire to suffer again that loving pain the spark causes.

Here there is no reason to wonder whether the experience is brought on naturally or caused by melancholy, or whether it is some trick of the devil or some illusion. It is something that leaves clear understanding of how this activity comes from the place where the Lord who is unchanging dwells. The activity is not like that found in other feelings of devotion, where the great absorption in delight can make us doubtful. Here all the senses and faculties remain free of any absorption, wondering what this could be, without hindering anything or being able, in my opinion, to increase or take away that delightful pain.

Anyone to whom our Lord may have granted this favor—for if He has, that fact will be recognized on reading this—should thank Him very much. Such a person doesn't have to fear deception. Let his great fear be that he might prove ungrateful for so generous a favor, and let him strive to better his entire life, and to serve, and he will see the results and how he receives more and more. In fact, I know a person who received this favor for some years and was so pleased with it that had she served the Lord through severe trials for a great number of years she would have felt well repaid by it. May He be blessed forever, amen.

You may wonder why greater security is present in this favor than in other things. In my opinion, these are the reasons: First, the devil never gives delightful pain like this. He can give the savor and delight that seem to be spiritual, but he doesn't have the power to join pain—and so much of it—to the spiritual quiet and delight of the soul. For all of his powers are on the outside, and the pains he causes are never, in my opinion, delightful or peaceful, but disturbing and contentious. Second, this delightful tempest comes from a region other than those regions of which he can be lord. Third, the favor brings wonderful benefits to the soul, the more customary of which are the determination to suffer for God, the desire to have many trials, and the determination to withdraw from earthly satisfactions and conversations and other similar things.

That this favor is no fancy is very clear. Although at other times the soul may strive to experience this favor, it will not be able to counterfeit one. And the favor is something so manifest that it can in no way be fancied. I mean, one cannot think it is imagined, when it is not, or have doubts about it. If some doubt should remain, one must realize that the things experienced are not true impulses; I mean if there should be doubt about whether the favor was experienced or not. The favor is felt as clearly as a loud voice is heard. There's no basis for thinking it is caused by melancholy, because melancholy does not produce or fabricate its fancies save in the imagination. This favor proceeds from the interior part of the soul.

God has another way of awakening the soul. Although it somehow seems to be a greater favor than those mentioned, it can be more dangerous, and therefore I shall pause a little to consider it. There are many kinds of locutions given to the soul. Some seem to come from outside oneself; others, from deep within the interior part of the soul; others, from the superior part; and some are so exterior that they come through the sense of hearing, for it seems there is a spoken word. Sometimes, and often, the locution can be an illusion, especially in persons with a weak imagination or in those who are melancholic, I mean who suffer noticeably from melancholy.

In my opinion no attention should be paid to these latter two kinds of persons even if they say they see and hear and understand. But neither should one disturb these persons by telling them their locutions come from the devil; one must listen to them as to sick persons. The prioress or confessor to whom they relate their locutions should tell them to pay no attention to such experiences, that these locutions are not essential to the service of God, and that the devil has deceived many by such means, even though this particular person, perhaps, may not be suffering such deception. This counsel should be given so as not to aggravate the melancholy, for if they tell her the locution is due to melancholy, there will be no end to the matter; she will swear that she sees and hears, for it seems to her that she does.

It is true that it's necessary to be firm in taking prayer away from her and to insist strongly that she pay no attention to locutions; for the devil is wont to profit from these souls that are sick in this way, even though what he does may not be to their harm but to the harm of others. But for both the sick and the healthy there is always reason to fear these things until the spirit of such persons is well understood. And I say that in the beginning it is always better to free these persons from such experiences, for if the locutions are from God, doing so is a greater help toward progress, and a person even grows when tested. This is true; nonetheless, one should not proceed in a way that is distressing or disturbing to a soul, because truly the soul can't help if it these locutions come.

Now then, to return to what I was saying about locutions, all the kinds I mentioned can be from God or from the devil or from one's own imagination. If I can manage to do so, I shall give, with the help of the Lord, the signs as to when they come from these different sources and when they are dangerous; for there are many souls among prayerful people who hear them. My desire, Sisters, is that you realize you are doing the right thing if you refuse to give credence to them, even when they are destined just for you (such as, some consolation, or advice about your faults), no matter who tells you about them, or if they are an illusion, for it doesn't matter where they come from. One thing I advise you: do not think, even if the locutions are from God, that you are better because of them, for He spoke frequently with the Pharisees. All the good comes from how one benefits by these words; and pay no more attention to those that are not in close conformity with Scripture than you would to those heard from the devil himself. Even if they come from your weak imagination, it's necessary to treat them as if they were temptations in matters of faith, and thus resist them always. They will then go away because they will have little effect on you.

Returning, then, to the first of the different kinds of locutions; whether or not the words come from the interior part of the soul, from the superior part, or from the exterior part doesn't matter in discerning whether or not they are from God. The surest signs they are from God that can be had, in my opinion, are these: the first and truest is the power and authority they bear, for locutions from God effect what they say. . . .

The third sign is that these words remain in the memory for a very long time, and some are never forgotten, as are those we listen to here on earth—I mean those we hear from men. For even if the words are spoken by men who are very important and learned, or concern the future, we do not have them engraved on our memory, or believe them, as we do these. The certitude is so strong that even in things that in one's own opinion sometimes seem impossible and in which there is doubt as to whether they will or will not happen, and the intellect wavers, there is an assurance in the soul itself that cannot be overcome. . . .

9

Melancholy

BRIGHT

BORN MIDWAY THROUGH the sixteenth century in Cambridge, England, Timothie Bright wrote several medical works, the best remembered of which was his *Treatise of Melancholy* (1568), from which the following excerpts are taken. As one of the first book-length works about mental disorder understood within a consistently medical frame of reference, this book is important in itself. It is also important as a source for other, better known Renaissance works. In his *Anatomy of Melancholy,* Robert Burton makes evident his debt to Bright (Bright's is the only English name among authors on melancholy whom Burton acknowledges); indeed, the better known *Anatomy* is in certain respects modeled on Bright's *Treatise*. Less established is the link between Bright's book and Shakespeare's frequent remarks on melancholy and madness. Evidence for the belief that Shakespeare was familiar with Bright's work derives from two sources: the similarity between particular descriptions in the plays and passages from Bright's book, and the claim that as a young man and at the time of its publication, Shakespeare worked as a proofreader in the small London publishing house of Thomas Vautrollier, which brought out Bright's *Treatise.*

Bright was born in 1550; his father is believed to have been one William Bright, mayor of the town of Cambridge in 1571. Timothie attended Trinity College in Cambridge between 1564 and 1570; he then traveled abroad, where he witnessed and was much influenced by the terror of the Saint Bartholomew's Day Massacre in Paris in 1572. He returned to England to complete medical studies at Cambridge, where he became a doctor of medicine in 1579. After this he practiced medicine, lectured on medicine at Cambridge, published a number of medical treatises, and eventually, through powerful patrons, in 1585 gained an appointment as physician to Saint Bartholomew's Hospital in London. A year later came the publication of *A Treatise of Melancholy.* Bright's interest in medicine subsequently declined, eclipsed by two other concerns, shorthand and religion. He had developed a form of shorthand, a skill known to the ancient world but reinvented by Bright, and devoted much energy to ensuring its widespread adoption. In addition, he published a popular abridged version of the religious classic, John Foxe's *Book of Martyrs*. By 1591, he was so negligent of his medical duties at Saint Bartholomew's that he was dismissed. From then until his death in 1615, Bright was employed as a member of the clergy, although he continued to see patients.

Bright's dual interest in religion and medicine is apparent in his *Treatise*. The dedicatory epistle promises to show the difference between natural melancholy and "the heavy hand of God upon the afflicted conscience," and throughout the text he offers remedies for the one, and spiritual consolation for the other. The work has been described as an early essay in psychiatry for its recognition of the interaction of body and mind, and of the influence of an afflicted mind upon the health of the body.

The classification with which Bright orders his discussion is confusing. He divides melancholia the disease ("a doting of reason through vaine feare procured by fault of the melancholie humour") from the melancholy humor, and he distinguishes among instances of the melancholy humor between those that are natural and unnatural. As a result of bodily heating of various kinds, the natural melancholy humor could become unnatural, and thus lead to melancholia the disease.

Bright's characterization of the affective states of melancholy is clearer: They are for the most part sadness and fear, together with related and resultant states such as distrust, doubt, diffidence, and despair. And he is at pains to emphasize that these states are often without apparent or external cause or occasion. (They are sadness and fear, "whereof no occasion was at any time before, nor like to be given hereafter"; the states they respond to are not external but "domestical" terror.) Of internal causes, however, they have plenty. Bright's elaborations on the interaction between the body, the brain, and the heart is complex. First, melancholy humor and splenetic vapors disturb the functions of the brain, distorting perception, belief, judgment ("discretion"), memory, and imagination so that these faculties in turn forge, as he says "monstrous fictions." Now the heart responds ("the heart answers his [the brain's] passion"), itself forging "new matters of sadness and fear," and sowing disorder, as Bright puts it, of the whole regiment of human nature, in both judgment and affection. Through time, what we would call a feedback system ensues. The heart comes to fear everything, and the brain, "sympathetically partaking with the heart's fear," further embroiders the sources inviting doubt, distrust, sadness, and suspicion.

Also complex is Bright's account of the initiating cause of this ever-elaborating, though purely "domestic" or internal, terror. The melancholy humor affected the brain in several ways. By an overheating of the blood, it gave off obscuring vapors. Rising from the "puddle" of the spleen to the brain, those brought confusion and errors of all kinds. In "excrement" or residue form it also corrupted the mind, giving it a "habit of depraved conceit, whereby it fancies not according to truth." More advanced and more extreme cases of melancholia resulted from the "putrification" of black bile.

Bright labors to distinguish from melancholic states the relatively greater suffering engendered by a sense of sin. These are contrasted as spiritual versus bodily. Only a sense of sin is susceptible to spiritual cure and springs from a spiritual cause (the body "works nothing on the [afflicted] soul"); and comfort for melancholic states but not spiritual states may be procured by "corporeal instruments."

• ⌣ • ⌣ •

From Timothie Bright, *A Treatise of Melancholy* (1586)

How Diverslie the Word "Melancholie" Is Taken

Before I enter to define the nature of melancholie, and what it is, for the cleare understanding of that wherein my purpose is to instruct you, it shall be necessarie to lay forth diverse manners of taking the name of melancholie, and whereto the name being one, is applied diversly. It signifieth in all, either a certaine fearfull disposition of the mind altered from reason, or else an humour of the body, comonly taken to be the only cause of reason by feare in such sort depraved. This humour is of two sorts: naturall, or unnaturall, naturall is either the grosser part of the bloud ordained for nourishment, which either by abundance or immoderate hotenesse, passing measure, surchargeth the bodie, and yeeldeth up to the braine certain vapors, whereby the understanding is obscured, or else is an excrement ordained to be avoyded out of the bodie, through so many alterations of naturall heate, and variety of concoction, having not a drop of nourishing juyce remaining, whereby the body, either in power or substance, may be relieved. This excrement, if it keepeth the bounds of his owne nature, breedeth less perturbance either to bodie or minde: if it corrupt and degenerate farther from it selfe and the qualite of the bodie, then are all passions more vehement, and so outrageously oppress and trouble the quiet feate of the mind, that all organicall actions thereof are mixed with melancholie madnesse, and reason turned to a vaine feare, or playne desperation, the braine being altered in his complexion, and as it were transported into an instrument of another make than it was first ordained: these two . . . do diversly affect the understanding, and do alter the affection, especiallye if by corruption of nature or evil custom of manners the partye bee over passionate. The unnatural is an humour rising of melancholie before mentioned, or else from bloud or cholor, whollie chaunged into another nature by an unkindly heate, which turneth these humors, which before were raunged under natures government, and kept in order, into a qualitie whollie repugnant, whose substance and vapor giveth such annoyance to all the parties, that as it passeth or is seated maketh strange alterations in our actions, whether they be animal or voluntarie, or naturall not depending upon our will, and these are all which the name of melancholie doth signifie: now the definition and what it is. As the things be divers, so it also followeth the suite, and is likewise diverse either of the humor or of the passion, and the humour being either a nutritive juyce or an excrement unprofitable thereunto, I define the humor no otherwise than that part of that bloud which naturally of the rest is most grosse, and the excrement the superfluitie of the same: which if it putrifieth, bestoweth still the name of a farre diverse thing both in temper & nature, called black cholor. The melancholie passion is a doting of reason through vayne fear procured by fault of the melancholie humour. Thus briefly & clearly do you understand what the nature of melancholie is. . . .

How Melancholie Procureth Feare, Sadness, Despair, and Such Other Passions

Now let us consider what passions they are that melancholie driveth us into and the reason how it doth so diversly distract those that are oppressed therewith. The perturbations of melancholie are for the most parte, sadde and fearfull, and such as rise of them: as distrust, doubt, diffidence, or despair, sometimes furious, and sometimes merry in apparaunce, through a kind of Sardonia, and false laughter, as the humour is disposed that procureth these diversities. Those which are sad and pensive, rise of that melancholick humour, which is the grossest part of the bloud, whether it be juyce or excrement, not passing the naturall temper in heat whereof it partaketh, and is called colde in comparison only. This for the most part is setled in the splene, and with its vapours annoyeth the heart and passing up to the braine, counterfetteth terrible objects to the fantasie, and polluting both the substance, and spirits of the braine, causeth it without external occasion, to forge monstrous fictions, and terrible to the conceite, which the judgment taking as they are presented by the disordered instrument, deliver over to the harte, which hath no judgment of discretion in itself but giving credite to the mistaken report of the braine, breaketh out into that inordinate passion, against reason. This cometh to passe, because the instrument of discretion is depraved by these melancholick spirites, and a darknes & clouds of melancholie vapours rising from that pudle of the splene obscure the clearnes which our spirits are indued with, and is requisite to the due discretion of outward objects. This at the first is not so extreame, neither doth it shewe so apparauntly, as in processe of time, when the substaunce of the brayne hath plentyfull drunk of that splenetic fogge, whereby his nature is become of the same qualitye, and the pure and bright spirits so defiled, and eclipsed, that their indifference alike to all sensible thinges, is now drawn to a partiality, and inclination, as by melancholy they are enforced. For where that naturall and internall light is darkened, their fancies arise vaine, false, and voide of ground: even as in the externall sensible darkness, a false illusion will appeare unto our imagination, which the light being brought in is discerned to be an abuse of fancie: nowe the internal darknesse affecting more nigh our nature, than the outward, is cause of greater feares, and more molesteth us with terror, than that which taketh from us the sight of sensible things: especially arising not of absense of light only, but by a preference of substauncial obscurity, which is possessed with an actuall power of operation, this taking hold of the braine by processe of time giveth it an habite of depraved conceite, whereby it fancieth not according to trueth: but as the nature of that humour leadeth it, altogether gastely and feareful. This causeth not only fantastical apparitions wrought by apprehension only of common sense, but fantasie, an other parte of internal sense compoundeth, and forgeth disguised shapes, which give great terror to the heart, and cause it with the huely spirit to hide it self as wel as it can, by contraction in all partes, from those conterfet goblins, which the braine dispossessed of right discerning, fayneth unto the heart. Neither only is common sense, and fantasie thus overtaken with delusion, but memory also receiveth a wound therewith: which disableth it both to keepe in memory, and after, therewith are defaced. For as the common sense and fantasye, which doe offer unto the memory to lay up, deliver by fables instead of true report, and those tragicall that dismay all the sensible frame of our bodies, so either is the memorie wholly distract by importunitie of those doubtes and fears, that it neglecteth the custodie of other store or else it recordeth and apprehendeth only such as by this importunity is thrust thereupon nothing but darkness, peril, doubt, frightes and whatsoever the harte of man most doeth abhor. And these the senses do so melancholickly deliver to the mindes configuration (which judging of such things as bee offered, not having farther to do in the deeper examination) that it applyeth those certaine ingenerate pointes of reason and wisdom to a deceitful cases, thought it be alwaies in the generall, and if particularities bee delivered up a right, in them also most certain and assured. For those things which are sensible, and are as it were the counterfettes of outward creatures, the report of them is committed by God's ordinance to the instruments of the braine furnished with his spirit, which it bee, as the thinges are in nature, so doeth the minde judge and determine, no farther submitting to it selfe to examine the credite of these senses which (the instruments being faultless and certain other configurations required necessary, agreeable unto their integrity) never faile in their busines, but are the very first groundes of all this corporall action of life and wisdome, that the mind for the most parte here outwardly practiceth. If they be contrary, so also doth the mind judge, and pursueth or shunneth for these sensible matters reposing trust in the corporall ministers, whose misreport, no more ought to discretite the minde, or draw it into an accessory cryme of error, then the judiciall sentence is to be blamed, which pronounceth upon the oth and credite of a jurie empanelled of such as are reported men of honesty, credite, and discretion though their verdict bee not peradventure according to the cause committed to them doth require. The memorie being thus fraight with perils paste: and embracing onely thorough the braynes disorder that which is of discomforte, causeth the fantasie out of such recordes, to forge newe matters of sadnes and feare, whereof no occasion was at any time before, nor like to be given hearafter: to these fancies the hart answering with like melancholicke affection, turneth all hope into feare, assurance into distrust and dispaire, joye into discomforte: and as the melancholie nature, or bodie any way corrupt defileth the pure and holesome nourishment, & converteth it into the same kinde of impuritie: and as the fire of all kinde of matter giveth increase of heat, whether it be wood, stone, metal or liquor so the body thus possessed with the uncheerfull, & discomfortable darkness of melancholie, obscureth the Sunne and Moone, and all the comfortable planets of our natures, in such sort that they appeare all darke and more than halfe eclipsed of this mist of blacknes, rising from that hidious lake: and in all thinges comfortable, either curiously prieth out, and snatcheth at whatsoever of mistake may be drawne to the nourishment of it self: or else neglecteth altogether that which is of other quality, then foode, and pasture of those monsters, which nature never bred, nor perfect sense conceived, nor memorie uncorrupt would ever allow entertainment, but are hatched out of this muddy humor, by an unnaturall temper & bastard spirite, to the disorder of the whole regiment of humane nature, both in judgement and affection. Thus the heart a while being acquaintet with nothing else, but domestical terror, feareth every thing and the braine simpathetically partaking with the hartes fear, maketh doubt, distrusteth, & suspecteth without cause, alwaies standing in awe of grievaunce: wherewith in time it becommeth so tender, that the least touch, as it were ones naile in an ucler, giveth discouragement thereto, rubbing it upon the gale of exculcerate with sorrow and feare: neither only doubleth it sorrow upon smal occasion, but taketh it where none is offered: even as the cholerick man feedeth his passion with ridiculous cases of displeasure. For first (the generall being in al natures actions before the particular) the heart by the braine solicited to passion & used to grief & fear, taketh the accustomed way of flight and annoyance, abhorring & fearing those thinges which of themselves are most amiable and gratefull: at the first not being aduised, whereto to apply the passion: even as one condemned to death with undoubted expectation of execution, fearing every knock at the prison door, hath horrour, though the messenger of pardon with knock require to be admitted & let in, and every messenger, where daunger is feared, though he come with cheareful countenance, giveth cause of distrust when there may be assurance, even so, the heart overcome with inward heavines, and skared with inward feares, faireth as though whatsoever cause of affection and perturbation were minister of present griefe, or messenger of future daunger, by mistaking only, and withdraweth it selfe, and shroudeth it as secrete and closse, as nature will suffer, from that, which if custome had not bent it another way, uppon aduisement (Now banished through swiftnes and vehemecy of passion) it would have with joyful cheare embraced. For eve as we see in outward *sense*. The eie or the eare long and vehemently affected with coulour, or found, or the nose with strong sent, retaine the very coulour, sound, and sent in the instrumentes, though the thing be removed that yeelded such qualities, so the internall senses molested continually with this fearefull object of internal darknes, esteemeth everie thing of that nature: the true qualitie thereof being obscure, by that which hath taken possession of the before. The braine thus affected, and the heart answering his passion thereafter, driveth us into those extremities of heavie mood, which assaile and dispossesse of right use of reason those who are melancholicklie disposed: much more if the heart be as melancholickly bent, as the braine: then diverse times doeth it prevent the fancie with feare, and as a man transported with passio is utterly bereft of aduisemet causeth the senses both outward & inwarde preposterously to conceive, as the heart vainely feareth. This melancholy as the partes are diverse & actions vary, so doth it as it is *septed*, or passeth this or that way, breed diversitie of passion: as in the heart a trembling, in the stomach a greedy appetite: in the braine false illusions, and in the other partes as theie are disposed: so depraving their actions, it causeth much variety of effects, which are not in the nature of the humor, but as it disturbeth the active instrumentes, no more than darknes causeth some to stuble, othersom to go out of their way, & wander, & other some to bright to passe such purposes, as light would betray & hinder, al as they be disposed & occupied which take to their busines in the dark & not through anie such effectual operation of darknes, which is nought else but meere absence of light. Neither doth so many straunge sorts of accidents following melancholy through diversity of parts only: but as the custome of life hath bin before, & the fancie, & hart some way vehemently occupied: there through this humour all the faculties afore named, are carried the same way, as it were with the streame of a tide, driven with a boysterous winde; which causeth that melancholicke men, are not all of one nature passionate this way: the one taking his dolorous passion from his love, another from his wealth: the other fro his pleasures, whereof his melancholie beareth him in hand the present losse, or imminent daunger of that wherein affection in former times had surest footing: & on the other part, which before a man most abhorred, that nowe the humor urgeth with most vehemencie. Againe as it is mixed with other humours, either keeping mediocrity, or abounding, so likewise breaketh it forth into such diversities, & many times into plaine contrareities of conceit and perturbation. Thus you understande, howe feares and sorrowes rise, without cause from naturall melancholie, whether it bee juyce, or excrement, not through chiefe action as from worke of facultie, but by abuse of instrument through occasion. If the spleneticke excrement surcharge the bodie, not being purged by helpe of the splene: then are these perturbations farre more outragious, and harde to be mitigated by counsell or persuasion: and more do they enforce us, the partes being altered with corporall humour, then with spiritual vapour: and so are the passions longer in continuance, and more extreme in vehemencie. For as the flame carrieth not such force of burning as the cole, neither contayneth the heate so longe, even so the partes affected with the humour, which carriety both grossenesse of substance, with continuall supplie of that dimme vapour, setleth a more fixed passion of feare and heavinesse, then that which riseth from the vapour onley, partly of the owne accorde more easily vanishing and partly with greater facillitie wafted by natures strife and resistance. Nowe it followeth to declare, howe the other unnaturall melancholy annoyeth with passions, & abuseth us with counterfet cause of perturbation, whereof there is no ground in truth, but onley a vaine and fantasticall conceit. . . .

The Particular Difference betwixt Melancholy, & the Distressed Conscience in the Same Person

Whatsoever molestation riseth directly as a proper object of the mind, that in that respect is not melancholicke, but hath a farther ground than fancie, and riseth from conscience, condemning the guylty soule of those ingraven lawes of nature, which no man is voyde of, be he never so barbarous. . . . This taketh nothing of the body, nor intermedleth with humour, but giveth a direct wounde with those firie dartes, which men so afflicted make their mone of. Of this kinde Saul was possessed, to whom the Lord sent an evill spirite to encrease the torment; and Judas the traytor, who took the revenge of betraying the innocent uppon him selfe with his owne handes, suche was the anguish that Esau felt when he founde no repentance, after he had solde his birthright for a messe of pottage; and such is the estate of all defiled consciences with hainous crimes; whose harts are never free from the worme, but with deadly bite thereof are driven to despaire. These terrible objects which properly appertain unto the minde, are such as onley affect it with horror of Gods justice for breach of those lawes naturall, or written in his word, which by duetie of creation, we are holden to obey. . . . On the contrarie part, when any conceite troubleth you that hath no sufficient grounde of reason, but riseth only upon the frame of your brayne, which is subject (as hath bene before shrewed) unto the humour, that is right melancholicke and so to be accounted of you. These are false points of reason deceaved by the melancholie brayne, and disguised fearres of the heart, without abilitie to worke the pretenced annoyaunce: neither do they approach the substaunce, and the substantiall and soveraigne actions of the soule, as the other doth. The estate happeneth by degrees, and getteth strength in time, to the encumberance of all the instrumentall actions, and . . . obscure the cleare light of reason. Here the humour purged, and the spirite attenuate and refreshed with remedie convenient, the brayne strengthened, and the heart comforted with cordials, are means most excellent ordayned of God for this infirmitie. And to deliver you in a word the difference, whatsoever is besides conscience of sinne in this case, it is melancholye: which conscience terrified, is of such nature, so beset with infinite feares and distruft, that it easily wafteth the pure spirit, congeleth the livelye bloud, and striketh our nature in such sort, that it soone becommeth melancholicke, vile and base, and turneth reason into foolishnesse, and disgraceth the beauty of the countenance, and transformeth the stoutest. . . . Besides this in you, vaine feares, and false conceites of apparitions, imagination of a voice sounding in your ears, frightfull dreames, distrust of the consumption, and putrifying of one part or other of your body, & the rest of this crue, are causes of this molestation, which are whelpes of that melancholicke litter, & are bred of the corrupted state of the body altered in spirite, in bloud, in substance and complexion, by the aboundance of this setling of the bloud which we call melancholy. This increaseth the terrour of the afflicted minde, doubling the feare & discouragement, & shutteth up the meanes of consolatio, which is after another sort to be conveyed to the minde, then the way which the temptation taketh to breed distrust of Gods mercy, & pardon. For that hath sinne the meanes which needeth no conveyaunce, but is bred with us & entreth even into our conceptio: neither is the guiltinesse brought unto us by foreine report but the knowledge riseth from the conscience of the offender: the meanes (I meane the outwarde meanes of consolation and cure) must needs passe by our senses to enter the mind whole instrument being altered by the humour, & their sincerity stained with the obscure & darke spots of melancholy, receive not indifferently the medicine of cosolatio. So it both mistaketh, that which it apprehendeth, and delivereth it imperfectly to the minds consideratio. As their brains are thus evill disposed, so their harts in no better case, & acquainted with terror, & overthrown with that fearful passio, hardly set free the cherful spirits, feebled with the corporall prison of the body, & hardly yeeld to persuasion of comfort what soever it bringeth of assurance. This causeth the release of the afflictio to be long & hard, and not answerable to the swiftnesse of the procuring cause, having so many wayes to *passe* & encountring so many lets before it meet with the fore. For as the cause respecteth not time nor place, no circumstance of person, nor condition, seeketh no opportunity of corporal imbecillity, but breaketh through all such considerations, & beareth down all resistaunce: so the comfort requireth them all agreeable, & missing any one worketh feble effects & flow. . . . Thus I conclude this point of difference, & marke betwixt melancholy and the soules proper anguish, whose only cause proceedeth from Gods vengeance and wrath apprehended of the guilty soule: neither does melancholy alone (though it may hinder the outward meanes of consolation, as it hath bin before shewed) any thing make me more subject unto this kind of afflictio. First because the body worketh nothing upon the soule altogether impatible of any other saving of god alone. 2. The torment is such as riseth fro an efficient that requireth noe dispositio of means, god himself. 3. The cofort is not procured by any corporal instrumets, so neither is the discomfort procured or increased that way, moreover the cause, the subject, the proper effects are other than corporall. For although in that case the hart is heavy, delivering a passio answerable to the feareful apprehension, yet the sense of those that are under this crosse feele an anguish far beyond all affliction of naturall passion coupled with that organicall feare and heavinesse of heart. The melancholie disposeth to feare, doubt, distrust and heavines, but all either without cause, or where there is cause above it inforceth the passion. Here both the most vehement cause urgeth, and alwaies carrieth a passion therwith above the harts affection, even the entry of those torments, which canot be conceaved at full, as our nature now stadeth, nor delivered by report. Here in this passion, the case is not feare nor passionate griefe, but a torment procuring these affections: and even as the punishment of bodily racking is not the passion of the hart, but causeth it onely, so the hart fareth under this sore of the minde, which her properlye fretteth and strayneth the sinners of the soule, where from the heart taketh his grievous discouragement, and fainteth under Gods justice. Hitherto you have described that which your soule feeleth, not to instruct you, but that other may more truly judge of the case, and the distinction betwixt melancholy and it, may be more apparent.

10

•

Melancholic States

BURTON

ROBERT BURTON WAS BORN the fourth of nine children in 1577. His birthplace was a village in Leicestershire. He died in 1640 in his college rooms after an outwardly quiet, scholarly life spent at Oxford.

Burton's education at Oxford began when he was only sixteen. He was admitted as a commoner at Brasenose College and then in 1599 was elected a student of Christ Church College. In 1614 he was awarded his bachelor of divinity, after which he was both tutor and librarian at Christ Church College, as well as serving as vicar of Saint Thomas' Church in 1616 and rector of Seagrave in Leicestershire in 1630, appointments he was able to combine with his duties at Christ Church. Because he was an Oxford fellow, Burton was not permitted to marry. He led the quiet life of a scholar, reading books from the college library and the Bodleian collection, writing, and amassing his own large library, which eventually numbered 2,000 volumes. Considered retiring, he nonetheless found his enforced single state a burden—he complains of it as "abominable, impious, adulterous, and sacrilegious."

As a student, Burton had written Latin verses and two Latin comedies, *Alba* and *Philosophaster*. Once established at Christ Church, he devoted himself to the research and writing that led in 1621 to the first edition of *The Anatomy of Melancholy*. Although the first edition was 900 pages, Burton managed to expand upon this for subsequent editions in 1624, 1628, 1632, 1638, and 1651 (published posthumously). All of Burton's adult efforts were devoted to the several editions of *The Anatomy*. As one commentator has remarked, *The Anatomy* was Burton's life, not merely his life's work (Burton, [1621] 1979).

The Anatomy is unmatched as a compendium of human failing, folly, anxiety, suffering, and variation, written in a style that is so eccentric yet so acute and vital that it is one of the most beloved of English books. Dr. Johnson remarked that Burton's *Anatomy* was the only book that ever took him out of bed two hours earlier than he wanted to rise! Despite Johnson's enthusiasm, the popularity of Burton's work lapsed briefly during the eighteenth century. But with the beginning of the nineteenth century a strong revival occurred, and interest in *The Anatomy* has never since abated.

The Anatomy of Melancholy is rich with reference to classical ideas (for instance, Burton's humoral account of melancholy derives from Hippocrates and Galen). He has been accused of making up some of his quotations, and he is guilty of misquotation. But as one authority points out, Burton's thousands of Latin tags were not, in a bilingual age, quaint pedantry, and they remain "an unceasing reminder that Burton was a Renaissance humanist for whom the ancients had given final expression to all the commonplaces of experience" (Bush, 1962:281).

One of the most important sources for *The Anatomy* was the authority referred to as "Laurentius." This was the sixteenth-century French physician André Du Laurens (1560?–1609), whose influential *Discourse de la melancholie* was known throughout Europe. Du Laurens had characterized melancholia, as Burton was to do after him, as "a kind of dotage without any fever."

Burton's treatise is presented in the voice of Democritus Jr., an imaginary heir to the Greek philosopher of that name. The writing reflects a fullness of style or prolixity that, as Burton himself remarks, makes Democritus seem like "a ranging spaniel that barks at every bird he sees, leaving his game." In a further description of his own style, he also notes "other faults," of "barbarism, extemporanean style, tautologies, apish imitation, a rhapsody of rages gathered together from several dunghills, excrements of authors, toys and fopperies confusedly tumbled out, without art, invention, judgment, wit, learning, harsh, raw, rude, phantastical, absurd, insolent, indiscreet, ill-composed, indigested, vain, scurrile, idle, dull and dry." This confusion of attributes aptly captures the confusion in the work itself, where Democritus Jr. leaves his game again and again to bark at every bird he sees, yet does so with such exuberance, humor, and vitality that we want to read on. As well as a reflection of the fashionable melancholy of the times, *The Anatomy* also reveals Burton's own personal struggles with disheartened and dispirited moods and states of despair. Yet to quote once more from Bush: "Even a summary sketch of Burton cannot fail to suggest his sanity of mind and largeness of heart, his love of life and of human beings, his capacity alike for robustness or bitter laughter and for sensitive exploration of the darker places of the soul. His matter is never dull, but more than half of our pleasure is in his manner, the revelation of himself" (Bush, 1962:285).

Burton distinguishes the melancholy undergone by women from that of men, relating women's suffering to "those vicious vapours" that come from menstrual blood. His account of the suffering of women, and his prescription for its cure ("to see them well placed, and married to good husbands in due time") is dealt with cursorily. It shows, in the words of one commentator, "Burton's stereotype of woman and her ailments: woman is undisciplined and her ailments stem from this lack of regulation and the hazards associated with her sexuality" (Skultans, 1979:81).

Its misogyny aside, Burton's rambling, eclectic, and ebullient *Anatomy* remains the most enduring and endearing among English works on melancholy.

• ⌣ • ⌢ •

From Robert Burton, *The Anatomy of Melancholy* (1621)

Melancholy in Disposition, Improperly So Called, Æquivocations

Melancholy, the subject of our present Discourse, is either in Disposition, or Habite. In Disposition, is that transitory *Melancholy,* which goes & comes upon every small occasion of sorrow, need, sicknesse, trouble, feare, griefe, passion, or perturbation of the Minde, any manner of care, discontent, or thought, which causeth anguish, dulnesse, heavinesse and vexation of the spirits, any wayes opposite to pleasure, mirth, joy, delight, causing frowardnesse in us, or a dislike. In which Æquivocall and improper sense, we call him Melancholy, that is dull, sad, sowre, lumpish, ill disposed, solitary, any way moved, or displeased. And from these Melancholy Dispositions, no man living is free, no *Stoicke,* none so wise, none so happy, none so patient, so generous, so godly, so divine, that can vindicate himselfe, so well composed, but more or lesse some time or other, he feeles the smart of it. Melancholy in this sence is the Character of Mortalitie. *Man that is borne of a woman, is of short continuance, and full of trouble.* . . .

. . . We are not here as those Angells, celestiall powers and Bodies, Sunne and Moone, to finish our course without all offence, with such constancy, to continue for so many ages: but subject to infirmities, miseries, interrupt, tossed and tumbled up and downe, carried about with every small blast, often molested and disquieted upon each slender occasion, uncertaine, brittle, and so is all that we trust unto. *And he that knowes not this, and is not armed to indure it, is not fit to live in this world* (as one condoles our time) *he knowes not the condition of it, where with a reciprocall tye, pleasure and paine are still united, and succeed one another in a ring. Exi è mundo,* get thee gone hence, if thou canst not brooke it, there is no way to avoide it, but to arme they selfe with patience, with magnanimitie, to oppose they selfe unto it, to suffer affliction as a good souldier of *Christ;* (as *Paul* adviseth) constantly to beare it. But forasmuch as so few can imbrace this good counsell of his, or use it aright, but rather as so many brute beasts, give a way to their passions, voluntarily subject and precipitate themselves into a Labyrinth of cares, woes, miseries; and suffer their soules to be overcome by them, cannot arme themselves with that patience as they ought to doe, it falleth out oftentimes that these *Dispositions* become *Habits,* and *many Affects con-*

temned, (as *Seneca* notes) *make a disease. Even as one Distillation, not yet growne to custome, makes a cough; but continuall and inveterate causeth a consumption of the lungs:* so doe these our Melancholy provocations: and according as the humor it selfe is intended, or remitted in men, as their temperature of Body, or Rationall soule is better able to make resistance; so are they more or lesse affected. For that which is but a flea-biting to one, causeth insufferable torment to another, & which one by his singular moderation, & well composed carriage can happily overcome, a second is no whit able to sustaine, but upon every small occasion of misconceaved abuse, injurie, griefe, disgrace, losse, crosse, rumor, &c. (if solitary, or idle) yeelds so farre to passion, that his complexion is altered, his digestion hindred, his sleepe gone, his spirits obscured, and his heart heavy, his Hypocondries misaffected, winde, crudity, on a sudden overtake him, and he himselfe over come with *Melancholy.* And as it is with a man imprisoned for debt, if once in the goale, every Creditor will bring his action against him, and there likely hold him: If any discontent sease upon a patient, in an instant all out perturbations (for ———— *quâ data porta ruunt)* will set upon him, and then like a lame dogge or broken winged goose hee droopes and pines away, and is brought at last to that ill habit or malady of melancholy it selfe. So that as the Philosophers make eight degrees of heat and cold: we may make 88 of *Melancholy,* as the parties affected are diversely seized with it, or have beene plunged more or lesse into this infernall gulfe, or waded deeper into it. But all these *Melancholy* fits, howsoever pleasing at first, or displeasing, violent & tyrannizing over those whom they seize on for the time, yet these fits I say or men affected are but improperly so called, because they continue not; but come & goe, as by some objects they are moved. This *Melancholy* of which we are to treat, as in Habit, *morbus sonticus* or *Chronicus,* a Chronicke or continuate disease, a setled humor, as *Aurelianus,* and others call it, not errant but fixed, and as it was long increasing, so now being (pleasant, or painefull) growne to an habit, it will hardly be removed.

Division of the Body Humors, Spirits

Of the parts of the Body, there be many divisions: The most approved is that of *Laurentius,* out of *Hippocrates:* which is, into parts *Contained,* of *Containing. Contained,* are either *Humours,* or *Spirits.*

A humour is a liquid or fluent part of the Body, comprehended in it, for the preservation of it, and is either innate and borne with us, or adventitious and acquisite. The Radicall or innate, is daily supplied by nourishment, which some call *Cambium,* and make those secondary humours of *Ros* and *Gluten* to maintaine it: or acquisite, to maintaine these foure first primary Humours, comming and proceeding from the first concoction in the Liver, by which meanes *Chylus* is excluded. Some divide them into profitable, and excrementitious humours: *Pituita,* and *Blood* profitable; the other two excrementitious. But *Crato* out of *Hippocrates* will have all foure to bee juyce, and not excrements, without which no living creature can bee sustained: which foure through they bee comprehended in the Masse of *Blood,* yet they have their severall affections, by which they are distinguished from one another, and from those adventitious, *peccant, or diseased humours,* as *Melancthon* calls them.

Blood, is a hot, sweet, temperate, red humour, prepared in the *Meseraicke* veines, and made of the most temperate parts of the *Chylus* in the liver, whose office is to nourish the whole body, to give it strength and colour, being dispersed by the veines, through every part of it. And from it *Spirits* are first begotten in the heart, which afterwards by the *Arteries,* are communicated to the other parts.

Pituita, or Fleagme, is a cold and moist humour, begotten of the colder part of the *Chylus,* (or white juyce comming of the meat digested in the stomacke) in the Liver; his office is to nourish, and moisten the members of the body, which as the tongue, are moved, that they be not over dry.

Choler, is hot and dry, bitter, begotten of the hotter parts of the *Chylus,* and gathered to the Gall: it helpes the naturall heat and senses, and serves to the expelling of excrements.

Melancholy, cold and drie, thicke, blacke, and sowre, begotten of the more fæculent part of nourishment, and purged from the spleene, is a bridle to the other two hot humors, *Blood* and *Choler,* preserving them in the Blood, and nourishing the bones: These foure humors have some analogie with the foure Elements, and to the foure ages in man. . . .

Immoderate Exercise a Cause, and How
Solitarinesse, Idlenesse

Nothing so good, but it may be abused: nothing better than Exercise (if opportunely used) for the preservation of the Body: nothing so bad, if it be unseasonable, violent, or overmuch. *Fernelius* out of *Galen, Path. lib. 1. cap. 16.* saith, *that much exercise and wearinesse consumes the spirits and substance, refrigerates the body; and such humors which Nature would have otherwise concocted & expelled, it stirres up, and makes them rage: which being so inraged, diversly affect, and trouble the body and minde.* So doth it, if it be unseasonably used, upon a full stomacke or when the body is full of crudities, which *Fuchsius* so much inveighs against, *lib. 2. instit. sec. 2. cap. 4.* giving that for a cause, why schoole-boyes in *Germany* are so often scabbed, because they use exercise presently after meats. *Bayrus* puts in a caveat against such exercise, because *it corrupts the meat in the stomacke, and carries the same juyce raw, and as yet undigested, into the veines* (saith *Lemnius*) *which there putrifies, and confounds the animal spirits. Crato consil. 21. lib. 2.* protests against all such exercise after meat, as being the greatest enimie to concoction that may bee, and cause of corruption of humors, which produce this, and many other diseases. Not without good reason then, doth *Salust. Salvianus lib. 2. cap. 1. & Leonartus Facchinus in 9. Rhasis, Mercurialis, Arculanus,* and many other, set downe immoderate exercise, as a most forcible cause of melancholy.

Opposite to Exercise is Idlenesse, (the badge of gentry) or want of Exercise, the bane of body and minde, the nurse of naughtinesse, step-mother of discipline, the chiefe author of all mischiefe, one of the seaven deadly sinnes, & a sole cause of this and many other maladies, the Divels cushion, as *Gualter* cals it, his pillow, and chiefe reposall. *For the minde can never rest, but stil mediates on one thing or other, except it be occupied about some honest busines, of his owne accord it rusheth into melancholy. As too much and violent exercise offends on the one side, so doth an idle life on the other* (saith *Crato*) *it fils the body full of fleagme, grosse humours, and all manner of obstructions, rhumes, catarres, &c. Rhasis cont. lib. 1. tract. 9.* accounts of it as the greatest cause of Melancholy: *I have often seene* (saith hee) that idlenesse begets this humour more than any thing else. Montaltus cap. 1. seconds him out of his experience, *they that are idle are farre more subject to melancholy, then such as are conversant or employed about any office or businesse. Plutarch* reckons up idlenesse for a sole cause of the sicknesse of the Soule: *There are they* (saith hee) *troubled in minde, that have no other cause but this. Homer Iliad. 1.* brings in *Achilles* eating of his owne heart in his Idlenesse, because he might not fight. *Mercurialis consil. 86.* for a melancholy young man urgeth it as a chiefe cause; why was he melancholy? because idle. Nothing begets it sooner, encreaseth and continueth it oftner than idlenesse. A disease familiar to all idle persons, an inseparable companion to such as live at ease, *pingui otio desidiosè agentes,* a life out of action, and have no calling or ordinary imployment to busie themselves about, that have small occasions; and though they have, such as their lasinesse, dulnesse; they will not compose themselves to doe ought, they cannot abide worke, though it bee necessary, easie, as to dresse themselves, write a letter or the like, yet as he that is benummed with cold, sits still shaking that might relieve himselfe with a little exercise or stirring, doe they complaine, but will not use the facile and ready meanes to doe themselves good: and so are still tormented with melancholy. . . .

Cosen German to Idlenesse, & a concomitant cause, which goes hand in hand with it, is *nimia solitudo,* too much solitarinesse, by the testimony of all Physitians, Cause & Symptome both: but as it is here put for a cause, it is either coact, enforced, or else voluntary. Enforced solitarinesse is commonly seene in Students, Monks, Friers, Anchorites, that by their order & course of life, must abandon all company, society of other men, and betake themselves to a private cell, *Otio supersititioso seclusi,* as *Bale and Hospinian* well tearme it, such as are the *Carthusians* of our time, that eat no flesh (by their order) keepe perpetuall silence, never goe abroad. Such as live in prison, or in some desart place, and cannot have company, as many of our countrey Gentlemen doe in solitary houses, they must either be alone without companions or live beyond their meanes, and entertaine all commers as so many hostes, or else converse with their servants and hindes, such as are unequall, inferior to them, and of a contrary disposition; or else as some doe, to avoide solitarinesse, spend their time with lewd fellowes in Tavernes, and in Ale-houses, and thence addict themselves to some unlawfull disports, or dissolute courses. Diverse againe are cast upon this rocke of solitarines for want of meanes, or out of a strong apprehension of some infirmity, disgrace or through bashfulnesse, rudenesse, simplicity, they cannot apply themselves to others company. *Nullum solum infælici gratius solitudine, ubi nullus sit qui miseriam exprobret,* this enforced solitarinesse takes place, and produceth his effect soonest in such, as have spent their time Jovially peradventure in all honest recreations, in good company, in some great family or populous citty, & are upon a sudden confined to a desert country cottage farre off, restrained of their liberty, and barred from their ordinary associats: solitarinesse is very irkesome to such, most tedious, and a sudden cause of great inconvenience. . . .

Passions and Perturbations of the Minde, How They Cause Melancholy

As that *Gymnosophist* in *Plutarch,* made answere to *Alexander,* (demanding which spake best) Every one of his fellows did speak better then the other: so may I say of these causes; to him that shall require which is the greatest, every one is more grievous then other, and this of Passion the greatest of all. A most frequent and ordinary cause of Melancholy, *fulmen perturbationum* (*Piccolomineus* calls it) this thunder and lightning of perturbation, which causeth such violent and speedy alterations in this our Microcosme, and many times subverts the good estate and temperature of it. For as the Body workes upon the minde, by his bad humours, troubling the Spirits, sending grosse fumes into the Braine; and so *per consequences* disturbing the Soule, and all the faculties of it,

> ———— *Corpus onustum*
> *Hesternis vitiis animum quoque prægravat unà,*

with feare, sorrow, &c. which are ordinary symptomes of this Disease: so on the other side, the minde most effectually workes upon the Body, producing by his passions and perturbations, miraculous alterations; as Melancholy, despaire, cruell diseases, and sometimes death it selfe. Insomuch, that it is most true which *Plato* saith in his *Charmides: omnia corporis mala ab animâ procedere;* all the mischiefes of the Body, proceed from the Soule: and *Democritus in Plutarch* urgeth, *Damnatam iri animam à corpore,* if the body should in this behalfe, bring an action against the Soule, surely the Soule would be cast and convicted; that by her supine negligence, had caused such inconveniences, having authority over the Body, & using it for an instrument, as a Smith doth his hammer (said *Cyprian*) imputing all those vices and maladies to the Minde. Even so doth *Philostratus, non coinquinatur corpus, nisi consensu animæ;* the Body is not corrupted, but by the Soule. *Lodov. Vives* will have such turbulent commotions proceed from *Ignorance,* and *Indiscretion.* All Philosophers impute the miseries of the Body to the Soule, that should have governed it better, by command of reason, and hath not done it. . . .

Of the Force of Imagination

What Imagination is, I have sufficiently declared in my *Digression of the Anatomie of the Soule.* I wil only now point at the wonderfull effects and power of it; which, as it is eminent in all, so most especially it rageth in melancholy persons, in keeping the species of objects so long, mistaking, amplifying them by continuall and strong medication, until at length it produceth in some parties reall effects, causeth this and many other maladies. And although this *Phantasie* of ours, be a subordinate facultie to reason, and should bee ruled by it, yet in many men, through inward or outward distemperatures, defect of Organs, which are unapt or hindered, or otherwise contaminated, it is likewise unapt, hindred, and hurt. This we see verified in sleepers, which by reason of humours, and concourse of vapours troubling the *Phantasie,* imagine many times absurd and prodigious things, and in such as are troubled with *Incubus,* or Witch ridden (as we call it) if they lie on their backes, they suppose an old woman rides, & sits so hard upon them, that they are almost stifled for want of breath; when there is nothing offends, but a concourse of bad humours, which trouble the *Phantasie.* . . .

Love of Learning, or Overmuch Study
With a Digression of the Misery of Schollers,
and Why the Muses Are Melancholy

Leonartus Fuchsius Instit. lib. 3. sect. 1. cap. 1. Fælix Plater lib. 3. de mentis alienat. Herc. de Saxonia Tract. post. de melanch. cap. 3 speake of a peculiar *Fury,* which comes by overmuch study. *Fernelius lib. 1. cap. 18.* puts *Study,* contemplation, and continuall meditation, as an especiall cause of madnesse: and in his *86. consul.* cites the same words. *To: Arculanus in lib. 9. Rhasis ad Almansorem cap. 16.* amongst other causes, reckons up *studium vehemens:* so doth *Levinus Lemnius, lib. de occul. nat.*

mirac. lib. 1. cap. 16. Many men (saith he) *come to this malady by continu-*
all study, and night-waking, and of all other men, Schollers are most subject
to it: and such *Rhasis* addes, *that have commonly the ifnest wits, Cont. lib.*
1. tract. 9. Marsilius Ficinus de sanit. tuenda. lib. 1. cap. 7. puts Melancholy amongst one of those five principall plagues of Students, 'tis a
common maule unto them all, and almost in some measure an inseparable companion. *Varro* belike for that cause calls *Tristes Philosophos &*
severos, severe, sad, dry, tetricke, are common Epithites to Schollers:
And *Patritius* therefore in the institution of Princes, would not have
them to be great students. For (as *Machiavel* holds) study weakens their
bodies, dulls the spirits, abates their strength and courage; and good
schollers are never good souldiers; which a certaine *Gothe* well
perceaved, for when his countrymen came into *Greece,* & would have
burned all their books, he cryed out against it, by al meanes they should
not doe it, *leave them that plague, which in time will consume all their*
vigor, and martiall spirits. The *Turkes* abdicated *Cornutus* the next heire,
from the Empire, because he was so much given to his booke: and 'tis
the common *Tenet* of the world, that Learning dulls and diminisheth
the spirits, and so *per consequens* produceth melancholy.

Two maine reasons may be given of it, why students should be more
subject to this malady then others. The one is, they live a sedentary,
solitary life, *sibi & musis,* free from bodily exercise, and those ordinary
disports which other men use: and many times if discontent and idlenesse concurre with it, which is too frequent, they are precipitated into
this gulfe on a sudden: but the common cause is overmuch study; too
much learning (as *Festus* told *Paul*) hath made thee mad; 'tis that other
extreame which effects it. So did *Trincavellius lib. 1. consil. 12. & 13.*
finde by his experience, in two of his Patients, a young Baron, and another, that contracted this malady by too vehement study. So *Forestus*
observat. lib. 10. observ. 13. in a young Divine in *Lovain,* that was mad,
and said, *he had a Bible in his head: Marsilius Ficinus de sanit. tuend. lib.*
1. cap. 1. 3. 4. & lib. 2. cap. 16. gives many reasons, *why students dote*
more often then others: The first is their negligence: *other men looke to*
their tooles, a Painter will wash his pencills, a Smith will looke to his ham-
mer, anvill, forge: an husbandman will mend his plough-irons, and grinde
his hatchet if it be dull; a faulkner or huntsman will have an especiall care
of his haukes, hounds, horses, dogges, &c. a Musitian will string and un-
string his Lute, &c. only scholiers neglect that instrument, their braine and
spirits (1 meane) which they daily use, and by which they range over all the
world, which by much study is consumed. Vide (saith *Lucian) ne funiculum*
nimis intendo, aliquandò abrumpas: See thou twist not the rope so hard,
till at length it break. *Ficinus* in his fourth cap. gives some other reasons; *Saturne & Mercury,* the patrones of Learning, are both dry Planets: & *Origanus* assignes the same cause, why *Mercurialists* are so poore,
and most part beggers: for that their President *Mercury* had no better
fortune himselfe. The Destinies of old, put poverty upon him as a pun-

ishment; since when, Poetry and Beggery, are *Gemelli,* twin-borne brattes, inseparable companions:

> *And to this day is every choller poore,*
> *Grosse gold from them runnes headlong to the boore:*

Mercury, can helpe them to knowledge but not to money. The second is contemplation, *which dries the braine, and extinguisheth naturall heat; for whilst the spirits are intent to mediation above in the head, the stomacke and liver are left destitute, and thence come blacke blood and crudities by defect of concoction, and for want of exercise, the superfluous vapours cannot exhale, &c.* The same reasons are repeated by *Gomesius lib. 4. cap. 1. de sale, Nymannus orat. de Imag. To. Voschius lib. 2. cap. 5. de peste:* and something more they adde, that hard students are commonly troubled with gouts, catarrhes, rhumes, *cacexia, bradiopepsia,* bad eyes, stone and collick, crudities, oppilations, *vertigo,* windes, crampes, consumptions, and all such diseases as come by overmuch sitting; they are most part leane, dry, ill coloured, spend their fortunes, loose their wits, and many times their lives, and all through immoderate paines, and, extraordinary studies. . . .

Symptomes, or Signes of Melancholy in the Body

Parrhasius a painter of *Athens,* amongst those *Olynthian* captives *Philip of Macedon* brought home to sell, bought one very old man; and when he had him at *Athens,* put him to extreame torture and torment, the better by his example, to expresse the paines and passions of his *Prometheus,* whom he was then about to paint. I need not be so barbarous, inhumane, curious or cruell for this purpose to torture any poore melancholy man, their symptomes are plaine, obvious and familiar, there needs no such accurate observation or farre fetched object, they delineate themselves, they voluntarily bewray themselves, they are too frequent in all places, I meete them still as I goe, they can not conceale it, their grievances are too well knowne, I neede not seeke farre to describe them. . . .

. . . as wine produceth diverse effects, or that hearbe *Tortocolla* in *Laurentius, which makes some laugh, some weepe, some sleepe, some dance, some sing, some howle, some drinke, &c.* So doth this our melancholy humour, worke severall signes in severall parties.

But to confine them, these generall Symptomes may be reduced to those of the *Body* or the *Minde.* Those usuall signes appearing in the *Bodies* of such as are melancholy be these, cold and dry, or they are hot and dry, as the humour is more or lesse adust. From these first qualities arise many other second, as that of colour, blacke, swarty, pale, ruddy, &c. some are *impense rubri,* as *Montaltus cap. 16.* observes out of *Galen lib. 3. de locis affectis,* very red and high coloured. *Hippocrates* in his booke *de Insaniâ & melan.* reckons up these signes, that they are *leane, withered, hollow-eyed, looke olde, wrinckled, harsh, much troubled with winde, and a griping in their bellies, or belly-ake, belch often, dry bellies and hard, dejected lookes, flaggy beards, singing of the eares, vertigo, light headed, little or no sleepe, and that interrupt, terrible and fearefull dreames. Anna soror, quæ me suspensam insomnia terrent?* The same Symptomes are repeated by *Melanelius* in his booke of Melancholy, collected out of *Galen, Ruffus, Ætius, by Rhasis, Gordonius,* and all the Juniors, *continuall, sharpe, and stinking belchings, as if their meat in their stomacke were putrified, or that they had eaten fish, dry bellies, absurd and interrupt dreames, and many phantasticall visions about their eyes, vertiginous, apt to tremble, and prone to Venery.* Some adde palpitation of the heart, cold sweat, as usuall Symptomes, and a leaping in many parts of the body, *saltum in multis corporis partibus,* a kinde of itching, saith *Laurentius* on the superficies of the skin, like a flea-biting sometimes. *Montaltus cap. 21.* puts fixed eyes and much twinkling of their eyes for a signe, and so doth *Avicenna, oculos habentes palpitantes, trauli, vehementèr rubicundi, &c. lib. 3. Fen. 1. Tract. 4. cap. 18.* They stutte most part, which hee tooke out of *Hippocrates Aphorismes. Rhasis* makes *head ach and a binding heavinesse* for a principall token, *much leaping of winde about the skinne, as well as stutting, or tripping in speech, &c. hollow eyes, grosse veines, & broad lips.* To some too, if they be far gone mimical gestures are too familiar, laughing, grinning, fleering, murmuring, talking to themselves, with strange mouthes and faces, inarticulate voices, exclamations, &c. And although they be commonly leane, hirsute, unchearefull in countenance, withered, & not so pleasant to behold, by reason of those continuall feares, griefes, and vexations, dull, heavy, lazye, restlesse, unapt to goe about any businesse; yet their memories are most part good, they have happy wits, and excellent apprehensions. Their hot and dry braines make them they cannot sleepe, *Ingentes habent & crebras vigilias (Areteus)* Mighty and often watchings, sometimes waking for a month, a yeare together. *Hercules de Saxoniâ* faithfully averreth, that hee hath heard his mother sweare, she slept not for seaven months together: *Trincavellius Tom. 2. cons. 10.* speakes of one that waked 50. dayes, and *Schenkius* hath examples of two yeares, and all without offence. In naturall actions their appetite is greater than their concotion, *multa appetunt, pauca digerunt,* as *Rhasis* hath it, they covet to eat, but cannot digest. And although they *doe eat much, yet they are leane, ill liking,* saith *Areteus, withered and hard, much troubled with costivenesse,* crudities, oppilations, spitting, belching, &c. Their pulse is rare and slowe, except it be of the *Carotides* which is very strong; but that varies according to their intended passions or perturbations, as *Struthius* hath proved at large, *Spigmaticæ artis lib. 4. cap. 13.* To say truth, in such Chronick diseases the pulse is not much to bee respected, there being so much superstition in it, as *Crato* notes, and so many differences in *Galen,* that he dares say they may not bee observed, or understood of any man.

Their urine is most part pale, and low coloured, *Urina pauca, acris, biliosa, (Areteus)* Not much in quantity, but this in my judgement, is all out as uncertaine as the other, varying so often according to severall persons, habits, & other occasions, not to be respected in Chronicke diseases. *Their melancholy excrements in some very much, in others little, as the Spleene playes his part,* and thence proceeds winde, palpitation of the heart, short breath, plenty of humidity in the stomacke, heavinesse of heart and heart ake, and intolerable stupidity and dulnesse of spirits. Their excrements or stoole hard, black to some and little. If the heart, braine, liver, splene, bee misaffected, as usually they are, many inconveniences proceed from them, many diseases accompany, as Incubus, Apoplexy, Epilepsie, Vertigo, those frequent wakings and terrible dreames, intempestive laughing, weeping, sighing, sobbing, bashfulnesse, blushing, trembling, sweating, swouning, &c. All their senses are troubled, they think they see, heare, smell, and touch, that which they doe not, as shall be proved in the following discourse.

Symoptomes or Signes in the Minde

Arculanus in 9. Rhasis and Almansor. cap. 16. will have these Symptomes to be infinite, as indeed they are, varying according to the parties, *for scarce is there one of a thousand that dotes alike, Laurentius cap. 16.* Some few of greater note I will point at; and amongst the rest, *Feare* and *Sorrow,* which as they are frequent causes, so if they persever long, according to *Hippocrates* & *Galen's* Aphorismes, they are most assured signes, inseparable companions, and characters of melancholy; Of present melancholy, and habituated, saith *Montaltus cap. 21.* and common to them all, as the said *Hippocrates, Galen, Avicenna,* and all Neotericks hold. But as hounds many times run away with a false cry, never perceiving themselves to be at a fault, so doe they. For *Diocles* of old, (whom *Galen* confutes) and amongst the *Juniors, Hercules de Saxoniâ,* with *Lod. Mercatus cap. 17. lib. 1. de melan.* take just exceptions at this Aphorisme of *Hippocrates,* tis not alwayes true, or so generally to be understood, *Feare* and *Sorrow* are no common Symptomes to all melancholy, *upon more serious consideration, I finde some* (saith he) *that are not so at all. Some indeed are sad, and not fearefull; some fearefull and not sad, some neither fearefull, nor sad, some both.* Foure kindes he excepts, fanaticall persons, such as were *Cassandra, Manto, Nicostrata, Mopsus, Proteus,* the *Sybills,* whom *Aristotle* confesseth to have beene deepely melancholy, *Baptista Porta* seconds him, *Physiog. lib. 1. cap. 8.* they were *atrâ bile perciti:* dæmoniacall persons, and such as speake strange languages, are of this ranke; some Poets, such as laugh alwayes, and thinke themselves Kings, Cardinalls, &c. sanguine they are, pleasantly disposed most part, and so continue. *Baptista Porta* confines Feare and Sorrow to them that are cold; but Lovers, Sybilles, Enthusiastes, hee wholly excludes. So that I thinke I may truely conclude, they are not alwayes sad and fearefull, but usually so: & that *without a cause, timent de non timendis, (Gordonius:) quæque momenti non sunt, although not all alike* (saith *Altomarus) yet all likely feare, some with an extraordinary and a mighty feare. Areteus. Many feare death, and yet in a contrary humour, make away themselves, Galen lib. 3. de loc. affect. cap. 7.* Some are afraid that heaven will fall on their heads: some, they are damned, or shall be. *They are troubled with scruples of conscience, distrusting Gods mercies, thinke they shall goe certainely to Hell, the Divell will have them, and make great lamentation, Jason Pratensis.* Feare of Divels, death, that they shall bee so sick, of same such or such disease, ready to tremble at every object, they shall dye themselves forthwith, or that some of their deare friends or neere allies are certainely dead; imminent danger, losse, disgrace still torment others, &c. that they are all glasse, and therefore will suffer no man to come neere them; that they are all corke, as light as feathers; others as heavy as lead, some are afraid their heads will fall off their shoulders, that they have frogs in their bellies, &c. *Montanus consil. 23.* speakes of one *that durst not walke alone from home, fir feare hee should sowne, or die.* A second *feares every man he meets will rob him, quarrell with him, or kill him.* A third dares not venture to walke alone, for feare he should meet the Divell, a theefe, bee sicke; feares all old women as witches, and every black dog or cat he sees, hee suspecteth to be a Divell, every person comes neere him is maleficiated, every creature, all intend to hurt him, seeke his ruine: another dares not goe over a bridge, come neere a poole, rock, steep hill, lye in a chamber where crosse beames are, for feare he be tempted to hang, drowne, or præcipitate himselfe; If he be in a silent auditory, as at a sermon, he is afraid he shall speake aloud at unawares, something undecent, unfit to be said. If he be locked in a close roome he is afraid of being stifled for want of ayre, and still carries Bisket, Aquavitæ, or some strong waters about him, for feare of *deliquiums,* or being sicke, or if he be in a throng, middle of a Church, multitude, where he may not well get out, though he sit at ease, he is so misaffected. He will freely promise, undertake any businesse beforehand, but when it comes to be performed, he dare not adventure, but fears an infinite number of dangers, disasters, &c. Some are *afraid to be burned, or that the ground will sinke under them, or swallow them quicke, or that the King will call them in question for some fact they never did (Rhasis cont.)* and *that they shall surely bee executed.* The terrour of such a death troubles them, and they feare as much, and are equally tormented in minde, *as they that have committed a murder, and are pensive without a cause, as if they were not presently to be put to death. Plater. cap. 3. de mentis alienat.* They are afraid of some losse, danger, that they shall surely loose their lives, goods, and all they have, but why they knowe not. *Trincavellius consil. 13. lib. 1.* had a patient that would needs make away himselfe, for feare of being hanged, and could not be perswaded for three yeares together, but that hee had killed a man. *Plater. observat. lib. 1.* hath two other examples, of such as feare to bee executed without a cause. If they come in a place where a robbery, theft, or any such offence hath beene done, they presently feare they are suspected, and many times betray themselves without a cause. *Lewis the 11.* the French King, suspected every man a traitor that came about him, durst trust no officer. *Alii formidolosi omnium, alii quorundam* (*Fracastorius lib. 2. de Intellect.*) *some feare all alike, some certaine men,* & cannot endure their companies, are sick in them, or if they be from home. Some suspect treason still, others *are afraid of their dearest and nearest friends* (*Melanelius è Galeno, Ruffo, Ætio,*) and dare not bee alone in the darke, for feare of hobgoblins and divells: hee suspects every thing he heares or sees to be a Divell, or enchanted, and imagineth a thousand Chimeras and visions, which to his thinking he certainely sees, like bugbeares, talkes with black men, Ghosts, goblins &c.

Omnes se terrent auræ, sonus excitat omnis.

Another through bashfulnesse, suspition and timorousnesse will not be seene abroad, *loves darknesse as life, and cannot endure the light,* or to sit in lightsome places, his hat still in his eyes, hee will neither see, nor be seene by his good will, *Hippocrates lib. de Insaniâ & Melancholiâ.* Hee dare not come in company for feare hee should be misused, disgraced, overshoot himselfe in gesture or speeches, or bee sicke, he thinkes every man observes him, aimes at him, derides him, owes him malice. Most part *they are afraid, they are bewitched, possessed, or poisoned by their enimies,* and sometimes they suspect their neerest friends: *hee thinkes something speakes or talkes within him, or to him, and he belcheth of the poyson. Christophorus à Vega lib. 2. cap. 1.* had a patient so troubled, that by no perswasion or Physicke, he could be reclaimed. Some are afraid that they shall have every fearefull disease they see others have, heare of, or read, and dare not therefore heare or read of any such subject, no not of melancholy it selfe, least by applying to themselves that which they heare or read, they should aggravate and increase it. If they see one possessed, bewitched, an Epilepticke Paroxisme, a man shaking with the palsie, or giddy headed, reeling or standing in a dangerous place &c. for many dayes after it runnes in their minds; they are afraid they shall be soo too, they are in like dangers, as *Perkins cap. 12. sect. 2.* well observes in his Cases of Conscience, and many times by violence of Imagination they produce it. They cannot endure to see any terrible object, as a Monster, a man executed, a carcase, heare the divell named, or any Tragicall relation seene, but they quake for feare; *Hecatas somniare sibi videntur* (*Lucian*) they dreame of Hobgoblins, and may not get it out of their minds a long time after: they apply (as I have said) all they heare, see, read, to themselves; as *Felix Plater* notes of some young Physitians, that studying to cure diseases, catch them themselves, will be sicke, and appropriate all symptomes they finde related of others, to their owne persons. And therefore (quod iterum moneo, utcunque nauseam paret lectori, malo decem verba decies repetita licet abundare, quam unum desiderari) I would advise him, that is actually melancholy, not to read this Tract of Symptomes, lest he disquiet or make himselfe for a time worse, and more melancholy then he was before. Generally of them all take this, *de inanibus semper conqueruntur, & timent,* saith *Areteus;* they complaine of toyes, and feare without a cause, and still thinke their melancholy to be most grievous, none so bad as they are, though it be nothing in respect, yet never any man sure was so troubled, or in this sort. As really tormented and perplexed in as great an agony for toyes and trifles (such things as they will after laugh at themselves) as if they were most materiall and essentiall matters indeed worthy to be feared, and will not be satisfied. Pacifie them for one, they are instantly troubled with some other feare, alwaies afraid of some thing, which they foolishly imagine or conceive to themselves, which never peradventure was, never can be, never likely will be, troubled in minde upon every small occasion, unquiet, still complaining, grieving, vexing, suspecting, grudging, discontent, & cannot be freed so long as melancholy continues. Or if their minds be more quiet for the present, and they free from forraine feares, outward accidents, yet their bodies are out of tune, they suspect some part or other to be amisse, now their head akes, heart, stomake, spleene, &c. is misaffected, they shall surely have this or that disease; still troubled in body, minde, or both, and through winde, corrupt phantasie, some accidentall distemper continually molested. Yet for all this, a *Facchinus* notes, *in all other things they are wise, stayd, discreet, and doe nothing unbeseeming their dignity, person, or place, this foolish, ridiculous, and childish feare excepted;* which so much, so continually tortures, and crucifies their soules, like a barking dogge that alwaies bawles, but seldome bites, this feare ever molesteth, and so long as Melancholy lasteth, cannot be avoided.

Sorrow is that other Character, and inseparable companion, as individuall as Saint *Cosmus* and *Damian, fidus Achates,* as all writers witnesse, a common symptome, a continuall, and still without any evident cause, *mærent omnes & si roges eos reddere causam non possunt,* grieving still, but why, they cannot tell: *Agelasti, mæsti, cogitabundi,* they looke as if they had newly come forth of *Trophonius* denne. And though they laugh many times, and seeme to bee extraordinary merry (as they will by fits) yet extreame lumpish againe in an instant, dull and heavy, *semel & simul,* merry and sad, but most part sad: *Si qua placent, abuent; inimica tenaciù hærent,* sorrow sticks by them still, continually gnawing, as the vulture did *Titius* bowels, and they cannot avoid it. No sooner are their eyes open, but after terrible & troublesome dreames their heavy hearts begin to sigh: they are still fretting, chafing, sighing, grieving, complaining, finding faults, repining, grudging, weeping, *Heautontimorumenoi,* vexing themselves, disquieted in minde, with restlesse, unquiet thoughts, discontent, either for their owne, other mens, or publike affaires, such as concerne them not, things past, present, or to come, the remembrance of some disgrace, losse, injury, abuse, &c.

troubles them now being idle afresh as if it were new done, they are afflicted otherwise for some danger, losse, want, shame, misery, that will certainly come, as they suspect and mistrust. *Lugubris Ate* frownes upon them, insomuch, that *Areteus* well calls it, *angorem animi,* a vexation of the minde, a perpetual agony. They can hardly bee pleased, or eased, though in other mens opinion most happy, goe, tarry, run, ride,

> *post equitem sedet atra cura:*

they cannot avoid this ferall plague, let them come in what company they will, *hæret lateri lethalis arundo,* as to a Deere that is strucke, whether hee runne, goe, rest, with the herd, or alone, this griefe remaines: irresolution, inconstancy, vanity of minde, their feare, torture, care, jealousie, suspition, &c: continues, and they cannot be relieved. So he complained in the Poet.

> *Domum revortor mæstus, atque animo ferè*
> *Perturbato, atque incerto præ ægritudine,*
> *Adsido, accurrunt servi soccos detrahunt:*
> *Video alios festinare, lectos sternere,*
> *Cænam apparare, pro se quisque sedulo*
> *Faciebant; quo ilam mihi lenirent miseriam.*

He came home sorrowfull, & troubled in his mind, his servants did all they possibly could to please him; one pulled off his socks, another made ready his bed, a third his supper, all did their utmost indeavours to ease his griefe, and exhilerate his person, he was profoundly melancholy, he had lost his sonne, *illud angebat,* that was his *Cordolium,* his paine, his agony which could not be removed. Hence it proceeds many times, that they are weary of their lives, and ferall thoughts to offer violence to their owne persons, come into their mindes, *tædium vitæ* is a common symptome, *tarda fluunt, ingrataque tempora,* they are soone tired with all things; they will now tarry, now bee gone; now in bed they will rise, now up, then goe to bed, now pleased, then againe displeased; now they like, by and by dislike all, weary of all, *sequitur nunc vivendi, nunc moriendi cupido,* saith *Aurelianus lib. 1. cap. 6.* but most part *vitam damnant,* discontent, disquieted, perplexed upon every light, or no occasion, object: often tempted, I say, to make away themselves; *Vivere nolunt, mori nesciunt;* they cannot dye, they will not live: they complaine, weepe, lament, and thinke they lead a most miserable life, never was any man so bad, or so before, every poore man they see is most fortunate in respect of them, every begger that comes to the doore is happier than they are, they could be contented to change lives with them, especially if they be alone, idle, and parted from their ordinary company, molested, displeased, or provoked: griefe, feare, agony, discontent, wearisomenesse, lazinesse, suspition, or some such passion forcibly seizeth on them. Yet by and by when they come in company againe, which they like or be pleased, *suam sen-*

tentiam rursus damnant, & vitæ solatio delectantur, as *Octavius Horatianus observes lib. 2. cap. 5.* they condemne their former mislike, and are well pleased to live. And so they continue, till with some fresh discontent they bee molested againe, and then they are weary of their lives, weary of all, they wil die, and shew rather a necessity to live, then a desire. *Claudius* the Emperour, as *Sueton* describes him, had a spice of this disease, for when hee was tormented with the paine of his stomacke, he had a conceipt to make away himselfe. *Jul. Cæsar Claudinus consil. 84.* had a *Polonian* to his Patient, so affected, that through feare and sorrow, with which he was still disquieted, hated his owne life, wished for death every moment, and to be freed of his misery. *Mercurialis* another, and another, that was often minded to dispatch himselfe, and so continued for many yeares.

Suspition, & Jealousie, are generall Symptomes: they are commonly distrustfull, timorous, apt to mistake, & amplifie, *facile irascibles,* testy, pettish, peevish, & ready to snarle upon every small occasion, *cum amicissimis,* & without a cause, *datum vel non datum,* it will be *scandalum acceptum.* If they speak in jest, hee takes it in good earnest. If they bee not saluted, invited, consulted with, called to counsell &c., or that any respect, small complement, or ceremony be omitted, they thinke themselves neglected, and contemned for a time that tortures them. If two talke together, discourse, whisper, jest, or tell a tale in generall, he thinkes presently they meane him, applies all to himselfe *de se putat omnia dici.* Of if they talke with him, he is ready to misconstrue every word they speake, and interpret it to the worst, hee cannot endure any man to looke steedily on him, speake to him almost, laugh, jest, or be familiar, or hem, or point, cough, or spit, or make a noise sometimes, &c. Hee thinks they laugh or point at him, or doe it in disgrace of him, circumvent him, contemne him; every man lookes at him, he is pale, red, sweates for feare and anger, lest some body should observe him. He workes upon it, and long after, this falce conceipt of an abuse, troubles him. *Montanus consil. 22.* gives instance in a melancholy Jew, that was *Iracundior Adria,* so waspish and suspitious, *tam facilè iratus,* that no man could tell how to carry himselfe in his company.

Inconstant they are in all their actions, vertigenous, restlesse, unapt to resolve of any businesse, they will, and will not, perswaded to & fro upon every small occasion, or word spoken: and yet if once they bee resolved, obstinate, hard to be reconciled. If they abhorre, dislike, or distast, once setled, though to the better by oddes, by no counsell or perswasion to be removed. Yet in most things wavering, irresolute, unable to deliberate, through feare, *faciunt, & mox facti pænitent (Areteus) avari, & paulò post prodigi.* Now prodigall, and then covetous; they doe, and by-and-by repent them of that which they have done, so that both waies they are troubled, whether they doe or doe not, want or have, hit or misse, disquieted of all hands, soone weary, and still seeking change, restlesse, I say, fickle, fugitive, they may not abide to tarry in one place long,

> *Romæ rus optans, absentem rusticus urbem*
> *Tollit ad astra,———*

no company long, or to persever in any action or businesse.

> *Et similis regum pueris pappare minutum*
> *Poscit, & iratus mammæ lallare recusat,*

eftosoones pleased, and anon displeased, as a man thats bitten with fleas, or that cannot sleepe, turnes to and fro in his bed, their restlesse mindes are tossed and varie, they have no patience to read out a booke, to play out a game or two, walke a mile, sit an houre, &c. erected and dejected in an instant; animated to undertake, and upon a word spoken againe discouraged.

Extreame *Passionate, Quicquid volunt, valdè volunt;* and what they desire, they doe most furiously seeke: anxious ever & very sollicitous, distrustfull and timorous, envious, malitious, profuse one while, sparing another, but most part covetous, muttering, repining, discontent, and still complaining, grudging, peevish, *injuriarum tenaces,* prone to revenge, soone troubled, and most violent in all their imaginations, not affable in speech, or apt to vulgar complement, but surly, dull, sad, austere; *cogitabundi* still, very intent, and as *Albertus Durer* paints melancholy, like a sad woman leaning on her arme with fixed lookes, neglected habit &c. held therefore by some proud, soft, sottish, or halfe mad, as the *Abderites* esteemed of *Democritus:* and yet of a deepe reach, excellent apprehension, judicious, wise and witty: for I am of that Noblemans mind, *Melancholy advanceth mens conceipts, more than any humour whatsoever,* improves their meditations more than any strong drinke, or sacke. They are of profound judgement in some things, although in others, *non rectè judicant inquieti,* saith *Fracastorius lib. 2. de Intell.* and as *Arculanus cap. 16. in 9. Rhasis,* tearmes it, *Judicium plerumque perversum, corrupti, cum judicant honesta, inhonesta; & amicitian habent pro inimicitiâ:* They count honesty, dishonesty; friends as enimies; they will abuse their best friends, and dare not offend their enimies. Cowards most part, *& ad inferendam injuriam timidissimi,* saith *Cardan lib. 8. cap. 40. de rerum varietate,* Loath to offend; and if they chance to over-shoot themselves in word, or deed, or any small businesse or circumstance be omitted, forgotten, they are miserably tormented, & frame a thousand dangers and inconveniences to themselves, *ex muscâ elephantum,* if once they conceit it: overjoyed with every good rumour, tale, or prosperous event, transported beyond themselves: with every small crosse againe, bad newes, misconceaved injury, losse, danger, afflicted beyond measure, in greaty agony, perplexed, dejected, astonished, impatient, utterly undone. Fearefull, suspitious of al. Yet againe, many of them desperate harebraines, rash, carelesse, fit to bee Assasinates, as being void of all feare and sorrow, according to *Hercules de Saxonia, Most audacious, and such as dare walke* *alone in the night, through desarts and dangerous places, fearing none. They are prone to love,* and easie to be taken: *Propensi ad amorem & excandescentiam,* (*Montaltus cap. 21.*) *quickly inamored, and dote upon all; love one dearely, till they see another, and then dote on her,* Et hanc, & hanc, & illam, & omnes, the present moves most and the last commonly they love best. Yet some againe *Anterotes,* cannot endure the sight of a woman, abhorre the sexe, as that same melancholy Duke of *Muscovy,* that was instantly sicke, if he came but in sight of them: and that Anchorite, that fell into a cold palsie, when a woman was brought before him.

Humorous they are beyond all measure, sometimes profusely laughing, extraordinary merry, and then againe weeping without a cause, (which is familiar with many Gentlewomen) groaning, sighing, pensive, sad, almost distracted, *multa absurda fingunt, & à ratione aliena* (saith *Frambesarius*) they faigne many absurdities, vaine, void of reason: one supposeth himselfe to be a Dog, Cock, Beare, Horse, Glasse, Butter, &c. He is a Giant, a Dwarfe, as strong as an hundred men, a Lord, Duke, Prince, &c. And if he be told hee hath a stinking breath, a great nose, that he is sicke, or inclined to such or such a disease, he beleeves it eftsoones, and peradventure by force of imagination, will worke it out. Many of them are immoveable, and fixed in their conceipts, others vary upon every object, heard or seene. If they see a stage-play, they runne upon that a weeke after; if they heare Musicke, or see dancing, they have naught but bag-pipes in their braine; if they see a combat, they are all for armes. If abused, an abuse troubles them long after; if crossed, that crosse &c. Restlesse in their thoughts, and actions, continually meditating, *Velut ægri somnia, vanæ finguntur species;* More like dreamers, then men awake, they faine a company of Anticke, phantasticall conceipts, they have most frivolous thoughts, impossible to be effected, or sometimes thinke verily they heare and see present before their eyes, such phantasmes or goblins, they feare, suspect, or conceave, they still talke with, and follow them; In fine, *cogitationes somniantibus similes, id vigilant, quod alii somniant cogitabundi;* Still, saith *Avicenna,* they wake, as others dreame, and such for the most part of their imaginations and conceipts, absurd, vaine, foolish toies, yet they are most curious and sollicitous, continuall, & *supra modum, Rhasis cont. lib. 1. cap. 9. præmeditantur de aliquâ re.* As serious in a toye, as if it were a most necessary businesse, of great moment, importance, and still, still, still thinking of it: *sæviunt in se,* macerating themselves. Though they doe talke with you, and seeme to be otherwise employed, and to your thinking, very intent and busie, still that toy runnes in their minde, that feare, that suspition, that abuse, that jealousy, that agony, that vexation, that crosse, that castle in the ayre, that crochet, that whimsie, that fiction, that pleasant waking dreame whatsoever it is. *Nec interrogant* (saith *Fracastorius*) *nec interrogatis rectè respondent,* They doe not much heed what you say, their minde is on another matter; aske what you will, they doe not attend, or much intend that businesse they are about, but forget themselves what they are saying, doing, or should otherwise say or doe, whither they are going, distracted with their owne melancholy thoughts. One laughs upon a sudden, another smiles to himselfe, a third frownes, calls, his lips goe still, he acts with his hand, as he walkes, &c. 'Tis proper to all melancholy men, saith *Mercurialis consil. 11. What conceit they have once entertained, to be most intent, violent, and continually about it. Invitis occurrit,* doe what they may, they cannot be rid of it, against their wills they must thinke of it a thousand times over, *Perpetuò molestantur, nec oblivisci possunt,* they are continually troubled with it, in company, out of company; at meat, at exercise, at all times and places, *non desinunt ea, quæ minimè volunt, cogitare,* if it bee offensive especially, they cannot forget it, they may not rest or sleep for it, but still tormenting themselves, *Sysiphi saxum volvunt sibi ipsis,* as *Brunner* observes, *Perpetua calamitas & miserabile flagellum.*

Crato, Laurentius, and *Fernelius,* put bashfulness for an ordinary Symptome, *subrusticus pudor,* or *vitiosus pudor,* is a thing which much haunts and torments them. If they have beene misused, derided, disgraced, chidden, &c. or by any perturbation of minde misaffected, it so farre troubles them, that they become quite moped many times, & so disheartened, dejected, they dare not come abroad, into strange companies especially, or manage their ordinary affaires, so childish, timorous and bashfull, they can looke no man in the face; some are more disquieted in this kinde, some lesse, longer some, others shorter, by fits &c. though some on the other side (according to *Fracastorius*) be *inverecundi & pertinaces,* impudent and peevish. But most part they are very shamefast: and that makes them with *Pet. Blesensis, Christopher Urswick,* and many such, to refuse honours, offices, & preferments, which sometimes fall into their mouthes, they cannot speake or put forth themselves as others can, *timor hos, pudor impedit illos,* timorousnesse and bashfulnesse hinder their proceedings, they are contented with their present estate, unwilling to undertake any office, and therefore never likely to rise. For that cause they seldome visit their friends, except some familiars: *pauciloqui,* of few words, and oftentimes wholly silent, *Frambesarius* a Frenchman, had two such patients, *omninò taciturnos,* their friends could not get them to speake: *Rodericus à Fonseca consult. Tom. 2. 85. consil.* gives instance in a young man, of 27 yeares of age, that was frequently silent, bashfull, moped, solitary, that would not eat his meat or sleepe, and yet againe by fits, apt to bee angry, &c. most part they are, as *Plater* notes, *desides, taciturni, ægrè impulsi, nec nisi coacti procedunt, &c.* they will scarce be compelled to doe that which concernes them, though it be for their good, so diffident, so dull, of small or no complement, unsociable, hard to be acquainted with, especially of strangers; they had rather write their mindes, then speake, and above all things love *Solitarinesse. Ob voluptatem, an ob timorem soli sunt?* Are they so solitary for pleasure (one askes) or paine? for both: yet I rather thinke for feare and sorrow &c.

Hinc metuunt, cupiuntque dolent, fugiuntque nec auras
Respiciunt clausi tenebris, & carcere cæco.
Hence 'tis they grieve and feare, avoiding light,
And shut themselves in prison darke from sight.

As *Bellerophon* in *Homer,*

Qui miser in sylvis mærens errabat opacis,
Ipse suum cor edens, hominum vestigia vitans.
That wandered in the woods sad all alone,
Forsaking mens society, making great moane.

They delight in flouds and waters, desart places, to walke alone in orchards, Gardens, private walks, back-lanes, averse from company, as *Diogenes* in his tub, or *Timon Misanthropus,* they abhorre all companions at last, even their neerest acquaintance, and most familiar friends, for they have a conceipt (I say) every man observes them, will derive, laugh to scorne, or misuse them, confining themselves therefore wholy to their private houses or Chambers *fugiunt homines sine causa* (saith *Rhasis*) *& odio habent, cont. lib. 1. cap. 9.* they will diet themselves, feed and live alone. It was one of the chiefest reasons, why the Cittizens of *Abdera* suspected *Democritus* to bee melancholy and mad; because that as *Hippocrates* related in his Epistle to *Philopæmenes, he forsooke the Citty, lived in groves and hollow trees, upon a greene banke by a brooke side, or confluence of waters all day long, and all night. Quæ quidem* (saith he) *plurimùm atrâ bile vexatis, & melancholicis eveniunt, deserta frequentant, hominumque congressum aversantur;* Which is an ordinary thing with melancholy men. The *Ægyptians* therefore in their *Hieroglyphicks,* expressed a melancholy man by an Hare sitting in her forme, as being a most timorous and solitary creature, *Pierius Hieroglyph. lib. 12.* But this, and all precedent symptomes, are more or lesse apparent, as the humour is intended or remitted, hardly perceaved in some, or not at all, most manifest in others. Childish in some, terrible in others, to be derided in one, pitied or admired in another, to him by fits, to a second continuate: and howsoever these symptomes bee common and incident to all persons, yet they are the more remarkable, frequent, furious and violent in melancholy men. To speake in a word, there is nothing so vaine, absurd, ridiculous, extravagant, impossible, incredible, so monstrous a Chymera, so prodigious and strange, such as Painters & Poets durst not attempt, which they will not really feare, faine, suspect, and imagine unto themselves: And that which *Lod. Vives* said in jest of a silly country fellow, that kil'd his Asse for drinking up the Moone, *ut lunam mundo redderet,* you may truely say of them in earnest. They will act, conceave all extreames, contrarieties, and contradictions, and that in infinite varieties. *Melancholici planè incredibilia sibi persuadent, ut vix omnibus sæculis duo reperti sint, qui idem imaginati sint (Erastus de Lamiis)* scarce two of two thousand, that concurre in the same symptomes; The tower of *Babel* never yeelded such confusion of tongues, as this Chaos of melancholy doth variety of Symptomes. There is in all melancholy *similitudo dissimilis,* like mens faces, a disagreeing likenesse still; And as in a River we swimme in the same place, though not in the same numericall water: as the same instrument affords severall lessons, so the same disease yeelds diversity of Symptomes. Which howsoever they be diverse, intricate, and hard to be confined, I will adventure yet in such a vast confusion and generality, to bring them into some order, & so descend to particulars.

Particular Symptomes from the Influence of Starres, Parts of the Body, and Humours

Some men have peculiar Symptomes, according to their temperament and *Crisis,* which they had from the Starres and those celestiall influences, variety of wits and dispositions, as *Anthony Zara* contends, *Anat. ingen. sect. 1. memb. 11. 12. 13. 14. plurimum irritant influentiæ cælestes, unde cientur animi ægritudines & morbi corporum.* One saith, diverse diseases of the body and minde proceed from their influences, as I have already proved out of *Ptolomy, Pontanus, Lemnius, Cardan,* and others, as they are principall significators of manners, diseases, mutually irradiated, or Lords of the geniture, &c. *Ptolomeus* in his centiloquie, *Hermes,* or whosoever else the author of that Tract, attributes all these symptomes, which are in melancholy men, to celestiall influences: which opinion *Mercurialis de affect. lib. 1. cap. 10.* rejects; but as I say, *Jovianus Pontanus,* and others stifly defend. That some are solitary, dull, heavy, churlish: some againe blith, buxome, light, and merry, they ascribe wholly to the Starres. As if *Saturne* be predominant in his nativity, and cause melancholy in his temperature, then he shall be very austere, sullen, churlish, black of colour, profound in his cogitations, full of cares, miseries, and discontents, sad and fearefull, alwaies silent, solitary, still delighting in husbandry, in Woods, Orchards, Gardens, Rivers, Ponds, Pooles, darke walkes and close: *Cogitationes sunt velle ædificare, velle arbores plantare, agros colere, &c.* To catch Birds, Fishes, &c. still contriving and musing of such matters. If *Jupiter* domineeres, they are more ambitious, still meditating of kingdomes, magistracies, offices, honours, or that they are Princes, Potentates, & how they would carry themselves, &c. If *Mars,* they are all for warres, brave combats, Monomachies, testy, cholericke, harebraine, rash, furious, and violent in their actions. They will faine themselves Victors, Commanders, are passioate & satyricall in their speeches, great braggers, ruddy of colour. And though they be poore in shew, vile and base, yet like *Telephus* and *Pelus* in the Poet

Ampullas jactant & sesquipedalia verba,

their mouthes are full of Myriades, and tetrarchs at their tongues end. If the *Sunne,* they will be Lords, Emperours, in conceipt at least, &

Monarchs, give Offices, Honours, &c. If *Venus,* they are still courting of their mistresses and most apt to love, amorously given, they seeme to heare musicke, plaies, see fine pictures, dancers, merriments, and the like. Ever in love, and dote on all they see. *Mercurialists* are solitary, much in contemplation, subtile, Poets, Philosophers, and musing most part about such matters. If the *Moone* have a hand, they are all for peregrinations, sea voyages, much affected with travels, to discourse, read, mediate of such things; wandering in their thoughts, divers, much delighted in waters, to fish, fowle, &c.

But the most immediate Symptomes proceed from the Temperature it selfe, and the Organicall parts, as Head, Liver, Spleene, Meseraicke veines, Heart, Wombe, Stomacke, &c. and most especially from distemperature of Spirits (which as *Hercules de Saxoniâ* contends, are wholly immateriall) or from the foure humours in those seats, whether they be hot or cold, naturall, unnaturall, innate or adventitious, intended or remitted, simple or mixt, their diverse mixtures, and severall adustions, combinations, which may bee as diversely varied, as those foure first qualities in *Clavius,* and produce as many severall Symptomes and monstrous fictions as wine doth effects, which as *Andreas Bachius* observes *lib. 3. ve vino cap. 20.* are infinite. Of greater note be these.

If it be naturall Melancholy, as *Lod. Mercatus lib. 1. cap. 17. de melan. T. Bright cap. 16.* hath largely described, either of the Spleene, or of the veines, faulty by excesse of quantity, or thicknes of substance, it is a cold and dry humour, as *Montanus* affirmes *consil. 26.* the parties are sad, timorous, and fearefull. *Prosper Calenas* in his booke *de atrâ bile,* will have them to be more stupid then ordinary, cold, heavy, dull, solitary, sluggish, *Si multam atram bilem & frigidam habent.* . . .

. . . These Symptomes vary according to the mixture of the other humours not adust, or the mixture of those foure humours adust, which is unnaturall melancholy. For as *Trallianus* hath written *cap. 16. lib. 1. There is not one cause of this melancholy, nor one humour which begets it, but divers diversly intermixt, from whence proceeds this variety of Symptomes:* And those varying againe as they are hot or cold. *Cold melancholy* (saith *Benedic. Vittorius Faventinus pract. mag.) is a cause of dotage, and more mild Symptomes, if hot or more adust, of more violent passions, and furies. Fracastorius lib. 2. de intellect.* will have us to consider well of it, *with what kinde of Melancholy every one is troubled, for it much availes to knowe it, one is enraged by fervent heat, another is possessed by sad and cold, one is fearefull, shamefast; the other impudent and bold;* As *Ajax, Arma rapit superosque furens in prælia poscit:* quite mad or tending to madnesse: *Nunc hos, nunc impetit illos. Bellerophon* on the other side, *solis errat malè sanus in agris,* wanders alone in the woods, one despaires, weepes, and is weary of his life, another laughs, &c. All which variety is produced from the severall degrees of heat and cold, which *Hercules de Saxoniâ* will have wholly proceed from the distemperature of spirits alone, animall especially, and those immateriall, the next & immediat causes of Melancholy, as they are hot, cold, dry, moist, and from their agitation proceeds that diversity of Symptomes, which hee reckons up, in the 13. cap. of his Tract of Melancholy, and that largely through every part. Others will have them come from the divers adustion of the foure humours, which in this unnaturall melancholy, by corruption of blood, adust choler, or melancholy naturall, *by excessive distemper of heat turned, in comparison of the naturall, into a sharp lye by force of adustion, cause according to the diversity of their matter, diverse & strange Symptomes,* which *T. Bright* reckons up in his following chapter. So doth *Arculanus,* according to the foure principall humours adust, and many others.

For example, if it proceed from fleagme, (which is seldome and not so frequent as the rest) it stirres up dull Symptomes, and a kinde of stupidity, or impassionate hurt: they are sleepy, saith *Savanarola,* dull, slow, cold, blockish, asse-like, *Asininam melancholiam, Melancthon* calls it, *they are much given to weeping, and delight in waters, ponds, pooles, rivers, fishing, fowling, &c. (Arnoldus breviar. 1. cap. 18.)* They are pale of colour, sloathfull, apt to sleepe, heavy; *much troubled with head-ach,* continual meditation, & muttering to themselves, they dreame of waters, that they are in danger of drowning, and feare such things, *Rhasis.* They are fatter than others that are melancholy, paler, of a muddy complexion, apter to spit, sleep, more troubled with rheume then the rest, and have their eyes still fixed on the ground. Such a patient had *Hercules de Saxoniâ,* a widdowe in *Venice,* that was fat and very sleepie still: *Christophorus à Vega* another affected in the same sort. If it bee inveterate or violent, the Symptomes are more evident, they plainely dote & are ridiculous to others, in all their gestures, actions, speeches: imagining impossibilities, as hee in *Christophorus à Vega,* that thought hee was a tunne of Wine, and that *Siennois,* that resolved with himselfe not to pisse, for feare he should drowne all the towne.

If it proceed from blood adust, or that there bee a mixture of blood in it, *such are commonly ruddy of complexion, and high coloured,* according to *Salust. Salvianus,* and *Hercules de Saxoniâ.* And as *Savanarola, Vittorius Faventinus Emper.* farther adde, *the veines of their eyes be red, as well as their faces.* They are much inclined to laughter, wittie & merry, conceipted in discourse, pleasant, if they be not farre gone, much given to musicke, dancing, and to be in womens company. They meditate wholly on such things, and thinke *thee see or heare playes, dancing, and such like sports* (free from all feare and sorrow, as *Hercules de Saxoniâ* supposeth.) If they be more strongly possessed with this kinde of melancholy, *Arnoldus* addes, *Breviar. lib. 1. cap. 18.* Like him of *Argos* in the Poet, that sate laughing all day long, as if hee had been at a Theatre. Such another is mentioned by *Aristotle,* living at *Abydos* a towne of *Asia minor,* that would sit after the same fashion, as if hee had been upon a stage, and sometimes act himselfe, now clap his hands, and laugh, as if he had beene well pleased with the sight. *Wolfus* relates of a country fellow called *Brunsellius,* subject to this humour, *That being by chance at a sermon, saw a woman fall off from a forme halfe asleepe, at which object most of the company laughed, but hee for his part, was so much moved, that for three whole dayes after hee did nothing but laugh, by which meanes hee was much weakened, and worse a long time following.* Such a one was old *Sophocles,* and *Democritus* himselfe had *hilare delirium,* much in this vaine. *Laurentius cap. 3. de melan.* thinkes this kinde of melancholy, which is a little adust with some mixture of blood, to be that which *Aristotle* meant, when hee said melancholy men of all others are most witty, which causeth many times a divine ravishment, and a kinde of *Enthusiasmus,* which stirreth them up to bee excellent Philosophers, Poets, Prophets, &c. *Mercurialis consil. 110.* gives instance in a young man his patient, sanguine melancholy, *of a great wit, and excellently learned.*

If it arise from choler adust, they are bold and impudent, and of a more hairebraine disposition, apt to quarrell, and thinke of such things, battles, combats, and their manhood, furious, impatient in discourse, stiffe, irrefragable and prodigious in their tenets, and if they be moved, most violent, outragious, ready to disgrace, provoke any, to kill themselves and others, *Arnoldus* addes, starke mad by fitts, *they sleepe little, their urine is subtile and fiery (Guianerius.) In their fits you shall heare them speake all manner of languages, Hebrew, Greeke and Latine, that never were taught or knew them before. Apponensis in com. in 1. Prob. sec. 30.* speaks of a mad woman that spake excellent good Latine; and *Rhasis* knew another, that could prophecy in her fit, and foretell things truely to come. *Guianerius* had a patient could make Latine verses when the moone was combust, otherwise illiterate. *Avicenna* and some of his adherents will have these symptomes, when they happen, to proceed from the divell, and that they are rather *dæmoniaci,* possessed, then mad or melancholy, or both together, as *Jason Pratensis* thinkes, *Immiscent se mali genii,* &c. but most ascribe it to the humor, which opinion *Montaltus cap. 21.* stifly maintaines, confuting *Avicenna* and the rest, referring it wholy to the quality and disposition of the humour and subject. *Cardan de rerum var. lib. 8. cap. 10.* holds these men of all other fit to be assasinats, bold, hardy, fierce, and adventurous, to undertake any thing by reason of their choler adust. *This humor,* saith he, *prepares them to endure death it self, and all manner of torments with invincible courage, and 'tis a wonder to see with what alacrity they will undergoe such tortures, ut supra naturam res videatur:* hee ascribes this generosity, fury, or rather stupidity, to this adustion of choler and melancholy: but I take these rather to be mad or desperate, then properly melancholy, for commonly this humor so adust and hot, degenerats into madnesse.

If it come from melancholy it selfe adust, those men, saith *Avicenna, are usually sad and solitary, and that continually, and in excesse, more then ordinary suspitious, more fearefull, and have long, sore, and most corrupt Imaginations;* cold and blacke, bashfull, and so solitary, that as *Arnoldus* writes, *They will endure no company, they dreame of graves still, and dead men, and thinke themselves bewitched or dead:* if it bee extreame, they thinke they heare hideous noyses, see and talke *with blacke men, and converse familiarly with divells, and such strange Chimeras and visions,* (*Gordonius*) or that they are possessed by them, that some body talkes to them, or within them. *Tales melancholici plerumque dæmoniaci, Montaltus consil. 26. ex Avicenna. Valescus de Taranta,* had such a woman in cure; *that thought every night she had to doe with the divell:* and *Gentilis Fulgosus quæst. 55.* writes that hee had a melancholy friend, that *had a blacke man in the likenesse of a souldier,* still following him wheresoever hee was. *Laurentius cap. 7.* hath many stories of such as have thought themselves bewitched by their enimies; and some that would eate no meat as being dead. Anno 1550. an Advocate of *Paris* fell into such a melancholy fit, that he believed verily he was dead, hee could not be perswaded otherwise, or to eate or drinke, till a kinsman of his, a Scholler of *Bourges* did eate before him, dressed like a corse. The story, saith *Serres,* was acted in a Comœdy before *Charles* the ninth. Some thinke they are beasts, wolves, hogges and cry like dogges, foxes, bray like asses, and low like kine, as King *Prætus* daughters. *Hildesheim spicel. 2. de Maniâ,* hath an example of a Dutch Baron so affected, and *Trincavellius lib. 1. consil. 11.* another of a noble man in his country, *that thought hee was certainely a beast, and would imitate most of their voices,* with many such symptomes, which may properly be reduced to this kinde.

If it proceed from the severall combinations of these foure humours, or spirits, *Herc. de Saxon.* addes, hot, cold, dry, moist, darke, confused, settled, constringed, as it participates of matter, or is without matter, the symptomes are likewise mixt. One thinkes himselfe a giant, another a dwarfe; one is heavy as lead, another is as light as a feather. *Marcellus Donatus lib. 2. cap. 41.* makes mention out of *Seneca,* of one *Seneccio* a rich man, *that thought himselfe and every thing else he had, great: great wife, great horses, could not abide little things, but would have great pots to drinke in, great hose, and great shooes bigger than his feet.* Like her in *Trallianus,* that supposed *shee could shake all the world with her finger,* and was afraid to clinch her hand together lest shee should crush the world like an apple in peeces: or him in *Galen,* that thought he was *Atlas,* and sustained heaven with his shoulders. Another thinkes himselfe so little, that he can creepe into a mousehole: one feares heaven will fall on his head: a second is a cock, and such a one *Guianerius* saith hee saw at *Padua,* that would clap his hands together and crowe. Another thinkes he is a Nightingall, and therefore sings all the night long: another hee is all glasse, a pitcher, and will therefore let no body come neere him, and such a one *Laurentius* gives out upon his credit, that he knew in *France. Christophorus à Vega lib. 3. cap. 14. Schenkius & Marcellus Donatus lib. 2. cap. 1.* have many such examples, and one amongst the rest of a Baker in *Ferrara,* that thought hee was composed of butter, and durst not sit in the sunne, or come neere the fire for feare of being melted: of another that thought hee was a case of leath, stuffed with winde. Some laugh, weepe, some are mad, some dejected, moped, in much agony, some by fits, others continuate, &c. Some have a corrupt eare, they thinke they heare musicke, or some hideous noise as their phantasie conceaves, corrupt eyes, some smelling: some one sense, some another. *Lewis* the eleventh had a conceit every thing did stinke about him, all the odoriferous perfumes they could get, would not ease him, but still hee smelled a filthy stinke. A melancholy *French* Poet in *Laurentius,* being sicke of a fever, and troubled with waking, by his Physitians was appointed to use *unguentum populeum* to annoint his temples; but hee so distasted the smell of it, that for many yeares after, all that came neere him he imagined to sent of it, and would let no man talke with him but aloofe off, or weare any new clothes, because hee thought still they smelled of it; in all other things, wise and discreet, he would talke sensibly, save onely in this. A Gentleman in *Lymosen,* saith *Anthony Verdeur,* was perswaded hee had but one legge, affrighted by a wild boare, that by chance stroke him on the legge: he could not bee satisfied his legge was sound (in all other things well) until two *Franciscans* by chance comming that way, fully removed him from the conceipt. *Sed abundè fabularum audivimus.*

The Melancholy Character

ALTHOUGH BIOGRAPHICAL DETAILS are sparse, we know that Samuel Butler was born at Avon, England, early in the year 1612 to a family of well-to-do yeoman farmers; that he inherited a library from his grandfather to which he subsequently added; and that although he never attended a university, he received formal education at a school (probably King's School, Worcester) in which he would have been taught a rigorous classical curriculum of grammar, rhetoric, and logic, as well as Greek and Latin.

Butler published many works, including the long poem "Hudibras," which gained the approval of King Charles II, who gave him, for his efforts, 300 pounds sterling and a pension. It is this poem for which Butler is often known, and he is sometimes identified by the appellation "Hudibras" Butler, to distinguish him from a later author of the same given name as his, Samuel ("Erewhon") Butler (1835–1902).

The work *Characters,* from which the following sketch of the melancholy man is taken, was written between 1667 and 1669. Butler's volume of characters contains almost 200 different human types he observed in the society about him in Restoration England. As well as the melancholy man, he sketched the Bumpkin or Country Squire, the Hypocritical Man, the Huffing Courtier, the Catholic, the Curious Man, the Proud Man, and the Hypocritical Nonconformist. The poem "Hudibras" is ostensibly about the religious politics of Butler's time, but it also reflects the satirical and cynical view of human folly and hypocrisy evident in the *Characters.*

The tradition of writing characters in this way is associated with the Greek philosopher and pupil of Aristotle, Theophrastus. With his characteristically witty style, revealing both learning and much astute observation, Butler is recognized as the English master of the tradition of character writing, in a time at which this genre was revived, and educators, moralists, and political satirists all tried their hand at developing such portraits.

Butler's characters are notable for their play on words and for their fresh and telling analogies. The portrait of the melancholy man offers two of the best of these analogies. The melancholy man leads his life as one leads a reluctant dog on a leash. And, while the mind of the melancholy man is full of thoughts, they are all empty like an empty nest of boxes.

Although the tradition of offering characters is one in which satirical oversimplification and exaggeration distort for effect, still Butler's portrait tells us much about the assumptions of his age when it comes to melancholy. Like thinkers before him, he identifies the spleen and fumes and vapors as the cause of the melancholy man's condition.

In this text, melancholy is portrayed both as a normal variation of human personality and as a pathological condition, and no tension seems to attach to this seeming contradiction. In keeping with the tradition of characters, Butler's melancholy man is at times no more than a dispositional type. On the other hand, the melancholy man is said to see visions and hear voices, and he seems incapable of distinguishing accurate from inaccurate perceptual experience. He is not a madman, for he is placed in contrast to the madman as "below him in degrees of frenzy." But neither is he an entirely normal person.

• ◞ • ◟ •

Samual Butler, "A Melancholy Man,"
from *Characters* (1659)

A melancholy man is one, that keeps the worst Company in the World, that is, his own; and tho' he be always falling out and quarrelling with himself, yet he has not power to endure any other Conversation. His Head is haunted, like a House, with evil Spirits and Apparitions, that terrify and fright him out of himself, till he stands empty and forsaken. His Sleeps and his Wakings are so much the same, that he knows not how to distinguish them, and many times when he dreams, he believes he is broad awake and sees Visions. The Fumes and Vapours that rise from his Spleen and Hypocondries have so smutched and sullied his Brain (like a Room that smoaks) that his Understanding is blear-ey'd, and has no right Perception of any Thing. His Soul lives in his Body, like a Mole in the Earth, that labours in the Dark, and casts up Doubts and Scruples of his own Imaginations, to make that rugged and uneasy, that was plain and open before. His Brain is so cracked, that he fancies himself to be Glass, and is afraid that every Thing he comes near should break him in Pieces. Whatsoever makes an Impression in his Imagination works it self in like a Screw, and the more he turns and winds it, the deeper it sticks, till it is never to be got out again. The Temper of his Brain being earthy, cold, and dry, is apt to breed Worms, that sink so deep into it, no Medicine in Art or Nature is able to reach them. He leads his Life, as one leads a Dog in a Slip that will not follow, but is dragged along until he is almost hanged, as he has it often under Consideration to treat himself in convenient Time and Place, if he can but catch himself alone. After a long and mortal Feud between his inward and his outward Man, they at length agree to meet without Seconds, and decide the Quarrel, in which the one drops, and the other slinks out of the Way, and makes his Escape into some foreign World, from whence it is never after heard of. He converses with nothing so much as his own Imagination, which being apt to misrepresent Things to him, makes him believe, that it is something else than it is, and that he holds Intelligence with Spirits, that reveal whatsoever he fancies to him, as the ancient rude People, that first heard their own Voices repeated by Echoes in the Woods, concluded it must proceed from some invisible Inhabitants of those solitary Places, which they after believed to be Gods, and called them *Sylvans, Fauns,* and *Dryads.* He makes the Infirmity of his Temper pass for Revelations, as *Mahomet* did by his falling Sickness, and inspires himself with the Wind of his own Hypocondries. He laments, like *Heraclitus* the Maudlin Philosopher, at other Men's Mirth, and takes Pleasure in nothing but his own un-sober Sadness. His Mind is full of Thoughts, but they are all empty, like a Nest of Boxes. He sleeps little, but dreams much, and soundest when he is waking. He sees Visions further off than a second-sighted Man in *Scotland,* and dreams upon a hard Point with admirable Judgment. He is just so much worse than a Madman, as he is below him in Degree of Frenzy; for among Madmen the most mad govern all the rest, and receive a natural Obedience from their Inferiors.

12

•

How to Help Melancholicks

MATHER

COTTON MATHER WAS A Puritan divine who lived between 1663 and 1728. He was born in Boston, and the son of Increase Mather, who was pastor of (Old) North Church. He was grandson of another Puritan clergyman, Richard Mather (1596–1669). Educated at Harvard, Cotton Mather was ordained in 1685 and later succeeded his father as the pastor of North Church. He is best known for his part in the Salem witch trials, the climate for which he helped create with his influential sermons and the 1689 publication of his work *Memorable Providences Relating to Witchcraft and Possession.* (A further work on witchcraft, *Wonders of the Invisible World,* followed this in 1693.) Mather was a man of extraordinary energy and seriousness of purpose, although few of the ends to which his efforts were directed seem admirable to us today. (He is usually dismissed as an example of the most narrow, severe, self-righteous, and joyless Puritan.) He was an indefatigable writer and, as the following excerpt from *The Angel of Bethesda* illustrates, a rather dry and witty stylist. Moreover, he was untiring in his support of the educational and cultural life of New England and was keenly interested in science. (He was the first native-born American to become a member of the Royal Society, and he supported the public-health measure of inoculation against smallpox even when, due to the unpopularity of that measure, his life was threatened.)

The Angel of Bethesda, Mather's last major work, was a medical compendium, offering a list of "the Common Maladies of Mankind," accompanied by remedies and by practical directions of a preventive kind. It was not published in his lifetime, remaining in manuscript form until parts of it were printed in the nineteenth century. As the only large inclusive medical work of the American colonial period, it is of immense medical and historical importance. But even when the manuscript was rediscovered by Oliver Wendell Holmes in 1869, it was treated with scorn: Holmes, it is said, "was opposed to medical writing by all non-physicians, and furthermore, modern medicine was evolving then, and practitioners of Holmes' generation felt very superior to all who had gone before" (Mather, 1972:xxxvi).

As well as his chapter "De Tristibus, or The Cure of Melancholy," excerpted here, Mather offers chapters on a multitude of remedies, in a manuscript that was more than 400 closely handwritten pages long. Chapters are devoted to "The Breast-beater, or a Cough Quieted," and "Breath Struggled for, or the Asthma and Short-Windedness, Releeved." The section on preventive medicine includes "A Physick-Garden" and "Great Things Done by Small Means, with Some Remarks on a Spring of Medicinal Waters, Which Every Body Is at Home, an Owner Of."

Cotton Mather's discussion on melancholy, which he ambitiously entitles "The Cure of Melancholy," is a curious blend of orthodox seventeenth-century ideas about melancholy derived from medical authorities such as Thomas Willis (1630–75) and Mather's own pragmatic New England emphasis on solutions to the social and practical problems melancholia raises for those such as himself, with pastoral responsibilities. He asks, What should be done with the melancholic? He acutely describes the failure of reasonable persuasion and sympathetic listening: "These melancholicks will go to, or send for Ministers, and with Long Impertinencies tell them How they seem unto themselves to be; And after the Ministers have spent many Hours in Talking with them, they still are, Just where they were before." Yet his solution, finally, involves offering a kindly spiritual consolation: "Get him fixed in the Resultions of Piety. . . . Comfort him, Comfort him speak thou comfortably to him. . . . Inculcate upon him, the Consolations of God."

About causes of melancholy Mather insists that it is safer to avoid speculation, and for the most part his concern lies with more practical questions. Nonetheless, his confidence in spiritual ministration for treating this disorder, and his own role as a cleric, require him to reject the reductionist mechanistic explanations of his day (explanations such as we see offered by Boerhaave). To espouse such accounts, he remarks, which make this trouble of mind "nothing but a Mechanical Business of our Animal Spirits," would ill become a minister of the Gospel.

Mather's interest in more scientific explanations is demonstrated in his keen reading of Thomas Willis, whose medical work, *Two Discourses Concerning the Souls of Brutes,* had been published in London in 1672. Although he spoke of the role of the animal spirits in melancholy, Willis had equated those with chemical substances ("Chymical Liquors") such as sulfur, salt, water, and earth, out of which he believed all bodies consisted. Thus Willis's work was the object of Mather's previously mentioned criticism, although Mather also lists respectfully the remedies Willis propounded.

Like many writing at the same time, Mather also points toward diabolical possession in explaining melancholy ("Some Devil is very busy with the poor Melancholicks"): The Devil fills the melancholics' minds with "Atheism," "Blasphemy," and a yearning for "Self Murder." But for one so intent on witchcraft, Mather interestingly does not accuse the melancholic of truck with the black arts.

Overall, Mather's attitudes toward those suffering melancholic states are remarkably humane, particularly in light of the severity with which he dealt with those accused of witchcraft. We must not resent the melancholics' utterances, he insists, even when they are hurtful, for "Tis not They that Speak; Tis their Distemper." He is compassionate but also practical and brisk ("With this, Bestow some Suitable Book upon them; And so take your Leave").

· ﹏ ● ﹏ ·

From Cotton Mather, *The Angel of Bethesda* (1724)

It has been a Maxim with some, *That a Wise Man will be Melancholy once a Day.* I suppose, they mean Something more than, *Serious,* and, *Thoughtful.* Such a Frame as *That,* is to be advised for more than, *Once a Day.* I must rather say, *My Son, Be thou in it all the Day long.* I am sure, a *Dying Man,* as thou art, has Reason to be so.

But, for a *Crasy Melancholy,* or a *froward Melancholy;* For this, *Once a Day,* is too much.

There is a Malady, which goes by the Name of *Melancholy.* Tis Commonly Called, The *Hypocondriac Melancholy:* [and for Brevity, and for *Division,* sake, often called, The *Hypo':*] because *Flatulencies* in the Region of the *Hypocondria,* often accompany it. And so, the poor *Spleen* frequently, but wrongfully Enough, comes to be Charged with it.

None are more Subject unto it, than such as have had Inveterate *Headakes* torturing of them; and Women who labour under *Obstructions.*

How the *System of our Spirits,* comes to be dulled, and sowred, in this Distemper, lett them, who *know,* Declare; They who can only *guess,* will be Modest and Silent.

The *Fancies* and *Whimsies* of People over-run with *Melancholy* are so Many, and so Various, and so Ridiculous, that the very Recital of them, one would think might somewhat serve as a little *Cure for Melancholy.* The Stories might be, what the Title of some silly Books have been; *Pills to purge Melancholy.* Tho' Truly unto a Reasonable and Religious Beholder of them, these Violations of *Reason,* are a *Melancholy-Spectacle.*

These *Melancholicks,* do sufficiently *Afflict themselves,* and are Enough their *own Tormentors.* As if this *present Evil World,* would not *Really* afford Sad Things Enough, they create a World of *Imaginary Ones,* and by *Mediatating Terror,* they make themselves as Miserable, as they could be from the most *Real Miseries.*

But this is not all; They *Afflict others* as well as *Themselves,* and often make themselves Insupportable *Burdens* to all about them.

In this Case, we must *Bear one anothers Burdens,* or, the *Burdens* which we make for One another.

Lett not the Friends of these poor *Melancholicks,* be too soon *Weary* of the *Tiresome Things,* which they must now *Bear with Patience.* Their

Nonsense and *Folly* must be *born with Patience, We that are Strong must bear the Infirmities of the Weak;* and with a patient, prudent, Manly Generosity, pitty them, and Humour them like *Children,* and give none but *Good Looks* and *good Words* unto them. And if they utter Speeches that are very *Grievous* (and like *Daggers*) to us. We must not Resent them as uttered by these Persons; Tis not *They* that Speak; Tis their *Distemper!*

The *Ministers* of the Gospel, undergo a very particular Trial on this Occasion. These *Melancholicks* will go to, or send for, *Ministers,* and with Long Impertinencies tell them *How they seem unto themselves to be;* And after the *Ministers* have spent many Hours in Talking with them, they still are, *Just where they were before.* Some Diligent and Vigilant Servants of God have observed Something that has look'd like a Sensible *Energy of Satan* operating in this Matter; inasmuch as the *Time,* which the *Melancholicks* often take, to pester them, has been, what the greatest Enemy of their more *Useful Studies,* would have chosen, to give them an Interruption at.

If I may offer my Opinion, unto those who are to *Watch for Souls,* I would say;

Syr, It will be Easy for you, to discover, whether your Patient, be really under the *Trouble of Mind,* that calls for the Skill of one who shall be, *Insignis Animarum tractandarum Artifex,* to be Exercised upon it. If you do really discover, That the Patient is under *Awakenings* from the SPIRIT of God, and under Apprehensions of the *Wrath Reveled from Heaven* against the *Ungodliness and Unrighteousness of Men,* God forbid, that you should make Light of the Matter. The Profane, Baneful, *Epicurean* Folly, of making such *Trouble of Mind,* nothing but a *Mechanical Business* in our *Animal Spirits,* very ill becomes a *Minister of the Gospel.* The *Pastoral Care* no better Exercised than so, would become the Men that are *Sensual, not having the Spirit.* No, All Possible and Exquisite Care must now be taken, to carry the *Troubled Sinner* through a *Process of Repentance;* And after a due Confession of his Guilt, and Impotency, and Unworthiness, *Lead him to the Rock:* Show Him a Glorious CHRIST, *Able to Save unto the Uttermost,* and *Willing to Cast out none that Come to Him.* Having obtained his *Consent,* that a Glorious CHRIST should accomplish all the Offices of Mighty and Holy *Redeemer* for him, then gett him fixed in the *Resolutions* of PIETY. And now, *Comfort him, Comfort him speak thou comfortably to him. Tell him* what the *very great and precious Promises* in the *Covenant of Grace* do now assure him of; inculcate upon him the *Consolations of God.*

But you may often see Cause to Suspect, that the *Spiritual Troubles* of your *Melancholicks* are not of such an *Original* as is pretended for. If you trace them, you may perhaps find out, that some very intolerable *Vexation,* or some *Temporal Troubles,* begun their Uneasiness, and first raised that *Ulcer* in their Minds, which now finds *New Matter* to work upon, and the *Old Matter* is no Longer Spoken of. If this be the Case,

Wisdome is profitable to direct, how the Patient is to be treated. A Cheerful, Courteous, Obliging Behaviour to them, with *Length of Time,* and some Notable Contrivance, if there be Opportunity, to *mend what is amiss* in their Condition, will do somehting towards the Cure.

If you *Melancholicks* are gott into a tedious Way, of *Complaining against Themselves,* why should not the Best Way be, to Allow that all their *Complaints* may be *True.* But then tell them, what is NOW to be done, that they may *do better* than they have done, and *all may be well* with them. Rebuke the *Pining, Moaning, Languid,* and *Slothful* Sort of Christians, and lett them know, that they must be rowsed out of their *Inactivity,* and abound more in *Direct* Acts, than in *Reflex* ones. Grant, that they have never yett *Repented,* and *Beleeved,* and Laid Hold on the *Covenant of Life;* But then, Demand it of them that they do all of it NOW; and plainly describe to them the *Acts* of a Soul Turning and Living unto God, Require them NOW to make a *Trial,* whether they can't, with the Aids of Heaven, *Do* those *Acts,* and keep at the *Repetition* of them, until they have some *Satisfaction,* that they have Heartily and Sincerely done them.

It is not without a Cause, that *Melancholy* has been called, *Balneum Diaboli.* Some *Devil* is often very Busy with the poor *Melancholicks;* yea, there is often a Degree of *Diabolical Possession* in the *Melancholy.* King *Saul* is not the only Instance to be produced for it. The *Diabolical Impression* appears very Sensible, Either when *Thoughts* full of *Atheism* of *Blasphemy* are shott like *Fiery Darts* into their Minds and so seriously infest them, that they are even *Weary of their Lives;* or, when their Minds are violently impelled and hurried on to Self-Murder, by *Starving,* or *Strangling,* or *Stabbing,* and the like. In this Case, Lett *Prayer with Fasting* be Employed; It may be the *Kind will go out no other Way.* But the astonishing Experiments that I have seen, of *Beseeching the Lord THRICE,* in this Way!—And of *Prayer* not prevailing, until the Number of THREE *Days* could be reached unto!—

As to Conferences with the *Melancholicks,* my Advice is, That if you would not *throw away much Time* to little Purpose, you would in short lett them know; That these are *Faithful Sayings, and Worthy of all Acceptation;* First, A Glorious CHRIST, is willing to make them *Righteous* and *Holy,* upon their *Cordial Consent* unto His doing so; and therefore Invites them to look unto Him for all the Blessings of His Plenteous Redemption. Secondly, That upon their *Looking up* to Him, with a soul consenting to be under His Gracious Influences, it is their *Duty* to entertain a *Persuasion,* That He has made them *Righteous* and will make them *Holy;* and so to Resolve upon always *Chusing the Things that please Him.* Lett them know, That when you have said all that you can say, *This* must be the *Sum,* and *Scope* of all. This is Enough. With This, Bestow some *Suitable Book* upon them; And so take your Leave. . . .

13
•

The Spleen

FINCH, COUNTESS OF WINCHILSEA

T HE ENGLISH POET Anne Finch lived between 1661 and 1720. She was the daughter of a Hampshire baronet. As maid of honor to the duchess of York and at the center of fashion around the court of James II, she met Heneage Finch, who was the duke of York's "gentleman of the bed-chamber." In 1685 she married Finch, who later became the fourth earl of Winchilsea. With the end of James's reign, the couple fled to their country estate of Eastwell Park, where they lived for the rest of their lives. Although not entirely part of the London literary circle of her day, Anne Finch had friendships with many in that circle, including Jonathan Swift and Alexander Pope, and is believed to have influenced Pope's writing about the spleen (Feder, 1980:174).

Anne Finch's nature poetry was admired by Wordsworth, and she is named with Thomson, Crabbe, and Cowper as a herald of the Romantic revival. Her country retreat was the setting she preferred, as the following lines, written to the countess of Thanet while she was still at the court, suggest:

> Give me, O indulgent Fate,
> Give me yet before I die,
> A sweet, but absolute retreat,
> Mongst paths so lost, and trees so high,
> That the world may ne'er invade,
> Through such windings and such shade,
> My unshaken liberty.

Alone in that age, it has been remarked of Anne Finch that she "truly loved the country, for its own sake, and had an eye to observe its features" (Gosse, 1891:125). Wordsworth was to describe her poems as "new images of external nature."

"Ardelia" was Anne Finch's pen name. The poem "The Spleen," reproduced here, is the best known of her works, a Pindaric ode that appeared in Charles Gildon's miscellany in 1701. (Pindaric form, after the Greek lyric poet Pindar, is marked by an irregular number of feet in different lines and the arbitrary disposition of the rhymes.) The only published collection of Finch's works in her own times was *Miscellany of Poems Written by a Lady,* published in 1701.

"The Spleen" is thought to be based on Finch's personal experience: she had constitutionally low spirits and suffered from melancholy. She believed the malady to be physical in origin and tried various nostrums, including tea, coffee, and mineral springs (she took the waters at Tunbridge Wells). Only two things, it has been said, could relieve her: the soothing influence of solitude with nature and the Muses, or the sympathetic presence of her husband (Gosse, 1891:127).

This poem captures many of the themes associated with melancholy from earlier writing. Melancholy is elusive and indefinable ("Thou Proteus to abus'd Mankind, Who never yet thy real Cause cou'd find"). Its characteristic subjectivity involves dull sorrow ("A Calm of Stupid Discontent") and ungrounded fear ("Thy gloomy Terrours"). Nightmares ("boading dreams") are frequent, as is insomnia. Delusions or hallucinations occur ("Thy fond Delusions cheat the Eyes"). It is the lot of great men ("sometimes thou dost presume, Into the ablest Heads to come"), as it was of Brutus. It is associated with blackness and darkness ("Thro' thy black Jaundice, I all Objects see, As Dark"). Its characteristic posture is drooping and absent ("the Head inclin'd, The thoughtful and composed Face, Proclaiming the withdrawn, the absent Mind").

In addition, certain themes associated with Finch's own century are evident, particularly its emphasis on melancholia as a defect of reason, not feeling and not, certainly, bile. ("The Cause, indeed, is a Defect of Sense, Yet it is the Spleen alledg'd, and still the dull Pretense"). Also reflective of the thinking of her own time is the reference to the "vapours": arising from overheated passions, these were believed to temporarily cloud the brain. Finally, "The Spleen" gives some suggestion that melancholy is a disorder of fashionable women, used for their own ends and acknowledged by their "Lordly" husbands only to humor them. In the eighteenth century such skeptical attitudes toward those who suffered from the "Spleen" were common. When in 1714 Finch's contemporary and friend Alexander Pope wrote of the "Cave of Spleen" in "The Rape of the Lock," his satirical dismissal of that fashionable melancholy known as "the Vapors" is unmistakable. In the gloomy cave of Spleen, Pope describes Affectation, who, "with a sickly mien,"

> Shows in her cheek the roses of eighteen,
> Practis'd to lisp, and hang the head aside,
> Faints into airs, and languishes with pride,
> On the rich quilt stinks with becoming woe,
> Wrapt in a gown, for sickness, and for show.
> The fair ones feel such maladies as these,
> When each new night-dress gives a new disease.

Unlike Pope's, Finch's poem clearly allows that some melancholy is a genuine disorder, and not merely a fashionable affectation. Yet Finch, in "The Spleen," acknowledges the possibility of the counterfeit as well as the real.

The commoner remedies of the eighteenbth century are included in "The Spleen," and we see what a diverse array they constitute: wine, society, religion, Indian leaf tea and some concoction with the Eastern berry, even music. All are applied in vain, however.

·⤳ • ⤦·

Anne Finch, Countess of Winchilsea, "The Spleen," from *Miscellany of Poems Written by a Lady* (1701)

A Pindarik Poem

What art thou, *SPLEEN,* which ev'ry thing dost ape?
    Thou *Proteus* to abus'd Mankind,
    Who never yet thy real Cause cou'd find,
Or fix thee to remain in one continued Shape.
    Still varying thy perplexing Form,
    Now a Dead Sea thou'lt represent,
    A Calm of stupid Discontent,
Then, dashing on the Rocks wilt rage into a Storm.
    Trembling sometimes thou dost appear,
    Dissolved into a Panick Fear;
    On Sleep intruding dost thy Shadows spread,
    Thy gloomy Terrours round the silent Bed,
And croud with boading Dreams the Melancholy Head;
    Or, when the Midnight Hour is told,
    And drooping Lids thou still dost waking hold,
    Thy fond Delusions cheat the Eyes,
    Before them antick Spectres dance,
Unusual Fires their pointed Heads advance,
    and airy Phantoms rise.
    Such was the monstrous *Vision* seen,
When *Brutus* (now beneath his Cares opprest,
And all *Rome's* Fortunes rolling in his Breast,
    Before *Philippi's* latest Field,
Before his Fate did to *Octavius* lead)
    Was vanquish'd by the *Spleen.*
    Falsly, the Mortal Part we blame
    Of our deprest, and pond'rous Frame,
    Which, till the first degrading Sin
    Let Thee, its dull Attendant, in,
    still with the Other did comply,
Nor clogg'd the Active Soul, dispos'd to fly,
And range the Mansions of it's native Sky.

Nor, whilst in his own Heaven he dwelt,
   Whilst Man his Paradice possest,
His fertile Garden in the fragrant East,
   And all united Odours smelt,
   No armed Sweets, until thy Reign,
   Cou'd shock the Sense, or in the Face
   A flusht, unhandsom Colour place.
Now the *Jouquille* o'ercomes the feeble Brain;
We faint beneath the Aromatick Pain,
Till some offensive Scent thy Pow'rs appease,
And Pleasure we resign for short, and nauseous Ease.

   In ev'ry One thou dost possess,
   New are thy Motions, and thy Dress:
   Now in some Grove a list'ning Friend
   Thy false Suggestions must attend,
Thy whisper'd Griefs, thy fancy'd Sorrows hear,
Breath'd in a Sigh, and witness'd by a Tear;
   Whilst in the light, and vulgar Croud,
   Thy Slaves, more clamorous and loud,
By Laughters unprovok'd, thy Influence too confess.
In the Imperious *Wife* thou Vapours art,
   Which from o'erheated Passions rise
   In Clouds to the attractive Brain,
   Until descending thence again,
   Thro' the o'er-cast, and show'ring Eyes,
   Upon her Husband's sofen'd Heart,
   He the disputed Point must yield,
Something resign of the contested Field;
Till Lordly *Man,* born to Imperial Sway,
Compounds for Peace, to make that Right away,
And *Woman,* arm'd with *Spleen,* do's servilely Obey.

   The Fool, to imitate the Wits,
   Complains of thy pretended Fits,
   And Dulness, born with him, wou'd lay
   Upon thy accidental Sway;
   Because, sometimes, thou dost presume
   Into the ablest Heads to come:
   That, often, Men of Thoughts refin'd,
   Impatient of unequal Sence,
Such slow Returns, where they so much dispense,
Retiring from the Croud, are to thy Shades inclin'd.
   O'er me alas! thou dost too much prevail:
   I feel thy Force, whilst I against thee rail;
I feel my Verse decay, and my crampt Numbers fail.
Thro' thy black Jaundice I all Objects see,

As Dark, and Terrible as Thee,
My Lines decry'd, and my Employment thought
An useless Folly, or presumptuous Fault:
        Whilst in the *Muses* Paths I stray,
Whilst in their Groves, and by their secret Springs
My Hand delights to trace unusual Things,
And deviates from the known, and common way;
        Nor will in fading Silks compose
        Faintly th'inimitable *Rose,*
Fill up an ill-drawn *Bird,* or paint on Glass
The *Sov'reign's* blurr'd and undistinguish'd Face,
The threatning *Angel,* and the speaking *Ass.*
        Patron thou art to ev'ry gross Abuse,
        The sullen *Husband's* feign'd Excuse,
When the ill Humour with his Wife he spends,
And bears recruited Wit, and Spirits to his Friends.
        the Son of *Bacchus* pleads thy Pow'r,
        As to the Glass he still repairs,
        Pretends but to remove thy Cares,
Snatch from thy Shades one gay, and smiling Hour,
And drown thy Kingdom in a purple Show'r.
When the *Coquette,* whom ev'ry Fool admires,
        Wou'd in Variety be Fair,
        And, changing hastily the Scene
        From Light, Impertinent, and Vain,
Assumes a soft, a melancholy Air,
And of her Eyes rebates the wand'ring Fires,
The careless Posture, and the Head reclin'd,
        The thoughtful, and composed Face,
Proclaiming the withdrawn, the absent Mind,
Allows the Fop more liberty to gaze,
Who gently for the tender Cause inquires;
        the Cause, indeed, is a Defect in Sense,
Yet is the *Spleen* alledg'd, and still the dull Pretence.
        But these are thy fantastic Harms,
        The Tricks of thy pernicious Stage,
        Which do the weaker Sort engage;
Worse are the dire Effects of thy more pow'rful Charms.
        By Thee *Religion,* all we know,
        That shou'd enlighten here below,
        Is veil'd in Darkness, and perplext
With anxious Doubts, with endless Scruples vext,
And some Restraint imply'd from each perverted Text.
        Whilst *Touch* not, *Taste* not, what is feely giv'n,
Is but thy niggard Voice, disgracing bounteous Heav'n.
        From Speech restrain'd, by thy Deceits abus'd,

To Deserts banish'd, or in Cells reclus'd,
Mistaken Vot'ries to the Pow'rs Divine,
Whilst they a purer Sacrifice design,
Do but the *Spleen* obey, and worship at thy Shrine.
In vain to chase thee ev'ry Art we try,
In vain all Remedies apply,
In vain the *Indian* Leaf infuse,
Or the parch'd *Eastern* Berry bruise;
Some pass, in vain, those Bounds, and nobler Liquors use.
Now *Harmony,* in vain, we bring,
Inspire the Flute, and touch the String.
From Harmony no help is had;
Musick but soothes thee, if too sweetly sad,
And if too light, but turns thee gayly Mad.
Tho' the Physicians greatest Gains,
Altho' his growing Wealth he sees
Daily increas'd by Ladies Fees,
Yet doft thou baffle all his studious Pains.
Not skilful *Lower* thy Source cou'd find,
Or thro' the well-dissected Body trace
The secret, the mysterious ways,
By which thou dost surprise, and prey upon the Mind
Tho' in the Search, too deep for Humane Thought,
With unsuccessful Toil he wrought,
'Till thinking Thee to've catch'd, Himself by thee was caught,
Retain'd thy Pris'ner, thy acknowledg'd Slave,
And sunk beneath thy Chain to a lamented Grave.

14
•

The Chronic Disease of Melancholy

BOERHAAVE

Herman boerhaave was a Dutch physician and humanist who lived between 1668 and 1738. Based in Leiden, a renowned medical center of that time, he was one of the most important influences on eighteenth-century medicine in Europe, and his fame even spread to China.

Boerhaave was educated for the ministry at the University of Leiden and took his doctoral degree in 1689 before graduating in medicine from the University of Harderwijk in 1693. In 1709 he succeeded to the chair of medicine and botany at the University of Leiden, where in 1714 he became professor of practical medicine and, four years later, professor of chemistry. His contribution to medical teaching practice was notable: he helped revive the Hippocratic method of bedside instruction, later carried throughout Europe by his students; he also insisted on postmortem examination of patients to demonstrate the relation between symptoms and underlying conditions.

Boerhaave was known for several works, including *Aphorisms: Concerning the Knowledge and Cure of Diseases,* published in 1735, from which the following passages are taken. Other works were the *Institutiones Medicinae,* published in 1708, and the *Elementa Chemiae,* published in 1732, both of which were standard textbooks for the greater part of the eighteenth century. In his discussion of melancholia in the *Aphorisms,* Boerhaave demonstrates the new mechanistic approach to medical explanation associated with seventeenth-century science, and particularly with Newtonian mechanics—an approach that challenged the earlier established humoral and chemical explanations. Boerhaave was a thoroughgoing adherent of the British natural philosophy of his day: Newtonian mechanics provided the model. The mechanical approach saw disease as explicable in terms of the movement and interaction of the various parts and subparts of matter. Thus, in an oration on the usefulness of the mechanical method in medicine, he observes: "The human body, then, is composed in such a manner that its united parts are able to produce several motions of very different kinds which derive—fully in accordance with the laws of mechanics—from the mass, shape, and the firmness of the parts and from the way in which they are linked together. . . . Therefore man has a body in the sense which the mechanicians give to that term and shows all the characteristics which are displayed by this clearly defined category," (Boerhaave [1703] 1983:96).

This shift in underlying assumptions is not immediately apparent because Boerhaave retains the humoral language of earlier traditions. The disease of melancholia, he remarks, arises from "that Malignancy of the Blood and Humors" that the ancients called "Black Choler." But rather than a naturally occurring chemical state, excesses of which resulted in melancholia, the black bile had for Boerhaave become a pathological by-product of purely mechanical actions in the blood. The atrabilious humor, or melancholy juice "already bred in the blood," as he puts it here, "doth yet infect equally all the circulating mass of humours" producing diseases (Boerhaave, 1735: no. 1094, p. 113).

Despite his innovations, Boerhaave adheres to several older features of melancholy. There is a lessened appetite, sorrowfulness, love of solitude, and indifference to "all other Matters," yet a great "Application to any sort of Study or Labor." Of the three principle causes of melancholy, he includes the "sharp, deep and penetrating Judgement" of a superior intellect. Faithful to the Galenic tradition, darkness and blackness are not only the colors of the atrabilious fluids but also the coloring of those most prone to the disorder.

Boerhaave classifies melancholia with other chronic diseases, those which, if bred in the body, "took their origin either from the defects of the liquids bred therein gradually, or from the defects left behind by acute diseases that have not been entirely cured" ([1735] 1775: no. 1050, p. 298).

Boerhaave's account of the forms of melancholia illustrates the seventeenth- and eighteenth-century notions of *the Spleen* or *hypochondriasis* (these terms were sometimes used as equivalents in that era). The least severe form of melancholic illness brought mild symptoms of disaffection and inactivity, resulting from a thickening and slowing of bodily fluids; the more severe second form, which he called a "Hypochondriac Disease: or "The Spleen," was still identified in terms of a sense of heaviness, fullness, and tightness resulting from further slowing and constriction. In the most severe form (Atra Bilis), steam or vapors from "putrified matter" are driven throughout the body, affecting all the functions and especially those of the brain. A matter of degree also differentiates "the sorrowful kind of melancholy" from madness, which Boerhaave describes as a "wild fury" and characterizes in terms of extreme delusions ("frightful fancies"). As the passages on madness illustrate, melancholy can be transformed into madness as the result of "the great motion of the liquid of the brain" (no. 1118, p. 323).

A new theme is sounded here in Boerhaave's definition of melancholy: the patient is "always intent upon one and the same subject." We find this notion of obsession on a single idea developed by Philippe Pinel and Benjamin Rush, each of whom would have been familiar with Boerhaave's work. On Rush's account, this notion is transformed into the idea of a partial insanity or partial derangement.

·⤳ ● ⤳·

From Herman Boerhaave, *Aphorisms: Concerning the Knowledge and Cure of Diseases* (1735)

Hitherto we have treated of the most remarkable internal and external *acute Diseases,* it is Time we come to the *Chronical.* These, if bred in the Body, took their Origin either from the Defects of the Liquids bred therein gradually, or from the Defects left behind by acute Diseases, that have not been entirely cured.

The Defects bred gradually in the Liquids proceed, 1. From the assumed Air, Meat, Drink, Sauces, Medicines, or Poisons, so foreign as not to be like unto the Liquids of our Body, or so strong, that they cannot be made like unto them by the Power of our Bowels and Liquids. And these are, α. *a Sharpness* β. *a Roughness,* consisting of a Sharpness and Earthiness joined to the first in a great Proportion, like unto that which we perceive in unripe Fruits, or astringent Juices, Wines, and the like; which do coagulate our Liquors, constrain the Vessels and make them narrower; whence they give Birth to hard Obstructions. It is cured with Diluters, fixed Alcalies, soapy Alcalies, used long and with Discretion. γ. *An aromatick Fatness,* from Meat, Drink, and Sauces, which appear hot to the Smell and Taste; these do produce a Heat, Attrition, an Injury of the smallest Vessels, hot Pains, Attenuation of the Liquors, a Putrefaction of the fame, Extravasation, and a great many more such Evils. They are cured with watery, mealy, gelatinous and acid Means. δ. *A sluggish Fatness,* from the too great Use of fat Things, either of Land-Animals, Fishes, or oil Vegetables; hence the Obstruction of a bilious Rustiness, an Inflammation, Corrosion, and worst sort of Putrefaction. This is cured with Diluters, soapy and acid Medicines and Diet. ε. *A briny Saltness,* from the Use of Salt or salt Things; this destroys the Vessels, breaks the Liquids, makes them sharp; hence a wasting, a Solution of the Vessels, Extravasations of the Liquids not putrifying soon, but producing Spots. 'Tis cured with Water, Acids, and the Use of Lime-water. ζ. *An Alcali* η. *A Glew* 2. From *a too great Power of our Faculties over the Things assumed* 3. From the spontaneous vicious Changes of our Humours.

Defects arise in the Humours of our Bodies in any Place from acute Diseases ill cured. α. *Purulent Diseases* which produce many Evils. They are cured according to β. *Ichorous Diseases* whose Effects are gnawing and consuming. They are cured with gentle, softening and thickening Means. γ. *Putrified Defects* . . . have been enumerated.

Acute Diseases ill cured in the solid or compound Parts, are apt to leave behind *Imposthumes, Fistulæ, Empyemas, Schirrous, Tumors, Cancers, a Caries.*

From these in simple Diseases or any way compound with themselves, it is usual for almost an Infinity of others to ensue as their Effects: which therefore may be throughly known and cured from the History of those well understood.

And as all chronical Diseases do, as it will be made evident, depend from thence, we must therefore fetch their general Doctrine and Division also from thence.

So that it is also plain at first Sight, that those Diseases are indeed numberless, on account of their Symptoms, and yet not of so compound a Nature as to their Origin, nor do require such Variety of Medicines or Intentions in the Cure; thence one may also perceive and guess the Reasons of the long Continuance of most, and the Impossibility of curing many; all which will be made more plain in treating of them separately. . . .

Of Melancholy

Physicians call that Disease a Melancholy, in which the Patient is long and obstinately delirious without a Fever, and always intent upon one and the same Thought.

This Disease arises from that Malignancy of the Blood and Humours, which the Ancients have called *Black Choler:* and again, though this Disease doth begin in what is called the Mind, it yet doth render the Choler black in the Body very soon.

It will be therefore needful to draw a small Sketch of this wonderful Disease, whose Doctrine is supposed commonly to be so dark, that Antiquity is unjustly blamed for it.

If the most moveable Parts of all the Blood be dissipated and have left the less moveable united, then will the Blood become thick, black, fat, and earthy. And this Defect will be called by the name of an *Atrabilair Humour,* or *Melancholy Juice.*

Whereof the Cause is whatever doth expel the most moveable, and fixes the rest: A violent Exercise of the Mind; the dwelling Night and Day mostly upon one and the same Object; a constant Wakefulness; great Motions of the Mind, whether of Joy or Sorrow; great and laborious Motions of the Body much repeated, chiefly in a very hot and dry Air; hereto refer also immoderate Venery: rough, hard, dry, earthy Aliments, long used without any Motion, or Exercise of the Body to digest them; the like Drink; Parts of Animals dried in Smoke, Air, or Salt, chiefly of old and tough ones; unripe Fruits; mealy unfermented Matters; astringent, coagulating, sticking, and cooling Medicines, and slow Poisons of the like Nature: Hot Fevers hanging about long, often returning without a good Crisis, and going off without the Help of diluting Means.

When this Evil already bred in the Blood and produced by these Causes doth yet infect equally all the circulating Mass of Humours, it will produce some Diseases, which will appear immediately, and are mostly as follow: The Colour of the Patient internally and externally is first paler, yellower, more tawny, livid, black with the like Spots; the Pulse slower; Coldness greater; Breathing slower; the Circulation through the Blood-vessels free, more sparing through the Side-vessels and less free; hence a slower, less, and thicker Separation of all the secretory and excretory Humours, a less wasting of them; a lessened Appetite; a Leanness; Sorrowfulness; Love of Solitude; all the Affections of the Mind violent and lasting; an Indifference to all other Matters; a Laziness as to Motion; and yet a very great and earnest Application to any sort of Study or Labour.

Its Matter therefore is the Earth and thick Oil of the Blood united and closed up together, which is worse in its Effects, and more difficult to cure, according to its Degrees of Fluidity, Softness, Driness, Thickness, intimate Mixture, and Time of being so. . . .

. . . And above all things, great Care must be taken to debar him [the melancholic] from all the Causes of the Illness.

But if that very Matter be from the same Causes grown thicker, tougher, and less moveable; it must necessarily be drove into the Hypochondriac Vessels; this the Nature of that Humour, the Seat and Condition of those Vessels, and the Laws of Motion of the Liquids do demonstrate. Here it will gradually stop, be accumulated and stagnate: Then it is called an *Hypochondriac Disease,* or in usual Terms in *England, The Spleen;* as it doth obsess the Spleen, Stomach, Pancreas, Caul, or Mesentery. . . .

When it is already grown . . . and has shewn itself such by its Effects . . . then ought no Time nor Means to be neglected towards the Cure, for otherways the Evil soon grows terrible in its Nature; and those Difficulties ought to be prevented if possible: If it continues in this State any time, it becomes incurable, and sometimes mortal, as will appear hereafter: If you attack it with purging Medicines, you only drive out the wholesome and moveable Humours, but the tough and bad ones do stay behind, whence the Disease grows worse still: If you attempt the Cure with stimulating and powerfully resolving Medicines, then doth often the loosened Matter grow very sharp, and throwing itself with a great Violence upon the tender Vessels of the Liver, it destroys them, whence many and incurable Ills.

So that, 1. The Matter is to be rendered moveable slowly, inquiring into the Nature of the predominant Acrimony, then giving soapy Medicines in which there is an Acrimony predominant over that which is in the peccant Matter; these must be continued till the unequal and weak Pulse, a nauseating or a continual Pressing to go to Stool, an Anxiety, and a small Fever, do signify that the Matter is put into Motion: And then, 2. Drive the same out immediately with a gentle opening Purge, A Glyster of the same kind, Milk-whey, Mineral-waters, and the like.

But if that very Matter [is] . . . already fixed, and drove in close, has been detained there long; the same begins already to grow sharp and gnawing by its Stagnation, the Motion of the Bowels and the Heat of surrounding Parts; new Matter is continually laid on, because the Obstruction is made already, and the same Causes do subsist; hence it extends, gnaws, and corrupts the Vessels by its increased Bulk, its present Acrimony, and continual Motion; hence the like Destruction of the Spleen, Stomach, Pancreas, Caul, Mesentery, Intestines, and Liver . . . [it disturbs] all the Functions, and above all, those of the Brain, by the constant Steam of the putrified Matter received into the Veins. And then may it be called by the true Name of *Atra Bilis*. . . .

From which the Nature of Melancholy and Hypochondriac Diseases as described is known: for it is evident, that from a long continued preceding Sorrowfulness, the Vessels of the abdomianl Bowels create a Stagnation, Alteration, and Accumulation of black Choler which insensibly increaseth, though the Body was very healthful but a little before: And also that the same black Choler, when bred from bodily Causes, doth produce . . . Delirium.

The apparent Causes of Melancholy therefore have been observed to be, 1. All things, which fix, exhaust, or confound the nervous Juices from the Brain; as great and unexpected frightful Accidents, a great Application upon any Object whatever, strong Love, Waking, Solitude, Fear, and hysterical Affections. 2. Those which hinder and confound the Confection, Refection, Circulation, the various secretions and Excretions of the Blood, chiefly if done in the Spleen, Stomach, Caul, Pancreas, Mesentery, Intestines, Liver, Womb, or hemorrhoidal Vessels: And consequently any hypochondriac Disease, acute ones imperfectly cured, and chiefly a Phrenitis, or a burning Fever; all exceeding Secretions and Excretions, eating, and drinking of cold, earthy, tough, rough, or astringent Aliments; too great a Heat long continued, which doth as it were roast the Blood; a stagnating, senny, or too shady Air. 3. A natural Disposition of the Body, such as a black, hoary, dry, lean, or manly one; a Middle Age; a sharp, deep, and penetrating Judgment.

If this Disease doth continue long, it occasions Foolishness, Epilepsies, Apoplexies, furious Madness, Convulsions, Blindness, wonderful Fancies, Laughters, Cryings, Singings, Sighings, Belchings, Anguishes; great Evacuations of Urine, sometimes clear like fair Water, at other times very thick; a Retention, Accumulation, often a sudden Excretion of bloody Fæces in the Vessels of the abdominal Viscera; an obstinate Costiveness, a thin and frequent Spitting, and they can endure to be without Sleep, Aliments, or Fire, even to a Wonder.

A Cure has often unexpectedly been obtained at the Appearance and Breaking out of a nasty Itch sometimes coming up and resembling a Leprosy, or numerous Varices and them very large; or flowing of the much swelled Piles; or at the voiding of black Choler upwards and downwards.

It grows much worse upon the taking of any Medicines, that weaken and evacuate roughly; or again upon the taking of such as put the Liquids into a violent Motion, whether they be Cordials, or cried up under any other Title.

So that the best Method to cure this Disease, is to apply different Remedies, and opposite to the different Sorts known from the exact Observation of the proximate Cause and different Constitution of the Patient.

The Indications will be therefore to excite, increase, and bring into a good Order the Liquids of the Brain and Nerves; which is done, α. By withdrawing the Mind from the usual Object to others contrary to the same. β. By causing and raising very artfully another Passion of the Mind, contrary to the constant melancholic one. γ. Sometimes by Siding with them in their false and depraved Fancies. δ. Or often by opposing the same with a great Force.

2. By opening, softening, cutting, stimulating the Obstructions, of the Cause, or the Effects of a false Imagination, with Mineral-waters, Milk-whey, Water and Honey, Splanchnick, Hepatic or Antihypochondriac Decoctions; Waters made effectual with the Addition of lixivious or compound Salts; loosening Mercurials, Vomits, Motions, Exercises, Riding, or going in a Boat; Medicines which evacuate from the Womb (as are the Aristolochia) or the Piles; Bathings, Ointments, or Plaisters.

3. Easing the Symptoms with bleeding, ducking into cold Water; by Carminatives and Opiates.

4. After the just mentioned Evacuations. By giving such as Experience doth shew us to be exhilarating, and to strengthen all the Parts of the Body.

From which it appears, that the Cure of this Disease is perfected in curing the black Choler. And that we must hence learn the Cure not only of this Disease, but of an infinite Number of others, which are wrongfully reputed incurable.

Of Madness

If Melancholy increases so far, that from the great Motion of the Liquid of the Brain, the Patient be thrown into a wild Fury, it is called *Madness.*

Which differs only in Degree from the sorrowful kind of Melancholy, is its Offspring, produced from the same Causes, and cured almost by the same Remedies.

In which Disease the Patient generally shews a great Strength of the Muscles, an incredible Wakefulness, a bearing to a wonder of Cold and Hunger, frightful Fancies, Endeavours to bite Men like Wolves, or Dogs, &c.

And we must take Notice, that by anatomical inspection it has been made evident, that the Brain of those is dry, hard, friable, and yellow in its Cortex; but the Vessels turgid, varicous, and distended with black and very tough Blood.

And also that almost all the Excretions are suspended.

The greatest Remedy for it is to throw the Patient unwarily into the Sea, and to keep him under Water as long as he can possibly bear it without being quite stifled.

When all Remedies have been tried in vain, it has sometimes happened that varicous Tumours, Piles, Dysenteries, Dropsies, great Hæmorrhagies come of themselves, and Tertian or Quartan Agues have cured this Disease.

This sort of Madness is occasioned sometimes after the Body has been exhausted by an autumnal, strong, obstinate intermitting Fever, and not only thus weakened by the Disease, but by repeated Bleedings, and Purges; which same will also occasion the Return of this Disease.

This sort is cured only with restorative, replenishing Cordials, strengthning Aliments and Medicines long continued: But if you attempt the Cure of it by Evacuations, you'll cause a Wasting, Weakness, and an insuperable Foolishness. "N.B. See *Sydenham's* Treatise of the intermitting kind of Fevers from the Year 1661 to 1664."

But a Madness bred in strong, hale, youthful, plethoric People of a hot Constitution, is cured by the same Means as that sort of Epilepsy . . . by repeated letting of Blood, and strong Purges between each Bleeding, and afterwards when you have laid his Fury, and have brought him to his Senses, then give him Cordials and Opiates.

15
•

Werther's Death

GOETHE

JOHANN WOLFGANG VON GOETHE was born in Frankfurt, Germany, in
1749 and died in 1832. He was one of the greatest geniuses of modern times, a lyric poet, dramatist, novelist, and scientist whose literary
and artistic output was remarkable. As a young man he went to
Leipzig to study law. He also studied art and music, and wrote plays,
songs, and poems. In 1775 Goethe was invited to visit Charles Augustus, duke of Saxe-Weimar, at whose court he spent the rest of his long
and productive life, holding several important government and artistic
positions in Weimar and also writing plays, poems, scientific tracts, and
novels, including *Wilhelm Meisters Lehrjahre* (*The Apprenticeship of Wilhelm Meister*), which was completed only at the end of his life. The
finest of Goethe's works is considered to be his dramatic poem *Faust,*
the first part of which was published in 1808 and the second part after
his death.

Not only were Goethe's artistic and literary achievements prodigious, he also became a legendary figure in his own time, a towering
symbol of German Romanticism. What was then his most popular
work, *The Sorrows of Young Werther,* from which excerpts are reproduced here, was published in 1774, a work of his youth. Goethe wrote
this novel out of despair over a broken heart. It tells the tragic tale of an
unrequited attachment that ends in a graphically described suicide.
The book brought Goethe enormous fame and was much translated.
Its effect on the public was intense: It inspired a condition of exaggerated sensibility that came to be known as *Wertherism.*

The passages included here are from the last pages of the novel.
Werther has resolved to end his life. Charlotte, whom he loves, is married to another (Albert). She has tried to persuade Werther to seek love
elsewhere and to curb his passionate and impossible attachment to her.
("'Werther . . . only control yourself! Oh! Why were you born with
that excessive, that ungovernable passion for everything that is dear to
you?' she asks.")

It is not easy for us today to recognize that *The Sorrows of Young
Werther* was a work of such artistic innovation. But as one authority has
put it, this short piece

181

elaborated a new form of novelistic discourse. . . . [It] unfolds its fictional world without tendentious moralizing and achieves in the shaping of its letters a lyrical intensity previously unknown in narrative prose. . . . The writing takes place in what might be called a pragmatic vacuum. Its function is not to communicate something to someone, but rather to make imaginatively accessible the tonality of a unique subjective experience. *Werther* is the first European novel in which subjectivity *per se* acquires aesthetic concretization. (Goethe [1774] 1988:283)

It is similarly difficult for us to admire the character type personified by Werther and Wertherism, or to avoid the conclusion that Werther deceives himself. As the poet W. H. Auden observed:

Living in the twentieth century, not the eighteenth, and knowing, as most of his contemporaries did not, Goethe's later work, Werther can still fascinate us, but in a very different way. To us it reads not as a tragic love story, but as a masterly and devastating portrait of a complete egoist, a spoiled brat, incapable of love because he cares for nobody and nothing but himself and having his way at whatever cost to others . . . the egoist who imagines himself to be a passionate lover. (Goethe [1774] 1971:xi)

Nonetheless, Werther's frustration, grief, and despair, elaborated in this work, captured and celebrated the Romantic notion of melancholy.

* • • • •

From Johann Wolfgang von Goethe,
The Sorrows of Young Werther (1774)

Werther returned home, took the candle from his servant, and retired to his room alone. He talked for some time with great earnestness to himself, wept aloud, walked in a state of great excitement through his chamber; till at length, without undressing, he threw himself on the bed, where he was found by his servant at eleven o'clock, when the latter ventured to enter the room, and take off his boots. Werther did not prevent him, but forbade him to come in the morning till he should ring.

On Monday morning, the 21st of December, he wrote to Charlotte the following letter, which was found, sealed, on his bureau after his death, and was given to her. I shall insert it in fragments; as it appears, for several circumstances, to have been written in that manner.

"It is all over, Charlotte: I am resolved to die! I make this declaration deliberately and coolly, without any romantic passion, on this morning of the day when I am to see you for the last time. At the moment you read these lines, O best of women, the cold grave will hold the inanimate remains of that restless and unhappy being who, in the last moments of his existence, knew no pleasure so great as that of conversing with you! I have passed a dreadful night—or rather, let me say, a propitious one; for it has given me resolution, it has fixed my purpose. I am resolved to die. When I tore myself from you yesterday, my senses were in tumult and disorder; my heart was oppressed, hope and pleasure had fled from me forever, and a petrifying cold had seized my wretched being. I could scarcely reach my room. I threw myself on my knees; and Heaven, for the last time, granted me the consolation of shedding tears. A thousand ideas, a thousand schemes, arose within my soul; till at length one last, fixed, final thought took possession of my heart. It was to die. I lay down to rest; and in the morning, in the quiet hour of awakening, the same determination was upon me. To die! It is not despair: it is conviction that I have filled up the measure of my sufferings, that I have reached my appointed term, and must sacrifice myself for thee. Yes, Charlotte, why should I not avow it? One of us three must die: it shall be Werther. O beloved Charlotte! this heart, excited by rage and fury, has often conceived the horrid idea of murdering your husband—you—myself! The lot is cast at length. And in the bright, quiet evenings of summer, when you sometimes wander towards the mountains, let your thoughts then turn to me: recollect how often you have watched me coming to meet you from the valley; then bend your eyes upon the churchyard which contains my grave, and, by the light of the setting sun, mark how the evening breeze waves the tall grass which grows above my tomb. I was calm when I began this letter, but the recollection of these scenes makes me weep like a child."

About ten in the morning, Werther called his servant, and, whilst he was dressing, told him that in a few days he intended to set out upon a journey, and bade him therefore lay his clothes in order, and prepare them for packing up, call in all his accounts, fetch home the books he had lent, and give two months' pay to the poor dependants who were accustomed to receive from him a weekly allowance.

He breakfasted in his room, and then mounted his horse, and went to visit the steward, who, however, was not at home. He walked pensively in the garden, and seemed anxious to renew all the ideas that were most painful to him.

The children did not suffer him to remain alone long. They followed him, skipping and dancing before him, and told him, that after to-morrow—and to-morrow—and one day more, they were to receive their Christmas gift from Charlotte; and they then recounted all the wonders of which they had formed ideas in their child imaginations. "To-morrow—and to-morrow," said he, "and one day more!" And he kissed them tenderly. He was going; but the younger boy stopped him, to whisper something in his ear. He told him that his elder brothers had written splendid New-Year's wishes—so large!—one for papa, and another for Albert and Charlotte, and one for Werther; and they were to be presented early in the morning, on New-Year's Day. This quite overcame him. He made each of the children a present, mounted his horse, left his compliments for papa and mamma, and, with tears in his eyes, rode away from the place.

He returned home about five o'clock, ordered his servant to keep up his fire, desired him to pack his books and linen at the bottom of the trunk, and to place his coats at the top. He then appears to have made the following addition to the letter addressed to Charlotte:—

"You do not expect me. You think I will obey you, and not visit you again till Christmas Eve. O Charlotte, to-day or never! On Christmas Eve you will hold this paper in your hand; you will tremble, and moisten it with your tears. I will—I must! Oh, how happy I feel to be determined!"

In the mean time, Charlotte was in a pitiable state of mind. After her last conversation with Werther, she found how painful to herself it would be to decline his visits, and knew how severely he would suffer from their separation.

She had, in conversation with Albert, mentioned casually that Werther would not return before Christmas Eve; and soon afterwards Albert went on horseback to see a person in the neighborhood, with whom he had to transact some business which would detain him all night.

Charlotte was sitting alone. None of her family were near, and she gave herself up to the reflections that silently took possession of her mind. She was forever united to a husband whose love and fidelity she had proved, to whom she was heartily devoted, and who seemed to be a special gift from Heaven to insure her happiness. On the other hand, Werther had become dear to her. There was a cordial unanimity of sentiment between them from the very first hour of their acquaintance, and their long association and repeated interviews had made an indelible impression upon her heart. She had been accustomed to communicate to him every thought and feeling which interested her, and his absence threatened to open a void in her existence which it might be impossible to fill. How heartily she wished that she might change him into her brother,—that she could induce him to marry one of her own friends, or could reestablish his intimacy with Albert.

She passed all her intimate friends in review before her mind, but found something objectionable in each, and could decide upon one to whom she would consent to give him.

Amid all these considerations she felt deeply but indistinctly that her own real but unexpressed wish was to retain him for herself, and her pure and amiable heart felt from this thought a sense of oppression which seemed to forbid a prospect of happiness. She was wretched: a dark cloud obscured her mental vision.

It was now half-past six o'clock, and she heard Werther's step on the stairs. She at once recognized his voice, as he inquired if she were at home. Her heart beat audibly—we could almost say for the first time—at his arrival. It was too late to deny herself; and, as he entered, she exclaimed, with a sort of ill-concealed confusion, "You have not kept your word!"—"I promised nothing," he answered. "But you should have complied, at least for my sake," she continued. "I implore you, for both our sakes."

She scarcely knew what she said or did, and sent for some friends, who, by their presence, might prevent her being left alone with Werther. He put down some books he had brought with him, then made inquiries about some others, until she began to hope that her friends might arrive shortly, entertaining at the same time a desire that they might stay away.

At one moment she felt anxious that the servant should remain in the adjoining room, then she changed her mind. Werther, meanwhile, walked impatiently up and down. She went to the piano, and determined not to retire. She then collected her thoughts, and sat down quietly at Werther's side, who had taken his usual place on the sofa.

"Have you brought nothing to read?" she inquired. He had nothing. "There in my drawer," she continued, "you will find your own translation of some of the songs of Ossian. I have not yet read them, as I have still hoped to hear you recite them; but, for some time past, I have not been able to accomplish such a wish." He smiled, and went for the manuscript, which he took with a shudder. He sat down; and, with eyes full of tears, he began to read.

"Star of descending night! fair is thy light in the west! thou liftest thy unshorn head from thy cloud; thy steps are stately on thy hill. What dost thou behold in the plain? The stormy winds are laid. The murmur of the torrent comes from afar. Roaring waves climb the distant rock. The flies of evening are on their feeble wings: the hum of their course is on the field. What dost thou behold, fair light? But thou dost smile and depart. The waves come with joy around thee: they bathe thy lovely hair. Farewell, thou silent beam! Let the light of Ossian's soul arise!

"And it does arise in its strength! I behold my departed friends. Their gathering is on Lora, as in the days of other years. Fingal comes like a watery column of mist! his heroes are around: and see the bards of song, gray-haired Ullin! stately Ryno! Alpin with the tuneful voice! the soft complaint of Minona! How are ye changed, my friends, since the days of Selma's feast! when we contended, like gales of spring as they fly along the hill, and bend by turns the feebly-whistling grass.

"Minona came forth in her beauty, with downeast look and tearful eye. Her hair was flying slowly with the blast that rushed unfrequent from the hill. The souls of the heroes were sad when she raised the tuneful voice. Oft had they seen the grave of Salgar, the dark dwelling of white-bosomed Colma. Colma left alone on the hill with all her voice of song! Salgar promised to come: but the night descended around. Hear the voice of Colma, when she sat alone on the hill!

"*Colma.* It is night: I am alone, forlorn on the hill of storms. The wind is heard on the mountain. The torrent is howling down the rock. No hut receives me from the rain: forlorn on the hill of winds!

"Rise moon! from behind thy clouds. Stars of the night, arise! Lead me, some light, to the place where my love rests from the chase alone! His bow near him unstrung, his dogs panting around him! But here I must sit alone by the rock of the mossy stream. The Stream and the wind roar aloud. I hear not the voice of my love! Why delays my Salgar; why the chief of the hill his promise? Here is the rock and here the tree! here is the roaring stream! Thou didst promise with night to be here. Ah! whither is my Salgar gone? With thee I would fly from my father, with thee from my brother of pride. Our race have long been foes; we are not foes, O Salgar!

"Cease a little while, O wind! stream, be thou silent a while! let my voice be heard around! let my wanderer hear me! Salgar! it is Colma who calls. Here is the tree and the rock. Salgar, my love, I am here! Why delayest thou thy coming? Lo! the calm moon comes forth. The flood is bright in the vale. The rocks are gray on the steep. I see him not on the brow. His dogs come not before him with tidings of his near approach. Here I must sit alone!

"Who lie on the heath beside me? Are they my love and my brother? Speak to me, O my friends! To Colma they give no reply. Speak to me: I am alone! My soul is tormented with fears. Ah, they are dead! Their swords are red from the fight. O my brother! my brother! why hast thou slain my Salgar? Why, O Salgar! hast thou slain my brother? Dear were ye both to me! what shall I say in your praise? Thou wert fair on the hill among thousands! he was terrible in fight! Speak to me! hear my voice! hear me, sons of my love! They are silent! silent forever! Cold, cold, are their breasts of clay! Oh, from the rock on the hill, from the top of the windy steep, speak, ye ghosts of the dead! Speak, I will not be afraid! Whither are ye gone to rest? In what cave of the hill shall I find the departed? No feeble voice is on the gale: no answer half drowned in the storm!

"I sit in my grief: I wait for morning in my tears! Rear the tomb, ye friends of the dead. Close it not till Colma come. My life flies away like a dream. Why should I stay behind? Here shall I rest with my friends, by the stream of the sounding rock. When night comes on the hill— when the loud winds arise, my ghost shall stand in the blast, and mourn the death of my friends. The hunter shall hear from his booth; he shall fear, but love my voice! For sweet shall my voice be for my friends: pleasant were her friends to Colma.

"Such was thy song, Minona, softly-blushing daughter of Torman. Our tears descended for Colma, and our souls were sad! Ullin came with his harp; he gave the song of Alpin. The voice of Alpin was pleasant, the soul of Ryno was a beam of fire! But they had rested in the narrow house: their voice had ceased in Selma! Ullin had returned one day from the chase before the heroes fell. He heard their strife on the hill: their song was soft, but sad! They mourned the fall of Morar, first of mortal men! His soul was like the soul of Fingal: his sword like the sword of Oscar. But he fell, and his father mourned: his sister's eyes were full of tears. Minona's eyes were full of tears, the sister of carborne Morar. She retired from the song of Ullin, like the moon in the west, when she foresees the shower, and hides her fair head in a cloud. I touched the harp with Ullin: the song of mourning rose!

"*Ryno.* The wind and the rain are past, calm is the noon of day. The clouds are divided in heaven. Over the green hills flies the inconstant sun. Red through the stony vale comes down the stream of the hill. Sweet are thy murmurs, O stream! but more sweet is the voice I hear. It is the voice of Alpin, the son of song, mourning for the dead! Bent is his head of age: red his tearful eye. Alpin, thou son of song, why alone on the silent hill? why complainest thou, as a blast in the wood—as a wave on the lonely shore?

"*Alpin.* My tears, O Ryno! are for the dead—my voice for those that have passed away. Tall thou art on the hill; fair among the sons of the vale. But thou shalt fall like Morar: the mourner shall sit on thy tomb. The hills shall know thee no more: thy bow shall lie in thy hall unstrung!

"Thou wert swift. O Morar! as a roe on the desert: terrible as a meteor of fire. Thy wrath was as the storm. Thy sword in battle as lightning in the field. Thy voice was a stream after rain, like thunder on distant hills. Many fell by thy arm: they were consumed in the flames of thy wrath. But when thou didst return from war, how peaceful was thy brow. Thy face was like the sun after rain: like the moon in the silence of night: calm as the breast of the lake when the loud wind is laid.

"Narrow is thy dwelling now! dark the place of thine abode! With three steps I compass thy grave, O thou who wast so great before! Four stones, with their heads of moss, are the only memorial of thee. A tree with scarce a leaf, long grass which whistles in the wind, mark to the hunter's eye the grave of the mighty Morar. Morar! thou art low indeed. Thou hast no mother to mourn thee, no maid with her tears of love. Dead is she that brought thee forth. Fallen is the daughter of Morglan.

"Who on his staff is this? Who is this whose head is white with age, whose eyes are red with tears, who quakes at every step? It is thy father, O Morar! the father of no son but thee. He heard of thy fame in war, he heard of foes dispersed. He heard of Morar's renown, why did he not hear of his wound? Weep, thou father of Morar! Weep, but thy son heareth thee not. Deep is the sleep of the dead,—low their pillow of dust. No more shall he hear thy voice,—no more awake at thy call.

When shall it be morn in the grave, to bid the slumberer awake? Farewell, thou bravest of men! thou conqueror in the field! but the field shall see thee no more, nor the dark wood be lightened with the splendor of thy steel. Thou hast left no son. The song shall preserve thy name, Future times shall hear of thee—they shall hear of the fallen Morar!

"The grief of all arose, but most the bursting sigh of Armin. He remembers the death of his son, who fell in the days of his youth. Carmor was near the hero, the chief of the echoing Galmal. Why burst the sigh of Armin? he said. Is there a cause to mourn? The song comes with its music to melt and please the soul. It is like soft mist that, rising from a lake, pours on the silent vale; the green flowers are filled with dew, but the sun returns in his strength, and the mist is gone. Why art thou sad. O Armin, chief of sea-surrounded Gorma?

"Sad I am! nor small is my cause of woe! Carmor, thou hast lost no son; thou hast lost no daughter of beauty. Colmar the valiant lives, and Annira, fairest maid. The boughs of thy house ascend. O Carmor! but Armin is the last of his race. Dark is thy bed, O Daura! deep thy sleep in the tomb! When shalt thou wake with thy songs?—with all thy voice of music?

"Arise, winds of autumn, arise: blow along the heath. Streams of the mountains, roar; roar, tempests in the groves of my oaks! Walk through broken clouds, O moon! show thy pale face at intervals; bring to my mind the night when all my children fell, when Arindal the mighty fell—when Daura the lovely failed. Daura, my daughter, thou wert fair, fair as the moon on Fura, white as the driven snow, sweet as the breathing gale. Arindal, thy bow was strong, thy spear was swift on the field, thy look was like mist on the wave, thy shield a red cloud in a storm! Armar, renowned in war, came and sought Daura's love. He was not long refused: fair was the hope of their friends.

"Erath, son of Odgal, repined: his brother had been slain by Armar. He came disguised like a son of the sea: fair was his cliff on the wave, white his locks of age, calm his serious brow. Fairest of women, he said, lovely daughter of Armin! a rock not distant in the sea bears a tree on its side; red shines the fruit afar. There Armar waits for Daura. I come to carry his love! she went—she called on Armar. Nought answered, but the son of the rock. Armar, my love, my love! why tormentest thou me with fear? Hear, son of Arnart, hear! it is Daura who calleth thee. Erath, the traitor, fled laughing to the land. She lifted up her voice— she called for her brother and her father. Arindal! Armin! none to relieve you, Daura.

"Her voice came over the sea. Arindal, my son, descended from the hill, rough in the spoils of the chase. His arrows rattled by his side; his bow was in his hand, five dark-gray dogs attended his steps. He saw fierce Erath on the shore; he seized and bound him to an oak. Thick wind the thongs of the hide around his limbs; he loads the winds with his groans. Arindal ascends the deep in his boat to bring Daura to land. Armar came in his wrath, and let fly the gray-feathered shaft. It sung, it sunk in thy heart, O Arindal, my son! for Erath the traitor thou diest. The oar is stopped at once: he panted on the rock, and expired. What is thy grief, O Daura, when round thy feet is poured thy brother's blood. The boat is broken in twain. Armur plunges into the sea to rescue his Daura, or die. Sudden a blast from a hill came over the waves; he sank, and he rose no more.

"Alone, on the sea-beat rock, my daughter was heard to complain; frequent and loud were her cries. What could her father do? All night I stood on the shore: I saw her by the faint beam of the moon. All night I heard her cries. Loud was the wind; the rain beat hard on the hill. Before morning appeared, her voice was weak; it died away like the evening breeze among the grass of the rocks. Spent with grief, she expired, and left thee, Armin, alone. Gone is my strength in war, fallen my pride among women. When the storms aloft arise, when the north lifts the wave on high, I sit by the sounding shore, and look on the fatal rock.

"Often by the setting moon I see the ghosts of my children; half viewless they walk in mournful conference together."

A torrent of tears which streamed from Charlotte's eyes and gave relief to her bursting heart, stopped Werther's recitation. He threw down the book, seized her hand, and wept bitterly. Charlotte leaned upon her hand, and buried her face in her handkerchief: the agitation of both was excessive. They felt that their own fate was pictured in the misfortunes of Ossian's heroes,—they felt this together, and their tears redoubled. Werther supported his forehead on Charlotte's arm: she trembled, she wished to be gone; but sorrow and sympathy lay like a leaden weight upon her soul. She recovered herself shortly, and begged Werther, with broken sobs, to leave her,—implored him with the utmost earnestness to comply with her request. He trembled; his heart was ready to burst: then, taking up the book again, he recommenced reading, in a voice broken by sobs.

"Why dost thou waken me, O spring? Thy voice woos me, exclaiming, I refresh thee with heavenly dews; but the time of my decay is approaching, the storm is nigh that shall wither my leaves. To-morrow the traveller shall come,—he shall come, who beheld me in beauty: his eye shall seek me in the field around, but he shall not find me."

The whole force of these words fell upon the unfortunate Werther. Full of despair, he threw himself at Charlotte's feet, seized her hands, and pressed them to his eyes and to his forehead. An apprehension of his fatal project now struck her for the first time. Her senses were bewildered: she held his hands, pressed them to her bosom; and, leaning towards him with emotions of the tenderest pity, her warm cheek touched his. They lost sight of every thing. The world disappeared from their eyes. He clasped her in his arms, strained her to his bosom, and covered her trembling lips with passionate kisses. "Werther!" she cried with a faint voice, turning herself away; "Werther!" and, with a feeble hand, she pushed him from her. At length, with the firm voice of virtue, she exclaimed, "Werther!" He resisted not, but, tearing himself from her arms, fell on his knees before her. Charlotte rose, and, with disordered grief, in mingled tones of love and resentment, she exclaimed, "It is the last time, Werther! You shall never see me any more!" Then, casting one last, tender look upon her unfortunate lover, she rushed into the adjoining room, and locked the door. Werther held out his arms, but did not dare to detain her. He continued on the ground, with his head resting on the sofa, for half an hour, till he heard a noise which brought him to his senses. The servant entered. He then walked up and down the room; and, when he was again left alone, he went to Charlotte's door, and, in a low voice, said, "Charlotte, Charlotte! but one word more, one last adieu!" She returned no answer. He stopped, and listened and entreated; but all was silent. At length he tore himself from the place, crying, "Adieu, Charlotte, adieu, forever!"

Werther ran to the gate of the town. The guards, who knew him, let him pass in silence. The night was dark and stormy,—it rained and snowed. He reached his own door about eleven. His servant, although seeing him enter the house without his hat, did not venture to say any thing; and, as he undressed his master, he found that his clothes were wet. His hat was afterwards found on the point of a rock overhanging the valley; and it is inconceivable how he could have climbed to the summit on such a dark, tempestuous night without losing his life.

He retired to bed, and slept to a late hour. The next morning his servant, upon being called to bring his coffee, found him writing. He was adding, to Charlotte, what we here annex.

"For the last, last time, I open these eyes. Alas! they will behold the sun no more. It is covered by a thick, impenetrable cloud. Yes, Nature! put on mourning: your child, your friend, your lover, draws near his end! This thought, Charlotte, is without parallel; and yet it seems like a mysterious dream when I repeat—this is my last day! The last! Charlotte, no word can adequately express this thought. The last! To-day I stand erect in all my strength—to-morrow, cold and stark, I shall lie extended upon the ground. To die! What is death? We do but dream in our discourse upon it. I have seen many human beings die; but, so straitened is our feeble nature, we have no clear conception of the beginning or the end of our existence. At this moment I am my own—or rather I am thine, thine, my adored!—and the next we are parted, severed—perhaps forever! No, Charlotte, no! How can I, how can you, be annihilated? We exist. What is annihilation? A mere word, an unmeaning sound that fixes no impression on the mind. Dead, Charlotte! laid in the cold earth, in the dark and narrow grave! I had a friend once who was every thing to me in early youth. She died. I followed her hearse; I stood by her grave when the coffin was lowered; and when I heard the creaking of the cords as they were loosened and drawn up, when the first shovelful of earth was thrown in, and the coffin returned a hollow sound, which grew fainter and fainter till all was completely covered over, I threw myself on the ground; my heart was smitten, grieved, shattered, rent—but I neither knew what had happened, nor what was to happen to me. Death! the grave! I understand not the words.—Forgive, oh forgive me! Yesterday—ah, that day should have been the last of my life! Thou angel!—for the first—first time in my existence, I felt rapture glow within my inmost soul. She loves, she loves me! Still burns upon my lips the sacred fire they received from thine. New torrents of delight overwhelm my soul. Forgive me, oh forgive!

"I knew that I was dear to you; I saw it in your first entrancing look, knew it by the first pressure of your hand; but when I was absent from you, when I saw Albert at your side, my doubts and fears returned.

"Do you remember the flowers you sent me, when, at that crowded assembly, you could neither speak nor extend your hand to me? Half the night I was on my knees before those flowers, and I regarded them as the pledges of your love; but those impressions grew fainter, and were at length effaced.

"Every thing passes away; but a whole eternity could not extinguish the living flame which was yesterday kindled by your lips, and which now burns within me. She loves me! These arms have encircled her waist, these lips have trembled upon hers. She is mine! Yes, Charlotte, you are mine forever!

"And what do they mean by saying Albert is your husband? He may be so for this world; and in this world it is a sin to love you, to wish to tear you from his embrace. Yes, it is a crime; and I suffer the punishment, but I have enjoyed the full delight of my sin. I have inhaled a balm that has revived my soul. From this hour you are mine; yes, Charlotte, you are mine! I go before you. I go to my Father and to your Father. I will pour out my sorrows before him and he will give me comfort till you arrive. Then will I fly to meet you. I will claim you, and remain in your eternal embrace, in the presence of the Almighty.

"I do not dream, I do not rave. Drawing nearer to the grave my perceptions become clearer. We shall exist; we shall see each other again; we shall behold your mother; I shall behold her, and expose to her my inmost heart. Your mother—your image!"

About eleven o'clock Werther asked his servant if Albert had returned. He answered, "Yes;" for he had seen him pass on horseback: upon which Werther sent him the following note, unsealed:—

"Be so good as to lend me your pistols for a journey. Adieu."

Charlotte had slept little during the past night. All her apprehensions were realized in a way that she could neither foresee nor avoid. Her blood was boiling in her veins, and a thousand painful sensations rent her pure heart. Was it the ardor of Werther's passionate embraces that she felt within her bosom? Was it anger at his daring? Was it the sad comparison of her present condition with former days of innocence, tranquillity, and self-confidence? How could she approach her husband, and confess a scene which she had no reason to conceal, and which she yet felt, nevertheless, unwilling to avow? They had preserved so long a silence towards each other—and should she be the first to break it by so unexpected a discovery? She feared that the mere statement of Werther's visit would trouble him, and his distress would be heightened by her perfect candor. She wished that he could see her in her true light, and judge her without prejudice; but was she anxious that he should read her inmost soul? On the other hand, could she deceive a being to whom all her thoughts had ever been exposed as clearly as crystal, and from whom no sentiment had ever been concealed? These reflections made her anxious and thoughtful. Her mind still dwelt on Werther, who was now lost to her, but whom she could not bring herself to resign, and for whom she knew nothing was left but despair if she should be lost to him forever.

A recollection of that mysterious estrangement which had lately subsisted between herself and Albert, and which she could never thoroughly understand, was now beyond measure painful to her. Even the prudent and the good have, before now, hesitated to explain their mutual differences, and have dwelt in silence upon their imaginary grievances, until circumstances have become so entangled, that in that critical juncture, when a calm explanation would have saved all parties, an understanding was impossible. And thus if domestic confidence had been earlier established between them, if love and kind forbearance had mutually animated and expanded their hearts, it might not, perhaps, even yet have been too late to save our friend.

But we must not forget one remarkable circumstance. We may observe from the character of Werther's correspondence, that he had never affected to conceal his anxious desire to quit this world. He had often discussed the subject with Albert; and, between the latter and Charlotte, it had not unfrequently formed a topic of conversation. Albert was so opposed to the very idea of such an action, that, with a degree of irritation unusual in him, he had more than once given Werther to understand that he doubted the seriousness of his threats, and not only turned them into ridicule, but caused Charlotte to share his feelings of incredulity. Her heart was thus tranquillized when she felt disposed to view the melancholy subject in a serious point of view, though she never communicated to her husband the apprehensions she sometimes experienced.

Albert, upon his return, was received by Charlotte with ill-concealed embarrassment. He was himself out of humor; his business was unfinished; and he had just discovered that the neighboring official, with whom he had to deal, was an obstinate and narrow-minded personage. Many things had occurred to irritate him.

He inquired whether any thing had happened during his absence, and Charlotte hastily answered that Werther had been there on the evening previously. He then inquired for his letters, and was answered that several packages had been left in his study. He thereon retired, leaving Charlotte alone.

The presence of the being she loved and honored produced a new impression on her heart. The recollection of his generosity, kindness, and affection had calmed her agitation: a secret impulse prompted her to follow him; she took her work and went to his study, as was often her custom. He was busily employed opening and reading his letters. It seemed as if the contents of some were disagreeable. She asked some questions: he gave short answers, and sat down to write.

Several hours passed in this manner, and Charlotte's feelings became more and more melancholy. She felt the extreme difficulty of explaining to her husband, under any circumstances, the weight that lay upon her heart; and her depression became every moment greater, in proportion as she endeavored to hide her grief, and to conceal her tears.

The arrival of Werther's servant occasioned her the greatest embarrassment. He gave Albert a note, which the latter coldly handed to his wife, saying, at the same time, "Give him the pistols. I wish him a pleasant journey," he added, turning to the servant. These words fell upon Charlotte like a thunderstroke: she rose from her seat half-fainting, and unconscious of what she did. She walked mechanically towards the wall, took down the pistols with a trembling hand, slowly wiped the dust from them, and would have delayed longer, had not Albert hastened her movements by an impatient look. She then delivered the fatal weapons to the servant, without being able to utter a word. As soon as he had departed, she folded up her work, and retired at once to her room, her heart overcome with the most fearful forebodings. She anticipated some dreadful calamity. She was at one moment on the point of going to her husband, throwing herself at his feet, and acquainting him with all that had happened on the previous evening, that she might acknowledge her fault, and explain her apprehensions; then she saw that such a step would be useless, as she would certainly be unable to induce Albert to visit Werther. Dinner was served; and a kind friend whom she had persuaded to remain assisted to sustain the conversation, which was carried on by a sort of compulsion, till the events of the morning were forgotten.

When the servant brought the pistols to Werther, the latter received them with transports of delight upon hearing that Charlotte had given them to him with her own hand. He ate some bread, drank some wine, sent his servant to dinner, and then sat down to write as follows:—

"They have been in your hands—you wiped the dust from them. I kiss them a thousand times—you have touched them. Yes, Heaven favors my design—and you, Charlotte, provide me with the fatal instruments. It was my desire to receive my death from your hands, and my wish is gratified. I have made inquiries of my servant. You trembled when you gave him the pistols, but you bade me no adieu. Wretched, wretched that I am—not one farewell! How could you shut your heart against me in that hour which makes you mine forever? O Charlotte, ages cannot efface the impression—I feel you cannot hate the man who so passionately loves you!"

After dinner he called his servant, desired him to finish the packing up, destroyed many papers, and then went out to pay some trifling debts. He soon returned home, then went out again notwithstanding the rain, walked for some time in the count's garden, and afterwards proceeded farther into the country. Towards evening he came back once more, and resumed his writing.

"Wilhelm, I have for the last time beheld the mountains, the forests, and the sky. Farewell! And you, my dearest mother, forgive me! Console her, Wilhelm. God bless you! I have settled all my affairs! Farewell! We shall meet again, and be happier than ever."

"I have requited you badly, Albert; but you will forgive me. I have disturbed the peace of your home. I have sowed distrust between you. Farewell! I will end all this wretchedness. And oh, that my death may render you happy! Albert, Albert! make that angel happy, and the blessing of Heaven be upon you!"

He spent the rest of the evening in arranging his papers: he tore and burned a great many; others he sealed up, and directed to Wilhelm. They contained some detached thoughts and maxims, some of which I have perused. At ten o'clock he ordered his fire to be made up, and a bottle of wine to be brought to him. He then dismissed his servant, whose room, as well as the apartments of the rest of the family, was situated in another part of the house. The servant lay down without undressing, that he might be the sooner ready for his journey in the morning, his master having informed him that the post-horses would be at the door before six o'clock.

"Past eleven o'clock! All is silent around me, and my soul is calm. I thank thee, O God, that thou bestowest strength and courage upon me in these last moments! I approach the window, my dearest of friends; and through the clouds, which are at this moment driven rapidly along by the impetuous winds, I behold the stars which illumine the eternal heavens. No, you will not fall, celestial bodies: the hand of the Almighty supports both you and me! I have looked for the last time upon the constellation of the Greater Bear: it is my favorite star; for when I bade you farewell at night, Charlotte, and turned my steps from your door, it always shone upon me. With what rapture have I at times beheld it! How often have I implored it with uplifted hands to witness my felicity! and even still— But what object is there, Charlotte, which fails to summon up your image before me? Do you not surround me on all sides? and have I not, like a child, treasured up every trifle which you have consecrated by your touch?

"Your profile, which was so dear to me, I return to you; and I pray you to preserve it. Thousands of kisses have I imprinted upon it, and a thousand times has it gladdened my heart on departing from and returning to my home.

"I have implored your father to protect my remains. At the corner of the churchyard, looking towards the fields, there are two lime-trees—there I wish to lie. Your father can, and doubtless will, do thus much for his friend. Implore it of him. But perhaps pious Christians will not choose that their bodies should be buried near the corpse of a poor, unhappy wretch like me. Then let me be laid in some remote valley, or near the highway, where the priest and Levite may bless themselves as they pass by my tomb, whilst the Samaritan will shed a tear for my fate.

"See, Charlotte, I do not shudder to take the cold and fatal cup, from which I shall drink the draught of death. Your hand presents it to me, and I do not tremble. All, all is now concluded: the wishes and the hopes of my existence are fulfilled. With cold, unflinching hand I knock at the brazen portals of Death.

"Oh, that I had enjoyed the bliss of dying for you! how gladly would I have sacrificed myself for you, Charlotte! And could I but restore peace and joy to your bosom, with what resolution, with what joy, would I not meet my fate! But it is the lot of only a chosen few to shed their blood for their friends, and by their death to augment, a thousand times, the happiness of those by whom they are beloved.

"I wish, Charlotte, to be buried in the dress I wear at present: it has been rendered sacred by your touch. I have begged this favor of your father. My spirit soars above my sepulchre. I do not wish my pockets to be searched. The knot of pink ribbon which you wore on your bosom the first time I saw you, surrounded by the children—Oh, kiss them a thousand times for me, and tell them the fate of their unhappy friend! I think I see them playing around me. The dear children! How warmly have I been attached to you, Charlotte! Since the first hour I saw you, how impossible have I found it to leave you. This ribbon must be buried with me: it was a present from you on my birthday. How confused it all appears! Little did I then think that I should journey this road. But peace! I pray you, peace!

"They are loaded—the clock strikes twelve. I say amen. Charlotte, Charlotte! farewell, farewell!"

A neighbor saw the flash, and heard the report of the pistol; but, as every thing remained quiet, he thought no more of it.

In the morning, at six o'clock, the servant went into Werther's room with a candle. He found his master stretched upon the floor, weltering in his blood, and the pistols at his side. He called, he took him in his arms, but received no answer. Life was not yet quite extinct. The servant ran for a surgeon, and then went to fetch Albert. Charlotte heard the ringing of the bell: a cold shudder seized her. She wakened her husband, and they both rose. The servant, bathed in tears, faltered forth the dreadful news. Charlotte fell senseless at Albert's feet.

When the surgeon came to the unfortunate Werther, he was still lying on the floor; and his pulse beat, but his limbs were cold. The bullet, entering the forehead, over the right eye, had penetrated the skull. A vein was opened in his right arm: the blood came, and he still continued to breathe.

From the blood which flowed from the chair, it could be inferred that he had committed the rash act sitting at his bureau, and that he afterwards fell upon the floor. He was found lying on his back near the window. He was in full-dress costume.

The house, the neighborhood, and the whole town were immediately in commotion. Albert arrived. They had laid Werther on the bed: his head was bound up, and the paleness of death was upon his face. His limbs were motionless; but he still breathed, at one time strongly, then weaker—his death was momently expected.

He had drunk only one glass of the wine. "Emilia Galotti" lay open upon his bureau.

I shall say nothing of Albert's distress, or of Charlotte's grief.

The old steward hastened to the house immediately upon hearing the news: he embraced his dying friend amid a flood of tears. His eldest boys soon followed him on foot. In speechless sorrow they threw themselves on their knees by the bedside, and kissed his hands and face. The eldest, who was his favorite, hung over him till he expired; and even then he was removed by force. At twelve o'clock Werther breathed his last. The presence of the steward, and the precautions he had adopted, prevented a disturbance; and that night, at the hour of eleven, he caused the body to be interred in the place which Werther had selected for himself.

The steward and his sons followed the corpse to the grave. Albert was unable to accompany them. Charlotte's life was despaired of. The body was carried by laborers. No priest attended.

16
•

Illnesses of the Cognitive Faculties

KANT

ONE OF THE GREATEST OF metaphysical philosophers, Immanuel Kant was born at and lived his entire quiet, scholarly life in or close to Königsberg, East Prussia (now Kalingrad, in the former Soviet Union). He was born in the first quarter of the eighteenth century (1724) and died just after the turn of the nineteenth century (1804). Kant was a tutor to several families before becoming a lecturer and later a professor of logic and metaphysics at the University of Königsberg, a position he held until the end of his life. During his long years as a professor, Kant achieved renown for his lecturing and writing. He was also known as an upright yet genial man, fond of company, although he never married, and with a great deal of curiosity about other peoples and places, although he never traveled far.

Kant published extensively, but he is best known for his "critical" philosophy, which came in the form of three great works. *The Critique of Pure Reason* was first published in 1781, followed by a second edition in 1787; it is primarily a work of epistemology and metaphysics, exploring fundamental questions about knowledge and reality. *The Critique of Practical Reason,* published in 1786, concerned moral understanding. Finally, *The Critique of Judgement,* published in 1790, put forth Kant's theory of aesthetics. In addition to these works, Kant lectured and wrote other, less philosophically monumental works, including the discursive, personal, and more loosely organized *Anthropology,* from which the following excerpts are drawn.

A feature common to the three critiques is Kant's emphasis on faculty psychological divisions, and these same divisions influence his thinking about mental disorder, as we shall see. In *The Critique of Pure Reason,* Kant attempted to reconcile two traditions, innate ideas and empiricism, by showing that sensory and conceptual elements were each required to yield an understanding of the world around us. To produce that synthesis, he postulated several cognitive faculties. Knowledge required a union of the faculties of sensibility and understanding, mediated by the faculty of imagination. Further faculty psychological divisions underlie the second and third critiques. None of this faculty psychology originated with Kant; indeed, faculty divisions can be traced to Plato. But Kant's work placed greater emphasis on faculty psychology and in that respect set the stage for the faculty divisions prominent in nineteenth-century psychology.

Anthropology from a Pragmatic Point of View was written at the same time but reflected rather different concerns than are found expressed in the three critiques. Although the publication of *Anthropology* occurred only at the end of his life, Kant had regularly lectured on the subject of anthropology—"man," or as we would say today, "human nature"—since 1772. Influenced by Rousseau, Kant's "pragmatic anthropology" was directed not only toward human nature but also toward achieving human perfection. Thus, in his anthropology lecture notes from 1765, we find the remark: "If there is any science which man really needs, it is the one I teach of how to fulfill properly that position in creation which is assigned to man, and from which he is able to learn what one must be in order to be a man." And he describes his pragmatic anthropology as a study of what man can and should make of himself.

Kant has been described as a typical example of a late eighteenth-century "armchair" disease classifier (Berrios and Beer, 1994:18). Quite without empirical study, he established the mental faculties whose functions might become impaired, and then identified the major kinds of mental disorder according to a two-part classification into melancholia and mania. The emphasis on the cognitive is notable in this scheme, as it is in that of Boerhaave, whom he is likely to have read. During the Age of Reason, madness was forms of "unreason," in Foucault's terminology. Mental disorder appeared in the reasoning faculties. Thus, Kant offers an intellectualistic definition. In mental disorder or mania a stream of thoughts runs contrary to, or is in disagreement with, the "rules of experience." Moreover, one of several forms of melancholy occurs when a "mere delusion of misery" is experienced. This suggest that for Kant the evidence of the subjective is discounted: melancholy is an essentially delusional disorder, always involving false belief. Similarly, it involves a problem of thought processing: the melancholy man cannot control the *course* or *sequence* of his thoughts.

Kant's classification of mental disorders proper, from which he carefully separates stupidity, and also mental retardation ("the simpleton"), breaks into three: melancholia, mental disorder or mania, and insanity or madness. One form of melancholy is *hypochondria,* a term Kant uses in the twentieth-century sense to convey a person who takes imaginary ills for something actual.

From Immanuel Kant, "On the Cognitive Faculties," in
Anthropology from a Pragmatic Point of View (1793)

General Division

The defects of the faculty of cognition are either mental weaknesses or
mental illnesses. The illnesses of the soul with regard to the cognitive
faculty can be listed under two main types. The one is melancholia
(hypochondria) and the other is mental disorder (mania). A melancholic man is well aware that the train of his thought does not move
properly, but he has not sufficient control over himself to direct, restrain, or control the course of his thought. Unjustified joy and grief
whimsically change in such a person like the weather which one has to
accept as it comes. Mental disorder indicates a voluntary stream of
thoughts which follows its own (subjective) law. The subjective law
runs contrary to the (objective) law which is in agreement with the
rules of experience.

With regard to sense perception, mental disturbance is either irrationality or insanity. As to perversity of judgment and reason, it is
known as delirium or imbecility. If a person habitually fails (by day-
dreaming) to compare his imagination with the laws of experience, he
is a visionary (a whimsical person). If he does so because of emotional
excitement, he is an enthusiast. Unexpected fits of the stricken person
are called attacks of fancy (*raptus*).

The simpleton, the imprudent, the stupid, the coxcomb, the fool,
and the buffoon are all different from the mentally disordered. They
differ not merely in degree but in the distinctive quality of mental discord. Despite their failings these people do not belong in a madhouse.
A madhouse is a place where people, not withstanding maturity and
age, must be controlled even as to their most trifling affairs of life by
someone else's reason. Insanity accompanied by emotional excitement
is called madness. It is often present from the beginning, but it may also
spring up unexpectedly like poetic inspiration (*furor poeticus*), and in
such cases it may border on genius. When such an attack of a facile but
uncontrolled flood of ideas affects reason, it is called fanaticism. Brooding over one and the same idea, to which there is no possible solution,
like the loss of a spouse who cannot be called back to life, is stupid foolishness. Such a person tries to find peace in the pain. Superstition is
more comparable to insanity, and fanaticism to delirium. The mental
derangement of the fanatic is often called (in mild terms) exaltation,
but it might also be called eccentricity.

The wild talk of persons in fever, or an attack of fury, akin to
epilepsy, which may occasionally be brought on sympathetically by

powerful imagination when someone is confronted merely with the blank, staring gaze of a madman (for this reason people with unsteady nerves are advised not to extend their curiosity to the cells where these unfortunates are kept), are not to be taken for insanity because of their temporary nature. But what is called a quirk (which is not a mental sickness, because we usually mean by mental sickness a sad melancholic derangement of the inner sense) is mostly a certain person's conceit which borders on insanity. Such a person's demand that others, upon comparison with him, should despise themselves, is a desire which runs counter to its own purpose (like that of a crazy man). By raising such a claim, he excites these people to check his vanity in every possible way, so that they are eager to tease him, and to expose him to ridicule because of his offensive foolishness. Milder is the expression of a whim (*marotte*) which someone entertains. It is supposed to be a popular fad that never meets the approval of intelligent people. For example, the gift of presentiment, inspirations similar to those of the genius of Socrates, and qualities purported to be grounded in experience but really based on such unaccountable influences as sympathy, antipathy, and idiosyncracy (*qualitates occultae*) are all chirping like a cricket in the person's head; but no one else can hear them. The mildest of all deviations across the borderline of sound understanding is the hobbyhorse. It reflects a fondness for the occupation with objects of the imagination, with which the understanding only plays for amusement. Rather than involving oneself with serious business, the hobbyhorse provides something like busy idleness. For old folks, retiring people, and the well-to-do who are returning again to the carefree life of childhood, this frame of mind is not only a health-bringing excitement which keeps one's vitality alive, but it is also something charming and at the same time, something to chuckle about, yet in such a way that the one laughed about can join in laughing happily with the others. However, with youths and busy people such hobby-riding also serves as recreation; and scoffers, who denounce these harmless little follies with pedantic seriousness, deserve Sterne's reprimand: "Let everybody ride his own hobbyhorse up and down the streets of the city, *as long as he does not make you sit behind him. . . .*"

On Mental Ailments

The major division, as already mentioned above, is the division into melancholia (hypochondria) and mental disorder (mania). The name of the former is derived as analogous to being startled by the chirping noise of a house-cricket in the quiet of the night. The noise disturbs the peace of mind necessary for sleep. The illness of the hypochondriac is such that certain inner, bodily sensations do not only disclose an actually existent illness inside the body, but they can also cause an illness because human nature, by virtue of a peculiar quality lacking in animals, can strengthen or sustain a feeling by centering attention on certain local impressions. On the other hand, either intentional abstraction, or abstraction caused by other distracting occupations, may weaken the symptoms and, if such abstraction becomes habitual, the illness may disappear altogether. In such a way hypochondria, considered as melancholia, becomes the cause for taking imaginary physical ills for something actual. The patient is well aware that these are imaginings, but from time to time he is unable to break loose from them. Or, conversely, from a genuine physical discomfort (like intestinal pressure caused from having eaten flatulent food), hypochondria will produce imaginings of all sorts of external events and concerns about one's intestinal tract. They will disappear completely as soon as digestion has been completed and flatulence has ceased. The hypochondriac is a capricious fellow (a visionary) of the most pitiful sort, obstinately unable to come to grips with his imaginings, always running to the physician, who has no end of trouble with him and who can only quiet the patient in the same way in which he quiets a child (that is, with pills containing bread crumbs instead of remedies). Moreover, when this patient, who despite his perpetual ailments never really falls ill, consults medical books, he becomes completely insufferable because now he believes that he feels in his body all the discomforts which he has read about in the books. Extraordinary gaiety, in the form of lively wit and happy laughter, serves as a symptom of this sick imagination to which the patient feels occasionally subjected; thus falling victim to the ever-changing sport of his moods. Anxious fear, childish in character, of the thought of death nourishes this sickness. But whoever does not tend to overlook these thoughts with manly courage will never enjoy life properly.

Still, on this side of the border of mental disorder is the sudden change of moods (*raptus*), an unexpected leap from one subject to a totally different one without apparent motivation. Occasionally the change precedes every disturbance as an indication; but frequently the mind is already so disorganized that such attacks of irregularity become the rule. Suicide is often just the result of a *raptus*. Because he who, in the violence of emotion, has slit his throat will soon after patiently allow it to be sewn up again.

Melancholy (*melancholia*) can also be a mere delusion of misery which the low-spirited self-tormentor (inclined toward feeling wretched) creates for himself. In itself it is not yet a mental disorder, but may easily lead to it. In other respects it is a mistaken but frequently used expression to speak of a melancholy mathematician . . . when one means only a profoundly thoughtful person.

17
●

Melancholia

PINEL

O NE OF THE GREATEST intellectual and moral figures in the history of psychiatry, Philippe Pinel was born in 1745 in the village of Saint Paul, near Castres, in the south of France, and died in 1826. His father was a country doctor. Pinel was to study theology but instead went to medical school in Toulouse, where he received his medical degree in 1773. He continued his studies at Montpellier, at that time an important medical center, and eventually moved to Paris. At first he did not practice medicine but wrote for scientific periodicals and translated medical works, including the writing on one of his greatest influences, the Englishman William Cullen (1710–90), while supporting himself by teaching. His interest in psychiatry is said to have been stimulated by two things. First, a young man whom Pinel had known well suffered a mental disorder, escaped to the woods, and was attacked and eaten by wolves. Then, a new hospital for the insane was opened, which employed more humane treatments for the patients, regarded now as sufferers of diseases rather than outcasts.

With the new regime after the Revolution, Pinel was given the task of overseeing Bicêtre, the largest institution for the insane in Paris. Like Salpêtrière, which he later reformed in the same way, Bicêtre contained unimaginable horrors. Mental patients were kept in chains and were housed with the sick, the feebleminded, and common criminals in poorly lit, poorly ventilated, vermin-infested stone buildings, sleeping on straw, and at the mercy of keepers recruited from the city's jails. Pinel's first act was to unchain the unfortunate patients; after two years, he had reformed Bicêtre and introduced a more humane regimen, a process he then went on to effect at Salpêtrière. Pinel was later appointed to the chair of hygiene, *physique medicale,* and pathology at the newly founded Paris School of Health.

Coming on the scene at a time of change and reform in every aspect of French medicine, Pinel was able to make a lasting mark on many aspects of medicine and psychiatry in his country. His humane character and progressive principles of treatment, no less than his knowledge and skill, shaped European as well as French thought. In his 1798 work *Nosographie Philosophique* (Philosophical Disease Taxonomy), Pinel revolutionized the approach to disease classification in internal medicine, linking symptoms and disorders more concisely and with a more logical medical rationale than had been previously employed. The work for which he is best known, however, is the one from which the following excerpt is drawn. Published first in 1801 and in a revised second edition in 1809, Pinel's *Treatise on Insanity* was a model of clarity and organization, in which he offered a simplified classification, an etiological analysis, a description of the phases of the disease, remarks on pathological anatomy, and a discussion of treatment. The following excerpts are from an English translation of the first edition published in 1806.

In this work, Pinel offered a five-part classification of mental disorders. There was melancholia (or, as he says, "delirium upon one subject exclusively"), mania without delirium, mania with delirium, dementia ("or the abolition of the thinking faculty"), and finally idiotism ("or obliteration of the intellectual faculties and affections"). Reproduced here, from the second edition, is part of his chapter devoted to melancholia, including a succinct diagnostic definition, which again emphasizes the limited nature of the disorder ("delirium exclusively upon one subject . . . free exercise in other respects of all the faculties of the understanding"). His account of melancholia indicates an overall category of enormous breadth: it includes cases where the disposition is one of "unruffled satisfaction," as well as those in which there is habitual depression and anxiety. It also seems to encompass long-term character traits in a normally functioning person, as well as more severe, and less habitual, conditions ending in suicide, or "degenerating" into mania.

Pinel's approach to the study of mental disorder emphasized careful observation over earlier thinkers' theorizing about obscure internal causes. He offers his methodological prescription in the *Treatise on Insanity:* "I must carefully refuse to consider all ideological theories, still contested, on the nature, the relation and the successive generation of the faculties of the human mind. It is wiser to limit oneself to the results of a strict observation of the impairments which the various faculties can experience and to learn to distinguish them by visible signs" (107). In keeping with this effort to eschew reference to unobservable causes, Pinel's etiological account of mental disorder was eclectic. He ascribed it to heredity, to ill treatment, to the horror of the Revolution, to irregular ways of living, to "spasmodic" and "weakening" passions; and melancholia, he explains by drunkenness, anomalies in skull structure, cranial traumata, skin conditions, various "moral" (we would now say psychological) causes such as domestic misfortunes and religious fanaticism and, in women, to menstruation and menopause.

In the emerging psychiatry of the nineteenth century, Pinel's influence was very great, both on future classifiers and theorists such as his famed student Jean-Etienne-Dominique Esquirol (1772–1840) and on those involved with the care and treatment of the mentally disordered.

From Philippe Pinel, "Melancholia, or Delirium Upon One Subject Exclusively," in *A Treatise on Insantiy, in Which are Contained the Principles of New and More Practical Nosology of Maniacal Disorders Than Has Yet Been Offered to the Public* (1801)

The Common Acceptation of the Term Melancholia

The symptoms generally comprehended by the term melancholia are taciturnity, a thoughtful pensive air, gloomy suspicions, and a love of solitude. Those traits, indeed, appear to distinguish the characters of some men otherwise in good health, and frequently in prosperous circumstances. Nothing, however, can be more hideous than the figure of a melancholic, brooding over his imaginary misfortunes. If moreover possessed of power, and endowed with a perverse disposition and a sanguinary heart, the image is rendered still more repulsive. Tiberius and Louis XI. are singular instances of this unhappy temperament. Gloomy taciturnity, austere moroseness and gravity, the inequalities of a mind abounding with acrimony and passion, love of solitude, and the timid embarrassment of an artful disposition, betrayed, from early youth, the melancholic temperament of Louis. Between the character of this prince and that of Tiberius, there are several striking traits of resemblance. Neither of them distinguished himself in war, excepting during the effervescence of youth. Imposing but ineffectual preparations, studied delays, illusive projects of military expeditions, and negociations conducted on the principles of intrigue and perfidiousness, distinguished their future lives. Before the commencement of their respective reigns, they passed several years in inglorious banishment, amidst the languors of private life; the one in the Isle of Rhodes, and the other in a retired province of Belgium. The profound dissimulation, the characteristic indecision, and equivocal answers of Tiberius upon his succession to the throne of Augustus are well known. Louis, throughout the whole of his life, was in like manner a model of the most refined and perfidious policy. Each of them a prey to dark suspicions, sinistrous prognostications and terrors ever new and imaginary, which increased with their advancing lives, they at length sought retirement from the effects of their tyranny; the one, in the château de Plessis-les-Tours; and the other, in the Island of Capreæ, on the coast of Campania, where they respectively buried themselves in unmanly and unlawful pleasures. The biography of persons of distinguished talents and reputation, affords many instances of melancholics of a very opposite character, who were remarkable for their ardent enthusiasm, sublime conceptions, and other great and magnanimous qualities. Others, occupying a less exalted station, charm society by the ardour of their affections, and give energy to its movements by their own impassioned turbulence and restlessness. Melancholics of this class are remarkably skilful in tormenting themselves and their neighbours, by imagining offences which were never intended and indulging in groundless suspicions. It is very common for physicians to be consulted by persons of this temperament for nervous palpitations or aneurism of the heart. Some fancy themselves under the influence of hydrophobic madness. Others believe that they have all the diseases which they read of in medical books. I have known many who had had the venereal disease, torment themselves, upon the appearance of the least indisposition, with the belief that the virus of siphilis was still operating; and they have gone for advice to every empyric that flattered their credulity.

Profound melancholia is frequently succeeded by actual derangement of the intellect. A lady, highly respectable for her talents and dispositions, seduced by the prospect of improving her rank and fortune, married a neighbouring gentleman, who was in a state of dementia. The desire of making herself agreeable in her family, united to a disposition truly amiable, enabled her for a long time to support the irksomeness of the connection. But the impassioned extravagances of her husband, and the disturbances which he made in the family and neighbourhood, admitted of no respite to her anxiety. The education of her two children, whom she tenderly loved, and the constant attention which she was disposed to pay to their health and improvement, were the only circumstances that served to palliate the severity of her disappointment, or to tolerate the insipidity of her existence. But they were not sufficient to arrest the progress of her melancholy. Her imagination daily suggested new causes of solicitude and apprehension. Some misfortune or other arrived every day of the week, but especially, as she supposed, on Friday. Hence she fancied that Friday was a day of ill omen and ill luck. She, at length, carried this notion so far, that she would not leave her room on that day. If the month began on a Friday, it rendered her extremely fearful and miserable for several days. By degrees, Thursday, being the eve of Friday, excited similar alarms. If ever she heard either of those days named in company, she immediately turned pale, and was confused in her manner and conversation, as if she had been visited by some fatal misfortune. Some months after the revolution it was determined to take my advice on her case. Conjoined to such moral management as her situation appeared to require, I advised a few simple and suitable remedies. The changes of 1789, succeeded by reverses of fortune, and the eventual emigration of the family, put it out of my power to learn the sequel of her history. But, I am disposed to think, that a new chain of ideas, change of scene and climate, and, perhaps, depressed circumstances, have long since dissipated her apprehensions and her melancholy.

Melancholia Considered Nosologically as a Species of Mental Derangement

Melancholics are frequently absorbed by one exclusive idea, to which they perpetually recur in their conversation, and which appears to engage their whole attention. At other times, they observe the most obstinate silence for many years, and friendship and affection are refused participation in their secret. On the contrary, there are some who betray no extraordinary gloom, and appear possessed of the soundest judgement, when an unforeseen circumstance happens and suddenly rouses their delirium. A commissary, one day, visited the hospital de Bicetre, for the purpose of dismissing such of its tenants as were supposed to be cured. Amongst others, he put some questions to an old vine dresser, who replied to him with great propriety and coherence. Upon which, the officer prepared the process verbal for his discharge, and according to custom, gave it him to sign. But, what was his surprise when he saw the old man sign himself CHRIST, and indulge in all the reveries suggested by that delusion.

Any cause of fear or terror may produce a habitual susceptibility to those emotions, and, by undermining the constitution, may induce dangerous debility and death. I have known two Austrian prisoners of war, fall victims to their apprehensions. The object of their terror was the guillotine.

A certain sourness of disposition, and a surly misanthropy of character, appear to determine some maniacs to shut themselves up in their own chambers, and to treat, with great rudeness and abuse, any person that should offer to molest their solitude. Fanatics, belonging to this class of madmen, often fancy themselves inspired and under divine requisition to perform some sacrificial act or acts of expiation. Those deluded and dangerous beings can commit most barbarous homicides in cold blood. An old monk, driven to a state of insanity by religious enthusiasm, believed that he had one night seen the virgin in a dream, and that he had received from her an express order to put to death a person of his acquaintance, whom he accused of infidelity. This projected homicide would, no doubt, have been executed, had the maniac, in consequence of betraying his purpose, not been timely and effectually secured.

Two Opposite Forms of Melancholia with Delirium

Nothing appears more inexplicable, at the same time that nothing can be more certain, than that melancholia with delirium, presents itself in two very opposite forms. Sometimes it is distinguished by an exalted sentiment of self-importance, associated with chimerical pretensions to unbounded power or inexhaustible riches. At other times, it is characterized by great depression of spirits, pusillanimous apprehensions and even absolute despair. Lunatic asylums afford numerous instances of those opposite extremes. The steward of a gentleman of fortune, lost his property by the revolution; and for his attachment to the old regime, he was committed to prison, where he was detained for some months. Overwhelmed by apprehensions for his life, which he perpetually harboured, and which the violence of the times were too much calculated to excite, he at length became insane. In that situation he was transmitted to the hospital de Bicetre, where he soon complimented himself with the title and prerogatives of the king of France. A jurisconsulte, deprived by requisition of an only son, for whom he entertained a most tender affection, yielded to a grief so poignant that it terminated in insanity; upon which, he assumed the character of the king of Corsica. A native of Versailles, ruined by the revolution, was soon after extatized by the fantastic illusion of being the sovereign of the world. On the other hand, there are instances of profound and distressing melancholy, being exasperated into active madness, without any change in the object of the hallucination. A simple timorous man, made use of some expressions of dissatisfaction with the government, in the second year of the republic. He was threatened with the guillotine. The consequences were, that he lost his sleep, was exceedingly perplexed, and forsook his ordinary employment. Soon after, he was confined in the Asylum de Bicetre. The idea of his ignominious death perpetually haunted him, and he daily solicited the execution of the decree which he fancied to have been passed against him. His mind was thoroughly unhinged and deranged. All my attempts to restore him proved unsuccessful.

It has not been without emotion, that I have seen many an interesting victim of sensibility and affection, sink under the loss of a near and dearly beloved relative, into a most distressing state of delirious melancholy. A young man, who had lost his reason amid the pangs of disappointed love, was influenced by so powerful an illusion, that he mistook every female visiter for his dear Mary Adeleine, the object of his unfortunate attachment. To hear his tender and impassioned addresses to every fair stranger that he met with, was calculated to soften the hardest heart.

May Not Melancholia of Several Years Standing Degenerate into Mania?

Melancholia remains often stationary for several years without any change in the object of its delirium, and without any other alteration of the moral and physical functions. Some melancholics of this class, have been confined at the Asylum de Bicetre, for twelve, fifteen, twenty and even thirty years; and, throughout the whole of that period, their hallucination has been confined to one subject. The functions of their monotonous existence chiefly consisted in eating and sleeping: and they have generally withdrawn from society to associate with phantoms of their own creation. But some of them who were endowed with a greater mobility of character, from constantly seeing the extravagances of their more furious associates, became themselves decided maniacs. Others, after the lapse of some years, and from no evident cause, have undergone a thorough revolution of character. The object of their hallucination has changed, or it has excited their interest in a new direction. A maniac of this description was under my care for about twelve years. For the first eight, he was perpetually haunted with the fear of being poisoned. He supposed that his relations wished to disown him, and to deprive him of his property. He was exceedingly reserved in his conversation; but what he said upon every subject, excepting that of his hallucination, was perfectly connected and correct. The idea of the poison made him extremely suspicious, and he durst not eat any victuals but what were cooked at the usual kitchen. Towards the eighth year of his confinement, his delirium suddenly changed its character. He then became a mighty potentate, sovereign of the world, equal to the creator, and supremely happy.

Melancholia with a Disposition to Commit Suicide

"The English," says Montesquieu, "frequently destroy themselves without any apparent cause to determine them to such an act, and even in the midst of prosperity. Among the Romans suicide was the effect of education; it depended upon their customs and manner of thinking: with the English it is the effect of disease, and depending upon the physical condition of the system." The propensity to this horrid deed as existing independent of the ordinary powerful motives to it, such as the loss of honour or fortune is by no means a disease peculiar to England: it is far from being of rare occurrence in France.

In a periodical journal of some time past, I published a case of this kind, of which the following history contains an abridged account. A young man, twenty-two years of age, was intended by his parents for the church. He disliked the profession exceedingly, and absolutely refused to take orders. For this act, at once of integrity and disobedience, he was forced to quit his father's house, and to exert his inexperienced energies for a precarious subsistence. He turned his thoughts to several different employments; and, at length, he went to reside with a family, where he was treated with great kindness, and where he appeared to enjoy a degree of tranquility. His enjoyment, however, was not of long continuance; for his imagination was again assailed by gloomy and distressing reflections. His life became gradually more and more burdensome to him, and he considered of different methods of putting an end to it. He one day formed the resolution of precipitating himself from the top of the house: but his courage failed him, and the execution of the project was postponed. Some days after, he took up a pistol with the same design of self-destruction. His perplexities and terrors returned. A friend of this unhappy youth, called upon me one day to inform me of the projected tragedy. We adopted every means of prevention that prudence could suggest: but the most pressing solicitations and friendliest remonstrances were in vain. The propensity to suicide unceasingly haunted him, and he precipitately quitted the family where he had experienced so many proofs of friendship and attachment. Financial considerations prohibited the suggestion of a distant voyage, or a change of climate. I, therefore, advised as the best substitute, some constant and laborious employment. The young melancholic, sensibly alive to the horror of his situation, entered fully into my views, and procured an engagement at Bled harbour, where he mingled with the other labourers, with a full determination to deserve his stipulated wages. But, completely fatigued and exhausted by the exertion of the two first days of his engagement, he was obliged to have recourse to some other expedient. He entered into the employ of a master mason, in the neighbourhood of Paris, to whom his services were peculiarly acceptable, as he devoted his leisure hours to the instruction of an only son. No situation, apparently, could have been more suitable to his case, then one of this kind, admitting of alternate mental and bodily exercise. Wholesome food, comfortable lodgings, and every attention due to misfortune, seemed rather to aggravate than to divert his gloomy propensities. After the expiration of a fortnight, he returned to his friend, and, with tears in his eyes, acquainted him with the internal struggles which he felt, and the insuperable disgust with life, which bore him irresistibly to self-destruction. The reproaches of his friend affected him exceedingly, and, in a state of the utmost anxiety and despair, he silently withdrew, probably to terminate a hated existence, by throwing himself into the Seine.

Specific Character of Melancholia

Delirium exclusively upon one subject: no propensity to acts of violence, independent of such as may be impressed by a predominant and chimerical idea: free exercise in other respects of all the faculties of the understanding: in some cases, equanimity of disposition, or a state of unruffled satisfaction: in others habitual depression and anxiety, and frequently a moroseness of character amounting even to the most decided misanthropy, and sometimes to an invincible disgust with life.

18
•

Hypochondriasis or Tristimania

RUSH

$\mathbf{B}$ENJAMIN RUSH WAS BORN IN 1745 in the town Byberry, now part of Philadelphia. He died in 1813. As a signer of the Declaration of Independence, a member of the Continental Congress who also served in the Continental army, a member of the Pennsylvania convention that ratified the federal Constitution, the founder of the first American antislavery society and of Dickinson College, and, from 1797 until his death, the treasurer of the U.S. mint, Rush played an important part in the public life of the new Republic. But his medical career was also remarkable, and he is known as the "father of American psychiatry."

Rush attended the College of New Jersey (now Princeton), received his medical training in Edinburgh, and upon his return became a professor of the institutes of medicine and clinical practice at the University of Pennsylvania. He was influenced in his ideas by William Cullen (1710–90), a European medical authority of the last part of the eighteenth century. Rush wrote extensive works, including *Medical Inquiries and Observations,* in five volumes (1794–98), and *Medical Inquiries and Observations upon the Diseases of the Mind* (1812). It was his writing on psychiatry for which he was best known as a medical authority.

Rush's work on melancholy was influential beyond America, being read by his contemporary in France, Esquirol (1772–1840). His particular contribution was to tighten, develop, and divide the hitherto loose notion of a partial insanity, or what he calls "partial intellectual derangement." The following passages from Rush's *Medical Inquiries and Observations upon the Diseases of the Mind* attempt to clarify the disorder category of partial insanity, and introduce new terminology to that end.

In relating these passages to other tests on melancholy, it is important to recognize that for Rush the notion of melancholia was very broad indeed, and was associated more with delusion than with a disorder of fear and sadness. In the breadth he accorded melancholia, Rush was closer to the Greek physicians than to the thinkers of his own time. Similarly, Rush seems to employ a somewhat outmoded sense of *hypochondriasis*. In the eighteenth century, hypochondriasis was usually viewed as a milder form of melancholia. By Kant's writing at the very end of the century, the term acquires a meaning close to the one in use today, in which the hypochondriac suffers imaginary ills. Yet there was an older meaning in which hypochondriasis implied the presence of delusion (Jackson, 1986), and it is to this that Rush appears to revert.

Partial derangement is defined as error in opinion and conduct upon some one subject only, with soundness of mind on other subjects. Thus Rush has characterized such derangement from the start in terms of false belief, or delusion, rather than in terms of the feelings or emotions associated with the condition. The presence or absence of feelings of distress over these delusions is not unimportant for the details of his taxonomy of different derangements. But like eighteenth-century classifiers such as Kant, Rush treats the faculty of reason as the center of all mental disturbance.

The different forms of partial derangement are usefully subdivided, Rush believes, although he objects to the grounds for division proposed by other "nosologists" (disease classifiers), who juxtapose melancholia with a condition misleadingly called *hypochondria*. Instead, Rush introduces the term *tristimania* to express forms of madness when the subject of the patient's distress is delusions about his person, affairs, or condition. And in place of the term *melancholia,* he substitutes *amenomania* to refer to delusions about the rest of the world around him, delusions that may or may not be distressing.

In another chapter of his book on the diseases of the mind, Rush enumerates the many remedies he or others have found useful for the form of partial insanity he calls tristimania: those remedies applied directly to the body, including bloodletting, purges, emetics, a reduced diet, stimulants and medicines such as laudanum and alcohol, warm baths, cold baths, friction (body rubbing), exercise, especially horseback riding ("By Degrees, People have Rid away Melancholy," he insists), and the infliction of mild pain; and those remedies whose effects work through the mind, such as terror and ridicule, a change of company, and "employment, or business of some kind."

Rush was a practical man, and, like his French contemporary Pinel, an empirical scientist. Nowhere do we find reference to the mysterious humors that haunted earlier writing on melancholy. Indeed, one of his objections to the earlier term *hypochondriasis* for the condition he has renamed tristimania is that it conveys the idea of "being seated in the liver, and derived from vitiated or obstructed bile." The seat of disease "appears to be in the brain," Rush firmly and confidently asserts, and "morbid or obstructed bile is evidently an accidental symptom of it."

From Benjamin Rush, "Of Partial Intellectual Derangement, and particularly of Hypochondriasis," in *Medical Inquiries and Observations Upon the Diseases of the Mind* (1812)

Partial derangement consists in error in opinion, and conduct, upon some one subject only, with soundness of mind upon all, or nearly all other subjects. The error in this case is two-fold. It is directly contrary to truth, or it is disproportioned in its effects, or expected consequences, to the causes which induce them. It has been divided by the nosologists according to its objects. When it relates to the persons, affairs, or condition of the patient only, and is attended with distress, it has been called hypochondriasis. When it extends to objects external to the patient, and is attended with pleasure, or the absence of distress, it has been called melancholia. They are different grades only, of the same morbid actions in the brain, and they now and then blend their symptoms with each other.

I wish I could substitute a better term than hypochondriasis, for the lowest grade of derangement. It is true the hypochondriac region is diseased in it; so it is after autumnal fevers, and yet we do not designate the obstructions induced by those fevers by that name. It would be equally proper to call every other form of madness hypochondriasm, for they are all attended with more or less disease or disorder in the liver, spleen, stomach and bowels, from which the name of hypochondriasm is derived. But I have another objection to that name, and that is, it has unfortunately been supposed to imply an imaginary disease only, and when given to the disease in question is always offensive to patients who are affected with it. It is true, it is seated in the mind; but it is as much the effect of corporeal causes as a pleurisy, or a bilious fever. Perhaps the term TRISTIMANIA might be used to express this form of madness when erroneous opinions respecting a man's person, affairs, or condition, are the subjects of his distress.

I object likewise to the term melancholia, when used, as it is by Dr. Cullen, to express partial madness from external causes.

1. Because it is sometimes induced by causes that are not external to the patient, but connected with his person, affairs, or condition in life; and,

2. Because it conveys an idea of its being seated in the liver, and derived from vitiated or obstructed bile. Now the seat of the disease, from facts formerly mentioned, appears to be in the brain, and morbid or obstructed bile is evidently an accidental symptom of it. Perhaps it would be more proper to call it AMENOMANIA, from the errors that constitute it, being generally attended with pleasure, or the absence of distress.

The hypochondriasis, or tristimania, has sometimes been confounded with hysteria, but differs from it. . . .

Hypochondriasis, or tristimania, is to hysteria what a typhus fever is to inflammatory fever. It is often combined with it, and sometimes alternates with it, and, when cured, it passes out of the system with symptoms of hysteria, in all those cases in which it was preceded by them. I beg the attention of the reader to this view of these two forms of disease. It is intended to destroy the nosological distinctions between them. As well might we divide the first and last stages of a fever by specific characters, as divide those two grades of morbid excitement by specific names.

I shall now deliver a history of the most characteristic symptoms of the two different forms of partial derangement that have been mentioned, and afterwards take notice of the remedies proper for each of them. I shall begin with *hypochondriasis,* or *tristimania.*

The symptoms of this form of derangement as they appear in the body are, dyspepsia; costiveness or diarrhœa, with slimy stools; flatulency pervading the whole alimentary canal, and called in the bowels borborigmi; a tumid abdomen, especially on the right side; deficient or preternatural appetite; strong venereal desires, accompanied with nocturnal emissions of semen; or an absence of venereal desires, and sometimes impotence; insensibility to cold; pains in the limbs at times, resembling rheumatism; cough; cold feet; palpitation of the heart; head-ache; vertigo; tenitus aurium; a thumping like a hammer in the temples, and sometimes within the brain; a disposition to faint; wakefulness, or starting in sleep; indisposition to rise out of bed, and a disposition to lie in it for days, and even weeks; a cool and dry skin, and frequently of a sallow colour, from the want of a regular discharge of bile from the liver, and its absorption into the blood.

While the alimentary canal is thus depressed, and the blood-vessels, nerves and muscles, robbed of nearly all their excitement, or possess it in parts of the body only, the lymphatic system is often preternaturally excited; hence we frequently observe in this disease a constant and increased discharge of urine.

The characteristic symptom of this form of derangement, as it appears in the mind, is *distress,* the causes of which are numerous, and of a personal nature. I shall enumerate some of them, as they have appeared in different people. They relate, 1, to the patient's body. He erroneously believes himself to be afflicted with various diseases, particularly with consumption, cancer, stone, and above all, with impotence, and the venereal disease. Sometimes he supposes himself to be poisoned, or that his constitution has been ruined by mercury, or that the seeds of the hydrophobia are floating in his system.

2. He believes that he has a living animal in his body. A sea captain, formerly of this city, believed for many years that he had a wolf in his liver. Many persons have fancied they were gradually dying, from ani-

mals of other kinds preying upon different parts of their bodies. 3. He magines himself to be converted into an animal of another species, such as a goose, a cock, a dog, a cat, a hare, a cow, and the like. In this case he adopts the noises and gestures of the animals into which he supposes himself to be transformed.

4. He believes he inherits, by transmigration, the soul of some fellow creature, but much oftener of a brute animal. There is now a madman in the Pennsylvania Hospital who believes that he was once a calf, and who mentions the name of the butcher that killed him, and the stall in the Philadelphia market on which his flesh was sold previously to his animating his present body.

5. He believes he has no soul. The late Dr. Percival communicated to me, many years ago, an account of a dissenting minister in England who believed that God had annihilated his soul as a punishment for his having killed a high-way man by grasping him by the throat, who attempted to rob him. His mind was correct upon all other subjects.

6. He believes he is transformed into a plant. In the Memoirs of the Count de Maurepas we are told this error took possession of the mind of one of the princes of Bourbon to such a degree, that he often went and stood in his garden, where he insisted upon being watered in common with all the plants around him.

7. The patient afflicted with this disease sometimes fancies he is transformed into glass. . . .

The mind, in its distress from all the above causes, is in a reverse state from that which was just now mentioned, in drawing erroneous, or disproportionate, conclusions from just premises. Thus the hypochondriac who possesses an income which he admits to be equal to all the exigencies of his family, reasons unjustly when he anticipates ending his days in a poor-house. In like manner the deranged penitent judges correctly when he believes that he has offended his Maker, but he reasons incorrectly when he supposes he has excluded him from his mercy.

In the hypochondriasis from all the causes that have been mentioned, the patients are for a while peevish and sometimes irascible. The lightest noises, such as the grating of a door upon its hinges, or its being opened and shut suddenly, produce in them anger or terror. They quarrel with their friends and relations. They change their physicians and remedies, and sometimes they discover the instability of their tempers by settling and unsettling themselves half a dozen times in different parts of their native country, or different foreign countries, in the course of a few years, leaving each of them with complaints of their climate, provisions, and the manners of their inhabitants.

The hypochondriasis, or tristimania, like most other diseases, has paroxysms, and remissions or intermissions, all of which are influenced by many circumstances, particularly by company, wine, exercise, and, above all, the weather.

A pleasant season, a fine day, and even the morning sun, often suspend the disease. Mr. Cowper, who knew all its symptoms by sad experience, bears witness to the truth of this remark, in one of his letters to Mr. Haley. "I rise," says he, "cheerless and distressed, and brighten as the sun goes on." Its paroxysms are sometimes denominated "low spirits." They continue from a day, a week, a month, a season, to a year, and sometimes longer. The intervals differ, 1, in being accompanied with preternatural high spirits. 2. In being attended with remissions only; and, 3, with intermissions, or, in other words, with correctness and equanimity of mind.

The extremes of low and high spirits which occur in the same person, at different times, are happily illustrated by the following case. A physician in one of the cities of Italy was once consulted by a gentleman who was much distressed with a paroxysm of this intermitting state of hypochondriasm. He advised him to seek relief in convivial company, and recommended to him in particular to find out a gentleman of the name of Cardini, who kept all the tables in the city to which he was occasionally invited in a roar of laughter. "Alas! Sir," said the patient, with a heavy sigh. "I am that Cardini." Many such characters, alternately marked by high and low spirits, are to be found in all the cities in the world.

But there are sometimes flashes of apparent cheerfulness, and even of mirth, in the intervals of this disease, which are accompanied with latent depression of mind. This appears to have been the case in Mr. Cowper: hence, in one of his letters to Mr. Hayley, he says, "I am cheerful upon paper, but the most distressed of all creatures." It was probably in one of these opposite states of mind that he wrote his humorous ballad of John Gilpin. . . .

But the most awful symptom of this disease remains yet to be mentioned, and that is DESPAIR. The marks of the extreme misery included in this word are sometimes to be seen in the countenances and gestures of hypochondriacs in a Hospital; but as it is difficult to obtain from such persons a history of their feelings, I shall endeavour to give some idea of them in the following account, communicated to me by a clergyman who passed four years and a half in that state of mind.

He said "he felt the bodily pains and mental anguish of the damned; that he slumbered only, but never slept soundly, during the long period that has been mentioned; that he lost his appetites, and passions, so as to desire and relish nothing, and to love and hate no one; that his feet were constantly cold, and the upper part of his body warm; that he lost all sense of years, months, weeks, days, and nights, and even of morning and evening; that in this respect, time was to him, no more." During the whole period of his misery, he kept his hands in constant motion towards his head and thighs, and ceased not constantly to cry out, "wretched man that I am! I am damned; oh, I am damned everlastingly."

Terrible as this picture of despair is, the disease has symptoms which mark a still greater degree of misery. It sometimes creates such a disgust of life, as to make the subjects of it wish to die. How undescribable, and even incomprehensible, must be that state of mind, which thus extinguishes the deep seated principle of the love of life! . . . Dreadful as this state of mind is, there is one still more distressing, and that is the desire, and fear of death operating alternately upon the mind. I have seen this state of hypochondriasm. It was in the lady who wished to be relieved from the horror of her thoughts by the complete loss of her reason.

After the history that has been given of the distress, despair, and voluntary death, which are induced by that partial derangement which has been described, I should lay down my pen, and bedew my paper with my tears, did I not know that the science of medicine has furnished a remedy for it, and that hundreds are now alive, and happy, who were once afflicted with it. Blessed science! which thus extends its friendly empire, not only over the evils of the bodies, but over those of the minds, of the children of men!

19

"Ode on Melancholy" and
"What the Thrush Said"

KEATS

BORN IN 1795, the English Romantic poet John Keats was the son of a livery-stable keeper in Moorfields, London. After some schooling, he was apprenticed to an apothecary and later trained to be a surgeon, but he abandoned surgery for poetry. With help from influential literary figures of his day such as Shelley, Leigh Hunt, and Hazlitt, he published poetry, including a number of longer poetic works, and some plays. "Ode on Melancholy" was one of four great odes, the others being "Ode on a Grecian Urn," "To a Nightingale," and "To Autumn." These were all written during the spring of 1819 and are widely judged to have been his best work.

Keats knew much suffering and died while still a young man. Consumptive and weak, he experienced many phases of despondency and moodiness. By the time he received recognition for his work, he was seriously ill with tuberculosis. He sailed for Rome in 1820 and died there soon after.

Keats's choice of subject matter in the "Ode on Melancholy," at least, may be accounted for. We know that he read Burton's writing on melancholy and that he suffered his own black moods. But the ode is difficult to understand and has given rise to extensive and sometimes conflicting interpretation. Some have read it as the triumph of joy over suffering; others have found in it perversity, masochism, sadism, and decadence. Three lines are particularly puzzling:

> Or if thy mistress some rich anger shows,
> Emprison her soft hand, and let her rave,
> And feed, deep, deep upon her peerless eyes.

These lines have been subject to intense scrutiny and interpretation. One critic has explained that, in the sense of the whole poem, Keats is not speaking, as some have supposed, of a physical mistress but of the personified figure of Melancholy herself, immediately addressed a "she" in the next stanza (Gittings, 1968:461). This reading enables us to see that Keats is echoing Burton. "If melancholy men be not as bad as he that is worst," Burton remarks, "'tis our *dame Melancholy* keep us so" ([1621] 1989:II.206, my emphasis).

As is true of his ode on indolence, the ode on melancholy starts with the world of darkness and pain, so vividly described that we are reminded that Keats wrote from personal experience. It ends with a more positive and happy resolution. We can identify a theme familiar from several of Keats's other works. Out of, and because of, suffering comes heightened joy, he seems to be saying. Only he who has felt the pain and darkness of melancholy can taste fully of pleasure—bursting "Joy grape against his palate fine."

This emphasis on what have been described as the "kinships" of Melancholy and Delight, and the "twin shrines of Melancholy and Pleasure" (Gittings, 1968:461) reflects a more general Romantic fascination with paradox that is powerfully conveyed in these works of Keats's. The soul, it was believed, grows and is exalted through its painful experiences. Similarly, with a passive failure to seek knowledge comes enlightenment. Both themes occur in the lovely verse on darkness (entitled "What the Thrush Said") reproduced here. The exalted pleasure of a "triple morn" comes only to "thou whose only book has been the light of supreme darkness." And he is awake who "thinks himself sleep."

Keats's evocation of these dual aspects of melancholy, this stress on the paradox uniting sensual pleasure, energy, and vitality, on the one hand, and despair, suffering, and passivity, on the other, elevates his writing on melancholy to a place beside that of Elizabethan authors.

·⁓ • ⌣·

John Keats, "Ode on Melancholy" (1819)

1.

No, no, go not to Lethe, neither twist
    Wolf's-bane, tight-rooted, for its poisonous wine;
Nor suffer thy pale forehead to be kiss'd
    By nightshade, ruby grape of Proserpine;
Make not your rosary of yew-berries,
    Nor let the beetle, nor the death-moth be
        Your mournful Psyche, nor the downy owl
A partner in your sorrow's mysteries;
    For shade to shade will come too drowsily,
        And drown the wakeful anguish of the soul.

2.

But when the melancholy fit shall fall
    Sudden from heaven like a weeping cloud,
That fosters the droop-headed flowers all,

And hides the green hill in an April shroud;
Then glut thy sorrow on a morning rose,
   Or on the rainbow of the salt sand-wave,
    Or on the wealth of globed peonies;
Or if thy mistress some rich anger shows,
   Emprison her soft hand, and let her rave,
    And feed deep, deep upon her peerless eyes.

3.

She dwells with Beauty—Beauty that must die;
   And Joy, whose hand is ever at his lips
Bidding adieu; and aching Pleasure nigh,
   Turning to poison while the bee-mouth sips:
Ay, in the very temple of Delight
   Veil'd Melancholy has her sovran shrine,
    Though seen of none save him whose strenuous tongue
Can burst Joy's grape against his palate fine;
   His soul shall taste the sadness of her might,
    And be among her cloudy trophies hung.

John Keats, "What the Thrush Said" (1819)

O thou whose face hath felt the Winter's wind
Whose eye has seen the snow-clouds hung in mist,
And the black elm tops, 'mong the freezing stars,
To thee the spring will be a harvest-time.
O thou, whose only book has been the light
Of supreme darkness which thou feddest on
Night after night when Phœbus was away!
To thee the Spring shall be a triple morn.
O fret not after knowledge—I have none,
And yet my song comes native with the warmth.
O fret not after knowledge—I have none,
And yet the Evening listens. He who saddens
At the thought of idleness cannot be idle,
And he's awake who thinks himself asleep.

20

•

Hypochondriasis and Melancholia

GRIESINGER

WILHELM GRIESINGER WAS BORN IN 1817. The son of a hospital administrator in the German city of Stuttgart, he pursued medical studies first in Tübingen, then in Zurich, and finally in Paris, before settling down to practice at the insane asylum in Winnenthal at the age of twenty-three. It was in Winnenthal that he conceived of his book *Mental Pathology and Therapeutics,* from which passages are reproduced here. Griesinger's interest in medicine went beyond mental disease. Starting in 1843, he took academic posts in medicine in several German universities and then from 1850 to 1852 worked in Egypt, where he completed important work on infectious diseases. Returning to Germany, he taught medicine and also psychiatry, first in Tübingen and later in Zurich. For the three years before his death in 1868, he taught neurology and psychiatry at the University of Berlin.

Griesinger will be remembered as one of the greatest influences on Emil Kraepelin, who was to dominate German psychiatry in the last two decades of the nineteenth century. More generally, Griesinger is credited with leading German psychiatry toward a position of preeminence in the second half of the nineteenth century, a place previously held by the French. He did so by resolving infighting between two polarized camps within German thinking about mental disorder, the "psychicists," who applied mentalistic language and presuppositions to mental disorder, and the "somaticists," whose materialistic metaphysics left them hostile to what they saw as the moralistic and overly poetic approach of their rivals. Griesinger sided with the "somaticists" at the level of metaphysics. He opens his book with the uncompromising assertion that "mental diseases are brain diseases." As a young man in the 1840s, moreover, he cofounded an anti-Romantic reform publication, the *Journal of Physiological Medicine.* Nonetheless, he recognized the importance of psychological symptoms (he called them the *pathophysiology)* in mental disease. Influenced by the philosopher and mathematician J. F. Herbart (1776–1841), he believed in the "unity of body and soul," and acknowledged that until underlying brain lesions could be identified, psychiatric nosology must conform to areas of psychological functioning. His confidence that brain lesions would eventually be found to underlie mental diseases led to a German emphasis on the anatomy and pathology of the brain throughout the second half of the century.

Although he wrote other works as well, including a book on infectious diseases, Griesinger is best remembered for *Mental Pathology and Therapeutics,* his great book on psychiatry. This text was first published in 1845, but in 1867 it appeared in the expanded second edition from which the following passages are drawn.

In its more than 500 pages, this work covers the causes and forms of mental disease, as well as its pathological anatomy (with chapters on the parts of the brain) and treatment (there are chapters on physical treatment, moral treatment, and lunatic asylums). The passages excerpted here from the third book, devoted to the forms of mental disease, and are selected to reveal Griesinger's view that there is but one mental disease, whose course includes an initial phase of melancholia. Griesinger adhered to the "unitary psychosis" classification until the very end of his life, when he was persuaded to accept in addition the existence of L. D. C. Snell's "Primary Verrucktheit," (corresponding to our present-day notion of paranoid states).

The classification of this part of Griesinger's work breaks into the three sorts of state he believed generally followed one another during the course of a single mental disorder. First were melancholic states, which were followed by states of mental exaltation or mania; finally, the patient ended in chronic dementia. Thus chapter 1 is devoted to states of mental depression, chapter 2 to states of mental exaltation, and chapter 3 to states of mental weakness. The passages that follow are from chapter 1, in which Griesinger offers a general account of "the melancholia which precedes insanity" and its subforms, which include hypochondriasis, melancholia with stupor, melancholia with destructive, including suicidal tendencies, melancholia with persistent excitement of the will, and "melancholia in a more limited sense," which corresponds most closely to the disposition and mood states we associated with earlier traditions on melancholy. Melancholia in a more limited sense is described as a state of mental pain, a "profound feeling of ill-being, of inability to do anything, of suppression of the physical powers, of depression and sadness."

Griesinger's confusing subclassification into melancholia "in a more limited sense," which allows a broader and a more exact notion of melancholic states, is revealing. It suggests a shift away from the delusional symptoms of melancholia emphasized in the eighteenth century toward symptoms centered on mood and feeling. In addition, it foreshadows a twentieth-century confusion, which still prevails, whereby *melancholia* sometimes is restricted. In contrast to the term *depression,* which encompasses a broader range of signs and symptoms, *melancholia* sometimes refers only to anhedonic mood states.

From Wilhelm Griesinger,
"States of Mental Depression—Melancholia,"
in *Mental Pathology and Therapeutics* (1867)

The fundamental affection in all these forms of disease consists in the morbid influence of a painful depressing negative affection—in a mentally painful state. This state may, at the outset, in the simplest and the most primitive form of melancholia, continue in the form of a vague feeling of oppression, anxiety, dejection, and gloom; generally, however, this obscure vague feeling of annoyance passes into a single, concrete, painful perception; there arise thoughts and opinions in harmony with the actual disposition of mind, and without external motive (false ideas)—a veritable delirium, revolving constantly upon some tormenting and painful subject, while at the same time the intellect presents some anomalous forms, is restrained in the exercise of its freedom, becomes slow and sluggish, and the thoughts monotonous and vacant. The normal reaction towards the external world is either weakened and blunted (mental anæsthesia, indifference even to actual stupor), or exaggerated in such a manner that all mental impressions are painful (mental hyperæsthesia); and very often these two forms are found in the same patient alternating with each other. Many disorders of the emotion and of the will are moreover associated with this. Their varieties form a basis for the distinction of the several principal forms of melancholia. Sometimes volition is directly diminished and weakened, at other times it is convulsively restricted (absence of energy and will); at others there appear certain desires and impulses of will to which material and object are afforded by the morbid mind; or, lastly, a high degree of moral pain excites various impulses of an aimless convulsive character, which manifest themselves in extreme restlessness, the continuance and increase of which cause these forms of melancholia to assume a different character, and to pass into quite another variety of that of mania.

> In employing the term "states of mental depression," we do not wish to be understood as implying that the nature of these states or conditions consists in inaction and weakness, or in the *suppression* of the mental or cerebral phenomena which accompany them. We have much more cause to assume that very violent *states of irritation* of the brain and excitation in the mental processes are here very often the cause; but *the general result* of these (mental and cerebral) processes is depression or a painful state of mind. It is sufficient to recall the analogy to physical pain; and to those who imagine that they make things better by substituting *"cerebral torpor"* and *"cerebral irritation"* for "depression" and "exaltation," it may fairly enough be objected that in melancholia there is also a state of irritation.

Observation shows that the immense majority of mental diseases commence with a state of profound emotional perversion, of a depressing and sorrowful character. Guislain was the first to elucidate this highly interesting fact, and make it at all serviceable. Of its general correctness there is no doubt, and we can have no hesitation in speaking of the *"stadium melancholicum"* as the initiatory period of mental disease. Of course there are exceptions. Thus, in senile dementia, in periodic mania, in meningitis, in the mental diseases consecutive to typhus fever, pneumonia, cholera, sun-stroke, &c., the outbreak of mania is generally observed without being preceded by melancholia; but the cases are much more frequent in which this *stadium melancholicum* only *appears* to be absent because it was less intense, and was not then recognised as a stage of mental disease.

The *"stadium melancholicum"* which precedes insanity is by some physicians designated as the period of incubation, or "prodromal stadium"; and, in their opinion, the outbreak of the disease dates only from the time when the patient is no longer able to control his actions. This limitation is to a certain extent arbitrary, but the circumstance that the stage of incubation has almost always a depressive character is interesting and of great importance.

The melancholia which precedes insanity sometimes appears externally as the direct continuation of some painful emotion dependent upon some objective cause (moral causes of insanity), *e.g.,* grief, jealousy; and it is distinguished from the mental pain experienced by healthy persons by its excessive degree, by its more than ordinary protraction, by its becoming more and more independent of external influences, and by the other accessory affections which accompany it. In other cases the melancholia originates without any moral cause, though most frequently there are such, but it does not originate as their direct continuation, but only shows itself after these affections have wrought considerable disturbances in the functions and nutrition of the nervous system, or have undermined the entire constitution. . . .

Melancholia in a More Limited Sense

Anomalies of self-consciousness, of the desires, and the will.—In many cases, after a period of longer or shorter duration, a state of vague mental and bodily discomfort, often with hypochondriacal perversion, depression and restlessness, sometimes with the dread of becoming insane, passes off, a state of mental pain becomes always more dominant and persistent, but is increased by every external mental impression. This is the essential mental disorder in melancholia, and, so far as the patient himself is concerned, the mental pain consists in a profound feeling of *ill-being,* of inability to do anything, of suppression of the physical powers, of depression and sadness, and of total abasement of self-consciousness. So soon as this condition of the sensorium attains a certain stage, the most important and wide-spread consequences, as regards the demeanour of the patient, result.

The disposition assumes an entirely negative character (that of abhorrence or repulsion). All impressions, even the slightest and formerly most agreeable, excite pain. The patient can no longer rejoice in anything, not even the most pleasing. Everything affects him uncomfortably, and in all that happens around him he finds new sources of pain. Everything has become repulsive to him; he has become irritable and angry. Every trifle puts him out of temper. The result is, either perpetual expressions of discontent, or—and this is more common—he endeavours to escape from all outward mental impressions, by withdrawing himself from the society of men, and, completely idle and unemployed, seeking solitude. This general feeling of aversion and indifference is often expressed by a dislike towards those by whom he is surrounded, his family, friends, and relatives, which often merges into absolute hatred—by a complete and unhappy change in his character.

We may sometimes observe in individuals apparently healthy (particularly among females) a similar though much more chronic state of habitual perversion of sentiment, accompanied by a capricious and morose disposition, with a tendency to contradiction and ill-nature. Nevertheless, it is very rarely that this is regarded as a morbid state, even although it differs widely from similar evil dispositions which we see sometimes displayed in those who are perfectly healthy,—through its frequent origin from palpable diseases, through its frequent remissions, which are explicable by no well-grounded mental motive, and through the fact that at times the patient feels himself constrained to yield to the evil disposition in direct opposition to the dictates of his conscience and his will, and although he is perfectly aware that such conduct is most unwarrantable.

In simple melancholia we frequently find a condition of the sensorium precisely analogous to that which we have described under the head of Hypochondria, in which the objects of the outer world, although they come into consciousness through the medium of the senses, and are indeed properly understood and recognised, still they produce an impression utterly different from what they were wont to do, of which the intelligent and educated sufferers can alone give a true description. "It appears to me," says such a melancholic, "that everything around me is precisely as it used to be, although there must have been changes. Everything around me wears the old aspect, everything appears as it was, and yet there must have been great changes," &c. This confounding by the patient of the subjective change of exterior things, and then objective change, is the commencement of that dreamy state, in which, when it has attained to a tolerably high degree, it appears to the patient as if the real world had actually and completely vanished,—that it has sunk, disappeared, or is dead, and all that now remains to him is an imaginary world, in the midst of which he is perpetually tormented by finding that he has still to live.

At the beginning of this state the patient is perfectly cognisant of the change which has taken place in his moral nature, in all his feelings and affections. Sometimes he seeks to hide it, and the inquiries concerning the cause of his peculiar behaviour weary and annoy him. He feels that his former enjoyment in everything that was honorable and estimable is fast passing into indifference and actual repugnance. He even complains himself that his sensations are no longer natural, that they are perverted; and when his evil genius constrains him to regard the worst side of the world, a new source of pain and sorrow is presented to him, viz., that he can rejoice about nothing, and must oppose everything. The unwonted impressions from the outer world excite his astonishment, grief, and fear. He feels himself excluded from his former intercourse with society; and this feeling of isolation, this exceptional position in which he finds himself, favours, on the one hand, the limitation of all ideas concerning the relation in which he stands to the world, and the relation of external objects to himself. On the other hand, there proceeds from this feeling of isolation, distrust, anxiety, and fear of all possible evils—sometimes a feeling of hatred and revenge towards the world, but more often a powerless, helpless withdrawal from society and concentration in himself.

That which weighs most heavily upon the mind of the patient at the commencement of his trouble, is that feeling of change which has taken place in his own personality, that vagueness and obscurity arising from this undefined feeling of annoyance. Yet at this stage he is sometimes perfectly aware that his fears are absurd, and that those uneasy thoughts which force themselves upon him are utterly false; and he is even conscious of his own actual state. But then, he perceives that it is impossible for him to feel, to think, to act otherwise than he does,—that he cannot resist, and how useless every effort at resistance is; then he receives from this overcoming of the *Ego* the idea of being ruled, of being irresistibly abandoned to some foreign influence, to which, afterwards, ideas of being governed by evil powers, of secret direction of the thoughts, of demoniacal possession, &c., correspond.

The limitation of the will, which is one of the fundamental disorders of melancholia, is manifested by inactivity, cessation of all employment, constant doubt and irresolution, incapacity of decision and absence of will. In the higher degrees, it shows itself in actual torpidity and dulness of feeling, inasmuch as impressions are no longer followed by a reaction of the will; in the more moderate degrees, as slowness, monotony, hesitation in movement and action, feeling of incapacity for the slightest mental exertion, lying in bed, &c.

Frequently there are sensations of intense anxiety, which often appear to spring from the epigastric and cardiac regions, and to mount upwards. "Here," say many of these patients, pointing to the epigastrium—"here it remains like a stone: would that I could get rid of it!" These feelings of anxiety sometimes increase to such an extent as to be almost unbearable; thus driving the patient into a state of despair, which generally passes into an attack of mania. Moreover, these states manifest themselves externally in many various forms, according to the former disposition of the patient, the moral causes, and accompanying physical anomalies, &c.: at times, with the outward signs of grief and care, or as silent melancholy, as self-concentration, or a dull, passionless, reserved bearing; sometimes as loud self-accusation, with weeping, wringing of the hands, and great restlessness; sometimes as morbid peculiarity and intractable obstinacy; or, finally, as a tendency to lay violent hands on self.

There are some melancholics who are always discontented, and whom nothing pleases; others to whom everything is alike indifferent, because their attention is completely absorbed in the contemplation of their own misfortune; and others who maintain that for them "everything is too good, and they cannot understand how it is that people do not despise such miserable creatures as they are."

All these varieties in the disposition of melancholics are at the commencement generally unaccountable, and do not depend on certain definite delirious conceptions; therefore it is that the patient himself is also, at this stage, perfectly incapable of giving any statement which might account for his present condition. "I am afraid," says such a patient; and if asked why, he can only reply, "I don't know, but I am afraid" (Esquirol). Hence, we are constrained to come to the conclusion—which, indeed, observation has led us to, and serves only every day to confirm—that exhortations, solicitude, and argument have not the slightest effect upon this state of depression, engendered by some cerebral lesion; and that the ideas which conduce to the development of this state must have an internal, subjective origin, and therefore a character of irrefutability, so that they render the patient wholly impervious to anything like argument, and at best only permit him to exchange one mournful train of ideas for another.

21

"Autumn Song" and "Spleen"

BAUDELAIRE

CHARLES BAUDELAIRE, a French poet of the Romantic era, lived between 1821 and 1867. His short life was troubled and erratic, and in his lifetime he published only one volume of poems, *Les Fleurs du Mal* (*The Flowers of Evil*). He was troubled, moody, rebellious, and given to religious mysticism. His life was marked by Bohemian excesses, illness, and despondent and despairing mood states such as we find conveyed in the two hauntingly sad poems reproduced here.

At the age of seventeen, after brilliant studies in Lyons and Paris, Baudelaire decided to become a poet. His parents worried about the excesses of his Bohemian life, and when he was twenty they sent him as a ship's apprentice on a boat bound for Calcutta. He did not get farther than Mauritius before returning home to the irregular life he had been leading in Paris, but he had been deeply impressed by the exotic charm of that island.

Baudelaire's first publications were in the field of art and poetry criticism. He believed criticism was the function of the poet, and he drew admiration for his critical writing. But *Les Fleurs du Mal,* first published in 1857, was initially condemned as obscene. (It later received recognition, and was enlarged and republished in 1861 and 1868.) A collection of poetic prose pieces was published posthumously (1869), as were two volumes of criticism (*Curiosites esthetiques* [1868] and *L'Art romantique* [1869]).

Baudelaire belonged to the symbolist school. His poetry, classical in form, established symbolic correspondences among sensory images such as sounds, scents, colors.

Both poems reproduced here are from *Les Fleurs du Mal.* "Chant D'Autonme" ("Autumn Song") is an expression of the poet's heavy sadness as the change of season conveys the imminence of death. The first section evokes the coming of winter, in the climate and in the soul; the familiar noises of the city seem like a scaffolding being erected, or his own coffin being built. In later stanzas not reproduced here, the poet turns to address the woman at his side. He will find comfort with her, although she cannot reconcile him with death.

The poem entitled "Spleen" is even more unremittingly mournful;

its portrait of the melancholy sensibility is unsurpassed. The inner state of the "plaintive soul prey to endless melancholy" is dark, without hope, frightening, painful, and full of tedium and despair.

Like Keats's conjunction of sadness with pleasure introduced earlier, Baudelaire's writing reflects the alignment between sadness and beauty common in Romantic poetry. "I have found the definition of beauty," wrote Beaudelaire in his journal. "It is something of ardor and sadness . . . of voluptuousness and sadness,—which conveys an idea of melancholy, of lassitude, even of satiation" ([1887] 1920:84). For the Romantics, as Mario Praz has put it, beauty was enhanced by exactly those qualities that seem to deny it, by those objects that produce horror: "The sadder, the more painful it was, the more intensely" they cherished it (Praz, 1968:27).

In his preface to the 1868 edition of *The Flowers of Evil,* the poet Théophile Gautier was to present Baudelaire's work as "decadent," and Baudelaire has subsequently come to be identified with the decadent movement of the last part of the nineteenth century. Gautier's famous description includes reference to "the morbidly rich tints of decomposition, . . . the bitumens blacked and browned in the depths of hell, and all that gamut of intensified colours, correspondent to autumn, and the setting of the sun, to overripe fruit, and the last hours of civilization" (Gautier, 1868, quoted in Gilman, 1979:89).

·～ ● ～·

From Charles Baudelaire, "Autumn Song,"
from *Flowers of Evil* (1857)

Soon will we plunge into the cold darkness;
Farewell, brilliant light of our too brief summers!
Already I hear the mournful thud
Of falling logs on the courtyard cobbles.

All of winter will enter my being: anger,
Hate, chills, horror, hard labor,
And like the sun in its polar hell,
My heart will turn a red and frozen block.

Trembling, I listen to each log fall;
The scaffold being raised has no duller echo.
My soul is as the crumbling tower
Under the heavy and ceaseless blows of the battering ram.

Lulled by the monotonous thud, it seems to me
That someone somewhere hastily nails a coffin.
For whom?—Yesterday it was summer; Fall has come.
This mysterious sound rings out like a passing. . . .

Charles Baudelaire, "Spleen,"
from *Flowers of Evil* (1857)

When the low and heavy sky weighs down like a damper
On the plaintive soul prey to endless melancholy,
And from the encircling horizon
Spills upon us a dark day gloomier than night;

When the earth becomes a damp cell
Where Hopefulness, like a bat,
Flaps its timid wing against the walls
And hits its head on rotting beams;

When the rain spreading its huge swath
Falls like the bars of a vast prison,
And a mute throng of repulsive spiders
Hangs its nets in the depths of our brains,

Suddenly bells strike furiously
And send their awful bellowing to the skies,
Like errant souls without a home
They begin their unrelenting moan.

—And long hearses, without drums or music,
Files past slowly in my soul: Hope,
Vanquished, weeps, and horrible despotic Despair,
Plants its black flag on my bowed head.

22

Green Sickness and Wertherism

ONE OF ELEVEN CHILDREN, Samuel Smiles was born in 1812, in the Scottish town of Haddington in East Lothian. Although his work is seldom read or remembered today, Smiles was an influential figure in the nineteenth-century "self-help" movement. As a youth he was trained to be a doctor, at first in Haddington and later at the University of Edinburgh. Until 1838, when he became a newspaper editor, he practiced medicine and wrote on medical subjects; after 1845 he gave up these pursuits to run the new Leeds and Thirsk Railway. He continued to be a prolific writer and speaker and published twenty-three books in his lifetime, including works on history, political and ethical tracts, and biography. He died in 1904.

Smiles's book *Self-help: With Illustrations of Character, Conduct and Perseverance* (1859) grew out of a series of lectures, designed for self-improvement, which he gave to young men as editor of the *Leeds Times* newspaper, and the following passages are from an 1862 American edition of that work. His theme was that diligent self-culture, self-control, and self-discipline held the key to human fulfillment; his motto: "It all depends on me." After the success of *Self-help,* Smiles went on to publish further on this theme, in works on character (1871), thrift (1875), duty (1880), and labor (1887).

"Green sickness" is an expression that captures the set of attributes— "a tendency toward discontent, unhappiness, inaction and reverie"— often associated with melancholy but known also, in Smiles's era, by the terms Byronism and Wertherism. That these traits are unhealthy, Smiles does not doubt. But he is also confident that they can be cured, as can all such character defects, by cultivating habits of cheerfulness, optimism, and physical exercise and activity.

Smiles's negative comments on Romanticism and the decadence he associates with it reflect a nineteenth century reaction to what had been an influential movement. Not only in England but also in America and continental Europe, Byron's poetry and life inspired, "Byronism," an approach to life characterized by contempt for conventional morality, combined with rather hectic and exaggerated elation, melancholy, and despair. "Weary of love, of life, devoured with spleen," Byron writes of himself ([1806] 1980:158). Wertherism was a movement following upon the publication of Goethe's *Sorrows of Young Werther* in 1774. This short epistolary novel was widely read and translated into several languages. Like Byronism, Wertherism was associated with Romantic excesses, heroic despair, and melancholy.

Dr. William Ellery Channing, to whom Smiles refers, was an American clergyman and thinker of the first half of the nineteenth century. To Channing's influence is attributed the elevated and religious spirit of the transcendentalist poetry of his contemporaries Emerson and Longfellow, and Channing shared Smiles's apprehension over the popularity of Byronism and other forms of perceived decadence.

The influence of thinkers like Smiles and Channing and the self-help movement Smiles generated are easily overlooked today. Yet this emphasis on and disgust with the unmanly, unmasculine quality of the Romantic melancholy popularized by Goethe and Byron may account in significant part for the curious gender reversal by which, toward the end of the nineteenth century melancholy, melancholia, and related responses came to be associated with women and the feminine.

·◡ ● ◡·

From Samual Smiles, *Self-help: Character, Conduct and Perseverance* (1862)

Cheerfulness is an excellent working quality, imparting great elasticity to the character. As a bishop has said, "Temper is nine-tenths of Christianity," so are cheerfulness and diligence nine-tenths of practical wisdom. They are the life and soul of success, as well as of happiness; perhaps the very highest pleasure in life consisting in clear, brisk, conscious working; energy, confidence, and every other good quality mainly depending on it.

In our day, [physical] exercises have somewhat fallen into disrepute, and education has become more exclusively mental; very much to the detriment of the bodily health. The brain is cultivated at the expense of the members, and the physical is usually found in an inverse ratio to the intellectual appetite. Hence, in this age of progress, we find so many stomachs weak as blotting-paper—hearts indicating "fatty degeneration,"—unused, pithless hands, calfless legs and limp bodies, without any elastic spring in them. But it is not merely health that suffers by neglect and disuse of bodily organs. The mind itself grows sickly and distempered, the pursuit of knowledge itself is impeded, and manhood becomes withered, twisted, and stunted. It is, perhaps, to this neglect of physical exercise that we find amongst students so frequently a tendency toward discontent, unhappiness, inaction and reverie—displaying itself in a premature contempt for real life, and disgust at the beaten tracks of men,—a tendency which in England has been called Byronism, and in Germany Wertherism. Dr. Channing noted the same growth in America, which led him to make the remark that, "too many of our young men grow up in a school of despair." The only remedy for this green-sickness in youth is abundant physical exercise—action, work, and bodily occupation of any sort.

It is indeed scarcely possible to over-estimate the importance of training the young to virtuous habits. . . . Even happiness itself may become habitual. There is a habit of looking at the bright side of things, and also of looking at the dark side. Dr. Johnson has said that the habit of looking at the best side of a thing is worth more to a man than a thousand pounds a year. And we possess the power, to a great extent, of so exercising the will as to direct the thoughts upon objects calculated to yield happiness and improvement rather than their opposites. In this way the habit of happy thought may be made to spring up like any other habit. And to bring up men or women with a genial nature of this sort, a good temper, and a happy frame of mind, is perhaps of even more importance, in many cases, than to perfect them in much knowledge and many accomplishments.

23

Affectivity in Mental Disorder

MAUDSLEY

Living between 1835 and 1918, Henry Maudsley oversaw and greatly shaped the development of British psychiatry in this crucial period. Moreover, before he died, he gave money to the London County Council for the purpose of building "a hospital for the treatment of mental diseases," and the Maudsley Hospital in London stand today as a testament to his vision and memory.

Maudsley was born on the west coast of Yorkshire, into an old farming family, schooled in the local town of Giggleswick, and then sent to boarding school before attending London University and undertaking the five-year medical apprenticeship and training program at the University Hospital. Graduating in 1856, he took work in small Yorkshire asylums until he was appointed to the position of medical superintendent of the Manchester Asylum, a position he held for three years. During this time he had begun to write for the prestigious *Journal of Mental Science,* and he was employed as joint editor and eventually editor of this publication for many years. In this role, he advocated an increase in clinical education and encouraged the introduction of European ideas (interestingly, Maudsley was himself much influenced by the great German classifier Griesinger).

In the 1870s Maudsley was appointed to the chair of medical jurisprudence at University College, London, and he wrote extensively on legal and forensic matters during that period. The best known example of this writing is *Responsibility and Mental Disease* (1874), widely read in England and the United States. In addition, he wrote about other issues relating to mental illness, in books, journal articles, and also the editorials he produced for the *Journal of Mental Science.*

One of Maudsley's themes was the physiological basis for all mental disorders. This emphasis is central in *The Physiology and Pathology of the Mind,* from which the following excerpts are taken. This work, his classic, first appeared as a 442-page book in 1867 and was much expanded in subsequent editions; it eventually was published in two volumes entitled *Physiology of Mind* and *Pathology of Mind.* Maudsley's determination to treat all mental phenomena from a "physical" rather than a "metaphysical" point of view is announced in the preface, and is characteristic. Throughout his long career, one group of historians has observed, Maudsley "was to devote much of his considerable intellectual energy to a sustained and consistently hostile polemic against the 'absurdity' of metaphysical musings about insanity, denouncing again and again as 'fruitless' and 'unscientific' all attempts to study mind 'from the psychological point of view' . . ." (Scull, MacKenzie, and Hervey, 1996:235). This relentless effort led to Maudsley being credited with shifting the attention of British psychiatrists from a metaphysical focus to a physical one.

The psychological symptoms of insanity, then, were in certain respects relatively insignificant in Maudsley's view. They played an epiphenomenal role only. Nonetheless, they, rather than the physiological features of mental disorders, were for Maudsley the basis of a classification system, as the passages here reveal. And in this respect Maudsley's (internally felt) "symptom"-based classification differs markedly from the (externally observed) "sign"-based analyses of Kraepelin. By emphasizing the psychological symptoms and symptom clusters distinguishing one disorder from another, Maudsley put forward a classification that was *descriptive* rather than *etiological* (causal). He believed that organic causes would eventually be found to correspond to the surface descriptions permitted by his symptom-based classification. But he was unprepared to posit physiological divisions before such scientific discovery should take place.

Both Maudsley's emphasis on the physiological basis of mental disorder and his distinctive diagnostic classification, exemplified here in his division between different kinds of insanity, have been the source of disagreement among historians attempting to evaluate his contribution. Sir Aubrey Lewis, renowned director of the Institute of Psychiatry in London, considered the year 1867 a turning point in English psychiatry because it saw the publication of Maudsley's great classic. But G. Zilboorg, the American historian of psychiatry, dismisses Maudsley's contribution: his psychiatry was "purely materialistic and purely descriptive," and his classification unenlightened (Zilboorg and Henry, 1941).

Maudsley's classification is complex and somewhat confusing. The forms of insanity encompass those affecting the feelings (affective insanity) and those affecting ideational or intellectual functioning (ideational insanity). This is roughly the division between forms of insanity without and with delusions. Within this broad division, which guides the classification offered in chapter 3 of the 1867 edition reproduced here, melancholia and mania fall under the heading of ideational insanity (they involve delusions). But two additional features of Maudsley's scheme complicate this picture. Although Maudsley distinguishes affective insanity from the intellectual or ideational forms, *all* insanity for Maudsley is inaugurated by a "disturbance of the affective life" (1867:321). Affective disorder is the "fundamental fact": in the great majority of cases, affective disorder precedes intellectual disorder; it "coexists with" intellectual disorder during its course, and it persists after intellectual disorder has disappeared (302). Using the word *moral* to mean "of the feelings," Maudsley quotes with approval the French authority Esquirol, who remarks that moral alienation is the "proper," or we might say "real" or "central," characteristic of mental derangement.

As this emphasis on the pervasive presence of affective disturbance in all mental disorder suggests, Maudsley is employing the term *affective* in two distinct senses. When he marks the distinction between affective insanity and ideational insanity, he is concerned with feelings as the springs of action. He uses *affective* to denote volitional and even moral faculties. Thus, the two sorts of affective insanity concern impulsivity, and something close to our twentieth-century notion of psychopathy or sociopathy, where there is an inability or unwillingness to conform to societal norms. (This second notion, as Maudsley recognizes, he owes to the category of moral insanity put forward earlier by the English physician Prichard [1786–1848].)

This sense of affectivity places melancholia, with mania, in the nonaffective category. Nonetheless, the category of ideational insanity is now subdivided, as he says, "according to the character of the accompanying *feeling* (my emphasis). When there is "great oppression of the self-feeling with corresponding gloomy morbid idea," we have melancholia (Maudsley, 1867:320).

Finally, Maudsley proposes that the essential division between mental disorders should rest on the presence or absence of delusions. With such a division, he shows, we would find melancholia in several forms. Unaccompanied by delusions, it takes the form of a melancholic depression, or as simple melancholia. Accompanied by delusions, melancholia may be a form of partial insanity or a more general insanity, depending on the extent of those delusions.

•⤳ • ↜•

From Henry Maudsley, "Varieties of Insanity," from
The Physiology and Pathology of the Mind (1867)

There are certain mild forms of Insanity, or rather certain eccentricities of thought, feeling, and conduct, that scarcely reach the degree of positive insanity, which not unfrequently cause great difficulty when the question of legal or moral responsibility is concerned. Many people who cannot be called insane, notably have what may be called the insane temperament—in other words, a defective or unstable condition of nerve element, which is characterised by the disposition to sudden, singular, and impulsive caprices of thought, feeling, and conduct. This condition, in the causation of which hereditary taint is commonly detectable, may be described as the *Diathesis spasmodica,* or the *Neurosis spasmodica.*

1. *The Insane Temperament,* or *Neurosis spasmodica.*—It is characterised by singularities or eccentricities of thought, feeling, and action. It cannot truly be said of any one so constituted that he is mad, but he is certainly strange, or "queer," or, as it is said, "not quite right." What he does he must often do in a different way from all the rest of the world. If he thinks about anything, he is apt to think about it under strange and novel relations, which would not have occurred to an ordinary person; his feeling of an event is unlike that which other people have of it. He is sometimes impressionable to subtle and usually unrecognised influences; and now and then he does whimsical and apparently quite purposeless acts. There is in the constitution an innate tendency to act independently as an element in the social system, and there is a personal gratification in the indulgence of such disposition, which to lookers-on seems to mark great self-feeling and vanity. Such a one, therefore, is deemed, by the automatic beings who perform their duties in the social system with equable regularity, as odd, queer, strange, or not quite right.

This peculiarity of temperament, which undoubtedly predisposes to insanity, does nevertheless in some instances border very closely upon genius; it is the condition of the talent or wit which is allied to madness, only divided from it by thin partitions. The novel mode of looking at things may be an actual advance upon the accepted system of thought; the individual may be in a minority of one, not because he sees less than, or not so well as, all the world, but because he happens to see deeper, or to be favoured with a flash of intuitive insight. He may differ from all the world, not because he is wrong, and all the world is right, but because he is right, and all the world is wrong. Of necessity every new truth is at first in a minority of one; it is a rebellion against the existing system of belief; accordingly the existing system, ever thinking itself a finality, strives with all the weight of its established organization to crush it out. But by the nature of things that must happen, whether the novelty be a truth or an error. After all, it is only through the appearance of rebels in the social system that progress is effected; and precisely because individuality is a reproach, and sneered at as an eccentricity, is it well for the world, as Mr. J. S. Mill has said, that individuality or eccentricity should exist. It may be advisable to set this matter forth at greater length, to the end that we may, if possible, get a just conception of the real relation of certain sorts of talent to insanity. . . .

It is undoubtedly true, that where hereditary taint exists in a family, one member may sometimes exhibit considerable genius, while another is insane or epileptic; but the fact plainly proves no more than that in both there has been a great natural sensibility of nervous constitution which, under different outward circumstances, or internal conditions, has issued differently in the two cases. Now we may properly look at the functional manifestations of unstable nerve element from two different aspects—first, as regards the reception of impressions; and, secondly, as regards the reaction outwards. In the first case, for example, we may have one who is equal to the ordinary events of a calm life, but who, possessing no reserve power, breaks down under the stress of adverse events. And yet his extreme nervous susceptibility may render him capable of slighter shades and subtler delicacies of feeling and thought than a more vigorously constituted being is. The defect, then, is in some respects an advantage, although a rather perilous one, for it may approach the edge of madness: such men as Edgar Allan Poe and De Quincey illustrate this great subtlety of sensibility, amounting almost to disease, and so far give some colour to the extravagant assertion of a French author (Moreau de Tours), that a morbid state of nervous element is the condition of genius. It should not be lost sight of, however, that any one so constituted is nowise an example of the highest genius; for he lacks, by reason of his great sensibility, the power of calm, steady, and complete mental assimilation, and must fall short of the highest intellectual development. Feeling events with a too great acuteness, he is incapacitated from the calm discrimination of the unlike in them, and the steady assimilation of the like, by which the integration of the highest mental faculties is accomplished,—by which, in fact, the truly creative imagination of the greatest poet and the powerful and almost intuitive ratiocination of the greatest philosopher are fashioned. His insight may be marvelously subtle in certain cases, but he is not sound and comprehensive. Although it might be said, then, by one not caring to be exact, that the genius of an acutely sensitive and subjective poet denoted a morbid condition of nerve element, yet no one, after a moment's calm reflection, would venture to speak of the genius of such as Shakespeare, Goethe, and Humboldt, as arising out of a morbid condition. The impulse which instigates these men to their superior striving, is not so much one of dissatisfaction as one of nonsatisfaction— a craving, in fact, for appropriation: the internal potentialities display their endeavour towards realization through the concurrence of suitable external impressions by a feeling of want, a craving, or an unsatisfied instinct—not otherwise than as the lower organic elements manifest their sense of hunger, or as the sexual instinct reveals its want at puberty. The difference between the desires which are the motives to action of the highly endowed, well-balanced nature of the genius, and the desires which instigate the eccentric and violent acts of the incipient madman, is indeed very much the difference between the natural feeling of hunger in the healthy organism, and the perverted appetite for garbage and dirt which the hysterical person occasionally displays. In the former case the aspiration is sound, and directed towards perfecting a harmony between the individual and nature; in the latter, it is unsound, and tends to the production of an irreconcilable discord. . . .

Thus much concerning those peculiarities of temperament which do not reach the degree of positive insanity, although they strongly predispose to it. I shall now go on to treat of the different varieties of actual mental disease. On a general survey of the symptoms of these varieties it is at once apparent that they fall into two well-marked groups: one of these embracing all those cases in which the mode of *feeling* or the *affective* life is chiefly or solely perverted—in which the whole habit or manner of feeling, the mode of affection of the individual by events, is entirely changed; the other, those cases in which *ideational* or *intellectual* derangement predominates. More closely scanning the character and course of the symptoms, it will be seen that the affective disorder is the fundamental fact; that in the great majority of cases it precedes intellectual disorder; that it co-exists with the latter during its course; and that it frequently persists for a time after this has disappeared. Esquirol rightly then declared "moral alienation to be the proper characteristic of mental derangement." "There are madmen," he says, "in whom it is difficult to find any trace of hallucination, but there are none in whom the passions and moral affections are not perverted and destroyed. I have in this particular met with no exception." To insist upon the existence of delusion as a criterion of insanity is to ignore some of the gravest and most dangerous forms of mental disease.

2. *Affective Insanity.*—The feelings mirror the real nature of the individual; it is from their depths that the impulses of action spring; the function of the intellect being to guide and control. Consequently when there is perversion of the affective life, there will be morbid feeling and morbid action; the patient's whole manner of feeling, the mode of his affection by events, is unnatural, and the springs of his action are disordered; and the intellect is unable to check or control the morbid manifestations, just as, when there is disease of the spinal cord, there may be convulsive movement, of which there is consciousness, but which the will cannot restrain. In dealing with this kind of derangement, it will be most convenient, as in the investigation of the insanity of early life, to distinguish two varieties—impulsive or instinctive insanity, and moral insanity proper.

(a) *Impulsive Insanity.*—Fixing their attention too much upon the impulsive act of violence, to the neglect of the fundamental perversion of the feelings which really exists, many writers appear to have helped to increase the confusion and uncertainty which unfortunately prevail with regard to these obscure varieties of mental disorder. Already it has been pointed out, at sufficient length, that the first symptom of an oncoming insanity commonly is an affection of the psychical tone,—in other words, a perversion of the whole manner of feeling; and what we have here to fix in the mind is that *the mode of affection* of the individual by events is entirely changed: this is the fundamental fact, from which flow as secondary facts the insane impulses, whether erotic, homicidal, or suicidal. The result of the abnormal condition of nerve element is to alter the mode of feeling of impressions: in place of that which is for the individual good being agreeable, and exciting a correspondent desire, and that which is injurious being painful, and exciting an answering desire to eschew it, the evil impression may be felt and cherished as a good, and the good impression felt and eschewed as an evil. There are not only perverted appetites, therefore, but there are perverted feelings and desires, rendering the individual a complete discord in the social organization: the morbid appetites and feelings of the hysterical woman and the singular longings of pregnancy are mild examples of a perversion of the manner of feeling and desire, which may reach the outrageous form of morbid appetite exhibited by the pregnant woman who killed her husband and pickled his body in order to eat it. The sexual appetite may exhibit strange and painful perversions, which again of necessity involve the destruction of all those finer feelings of affection and propriety in the social system that are based upon it; for it is impossible that natural and healthy love should co-exist with morbid lust. The morbid perversion of feeling may be general, so that all sorts and conditions of abnormal feelings and desires are exhibited, or it may be specially displayed in some particular mode, so that one persistent morbid feeling or desire predominates. In the latter case we have such instances of madness as those in which there is a persistent morbid desire to be hanged, and the victim of the diseased feeling is actually impelled to a homicidal act to satisfy his unnatural craving; or, again, such insanity as that of the father or mother who kills a child with the sincere purpose of sending it to heaven. The act of violence, whatever form it may take, is but the symptom of a deep morbid perversion of the nature of the individual, of a morbid state which may at any moment be excited into a convulsive activity, either by a powerful impression from without producing some great moral shock, or by some cause of bodily disturbance—intemperance, sexual exhaustion, masturbation, or menstrual disturbance. There are women, sober and temperate enough at other times, who are afflicted with an uncontrollable propensity for stimulants at the menstrual period; and every large asylum furnishes examples of exacerbation of insanity or epilepsy coincident with that function. In fact, where there is a condition of unstable equilibrium of nerve element, any cause, internal or external, exciting a certain commotion, will upset its stability, just as happens with the spinal cord under similar circumstances. By his acts, as well as by his speech, does man utter himself; gesture-language is as natural a mode of expression as speech; and it is in insanity of action that this most dangerous form of affective insanity is expressed—most dangerous indeed, because so expressed.

(b) *Moral Insanity Proper*. Whatever name it may ultimately be thought best to give it, there can be no doubt of the necessity of recognising in practice the existence of such a form of disease. If, indeed, the evidence drawn from its own nature and causation were insufficient, the fact that it is often the immediate forerunner of the severest mental disease might suffice to teach its true pathological interpretation. When, therefore, a person in good social position, possessed of the feelings that belong to a certain social state, and hitherto without reproach in all the relations of life, does, after a cause known by experience to be capable of producing every kind of insanity, suddenly undergo a great change of character, lose all good feelings, and from being truthful, temperate, and considerate, become a shameless liar, shamelessly vicious, and brutally wicked, then it will certainly be not an act of charity, but an act of justice, to suspect the effects of disease. At any rate it behoves us not to be misled in our judgment by the manifest existence in such a patient of a full knowledge of the nature of his acts—of a consciousness, in fact, of right and wrong; but to remember that disease may weaken or abolish the power of volition, without affecting consciousness. Fortified by this just principle, we shall be far better prepared for a right interpretation of the facts of a particular case than when biassed or blinded by the opposite most false principle.

3. *Ideational Insanity.*—Under this general name may be included those different varieties of insanity usually described as *Mania or Melancholia:* the unsoundness affects *ideation,* and is exhibited in delusions and intellectual alienation. Cases of ideational insanity are easily recognised to be of two principal kinds, according to the character of the accompanying feeling: in one kind there is great oppression of the self-feeling with corresponding gloomy morbid idea; in the other there is excitement or exaltation of the self-feeling, with corresponding lively expression of it in the character of the thoughts or in the conduct of the patient. The former cases belong to *Melancholia;* the latter to *Mania,* acute or chronic. Again, on looking at cases of ideational insanity, it is easily seen that there is general intellectual derangement in some, while in others the alienation seems to be confined to a small number of fixed ideas; so that we might make a division of ideational insanity into (*a*) general and (*b*) partial. If we did so, then partial ideational insanity would really correspond with what Esquirol called *Monomania,* though not with what is now usually called so; for under that name was included by him not only partial mania accompanied by an exciting or gay passion, but also partial intellectual insanity accompanied by a sad and oppressive passion; the latter he subdistinguished as *Lypemania,* but it is now commonly separated as *Melancholia.* Whether this is wisely done may admit of considerable doubt: there are met with in practice as many varieties of emotional perversion as there are varieties of morbid ideas, different patients exhibiting every degree and kind of passion, from the rapture of the exalted monomaniac to the deep gloom of the profound melancholic; and accordingly it is not always possible, under the present nomenclature, to determine satisfactorily whether a particular case belongs to monomania or to melancholia. Certain cases of melancholia do in point of fact furnish the best examples of monomania. Another reason against the present classification is that there are cases of acute melancholia in which the excitement and the derangement of ideas and conduct are so great that they run insensibly into acute mania, and might just as properly be called so: they are ex-

amples of acute ideational insanity, but whether they are classified as maniacal or melancholic is very much a matter of caprice or accident.

A third objection to an adherence to the present artificial classification is, that it has unquestionably fettered observation, and hindered the faithful study of the natural history of insanity. The different forms of affective insanity have not been properly recognised and exactly studied because they did not fall under the time-honoured divisions; and the real manner of commencement of intellectual insanity in a disturbance of the affective life has frequently been overlooked. It is true that Guislain and Griesinger have held that a melancholic stage of depression almost invariably precedes an outbreak of mania; and there can be no doubt that the sequence is traceable in very many cases. But it cannot be admitted, as some would have it, in every case. What has been overlooked even by those who have not overlooked the preliminary affective derangement is, that there is not only (*a*) a *melancholic perversion* of the affective life preceding intellectual derangement, but that there is also (*b*) a *maniacal perversion* of the affective life, so to speak—an affective insanity which is of an excited or expansive kind, in which the individual's self-feeling is greatly exaggerated or morbidly exalted. It is a maniacal disorder of the feelings, sentiments, and acts, without delirium, and it is expressed chiefly, as the corresponding affective melancholia is, not in delusion but in the conduct of the patient. Though frequently following a brief stage of melancholic depression, this condition is sometimes primary. It is displayed in a great change of moral character: the parsimonious becomes extravagant, the modes than presumptuous and exacting, the affectionate parent thoughtless and indifferent; there is great liveliness of manner, or a restless activity as of one half-intoxicated; an overweening self-esteem is very evident, and an extravagant expenditure of money, an excessive sexual indulgence, or other intemperance, is common. The tone of the mental nature is profoundly deranged; the foundations of the mental being are shattered; and the patient is often practically less fitted for his relations in life than at a subsequent stage of the disease, when matters have gone further and the morbid action is systematized in some definite delusions. In some cases there may be less *exaltation* manifest, while the *perversion* of the affective life is more marked,—in other words, the *moral alienation* more extreme; this condition being perhaps best witnessed in that profound moral derangement which sometimes precedes a series of epileptic fits, or takes the place of an epileptic fit.

So soon as we have recognised the existence of a deep perversion of the feelings, sentiments, and acts, having a brisk maniacal rather than a gloomy melancholic character, and preceding in some cases the outbreak of intellectual derangement, we fail not to perceive how closely it is allied to, or rather how it is fundamentally identical with, those stages of insane degeneration already described as varieties of affective insanity. In fact, the *Mania sine delirio* of Pinel, the *Monomanie raisonnante ou sans délire* of Esquirol, the *Monomanie affective* of the same author, and the *Moral Insanity* of Prichard,—all are varying phases of this affective disorder, which, continued, usually ends in positive intellectual disorder or dementia. Though an earlier stage of mental degeneration than intellectual insanity, it is really, from a social point of view, a more dangerous form of mental disease; for its natural tendency is to express itself, not in words, as ideational insanity does, but in actions. It is a condition in which dangerous hallucinations and dangerous impulses are both apt to arise suddenly and to hurry the patient into some desperate act. Once more then let it be repeated, that man is not only a consciously active being, but also an unconsciously active being; and that, although the unconscious mental function is, in the state of perfect bodily health, subordinated to the directing power of the will, yet, when disease has disturbed the harmony of parts, the unconscious activity displays its effects independently of the will or even of consciousness.

For the foregoing reasons I hold that it would conduce to greater precision of knowledge, and would be followed by some valuable practical results, if the present artificial classification, which is not really in conformity with nature, and which assumes an entirely fictitious exactness, were considerably modified. If a broad division were made of insanity into two classes, namely, insanity without positive delusion and insanity with delusion, in other words, into *affective* insanity and *ideational* insanity; and if the subdivisions of these into varieties were subsequently made—would not the classification, general as it may appear, and provisional as it should be deemed, be really more scientific than one which, by postulating an exactness that does not exist, is a positive hindrance to an advance in knowledge? One desirable result of great practical consequence could not fail to follow; that is, the adequate recognition of those serious forms of mental degeneration in which there are no delusions. I have ventured accordingly in a former publication to put forward the following classification:—

I. AFFECTIVE OR PATHETIC INSANITY.

1. MANIACAL PERVERSION OF THE AFFECTIVE LIFE. MANIA SINE DELIRIO.
2. MELANCHOLIC DEPRESSION WITHOUT DELUSION. SIMPLE MELANCHOLIA.
3. MORAL ALIENATION PROPER. Approaching this, but not reaching the degree of positive insanity, is the INSANE TEMPERAMENT.

II. IDEATIONAL INSANITY.

1. GENERAL.
   a. Mania. ⎤ Acute and
   b. Melancholia. ⎦ Chronic.
2. PARTIAL.
   a. Monomania.
   b. Melancholia.
3. DEMENTIA, primary and secondary.
4. GENERAL PARALYSIS.
5. IDIOCY, including IMBECILITY.

The cases of so-called *impulsive* insanity, which for practical purposes has just been illustrated separately as a variety of affective insanity, will really fall under one or other of its above-mentioned varieties: in all of them dangerous impulses are apt to arise, and to express themselves in convulsive action; and, where a desperate impulse displays itself without any apparent affective disorder, it is only that the outward violence makes the internal derangement.

Whatever classification be adopted in the present state of our knowledge of so obscure a subject, it must be provisional. What meanwhile it is most important to bear in mind is, that the different forms of insanity are not actual pathological entities, but different degrees or kinds of the degeneration of the mental organization,—in other words, of deviation from healthy mental life; they are consequently sometimes found intermixed, replacing one another, or succeeding one another, in the same person. There is in the human mind a sufficiently strong propensity not only to make divisions in knowledge where there are none in nature, and then to impose the divisions upon nature, making the reality thus comfortable to the idea, but to go further, and to convert the generalizations made from observation into positive entities, permitting for the future these artificial creations to tyrannise over the understanding. A typical example of madness might be described as one in which the disorder, commencing in emotional disturbance and eccentricities of action—in derangement of the affective life, passes thence into melancholia or mania, and finally, by a further declension, into dementia. This is the natural course also of mental degeneration when proceeding unchecked through generations. Although then we may have the different stages passed through within the brief spaces of a single life, this is not a sufficient reason why they should not be distinguished and separately treated of; for not only may a person suffer from one kind of mental derangement without ever falling victim to another, but the different varieties run their particular course, call for their special prognosis, and require their special treatment.

(*a*) *Partial Ideational Insanity.*—This division will correspond with that originally described as monomania by Esquirol, and will include not only delusion accompanied by an exalted passion, but also delusion accompanied by a sad and oppressive passion—monomania proper and ordinary melancholia. In the former an exalted self-feeling gets embodied in a fixed delusion, or in a group of delusions, which fails not to testify an overweening self-esteem; it is clothed in a corresponding delusion of power or grandeur, and the personality of the patient, who may fancy himself king, prophet, or divine, is transformed accordingly: in the latter, the feeling of oppression of self becomes condensed into a painful delusion of being overpowered by some external agency, demonic or human, or of salvation lost through individual sins. In both cases we have a partial ideational insanity—in the one case with overweening esteem of self, in the other with oppression of self—with fixed delusion or delusions upon one subject or a few subjects, apart from which the patient reasons tolerably correctly. Pathologically, there is a systematization of the morbid action in the supreme cerebral centres, the establishment of a definite type of morbid nutrition in them.

A morbid idea, or a delusion, engendered in the mind and persisting there, may be compared with a morbid growth in some organ of the body, or with a chronic morbid action, which cannot be brought under the correcting influence of the surrounding healthy tissues, and restored to a sound type. Similarly, the morbid idea does not, as in health, call up other ideas which may supersede it, its energy being transferred, and itself becoming latent or statical under the unconscious assimilating influence of the cerebral centres, so that the present is brought into accord with the past, or with that mental organization which by an abstraction we call the *ego;* but the morbid idea is not assimilable, cannot be made of the same kind with compound elements of the mental organization, is in entire contradiction with the past, and remains unaffected by reflection, because it cannot really enter into any reflection: like a cancer, or any other strange morbid growth, it continues its own morbid life, and the whole conscious life may at any moment be brought under its dominating influence: it represents a partial automatic morbid action, like a spasm beyond the control of volition, though, like a spasm, not always beyond the knowledge of consciousness. A young man, for example, who had previously had a few epileptic fits, became extremely melancholic, being possessed with the morbid idea that he was to be murdered in his father's house; he made frequent attempts to escape from it, and the precautions taken to prevent his escape only served to strengthen his delusion. Reasoning with him was of no use, for the notion was not explicable on any reasonable principles: if a looker-on could truly enter into the steps of the mental processes by which such a delusion was generated, he would be as mad as the patient; and if the patient could appreciate the force of the reasoning by which the looker-on proves the notion to be madness, why then he would not be mad at all. It is the patient's disease that he cannot: when the constitution of his nervous element is such that an absurd delusion of that kind could persist and not be corrected by the stored-up results of past mental acquisitions—whether such as might be consciously recalled, or such as existed as statical faculties interworking in unconscious assimilating action—then it is the sure testimony of fundamental damage to the mechanism of mental action, the consequences of which are a disorder and incoherence of action inconsistent with, and therefore unintelligible to, the experience of the sound mind. The very fact that such a notion is not self-annihilating is evidence of a fundamental disorder, which, if it should not actually prepare us to look for, at any rate should make us receive without surprise, any further irrational exhibition by the patient. Hence also it is that if we admit the false premisses of the madman's delusion, he cannot follow us in rational deductions from them; he does not generally, as Locke supposed, reason correctly from false premisses; he is not logically mad; but his whole manner of action is more or less incoherent, and betrays the disease of which the delusion is a symptom. In vain do men pretend that the mind of the monomaniac is sound, apart from his delusion: not only is the diseased idea a part of the mind, and the mind, therefore, no more sound than the body is sound when a man has a serious disease of some vital organ, but the exquisitely delicate and complex mechanism of mental action is radically deranged: the morbid idea could not else have been engendered and persist. The mind is not unsound upon one point, but an unsound mind expresses itself in a particular morbid action. Moreover, when the delusion is once produced, there is no power of drawing a sanitary cordon round it, and thus, by putting it in quarantine as it were, preserving all other mental processes from infection: on the contrary, the morbid centre reacts injuriously on the neighbouring centres, and there is no guarantee that at any moment the most desperate consequences may not ensue. That was precisely what did happen in the case which we have taken for illustration: the young man, whose father was a butcher, becoming calmer after a time, and being thought trustworthy, was permitted at his own request to be present at the slaughter of an ox; but, when all was finished, he did not wish to return home. His friends, however, pressed him, and two of them, taking him by the arm in a friendly manner, accompanied him towards his home; but, just as he approached the door of his house, he suddenly drew out a butcher's knife which he had concealed, and stabbed to the heart one of them, fleeing immediately to the forest, where he passed the night. Next morning he went to the house of a relative who lived some distance off, and said that he had run away from home, as they wished to kill him there. In this case the homicidal act had a discoverable relation to the delusion, although a very insane one; but in some cases of monomaniacal delusion there is no relation whatever discoverable between the delusion and the act of violence, while in others the patient may subsequently make known a most absurd and incoherent connexion which the most sagacious looker-on would never have suspected, and cannot understand.

The signification of a persistent delusion in the mind; in regard to those intimate organic processes on which rests the integrity of mental action, is threefold: first, the fact of the delusion betokens a fundamental disorder in the organic processes as the condition of its existence, the extent of such disorder being nowise necessarily limited to its production; secondly, the existence of a centre of morbid action in the midst of numerous most sensitive nervous centres, which are connected in the most delicate, intimate, and complex manner, will tend to produce by sympathy, infection, or induction, or reflex action, call it as we may, some derangement in them; and, thirdly, the automatic activity of the morbid centre, reaching a certain intensity, may become an uncontrollable impulse, and, irresistibly uttering itself, hurry the patient into some insane action instigated by it. In other words, psychologically speaking, the existence of a delusion indicates fundamental disorder of mental action—radical insanity; secondly, the delusion reacts injuriously upon other mental phenomena, interfering secondarily with correct ratiocination, or due co-ordination of function, and predisposing to convulsive mental phenomena; and, thirdly, while it cannot be subordinated to reflection, the individual may at any moment be subordinated to it, and act under its instigation. The mind then which suffers from positive ideational insanity, however seemingly partial, is, being unsound, not to be relied upon, nor to be held responsible; disease is going on in it, and it does not depend upon the individual wishes or will what course it shall take or what height it shall reach, any more than the health of a man bodily sick depends upon the desire which he may have to rise, take up his bed, and walk.

Certainly, in some cases of so-called monomania or partial ideational insanity, there does appear to be but little evidence of insanity apart from the particular morbid ideas; but such cases are generally met with in an asylum, where the patient is removed from those particular relations in which the moral perversion might be expected to display itself, and where the quiet regularity of life and the absence of all exciting impressions favour the latency of the affective insanity. Allow those patients who are so calm and serviceable in the asylum, to return to active life, and to be subjected to the strain of trying circumstances, or the stress of adverse events, and they soon suffer from attacks of general excitement, if they do not perpetrate acts of dangerous violence; even in the asylum they have now and then their bad times, in which they are morose, uncertain, and excitable. Nothing is more surprising to the inexperienced person than the extreme passionate excitement and utter irrationality, when they do break out, of these monomaniacs, whom he has hitherto regarded as quite sensible apart from their delusion, and as harmlessly interesting perhaps by reason of it. They will mostly tolerate with great composure the annoyances of their fellow-patients, because they look down upon them with pity as mad; but once let them be offended and excited, it is rendered very plain how unstable and dangerous is their state of mind.

It is necessary to guard against the mistake of supposing the delusion to be the cause of the passion, whether painful or gay, that may accompany partial ideational insanity. In cases of simple melancholia there may be no delusion: the patient's feeling of external objects and events may be perverted so that he is conscious of being strangely and unnaturally changed; impressions which should be agreeable or indifferent are painful; he feels himself strangely isolated, and cannot take any interest in his affairs; he is profoundly miserable and shuns society, perhaps lying in bed all day. All this while he may be quite conscious of his unnatural state, and may strive to conceal it from his friends. Suddenly, it may be, an idea springs up in his mind that he is lost for ever, or that he must commit suicide, or that he has committed murder and is about to be hanged; the vast and formless feeling of profound misery has taken form as a concrete idea—in other words, has become condensed into a definite delusion, this now being the expression of it. The delusion is not the cause of the feeling of misery, but is engendered of it,—is precipitated, as it were, in a mind saturated with the feeling of inexpressible woe; and it takes different forms according to the degree of the patient's culture, and the social, political, and religious ideas prevailing at the particular epoch. In some cases it is striking how disproportionate the delusion is to the extreme mental anguish, the patient assigning some most ridiculously inadequate cause for his gloom: one man under my care, whose suffering was very great, said that it was because he had drunk a glass of beer which he ought not to have done, and another man was, as he thought, lost for ever because he had muttered a curse when he ought to have uttered a prayer. With him who believes that he is doomed to infinite and eternal misery, it is not the delusion but the affective disorder that is the fundamental fact; there cannot be an adequate or definite idea in the finite mind of the infinite or the external; and the insane delusion of eternal damnation is but the vague and futile attempt to express an unutterable real suffering. In all these cases of melancholia the deep sense of individual restriction which exists, the wretched feeling of the oppression of self, is interpreted as due to some external agency; and as the existence of any passion notably intensifies an idea that is congruous with it, the delusion ultimately attains great vividness. So with regard to other passions, whether excited by some external event or some internal commotion; when vehement and long continued, they are apt to end in some positive delusion. The vain person who cherishes an ambitious passion may after a time be so entirely possessed by it that he is unable to see things as they really are, and his overweening self-esteem terminates perhaps in the delusion that he is emperor, king, or even divine. The essential nature of the delusion will depend upon the special nature of the passion in which the individual's self-feeling is engaged, but the particular form which it assumes will depend greatly upon the education and upon the circumstances of life in which he has been placed. Thus the vain and ambitious person who has had a religious training will assume a character in accordance with his sentiments, and will deem himself a prophet favoured of heaven, or even Jesus Christ; the politician will be a prime minister, or some great political character; the man of science will have solved the problem of perpetual motion, or will be the victim of complicated and ingenious persecution by means of electricity. When witchcraft was generally believed in, the insane frequently fancied themselves to be tormented by witches; but since the police have been established, they often believe the police to be in pursuit of them. At the time when Napoleon was setting up and pulling down kings, many people were admitted into French asylums who believed them-selves to be kings and emperors; and Esquirol thought that he could have written the history of the French Revolution from the character of the insanity which accompanied its different phases. The insanity of any time will be a more or less broken reflection of the character of the events that happen in it. . . .

It is noteworthy, in some of these cases, how sudden and complete may be the change from the deepest anguish and despair to a state of perfect calm and sanity. Thus one of my patients, who suffered from acute melancholy, who usually wandered about moaning grievously, or sat weeping profusely, and who had made several attempts against her own life, awoke one morning seemingly quite well, rational, cheerful, and wonderfully pleased at her recovery, remaining so for the rest of that day. Next morning, however, she had entirely relapsed, and it was some months before she finally recovered. Again Griesinger mentions the case of a woman with melancholia and delusions as to loss of prop-erty and persecution, who for the space of a quarter of an hour was quite herself, and then relapsed. Such cases are of interest in regard to the pathology of the disease, as they would seem to prove that there is no serious organic disease so far—that the condition of nerve-element is a polar modification which may soon pass away, not unlike, perhaps, the electrotonic state that may be artificially produced in nerve.

Miss S., [aged] twenty-two was rather a good-looking young lady, though with an irregularly formed head, and a deformity of one ear, and with a strangely wandering and occasionally vacant look. Her family is saturated with insanity, and the present is said to be her third attack. She is surcharged with grief, moaning continually, and weeping so abundantly as to surprise one how she can raise so many tears. She exclaims that she is utterly estranged from God, and sobs as though her little heart must break. Notwithstanding this extreme exhibition of mental suffering, one could not, on carefully observing her, but con-clude that she was not really so miserable as she looked, that her dis-tressing actions were in great part automatic. And there was truth in the instinctive suspicion; for in the midst of the most violent sobbing, she would sometimes, on the occasion of a ludicrous or sarcastic obser-vation, look up quite calmly, speak quietly, and even smile for a mo-ment, and thereupon relapse instantly into her extreme grief. She was quite conscious of her state, and threw all the blame of it upon her friends, who, she said, ought to have subjected her to proper restraint and discipline, instead of indulging her in every way, as they had done. Previously to being sent from home she had been very wilful and im-pulsive, sometimes starting out of the house, and saying that she must kill herself. After being in the asylum for a few days she became calm and composed, spoke quite rationally, and professed herself very well contented with her position, and with the course which her friends had taken on her behalf. And yet, while wearing this cheerful and contented manner, she was secretly positing letters to her friends, full of the bitterest complaints, moanings, and reproaches, sentence after sentence in them beginning, "Oh God!" Reminded of her inconsistency, she sank into the deepest self-accusation and abasement, said she was utterly wretched on account of her deceitfulness and wickedness, which she could not help, and that she was lost for ever. And, indeed, she could not help it. She was sincerely cheerful in her new relations when engaged in conversation, or in some occupation, but when she sat down to write home the old feelings returned, and the old automatic morbid activity broke out. Ultimately she recovered, the morbid tension gradually subsiding, and finally disappearing in the entirely changed relations. This example enables us to understand, in some sort, how it is that murderers in an asylum sometimes appear to be unconscious of what they have done, and, if they are conscious of their crime, never think they are to blame; for the automatic activity of their morbid nature has surprised them, and when they reflect upon the act of violence, if they do so, it is as upon an act done by some one else.

The foregoing cases will suffice to illustrate partial ideational insanity, although they all fall under that division of it usually called melancholia. In conversing with patients so afflicted, it is impossible to avoid being surprised at the strange discord or incoherency which their mental character exhibits: they are often, as it were, double beings—a rational and an insane being: the two beings cannot be brought into intercommunication and beneficial reaction upon one another, for the persistence of the delusion implies the cutting off of such interaction; as conscious manifestations they are independent, isolated. One day the sound being is in predominant or exclusive action; another day, the unsound being: on different occasions one might say—"Now I am talking with the rational being; now with the morbid being." Herein we have the explanation of the doubt which such patients sometimes have of themselves; they are not confident at times, and appear only to half believe in their delusion, because they are not then under its entire influence: their rational nature is in predominant action, and they act in their relations as if their delusion really was a delusion. It would be a mistake, however, to put any reliance on such seeming hesitation: let the delusion be excited into activity, all doubts vanish, and the sound being is brought into dangerous bondage to the unsound being.

In a complete account of partial ideational insanity, whether accompanied by a gloomy or a gay passion, the effects of the delusion should be considered—as was done when considering idea physiologically—first, upon sensation; secondly, upon the processes of nutrition and secretion; and, thirdly, upon the movements or general conduct of the patient. As the delusion is sometimes the final effect of a morbid organic stimulus resulting from bodily disease, so it in turn, however caused, reacts injuriously on the bodily nutrition and on sensibility. The latter is commonly much affected in melancholia. There may be general or partial diminution or perversion of the sensibility of the skin, or a local complete loss thereof; and complaints of precordial anguish and of strange epigastric or abdominal sensations testify to the perversion of organic sensibility. These complaints, causeless as they may seem, are not always without significance. Illusions and hallucinations of the special senses are frequent: one patient, believing himself lost, sees the devil in his room, another smells a corpse in his room, a third tastes poison in his food, a fourth hears voices which revile and accuse him, or which suggest impious thoughts and instigate violent deeds—it may be to imitate Abraham and sacrifice his child.

The general depression of tone in melancholia is felt throughout the processes of nutrition, although not usually in observable proportion to the great apparent suffering. So vast indeed does this seem in some cases that the wonder is that organic life can go quietly on. However, digestion mostly fails, and constipation becomes troublesome; the skin loses its freshness, and gets sallow, dry, and harsh; the temperature of the body is lowered, and the extremities are cold; the pulse is feeble, sometimes very slow, and even intermittent; the respiration is slow, moaning, and interrupted by frequent and long-drawn sighs; the urine is in some cases abundant in quantity and very pale in colour; the menstruation is generally irregular or suppressed. Everything indicates the depressing influence of the gloomy morbid idea on the organic life. There is usually a great want of sleep, although patients are apt to assert that they have not slept when they really have, so little has been the feeling of refreshment therefrom. Refusal of food, which is common and sometimes very persistent, may be due to other causes besides the want of appetite and general sluggishness of nutrition: it may be in consequence of a fear of poison in the food, or of a delusion that the intestines are sealed up, or in order to die by starvation, or in fancied obedience to a voice from heaven.

There is the same depressing influence exerted upon the voluntary movements; these, like the ideas, are sluggish generally, and the conduct of the patient accords with the character of his mental state. In an extreme form of melancholia known as melancholia with stupor, *M. attonita,* where the mind is entirely possessed with some terrible delusion, the patient sits or stands like a statue, and must be moved from place to place; the muscles are generally lax, or some of them are fixed in a cataleptic rigidity; the patient, as if in a trance or as one only partially awake, scarcely seems to see or hear; consciousness of time, place, and persons is lost; and the bodily wants and necessities are alike unheeded. Between this condition at one end of the scale, and those cases at the other end in which there is an acute utterance of the internal agony in gesture-language, though this is usually of a somewhat uniform or even monotonous character, there are of course cases representing every sort of intermediate stage. But where there is the most activity of movement in melancholia it is confined to the expression of the mental suffering, or to the common attempt to escape from it by suicide: there is an extreme aversion for the most part to exercise, employment, and activity of a beneficial kind.

In monomania proper, where the delusion is attended with an exalted feeling, its effects upon sensibility, nutrition, and movement are different. There appears to be no real diminution of general sensibility, though the sensations are not always attended to, by reason of the excited mental state; but hallucinations of the special senses are by no means uncommon, and they appear both as occasional consequences and occasional causes of the delusion, which in any case they fail not to strengthen. There is not usually any notable interference with the processes of nutrition. The behaviour of the patient often expresses with sufficient distinctness the character of his delusion: one may reveal his exalted notions in his gait, manner, and address, while another is not satisfied with the capabilities of ordinary language to express the magnificence of his ideas, but invents new and mysterious signs which, unintelligible to every one else, have wonderful meaning for him. A third makes perhaps sweeping plans and projects, enters upon vast undertakings, and sometimes goes through an immense amount of patient and systematic work in perfecting some impossible scientific invention.

The courses which melancholia and monomania run respectively are different. In melancholia remissions are common, but complete intermissions rare. It is striking in some cases how suddenly a great change may take place: Griesinger, as already said, quotes one case in which there was a perfectly lucid interval for the space of a quarter of an hour; and I have more than once seen a melancholic go to bed cheerful and seemingly quite well, and yet awake in the morning as bad as ever. It is never safe to trust to these sudden conversions from gloom to cheerfulness. When recovery does really take place, as it does in half or even more than half of the cases of melancholia, it is usually gradual, and takes place within from four to twelve months from the commencement of the disease. After twelve months a favourable result, though less probable, is still not hopeless, for there are instances on record in which recovery has taken place after the disease has lasted years. Of the cases that do not recover, about half decline into mental weakness or complete dementia, the rest remaining chronic or ending in death. Though death may take place in consequence of refusal of food and exhaustion, it is often due to intercurrent disease, phthisical, cardiac, or abdominal, and most often to phthisis. It was in melancholics who had died after long refusal of food that Guislain most frequently met with gangrene of the lung. I have met with it in one such case.

The course of monomania, once established, is very seldom towards recovery. The reasons of this are not far to seek: in the first place, monomania is often secondary to mania or melancholia, and represents therefore a further degree of mental degeneration than these diseases; and in the second place, when it is primary, the fixed delusion is commonly the exaggeration of some fundamental vice of character, and has been slowly developed. Whether primary or secondary, the fixed delusion marks the establishment of a definite type of morbid action of a chronic nature, such as is not easily got rid of in any organ of the body, much less so in an organ so delicate as the brain. Nevertheless recovery does sometimes take place under the prolonged influence of systematic moral discipline, or after some great shock to, or change in, the system—whether emotional, or produced by some intercurrent disease, or occurring at the climaeteric period. As a general rule it may be said that recovery does not take place when a fixed delusion has lasted for more than half a year. When it does not, the disease remains chronic, or passes into dementia: the more the exaggerated self-feeling which underlies and inspires the delusion wanes, and the more this, losing its inspiration, becomes a mere form of words, the nearer the case gets to incoherent dementia.

The reason why the prognosis is so much more favourable in partial ideational insanity with depression than in partial ideational insanity with exaltation, though sufficiently set forth already, might be roughly stated thus: that in the former the system is painfully sensible of its infirmity, depressed thereby, and feels the need of amendment, while in the latter it is abundantly satisfied with its condition, gay, and sensible of nothing to amend.

(*b*) *General Ideational Insanity.*—This division will include all those cases of intellectual alienation which are commonly described under *mania,* as well as many cases of general intellectual disorder in which, notwithstanding the excitement, the evidence of much mental suffering leads to their being placed under *melancholia.* In fact, it is not possible in practice to draw the line of distinction between acute mania and acute melancholia, which often blend, follow one another, or run into one another, in a way that defies exact division; for although we may properly say that there is in acute mania an excitement or exaltation of the self-feeling, the expression of which takes place chiefly in the actions of the patient, who sings, dances, declaims, runs about, pulls off his clothes, and in all ways acts most extravagantly, yet there may be equal excitement and restlessness of action in a patient who believes himself bewitched or lost, while another, exalted and furious one day, shall be frenzied with anguish next day. They all, however, agree in being examples of acute ideational insanity.

24
•

Depressive States

KRAEPELIN

EMIL KRAEPELIN WAS BORN IN 1856 and died in 1926. His life
thus spanned the most influential era in the formation of modern
psychiatry, and he is widely acknowledged to be the most influential psychiatrist of his time. He received his medical degree at Würzburg in 1878,
then completed research training with Wilhelm Wundt, the famous ex-
perimentalist. Following this, he became professor of psychiatry at the
University of Dorpat, and later at Heidelberg. In 1904 he was appointed
director of the Psychiatric Clinic in Munich, where he stayed, also occupying the chair of psychiatry at the university, until his retirement in 1922.

Kraepelin's system of classifying mental diseases is his lasting legacy.
He was not primarily a clinician or a theorist but a researcher and classifier. With the meticulous case records and large inpatient population
of the Psychiatric Clinic at his disposal, he observed, described, and
categorized what he took to be the natural kinds of disease entity
around him. His theoretical assumptions about disease were derived
from Rudolf Virchow, as were those of many of his colleagues undertaking clinical analysis at the end of the nineteenth century. More immediately, they came from his predecessor, Wilhelm Griesinger. Evidence for underlying, localized organic disease entities could be found
in the presence of observable and rule-governed signs and symptoms,
even though these underlying entities had not yet been identified.
Moreover, diseases had a "course," persisting and undergoing changes
through long stretches of time; thus, they required longitudinal study.

Kraepelin's clinical descriptions and classification of mental diseases
were published first in a *Compendium* (1883) and later in a *Short Textbook;* 1893 saw the fourth edition, 1896 the fifth, and 1899 the sixth,
now in two volumes. The seventh edition came out in 1903–4, and by
the eighth edition (1909–15) and the posthumous ninth edition published in 1927, the work was printed as four separate volumes. The passages from the eighth edition of the textbook (1909–15), included here,
reflect part of Kraepelin's unique contribution to psychiatric classification: the broad division between dementia praecox or what we would
today call schizophrenia, on the one hand, and manic-depressive insanity, or what today would usually be called mood or affective disor-

der, on the other. (Kraepelin begins his work on manic-depressive insanity in the eighth edition of the *Textbook* with an enumerative definition: manic-depressive insanity includes "on the one hand the whole domain of so-called periodic and circular insanity, on the other hand simple mania, the greater part of the morbid states termed melancholia and also a not inconsiderable number of cases of amentia (confusional or delirious insanity)" *(Kraepelin* [1909] 1921:1).

The division between dementia praecox and manic-depressive insanity was considered enormously valuable and has continued to influence both German psychiatric classification and twentieth-century English-language classification such as is found in the American Psychiatric Association's *Diagnostic and Statistical Manuals* and the World Health Organization's *International Classification of Diseases*. This influence is in part due to the efforts of George M. Robinson, first professor of psychiatry at the University of Edinburgh. Robinson arranged for translations of selections from Kraepelin's textbook, believing that the work on these two broad categories of dementia praecox and manic-depressive insanity represented Kraepelin's greatest achievements in psychiatry. The text reproduced here reflects Robinson's work. It is a 1921 translation of the eighth German edition of the *Textbook,* edited by Robinson.

The structure of Kraepelin's writing on manic-depressive insanity is elaborate and multidimensional. With chapters on psychic symptoms, bodily symptoms, manic states, depressive states (reproduced here), mixed states, fundamental states, course, prognosis, causes, delimitation, diagnosis, and treatment, he carefully addresses every aspect of the disorder. Depressive states are distinguished according to the presence of hallucinations and delusions (the distinction between *melancholia simplex* and *melancholia gravis*), as well as according to the coherence and content of the ideas entertained (*paranoid melancholia*), and finally according to the presence of fantastical delusions (*fantastic melancholia*). In the chapter reproduced here, we see Kraepelin's characteristic attention to clinical and phenomenological details, illustrated with liberal direct quotations from his patients themselves.

The second half of the nineteenth century had seen Germany emerge as the center of European psychiatric advances, and Kraepelin's monumental contribution to this new medical field has rightly earned him the name the "father of modern psychiatry."

·　·　·

From Emil Kraepelin, "Manic-depressive Insanity," in
Textbook of Psychiatry, 8th edition, 1909–15.

Melancholia Simplex

The slightest depressive states are characterised by the appearance of a *simple psychiatric inhibition without hallucinations and without marked delusions.* Thinking is difficult to the patient, a disorder, which he describes in the most varied phrases. He cannot collect his thoughts or pull himself together; his thoughts are as if paralysed, they are immobile. His head feels heavy, quite stupid, as if a board were pushed in front of it, everything is confused. He is no longer able to perceive, or to follow the train of thought of a book or a conversation, he feels weary, enervated, inattentive, inwardly empty; he has no memory, he has no longer command of knowledge formerly familiar to him, he must consider a long time about simple things, he calculates wrongly, makes contradictory statements, does not find words, cannot construct sentences correctly. At the same time complaints are heard that the patient must meditate so much, that fresh thoughts are always coming to him, that he has too much in his head, that he finds no rest, is confused.

The patients frequently describe that change of their inward state, which is usually called "depersonalisation." Their presentations lack sensuous colouring. The impressions of the external world appear strange, as though from a great distance, awake no response in them; their own body feels as if not belonging to them; their features stare quite changed from the mirror; their voice sounds leaden. Thinking and acting go on without the co-operation of the patient; he appears to himself to be an automatic machine. Heilbronner has pointed out that Goethe has described similar disorders in Werther, when he says:—

> "O, when this glorious nature lies before me so rigid, like a little varnished picture, and all the joy of it cannot pump a drop of bliss from my heart up to my brain," and "I stand as though in front of a cabinet of curiosities, and I see little men and little horses moving about in front of me, and I often ask myself whether it is not an optical delusion. I play with them, or rather I am played like a marionette, and I sometimes take hold of my neighbour by his wooden hand and start back shuddering."

Mood is sometimes dominated by a profound inward dejection and gloomy hopelessness, sometimes more by indefinite anxiety and restlessness. The patient's heart is heavy, nothing can permanently rouse his interest, nothing gives him pleasure. He has no longer any humour or any religious feeling,—he is unsatisfied with himself, has become indifferent to his relatives and to whatever he formerly liked best. Gloomy thoughts arise, his past and even his future appear to him in a uniformly dim light. He feels that he is worth nothing, neither physically nor mentally, he is no longer of any use, appears to himself "like a murderer." His life has been a blunder, he is not suited for his calling, wants to take up a new occupation, should have arranged his life differently, should have pulled himself together more. "I have always given advice, and then things have gone wrong," said a patient.

He feels solitary, indescribably unhappy, as "a creature disinherited of fate"; he is sceptical about God, and with a certain dull submission, which shuts out every comfort and every gleam of light, he drags himself with difficulty from one day to another. Everything has become disagreeable to him; everything wearies him, company, music, travel, his professional work. Everywhere he sees only the dark side and difficulties; the people round him are not so good and unselfish as he had thought; one disappointment and disillusionment follows another. Life appears to him aimless, he thinks that he is superfluous in the world, he cannot restrain himself any longer, the thought occurs to him to take his life without his knowing why. He has a feeling as if something had cracked in him, he fears that he may become crazy, insane, paralytic, the end is coming near. Others have the impression as though something terrible had happened, something is rising in their breast, everything trembles in them, they have nothing good to expect, something is happening.

Imperative Ideas of all kinds occasionally emerge in these states, agoraphobia, mysophobia, the fear of having been pricked by a splinter and having to die of blood-poisoning, the fear of having vicious or "unclean" thoughts, the idea of throwing people into water, the fear of having stolen bread or money, of having removed landmarks, of having committed all the crimes mentioned in the newspapers. A patient was tormented by the idea of having murdered people with his thoughts, and of having been guilty of the death of King Ludwig. A female patient, who in a former attack had thought that she was an empress with a court of dogs and cats, made convulsive efforts to get rid of the word empress which always forced itself upon her, the effort consisting in rubbing her teeth rhythmically with her hand. Another was very greatly tormented by being compelled to connect obscene sexual ideas with religious representations (crucifixes). A third patient wrote the following in a note:—

> It is really so, that I have now become unclean with what I always played with; from negligence and clumsiness I often do not now go at the right time to the closet and I pass something into my chemise, into my bed, and into my clothes, and, as I always put on the clothes again, it so happens that the petticoat is drawn on over the night-jacket, something on there and on to my head, from the petticoat on to the bodice; on to the hair and so on.

She was afraid also that something would fall out of her nose into a book; she often destroyed things supposed to be dirty; she would not sit down on a chair or give her hand in order not to soil anything. All these ideas she herself called "on-goings," in order to make herself interesting. The fear of knives, with the idea of being obliged to kill someone, occurs occasionally also. A patient went to bed in order not to do anything of that kind. One of my patients impulsively stole all sort of things which had no value for herself and of which she made no further use. She stated that she could not help it, it was an impulse, just as if she had been thirsty, she was uneasy if she did not yield to it. Gross by means of "psychoanalysis" has arrived at the result here, that the theft-impulse, being forced to do secretly what is forbidden, to take "something secretly into the hand," signifies a transference of sexual desires unsatisfied by the impotent lover, which has been further influenced by the question of a priest at confession whether she herself had introduced the organ in sexual intercourse. On other grounds also we may perhaps regard these imperative fears and impulses as the expression of a certain relationship between manic-depressive insanity and the insanity of degeneration.

The *Total Absence of Energy* is very specially conspicuous. The patient lacks spirit and will-power, like a wheel on a car, which simply runs but in itself has no movement or driving power. He cannot rouse himself, cannot come to any decision, cannot work any longer, does everything the wrong way about, he has to force himself to everything, does not know what to do. A patient declared that he did not know what he wanted, went from one thing to another. The smallest bit of work costs him an unheard-of effort; even the most everyday arrangements, household work, getting up in the morning, dressing, washing, are only accomplished with the greatest difficulty and in the end indeed are left undone. Work, visits, important letters, business affairs are like a mountain in front of the patient and are just left, because he does not find the power to overcome the opposing inhibitions. If he takes a walk, he remains standing at the house door or at the nearest corner, undecided as to what direction he shall take; he is afraid of every person whom he meets, of every conversation; he become shy and retiring, because he cannot any longer look at any one or go among people.

Everything new appears uncomfortable and unbearable. One of my patients insisted on leaving a post which he had been very anxious to get, but he was alarmed at the removal to a new residence, and importuned the authorities with contradictory requests, as his new position immediately appeared to him much worse than the former one. Finally the patient gives up every activity, sits all day long doing nothing with his hands in his lap, brooding to himself in utter dulness. His sorrowful features show no play of emotion; the scanty linguistic utterances are laboured, low, monotonous and monosyllabic, and even the addition of a simple greeting on a postcard is not attainable or only after much urging.

Sometimes a veritable passion for lying in bed is developed; the patients ever again promise to rise to-morrow, but have always new excuses to remain in bed. Just because of this severe volitional disorder it relatively seldom comes to more serious attempts at suicide, although the wish to die very frequently occurs. It is only when with the disappearance of inhibition energy returns while the depression still continues, that the attempts at suicide become more frequent and more dangerous. A patient with very slight moodiness hanged himself a few days before his discharge on a free pass when he already appeared quite cheerful.

Insight.—Sense and orientation are in spite of the great difficulty in perception and thinking completely retained. Generally a very vivid morbid feeling also exists, not infrequently even a certain morbid insight, in as far as the patients express their regret for former improprieties, and their fear lest they might again let themselves be carried away by excitement. Others, however, think that they are not ill, only destitute of will-power, that they could indeed pull themselves together, only will not; that they are simulating. Frequently the return of moodiness is connected with external accidents, unpleasant experiences, changes in circumstances and such things. To the unprejudiced observer it is clear that the psychic working of those influences has been produced by the morbid clouding of disposition. . . .

Stupor

In the highest grades for psychic inhibition described may go on to the development of marked stupor. The patients are deeply apathetic, are no longer able to perceive the impressions of the surroundings and to assimilate them, do not understand questions, have no conception of their position. A female patient who has made to leave her bed and go into the one beside it, said quite without understanding, "That is too complicated for me." Occasionally, it can be recognized that the inhibition of thought is slighter than the volitional disorder. A patient was able to give the result of complicated problems in arithmetic in the same time, certainly considerably prolonged, as that of the simplest addition.

Sometimes the occasional, detached utterances of the patients contain indications of confused, delusional ideas, that they are quite away from the world, have a crack through the brain, are being sold; down below there is an uproar. A definite affect is at the same time mostly not recognisable, yet in the astonished expression of the patients their helplessness in regard to their own perceptions, and further a certain anxious feeling of insecurity on attempting anything can usually be seen.

Volitional utterances are extremely scanty. As a rule, the patients lie mute in bed, give no answer of any sort, at most withdraw themselves timidly from approaches, but often do not defend themselves from pinpricks. Sometimes they display catalepsy and lack of will-power, sometimes aimless resistance to external interference. They sit helpless before their food; perhaps, however, they let themselves be spoon-fed without making any difficulty. They hold fast what is pressed into their hand, turn it slowly about without knowing how to get rid of it. They are, therefore, wholly unable to care for their bodily needs, and not infrequently they become dirty. Now and then periods of excitement may be interpolated. The patients get out of bed, break out in confused abuse, sing a folksong. . . . After the return of consciousness, which usually appears rather abruptly, memory is very much clouded and often quite extinguishes.

Melancholia Gravis

The picture of simple depression corresponding perhaps to the former *"melancholia simplex,"* experiences very varied elaboration through the development of hallucinations and delusions, which frequently follows; one might here perhaps speak of a *"melancholia gravis."* The patients see figures, spirits, the corpses of their relatives; something is falsely represented to them, "all sorts of devil's work." Green rags fall from the walls; a coloured spot on the wall is a snapping mouth which bites the heads off children; everything looks black. The patients hear abusive language ("lazy pig," "wicked creature," "deceiver," "you are guilty, you are guilty"), voices, which invite them to suicide; they feel sand, sulphur vapour in their mouth, electric currents in the walls. A patient, who reproached himself with having had connection with a cow, felt a cow's tail flicking his face.

Ideas of Sin usually play the largest part. The patient has been from youth up the most wicked being, an abomination, filled with malice, has led a horrible life, as far as possible has let others do his work, has not put his full strength into his calling, has sworn falsely in taking the military oath, has defrauded the sick fund. He has offended everyone, has borne false witness, has overreached some one in making a purchase, has sinned against the seventh commandment. He cannot work any more, has no more feeling, no more tears; he is so rough; something is lacking in his disposition. Frequently the self-accusations are connected with harmless occurrences which have often happened long before. The patient, when a child, communicated unworthily, did not obey his mother, told a lie before he was twelve years old. He has not paid for his beer and on this account will be imprisoned for ten years. A patient, fifty-nine years of age, alleged that as a boy he had stolen "apples and nuts," and "played with the genitals" of a cow. Conscience is roused. "Certainly it would have been better, if it had been roused sooner," he said in answer to the objection that up till then he had not been troubled about the supposed sin. Others have once turned away a beggar unkindly, have skimmed the cream from the milk. By renting a house, by undertaking some building, by a thoughtless purchase, a suicidal attempt, they have brought their family to misery; they should not have entered the institution; then it would all have come differently. Female patients have put too much water into the milk of their dead children, have not brought up their boys well, have neglected them in religion, have procured the abortion of a child, have not had patience in their confinements, have not kept their house properly; they do not put things in order, they are lazy. A female patient, because of this, would not stay in bed. When it was represented to another that it was a delusion, she replied, "It is only conscience; when I was at school it once came like this." Obviously she was speaking of a former depression.

The domain of *religion* is a peculiarly favourable soil for self-accusation. The patient is a great sinner, cannot pray any more, has forgotten the ten commandments, the creed, the benediction, has lost eternal bliss, has committed the sin against the Holy Ghost, has trafficked in divine things, has not offered enough candles. He has apostatized from God, is gripped firmly by Satan, must do penance. The spirit of God has left him; he feels that he dare not enter church any more. He is going to Hell, has only two hours to live; then the devil will fetch him; he must enter eternity with transgression, and redeem poor souls.

The following extract from a letter of a married peasant woman to her sister affords a glimpse into the spiritual state of such patients:—

> I wish to inform you that I have received the cake. Many thanks, but I am not worthy. You sent it on the anniversary of my child's death, for I am not worthy of my birthday; I must weep myself to death; I cannot live and I cannot die, because I have failed so much, I shall bring my husband and children to hell. We are all lost; we won't see each other any more; I shall go to the convict prison and my two girls as well, if they do not make away with themselves, because they were borne in my body. If I had only remained single! I shall bring all my children into damnation, five children! Not far enough to cut in my throat, nothing but unworthy confessions and communion; I have fallen and it never in my life occurred to me; I am to blame that my husband died and many others. God caused the fire in our village on my account; I shall bring many people into the institution. 'My good, honest John was so pious and has to take his life; he got nineteen marks on Low Sunday, and at the age of nineteen his life came to an end. My two girls are there, no father, no mother, no brother, and no one will take them because of their wicked mother. God puts everything into my mind; I can write to you a whole sheet full of nothing but significance; you have not seen it, what signs it has made. I have heard that we need nothing more, we are lost.

Besides the marked ideas of sin there is to be noted the delusional conviction, that her husband is dead and her son must take his life, but especially the tendency to find "signs" and "significance," which God sends (nineteen marks and nineteen years), the regret about the failure of an attempt at suicide by cutting her throat, lastly, the remark that her many sins have only now occurred to the patient.

His present activities also frequently give the patient the opportunity for continual self-reproach. He notices that he always commits fresh faults, talks at random so stupidly, says things which he does not wish to say, offends everyone. "What I do, is the wrong way about; I must always retract everything that I say," said a patient. He causes so much trouble, is to blame that the others are so distressed, that they are being taken away. "I have probably done all this," said a patient. He has brought in all his fellow-patients, must care for them all, is responsible for them, complains that he is really not able to feed the others, to do the work of the head-waiter, to pay for them all. Everyone must go hungry when he eats. A patient reported as follows about his "offences against the doctors":—

> The patient F. is very often vexed with himself when at the visit of the physicians he does not greet relatively thank in a more friendly way, he very often says: "I have the honour," which expression may be mis-interpreted. The better and more usual responses to greetings, as "Good morning," and expressions of gratitude, as "Many thanks for the kind visit," are often omitted. Then the patient must take offence at his position, that is the position and attitude of his body. Very often he does not assume the requisite demeanour towards such highly placed gentlemen. Just made another offence; I have omitted to rise from my seat when the chief physician went past. At the washstand I omitted to show a boy how to fill the basin. He of course might have asked me. But those who were near will certainly have blamed my conduct and not the boy's. Once I omitted to hand the water to a pa-tient, when he asked for it. It is true that he did not apply directly to me; he only called into the room; others were much nearer to him, but it would have been my duty to fulfil his request at once."

Ideas of Persecution frequently exist in the closest connection with the delusion of sin. Disgrace and scorn await the patient everywhere; he is dishonourable, cannot let himself be seen anywhere any more. People look at him, put their heads together, clear their throat, spit in front of him. They disapprove of his presence, feel it as an insult, can-not tolerate him any longer among them; he is a thorn in the side to all. Speeches in the club have reference to him; there is secret talking of stories about females; he is a bully, should hang himself, because he has no character. Everywhere he notices signs. The writer of the letter quoted above said that her twisted knot of hair signified that her hus-band had hanged himself, the scarfs of her fellow-patients that her chil-dren were drowned at home. A patient concluded from the remark, "Still waters run deep," that he should drown himself. The patient therefore asks for an explanation; he did not know that such was his state. "What is being done with me?" he asks anxiously. Things are so put before him as if every step in his life had been wrong. He defends himself, therefore, in despair against the supposed accusations and de-clares his innocence. But I have not done anything wrong, have stolen nothing, have not betrayed my country, such patients are heard to lament. They are afraid that on the death of a relative they may be sus-pected of poisoning ("Has poison been found?"), that they may be called to account for lese-majesty, or for a planned assault.

Everywhere danger threatens the patient. The girls read his letters; strange people are in the house, a suspicious motor-car drives past. People mock him, are going to thrash him, to chase him from his post in a shameful way, incarcerate him, bring him to justice, expose him publicly, deport him, take his orders from him, throw him into the fire, drown him. The people are already standing outside; the bill of indictment is already written; the scaffold is being put up; he must wander about naked and miserable, is quite forsaken, is shut out of human society, is lost body and soul. His relatives also are being tortured, must suffer; "I do hope they are still at home." His family is imprisoned; his wife has drowned herself; his parents are murdered; his daughter wanders about in the snow without any clothes on. Everything goes the wrong way; the household is going to ruin; there is nothing more there but rags; the clothes have been changed at the laundry. Things have been pawned; the money is not sufficient, is false; everything costs too much; everyone must starve. A woman said that her husband did not like her any longer; he wanted to kill her. Others release their husband, invite him to get a divorce.

His bodily state also appears to the patient to be frequently in a very dangerous condition, which may be connected with the dysæsthesiæ formerly described. He is incurably ill, half-dead, no longer a right human being, has lung-disease, a tapeworm, cancer in his throat, cannot swallow, does not retain his food, passes such thin and such frequent stools. Face and figure have changed; there is no longer blood in his brain; he does not see any longer, must become crazy, remain his whole lifetime in the institution, die, has already died. He has become impotent by onanism, has had a chancre from birth, has incurable blood-poisoning, infects everyone, he must not be touched. On this account a woman no longer had the bread baked in the house. The people in his surroundings become ill and yellow through the nasty exhalation of the patient, are already mentally disordered and weary of life. Female patients feel themselves pregnant, have been sexually ill used. . . .

Paranoid Melancholia

When ideas of persecution and hallucinations of hearing are frequently present and sense remains preserved, morbid states may occasionally arise, which readily call to mind alcoholic insanity, without alcohol having any causal significance ("paranoid melancholia"). The patients feel themselves watched, are pursued by spies and threatened by masked murderers; they catch sight of a dagger in their neighbour's hand. On the street, in the restaurant from the neighbouring table, they hear isolated remarks about themselves. In the next room a court of justice is deliberating on their case; intriguing is going on; experiments are made on them; they are threatened with secret words and with suspicious gestures. Delusional mistakes are made about people. One of my patients tried to escape from his persecutors by taking a journey, but noticed already in the station that they were accompanying him, and he walked only in the middle of the street because the voices threatened him with shooting as soon as he turned aside either to the right or to the left.

In the course of the forms here described consciousness is mostly clear, and sense and orientation are preserved. The patients perceive correctly the conversations and occurrences in their surroundings and then frequently misinterpret them in a delusional way. They think perhaps that they are not in the proper institution with proper physicians, but in the convict prison, that fellow-patients are acquaintances or members of their family; they address the physician as if he were the public prosecutor; their letters are falsified; what is said in the surroundings has a hidden meaning. Their train of thought is orderly and connected, although mostly very monotonous; the patients always move in the same circle of ideas; on an attempt being made to divert them, they return again immediately to the old track. All mental activity is as a rule made difficult. The patients are absent-minded, forgetful, are easily tired, progress slowly or not at all, and at the same time are sometimes most painfully precise in details. Often a certain morbid feeling exists. The head is darkened; the patient speaks of his chimeras; "I have something just like a mental disorder"; "understanding, reason, and the five senses are lacking." There is no question, however, of genuine morbid insight. Even if his attention is called to earlier similar attacks of which the patient had formed a correct opinion, it makes no impression on him. At that time everything was still quite different; now things are much worse; now every possibility of being saved is excluded.

Mood is gloomy, despondent, despairing. By persuasion or visits from relatives it may usually be somewhat influenced; sometimes on such an occasion lively excitement follows. On the other hand unpleasant news often makes little impression. What happens in the surroundings also usually affects the patients only slightly. "The noise does not annoy me, but the unrest in myself," said a female patient, when it was proposed that she should be transferred to another part of the building on account of the disturbing surroundings. The patients very frequently complain about the great inward excitement in spite of outwardly quiet behaviour; they may then give vent to it at times in violent outbursts of anxiety. Not infrequently it takes the form of an unquenchable home-sickness which drives the patients perpetually to try to get away, deaf to all reason. If one gives in to this, their state of mind deteriorates rapidly at home, as a rule. Many patients in regard to their delusions appear remarkably dull and indifferent, occasionally also perhaps good-humoured and even cheerful.

In the *Activities* of the patients their *volitional inhibition* on the one hand makes itself felt, on the other the influence of their *delusions* and *moods.* They feel tired, in need of rest, are no longer able to take care of themselves, neglect themselves, spend no more money, take no nourishment, wear very shabby clothes, refuse to sign the receipt for their salary, as indeed they have not done any work. They shut themselves up, go to bed, lie there rigidly with a troubled expression in a constrained attitude, sometimes with closed eyes, or sit timidly on the edge of the bed, because they do not venture to lie down. Indications of automatic obedience are not rare. In other patients anxious restlessness is predominant. They run off in a shirt, remain for days in the forest, beg for forgiveness, entreat for mercy, kneel, pray, pluck at their clothes, arrange their hair, rub their hands restlessly, give utterance to inarticulate cries. Their utterances are, as a rule, monosyllabic; it is very difficult to get anything out of them. They do not give information on their own initiative, are immediately silent again, but, at the same time, occasionally display in their writings a fluent and skilful diction. Speech is mostly low, monotonous, hesitating and even stuttering. Calligraphy is often indistinct and sprawling. There are also occasional omissions and doubling of letters.

Suicide.—The extraordinarily strong tendency to suicide is of the greatest practical significance. Sometimes it continually accompanies the whole course of the disease, without coming to a serious attempt owing to the incapacity of the patients to arrive at a decision. The patient buys a revolver, carries it about with him, brings it with him to the institution. He would like to die, begs that he may be beheaded, that he may be provided with poison; he ties a scarf round his neck, goes to the forest to search for a tree on which to hang himself; he scratches his wrist with his pocket-knife or strikes his head against the corner of the table. One of my female patients bought strychnine wheat and phosphorus paste, but luckily only took the first, because the phosphorus "smelt too filthy." Another stepped on to the window-sill in the second storey in order to throw herself down, but returned to the room, when a policeman, who by chance was passing, threatened her with his finger.

Nevertheless the danger of suicide is in all circumstances extremely serious, as the volitional inhibition may disappear abruptly or be interrupted by violent emotion. Sometimes the impulse to suicide emerges very suddenly without the patients being able to explain the motives to themselves. One of my female patients was occupied with household work, when the impulse came to her quite abruptly to hang herself; she at once did so and was only saved with difficulty. Subsequently she was not able to give any explanation of her deed, and had only a dim recollection of the whole occurrence.

Occasionally after indefinite prodromata the first distinct morbid symptom is a suicidal attempt. Only too often the patients know how to conceal their suicidal intentions behind an apparently cheerful behaviour, and then carefully prepare for the execution of their intention at a suitable moment. The possibilities at their command are numerous.

They may, while deceiving the vigilance of the people round them, drown themselves in the bath, hang themselves on the latch of the door, or on any projecting corner in the water-closet, indeed even strangle themselves in bed under the cover with a handkerchief or strips of linen. They may swallow needles, nails, bits of broken glass, even spoons, drink up any medicine, save up sleeping-powder and take it all at one time, throw themselves downstairs, smash their skull with a heavy object and so on. A female patient by sticking in pieces of paper managed to prevent the upper part of a window, where there was no grating, being properly shut, and then threw herself down from the second storey in an unwatched moment. Another who was shortly to have been discharged, was alone for a few minutes in the scullery; she took a little bottle of spirit and a match from the cupboard, which had been left open through negligence, and having poured the spirit over herself set herself on fire. Not at all infrequently the idea occurs to the patients to do away with the family also, because it would be better if none of them were alive. They then try to strangle their wife, to cut their children's throats, they go with them into the water, in order that they may not also be so unhappy, that they may not get stepparents.

Fantastic Melancholia

A further, fairly comprehensive group of cases is distinguished by a still greater development of *delusions*. We may perhaps call it "fantastic melancholia." Abundant *hallucinations* appear. The patients see evil spirits, death, heads of animals, smoke in the house, black men on the roofs, crowds of monsters, lions' cubs, a grey head with sharp teeth, angels, saints, dead relatives, the Trinity in the firmament, a head rising in the air. Especially at night extraordinary things happen. A dead friend sits on the pillow and tells the patient stories. The patient thinks that he is on a voyage; God stands beside the bed and writes down everything; the devil lies in wait behind the bed; Satan and the Virgin Mary come up out of the floor. God speaks in words of thunder; the devil speaks in church; something is moving in the wall. The patient hears his tortured relatives screaming and lamenting; the birds whistle his name; call out that he should be taken up. "There's a black one, a sozi," it is said, "a vagabond," "Do away with him, do away with him," "Look, that's the masturbator," "Now she's coming, now there'll be blood again," "Now we've caught her nicely," "You have nothing more," "You're going to hell." A woman is standing at the door and is giving information to the persecutors; there is a voice in his stomach, "You must still wait a long time till you are arrested; you are going to purgatory when the bells ring." The patient is electrified by the telephone, is illuminated at night by Röntgen-rays, pulled along by his hair; someone is lying in his bed; his food tastes of soapy water or excrement, of corpses and mildew.

Besides those genuine hallucinations there are also multifarious delusional interpretations of real perceptions. The patient hears murderers come; some one is slinking about the bed; a man is lying under the bed with a loaded gun; an electro-magnet crackles. People with green hats or black spectacles follow him on the street; in the opposite house someone is bowing conspicuously; the motor-cars are making a very peculiar noise; in the next room knives are being sharpened; the conversations on the telephone refer to him. Plays in the theatre, the serial story in the newspaper, are occupied with him; there is gross abuse written on a postcard; a female patient found her hat portrayed in a fashion proper for mockery. There is a great deal of talk, another said, and she imagined that it referred to her. What is said in the surroundings has a hidden meaning. Another one asserted that the physicians spoke a "universal language," in which they expressed all thoughts in a quite different form not understood by her. The most extraordinary conclusions are drawn from every perception; ravens flying signify that the daughter is being cut to pieces in the cellar; the son when he made his visit was wearing a black tie, so the youngest child must be dead. Everything is "so fateful," comedy and illusion. "Everything simulates, everything is talmi-gold," said a patient. The food is flesh and blood of their own relatives, the light is a funeral-light, the bed is an enchanted bed, the clattering cart outside is a hearse. It is quite another world, not the right town, quite another century. The clocks strike wrong; the letters are as if from strangers; the mortgages are exchanged; the savings-bank book is not valid. The trees in the forest, the rocks, appear unnatural, as if they were artificial, as if they had been built up specially for the patient, in fact, even the sun, the moon, the weather, are not as they used to be. One of my patients thought that the sun was artificial electric illumination, and he complained about the weakness of his eyes because he could not see the real sun (in the night).

The people, who visit the patient, are not the right people, are only false show. The physicians are only "figures"; he thinks that he is surrounded "by elemental spirits"; the children appear changed. The nurse is a disguised empress; a fellow patient (female) thinks that the patient (also female) is her husband; the attendants have false names. The wife is a witch, the child is a wild cat, a dog. A patient noticed that her husband looked black, and on this account attacked him with a bottle.

The numerous delusions are very extraordinary. The patient has committed mortal sins, has caused a derailment, has killed many people, has brought on himself a primeval sin, has murdered many souls; he has forged documents, been a legacy hunter, caused an epidemic. Because of sins of his youth he is in detention; he has committed bestiality; he is poisoning the whole world by his onanism. He has torn down the firmament, drunk up the fountain of grace, tormented the Trinity; cities and countries are on his account laid waste. The other patients are there by his fault, are beheaded on his account; every time that he eats or turns round in bed, someone is executed; the devil's mill is working over there; they are being killed there. Female patients have committed abortion, have been extravagant, have not been good house-wives, must be the devil's whore.

Because he is to blame for all misfortune, the patient is going to hell. The devil slipped down the chimney to take him away, has him by the nape of the neck, sits in his bosom as a black beast with sharp claws, speaks in his heart; he himself is changed into the devil; neither will his dead son come into heaven. His baseness is revealed in his expression; everyone knows of his crime. No one likes him any longer; he is sur-rounded by spies, is watched by the police, is continually followed by suspicious people; detectives wait for him; the judge is already there. He is dragged off to Siberia, to the convict prison; he is being electro-cuted, stabbed, shot, is having petroleum poured over him, is being tied to a corpse, run over by the motor car, hacked to pieces, cut up into a thousand bits, flayed, devoured by mice; naked in the wild forest he is being torn to pieces by wolves. His fingers are being chopped off, his eyes dug out, his sexual parts, his entrails cut off, his nails torn out; women have their womb drawn out. The last judgment is coming; the vengeance of God is at hand. To-day is the death-day, the last meal be-fore execution; the bed is a scaffold; the patient wishes to confess once more. Over his family also misfortune is poured out. His relatives are crucified by the mob; his daughter is in the convict prison; his son-in-law has hanged himself; parents and brothers and sisters are dead, his children are burned up. The husbands of female patients have been murdered. The sister was cut to pieces, sent away in a box; the son's corpse was sold for dissection.

At home the patient is teased by everyone, regarded as a fool, cheated; people have no respect for him, spit in his face; the servants take everything from him with their finger tips, because they think that he is syphilitic. All are in alliance together and vent their anger on him; many dogs are the death of the hare. The telephone conversations were listened to; the house was searched; the things sent to the laundry were lost; false keys were found on the ring; at night the children were ren-dered insensible by gas. The patient is surrounded by an international gang of robbers; his house is going to be blown up into the air. People knew his career and his thoughts. At night he is sent to sleep, taken away and made to carry out practical jokes, for which he is later held responsible. A female patient aged sixty-five complained of improper assaults, thought that she had been brought to a house of ill-fame and was pregnant. Another of the same age fancied that she was exposed to the persecutions of old bachelors, who lay down beside her in bed. A young girl asked if she would get a child. A woman forty-eight years of age declared that she was pregnant and that she had impregnated her-self. An elderly man thought that he was dragged about every night in brothels and there infected with syphilis. "I am here again," said a female patient everytime she was visited, as she thought that she was always being taken away each hour to a different place.

Hypochondriacal delusions usually reach a considerable development; they often completely resemble those of the paralytic. In the patient everything is dead, rotten, burnt, petrified, hollow; there is a kind of putrefaction in him. He has syphilis of the fourth stage; his breath is poisonous; he has infected his children, the whole town. His head is changing in shape, is as large as Palestine; his hands and feet are no longer as they were; the bones have become thicker, have slipped lower down; all his limbs are out of joint; his body is no longer compact; it stretches out and is shrivelled up. In his skull there is filth; his brain is melting; the devil has displaced it backwards by a discharge of blood. His heart no longer cooks any blood, is a dead piece of flesh; his blood-vessels are dried up, filled with poison; no circulation goes on any longer; the juices are gone. Everything is closed; in his throat a bone is sticking, a stone; stomach and bowel are no longer there. There is a worm in his body, a hairy animal in his stomach; his food falls down between his intestines into his scrotum; neither urine nor fæces are passed; his entrails are corroded. His testicles are crushed, have disappeared; his genitals are becoming smaller. His mucous glands have risen up; his life is lacerated; rolling about is going on at the navel. There is a hole in his nose; there is pus in his jaw, in all his limbs, and it passes away in great quantity with his motions and with hawking; his palate stinks. His skin is too narrow over the shoulders; worms are lying under it and are creeping about. A patient declared that for eleven years he had been a spirit, and had only the internal organs left; when some one died, death passed through him and took away his entrails; he still had the scar. A female patient asserted that there was iron in her and the bedstead attracted her. Another said that she would get a child with a cat's head. Many patients believe that they are bewitched inwardly, changed into a wild animal, that they must bark, howl and rage. Others cannot sit, cannot eat, cannot go a step, or give their hand.

The ideas of *annihilation,* already frequently indicated in the foregoing pages, may experience a further, wholly nonsensical elaboration. The patient has no longer a name, a home, is not born, does not belong at all to the world any more, is no longer a human being, is no longer here, is a spirit, an abortion, a picture, a ghost, "just only a sort of shape." He cannot live and he cannot die; he must hover about so, remain in the world eternally, is as old as the world, has been already a hundred years here. If he is beaten with an axe on his head, if his breast is cut open, if he is thrown into the fire, he still cannot be killed. "I cannot be buried any more," said a patient, "when I sit down on the weighing-machine, it shows zero!" The world has perished; there are no longer railways, towns, money, beds, doctors; the sea runs out. All human beings are dead, "poisoned with antitoxic serium," burned, dead of starvation, because there is nothing more to eat, because the patient has stuffed everything down into his enormous stomach, and has drunk the water-pipes empty. No one eats or sleeps any more; the patient is the only being of flesh and blood, is alone in the world. A female patient declared that there was no blood in her internal organs, therefore the electric light caught fire from her, so that the whole human race and the firmament were consumed. Another thought that a thunderstorm would destroy the whole world.

Consciousness is in this form frequently somewhat clouded. The patients perceive badly, do not understand what goes on, are not able to form clear ideas. They complain that they cannot lay hold of any proper thought, that they are beastly "stupid," confused in their head, do not know their way, also perhaps that they have so many thoughts in their head, that everything goes pell-mell. Many patients say that they have been made confused by medicines and much eating, that they have been hypnotized, that they continually talk nonsense, must profess sometimes one thing, sometimes another, that they have become crazy. But at the same time, when their delusions come into play, they are incapable of recognising the grossest contradictions or of correcting them; they assert that they cannot take a bit more while they are chewing with full cheeks. "This is my last," said a patient every time the contradiction was pointed out to her. Others beg to be sent out of the world by poison, although they assert that they cannot die at all.

Yet the train of thought is usually in general reasonable. They are frequently also able to give appropriate and connected information about their personal circumstances and more remote things, though certainly they are for the most part little inclined to engage in such conversations, but return immediately to their delusions again.

Mood is sometimes characterised by dull despondency, sometimes by anxious tension or excitement; at times the patients are also repellent, irritated, angry, inclined to violence. But not altogether infrequently we meet in the patients slight self-irony; they try to describe their sins and torments in excessively obtrusive colours, use the language of students, enter into a joke, allow themselves to smile; erotic moods also may be conspicuous. Especially in the last periods of the attack a grumbling, insufferable, perverse mood is developed, which only with complete recovery gradually disappears. A patient declared that she was envious of the other children of God.

The *Volitional Disorders* are also not quite uniform. The activity of the patients is frequently dominated by volitional inhibition; they are taciturn, even mute, cataleptic; they lie with vacant or strained expression of countenance in bed, often with closed eyes, do not ward off pricks, do not do what they are bidden, are resistive when taking nourishment, hide themselves under the cover, are occasionally unclean. The inward tension is, perhaps, only revealed by isolated whispered utterances ("Entreat for me," "What's the matter?"), convulsive grasping of the rosary, imploring looks, excitement during the visits of relatives. Many patients feel themselves not free, but under the influence of a higher power. A patient declared that people had him in their power, he had lost his will completely, and was a broken man. A female patient was obliged to kiss the floor and altar in church.

Anxious restlessness, however, seems to me to be more frequent, occasionally alternating with slight stuporous states. The patients do not remain in bed; they wander about, bewail and lament, often in rhythmical cadence, "Sinful creature, wicked creature." They beg for forbearance as they have not committed any fault; people want to kill them, to bury them alive, to throw them into the outermost darkness, into the river, into the fire, to poison them and then have them dissected, to chase them out naked into the forest, for choice when it is freezing hard. A patient begged to be let down for execution. They refuse nourishment, as they are not worthy of food, do not want to deprive others of nourishment, cannot pay, observe poison or filth in the dishes; they would like to nourish themselves on refuse and to sleep on bare boards. A patient ran about bare-footed in order to be accustomed to the cold when people chased him out into the snow.

At times more violent states of excitement may be interpolated. The patients scream, throw themselves on the floor, force their way senselessly out, beat their heads, hide away under the bed, make desperate attacks on the surroundings. A female patient knelt down in a public warehouse in front of religious pictures and tried to destroy secular ones. Another made herself conspicuous in the tramway car by her loud self-accusations. A third in great anxiety seized the full spittoon and emptied it. A patient, who was wholly disordered, suddenly proposed the health of the Prince Regent. Serious attempts at suicide are in these states extremely frequent. God commanded a female patient to kill her relatives.

Delirious Melancholia

From the form here described, which essentially corresponds to the "melancholia with delusions" of Griesinger, partly also to the "depressive insanity" of many investigators, gradual transitions lead to a last, delirious group of states of depression, which is characterized by *profound visionary clouding of conscience*. Here also numerous, terrifying hallucinations, changing variously, and confused delusions are developed. The appearance of people is changed; faces are distorted; it is like a "wandering of souls." His wife appears "queer" to the patient; mistakes are made about the nearest relatives; a stranger is mistaken for the loved one, a woman believed that her husband was mad. The patient sees the Virgin Mary, the Christ-child, spirits, devils, men, who wish to kill poor souls with the sword. Every one is in mourning; someone must have died. Clouds sink down; fire and flames rise upwards;

buildings with wounded men are burning; cannon are being brought up; the windows are turning round; the sky is falling down. The room stretches itself out into infinity, becomes heaven, in which God sits on his throne, or it becomes the narrow grave, in which the patient is suffocated, while outside prayers for the dead are muttered. On a high mountain sits a little manikin with an umbrella, who is always being blown down again by the wind. The patient hears shooting, the devil speaking, screams, terrifying voices; twenty-seven times it is said, "You are to die like a beast!" Outside the scaffold is being erected; a numerous company is watching him and scoffing at him; the stove makes snappish remarks; the patient is ordered to hang himself in order to bury his shame; he feels burning about his body.

He is in a wrong house, in the law-courts, in a house of ill-fame, in prison, in purgatory, on a rolling ship, attends the solemn burial of a prince with funeral music and a large retinue, flies about in the universe. The people round him have a secret significance, are historical celebrities, divinities; the Empress, disguised as a maid-servant, cleans the boots. The patient himself has become of another sex, is swollen like a barrel, suffers from ulcers in his mouth and cancer; he is of high descent, guardian-angel, the redeemer of the world, a war-horse. An action is brought against him; he is to blame for all misfortune, has committed treason, set the house on fire, is damned, forsworn, and accursed; it penetrates through his whole body. His lungs are to be torn out of him; wild beasts will devour him; he is made to wander about naked on the street, is exhibited publicly as a Siamese twin. A patient called from the window, "The devil is taking me away!" A female patient asked, "Am I allowed to die in open death?" The patient feels quite forsaken, does not know what wrong he has committed, cries aloud, "This is not true!" The children have been shot by their father; the husband wants to marry the sister, the father-in-law to kill the daughter; the brother is threatening murder. Everyone is lost; all is ruined; everything is falling to pieces; everything is undermined. Seething and burning are going on; there is revolution, murder, and war; in the house there is an infernal machine; the justice of God exists no longer. The whole world is burnt up and then again becomes frozen; the patient is the last man, the wandering Jew, alone in desolation, immured in Siberia.

During these changing visionary experiences the patients are outwardly for the most part strongly inhibited; they are scarcely capable of saying a word. They feel confused and perplexed; they cannot collect their thoughts, know absolutely nothing any longer, give contradictory, incomprehensible, unconnected answers, weave in words which they have heard into their detached, slow utterances which they produce as though astonished. The following transcript distinctly shows the great confusion.

One voice has choked the other—No, it wasn't so—It is something peculiar—It was quite different—The house is athwart—Everyone has poison—No, those ones cried out that—No, I've written it extra—Yes, now I eat nothing more—If you had only done it otherwise, then it would have been better—You would have written nothing at all—She alarmed everyone—It isn't really a right sentry up there—Now it will never be better—.

For the most part the patients lie in bed taking no interest in anything. They betray no pronounced emotion; they are mute, inaccessible; they pass their motions under them; they stare straight in front with vacant expression of countenance like a mask and with wide open eyes. Automatic obedience alternates with anxious resistance; at times the patients assume peculiar attitudes and make curious movements. Temporarily they become restless, get out of bed, wander slowly to and fro, force their way out, search round about, want to pull other people out of bed, wring their hands, cling to people, cry out, beg for pardon, protest their innocence. Suicidal attempts also occur. A female patient went with her children into the water and declared, "The devil and lightning and electricity were in me." The taking of food is frequently made very difficult owning to the resistance of the patients.

The *Course* of states of depression is in general fairly protracted, especially in more advanced age. Not infrequently their development is preceded by fluctuating, nervous disorders and slight irritable or depressive moodiness for years before the more marked morbid phenomena begin. Sometimes they appear only as an increase of a slight morbid state which had always existed.

The *Duration* of the attack is usually longer than in mania; but it may likewise fluctuate between a few days and more than a decade. The remission of the morbid phenomena invariably takes place with many fluctuations; not infrequently there is developed at the same time an impatient, grumbling, discontented behaviour, with restlessness and continual attempts to get away, which probably should be connected with the admixture of slight manic disorders.

When the depression disappears with remarkable rapidity, one must be prepared for a manic attack. The improvement of the physical state is for the observer already very conspicuous, while the patient feels himself not at all easier, indeed worse, than formerly. That is perhaps related to the fact that he is more distinctly aware of the disorder when the natural emotional stresses have returned, than at the height of the malady. Later an increased feeling of well-being may take the place of depression; this we must perhaps regard as a manic indication even when it acquires no real morbid extent. A female patient wrote as follows in a letter of thanks shortly after recovery from a rather long period of depression:—

I am now such a happy human being, as I never was before in my whole life; I simply feel that this illness, even though quite insane to endure, had to come. Now at last, after a hard struggle, I may look forward to a quiet future. My spirit is so fresh; I absolutely don't need to be trained, I cook with the greatest calmness . . . at the same time I keep my ideals, which, God be thanked, life has left to me in spite of all that is dreadful. And so my soul is in the greatest peace.

In other cases dejection, lassitude, lack of pleasure in work, sensitiveness still persist for a long time after the more conspicuous morbid phenomena have disappeared. Occasionally also one sees hallucinations, which have arisen at the height of the attack, disappear very gradually although the patients otherwise are perfectly unconstrained psychically and have acquired clear insight into the morbidity of the disorder. A female patient, after recovery from a severe, confused depression still for a number of weeks heard in decreasing strength "her brain chatter," and she made the following notes about it:—

I have nothing more, I do nothing more, I like no one any longer, you submissive thing, you; I have no intention—must come here—they must come here; I know no one any longer—O God, O God, what shall I do, when you have offended all here, in here, you impudent female, you . . .

The content of these auditory hallucinations, which betray a certain rhythm, is partly changing and disconnected, but on the whole lets the trains of thought be recognised, by which the patient was dominated in her depression.

25

Loss

FREUD

LIKE KRAEPELIN, the Austrian Sigmund Freud was born in 1856. His birthplace was Moravia, but he spent most of his life in Vienna. He fled to London in 1938 (a year before his death) when the National Socialists occupied Austria. Freud was trained as a physician and is known as the influential founder of the psychoanalytic movement. His medical studies began in Paris, where he worked with the renowned neurologist Jean-Martin Charcot. On his return to Vienna, Freud began a fruitful collaboration with Josef Breuer on the use of hypnosis in the treatment of hysteria. Later Freud rejected hypnosis and developed a technique of free association, which would allow emotionally charged repressed material to reenter consciousness.

By the beginning of the century, Freud's ideas were systematized and his efforts directed toward founding the psychoanalytic movement. In this he was joined by Swiss psychiatrists Paul Eugen Bleuler and Carl Jung, and the Austrian Alfred Adler. In 1910 the International Psychoanalytical Association was formed with Jung as its president. Later Jung and many of Freud's other followers broke away to form competing psychoanalytic schools. Between the publication of *Studies in Hysteria* with Breuer in 1895 and *The Ego and the Id* in 1923, Freud wrote extensively on psychoanalytic theory and technique. After 1923 his work was devoted more to the application of psychoanalytic ideas to cultural issues. His *Interpretation of Dreams* (1900), *Psychopathology of Everyday Life* (1904), *Three Essays on Sexuality* (1905), and *General Introduction to Psychoanalysis* (1910) are part of a long stream of books, essays, and lectures devoted to ever-developing and evolving theory, case studies, and discussions of analytic technique.

The period leading up to the publication of Freud's essay "Mourning and Melancholia," (written in 1915 but not published until 1917) was particularly fruitful. It is associated with what have come to be called Freud's metapsychological essays, which constitute the cornerstone of his theoretical efforts: "Formulations Regarding the Two Principles in Mental Functioning" and "On the Mechanisms of Paranoia," in 1911; "A Note on the Unconscious in Psychoanalysis," in 1912; "On Narcissism," in 1914; "Instincts and Their Vicissitudes," "Repression," and "The Unconscious," in 1915; and "Metapsychological Supplement to the Theory of Dreams," in 1916.

In the long essay reproduced here, considered by many to be one of his masterpieces, Freud develops a comparison between the normal sadness associated with grieving a lost loved one and the disturbance of self that results, he believes, in dispirited mood states and self-hatred associated with the clinical condition of melancholia. With its technical constructs and theoretical assumptions, Freud's essay is not easy to understand. But it is important for several reasons. It has gone largely unchallenged in psychoanalytic accounts of melancholia and depression through much of the twentieth century. Indeed, it introduced and develops what have become key concepts of psychoanalysis and object-relations theory, such as that of projective identification and introjection. And, with its emphasis on loss, it reconstrues melancholy and melancholia. From a state of imbalance and a mood of despondency, melancholia has become a frame of mind characterized by a loss of something.

Three aspects of "Mourning and Melancholia" distinguish it from earlier writing: the theme of loss, the emphasis on self-accusation and self-loathing in melancholic subjectivity, and the elaborate theory of narcissism, identification, and introjection it introduces. Melancholia represents loss of the "object," that is, the beloved parent whose love has been perceived to be withdrawn. Self-accusation and self-hatred, which Freud describes as central characteristics of the melancholic patient, are a form of rage redirected from the loved object to the self.

Such redirected rage can occur because the self is deeply identified with the other. (This identification is so strong that Freud speaks of the other person as *incorporated* by the self. *Introjection* is his technical term for this process of incorporation.) In developmental terms, the infant's love energy is at first directed exclusively upon the ego; later it turns to the other, a loved person with whom the infant is intimately identified. That identification allows the fantasy that the ego has incorporated the mother, or "object." In those suffering from melancholia, some adult sorrow or slight reignites those infantile experiences. Now with the characteristic ambivalence of the oral phase, the ego attacks the loved, introjected "object" in self-accusations whose curious quality of indifference, Freud believes, proves their true object to be not the self but the incorporated other.

Despite the essay's novelty, several features of the older, Renaissance tradition appear to have found their way into Freud's writing here. First in a sense that the category of melancholy and melancholia eludes definition in a form of words. Freud begins by admitting that "the definition of melancholia is uncertain; it takes on various clinical forms . . . that do not seem definitely to warrant reduction to a unity." Second, melancholia is characterized by loss of an object of which its subject *may be unconscious.* In this respect it seems to mimic the earlier characterizations of melancholy as a nebulous mood state of fear and sadness *without cause*. Finally, in choosing the character of Hamlet as an exemplar, and admitting that the melancholic "has a keener eye for the truth than others who are not melancholic," Freud seems to allow that melancholia may have a glamorous aspect.

•⤳ • ⤳•

Sigmund Freud, "Mourning and Melancholy" (1917)

Now that dreams have proved of service to us as the normal prototypes of narcissistic mental disorders, we propose to try whether a comparison with the normal emotion of grief, and its expression in mourning, will not throw some light on the nature of melancholia. This time, however, we must make a certain prefatory warning against too great expectations of the result. Even in descriptive psychiatry the definition of melancholia is uncertain; it takes on various clinical forms (some of them suggesting somatic rather than psychogenic affections) that do not seem definitely to warrant reduction to a unity. Apart from those impressions which every observer may gather, our material here is limited to a small number of cases the psychogenic nature of which was indisputable. Any claim to general validity for our conclusions shall be forgone at the outset, therefore, and we will console ourselves by reflecting that, with the means of investigation at our disposal to-day, we could hardly discover anything that was not typical, at least of a small group if not of a whole class of disorders.

A correlation of melancholia and mourning seems justified by the general picture of the two conditions.[1] Moreover, wherever it is possible to discern the external influences in life which have brought each of them about, this exciting cause proves to be the same in both. Mourning is regularly the reaction to the loss of a loved person, or to the loss of some abstraction which has taken the place of one, such as fatherland, liberty, an ideal, and so on. As an effect of the same influences, melancholia instead of a state of grief develops in some people, whom we consequently suspect of a morbid pathological disposition. It is also well worth notice that, although grief involves grave departures from the normal attitude to life, it never occurs to us to regard it as a morbid condition and hand the mourner over to medical treatment. We rest assured that after a lapse of time it will be overcome, and we look upon any interference with it as inadvisable or even harmful.

The distinguishing mental features of melancholia are a profoundly painful dejection, abrogation of interest in the outside world, loss of the capacity to love, inhibition of all activity, and a lowering of the self-regarding feelings to a degree that finds utterance in self-reproaches and self-revilings, and culminates in a delusional expectation of punishment. This picture becomes a little more intelligible when we consider that, with one exception, the same traits are met with in grief. The fall in self-esteem is absent in grief; but otherwise the features are the same. Profound mourning, the reaction to the loss of a loved person, contains the same feeling of pain, loss of interest in the outside world—in so far as it does not recall the dead one—loss of capacity to adopt any new object of love, which would mean a replacing of the one mourned, the same turning from every active effort that is not connected with thoughts of the dead. It is easy to see that this inhibition and circumscription in the ego is the expression of an exclusive devotion to its mourning, which leaves nothing over for other purposes or other interests. It is really only because we know so well how to explain it that this attitude does not seem to us pathological.

We should regard it as a just comparison, too, to call the temper of grief "painful." The justification for this comparison will probably prove illuminating when we are in a position to define pain in terms of the economics of the mind.[2]

Now in what consists the work which mourning performs? I do not think there is anything far-fetched in the following representation of it. The testing of reality, having shown that the loved object no longer exists, requires forthwith that all the libido shall be withdrawn from its attachments to this object. Against this demand a struggle of course arises—it may be universally observed that man never willingly abandons a libido-position, not even when a substitute is already beckoning to him. This struggle can be so intense that a turning away from reality ensues, the object being clung to through the medium of a hallucinatory wish-psychosis. The normal outcome is that deference for reality gains the day. Nevertheless its behest cannot be at once obeyed. The task is now carried through bit by bit, under great expense of time and cathectic energy, while all the time the existence of the lost object is continued in the mind. Each single one of the memories and hopes which bound the libido to the object is brought up and hypercathected, and the detachment of the libido from it accomplished. Why this process of carrying out the behest of reality bit by bit, which is in the nature of a compromise, should be so extraordinarily, painful is not at all easy to explain in terms of mental economics. It is worth noting that this pain[3] seems natural to us. The fact is, however, that when the work of mourning is completed the ego becomes free and uninhibited again.

Now let us apply to melancholia what we have learnt about grief. In one class of cases it is evident that melancholia too may be the reaction to the loss of a loved object; where this is not the exciting cause one can perceive that there is a loss of a more ideal kind. The object has not perhaps actually died, but has become lost as an object of love (*e.g.* the case of a deserted bride). In yet other cases one feels justified in concluding that a loss of the kind has been experienced, but one cannot see clearly what has been lost, and may the more readily suppose that the patient too cannot consciously perceive what it is he has lost. This, indeed, might be so even when the patient was aware of the loss giving rise to the melancholia, that is, when he knows whom he has lost but not *what* it is he has lost in them. This would suggest that melancholia is in some way related to an unconscious loss of a love-object, in contradistinction to mourning, in which there is nothing unconscious about the loss.

In grief we found that the ego's inhibited condition and loss of interest was fully accounted for by the absorbing work of mourning. The unknown loss in melancholia would also result in an inner labour of the same kind and hence would be responsible for the melancholic inhibition. Only, the inhibition of the melancholiac seems puzzling to us because we cannot see what it is that absorbs him so entirely. Now the melancholiac displays something else which is lacking in grief—an extraordinary fall in his self-esteem, an impoverishment of his ego in a grand scale. In grief the world becomes poor and empty; in melancholia it is the ego itself. The patient represents his ego to us as worthless, incapable of any effort and morally despicable; he reproaches himself, vilifies himself and expects to be cast out and chastised. He abases himself before everyone and commiserates his own relatives for being connected with someone so unworthy. He does not realize that any change has taken place in him, but extends his self-criticism back over the past and declares that he was never any better. This picture of delusional belittling—which is predominantly moral—is completed by sleeplessness and refusal of nourishment, and by an overthrow, psychologically very remarkable, of that instinct which constrains every living thing to cling to life.

Both scientifically and therapeutically it would be fruitless to contradict the patient who brings these accusations against himself. He must surely be right in some way and be describing something that corresponds to what he thinks. Some of his statements, indeed, we are at once obliged to confirm without reservation. He really is as lacking in interest, as incapable of love and of any achievement as he says. But that, as we know, is secondary, the effect of the inner travail consuming his ego, of which we know nothing but which we compare with the work of mourning. In certain other self-accusations he also seems to us justified, only that he has a keener eye for the truth than others who are not melancholic. When in his exacerbation of self-criticism he describes himself as petty, egoistic, dishonest, lacking in independence, one whose sole aim has been to hide the weaknesses of his own nature, for all we know it may be that he has come very near to self-knowledge; we only wonder why a man must become ill before he can discover truth of this kind. For there can be no doubt that whoever holds and expresses to others such an opinion of himself—one that Hamlet harboured of himself and all men—that man is ill, whether he speaks the truth or is more or less unfair to himself. Nor is it difficult to see that there is no correspondence, so far as we can judge, between the degree to self-abasement and its real justification. A good, capable, conscientious woman will speak no better of herself after she develops melancholia than one who is actually worthless; indeed, the first is more likely to fall ill of the disease than the other, of whom we too should have nothing good to say. Finally, it must strike us that after all the melancholiac's behaviour is not in every way the same as that of one who is normally devoured by remorse and self-reproach. Shame before others, which would characterize this condition above everything, is lacking in him, or at least there is little sign of it. One could almost say that the opposite trait of insistent talking about himself and pleasure in the consequent exposure of himself predominates in the melancholiac.

The essential thing, therefore, is not whether the melancholiac's distressing self-abasement is justified in the opinion of others. The point must be rather that he is correctly describing his psychological situation in his lamentations. He has lost his self-respect and must have some good reason for having done so. It is true that we are then faced with a contradiction which presents a very difficult problem. From the analogy with grief we should have to conclude that the loss suffered by the melancholiac is that of an object; according to what he says the loss is one in himself.

Before going into this contradiction, let us dwell for a moment on the view melancholia affords of the constitution of the ego. We see how in this condition one part of the ego sets itself over against the other, judges it critically, and, as it were, looks upon it as an object. Our suspicion that the critical institution in the mind which is here split off from the ego might also demonstrate its independence in other circumstances will be confirmed by all further observations. We shall really find justification for distinguishing this institution from the rest of the ego. It is the mental faculty commonly called conscience that we are thus recognizing; we shall count it, along with the censorship of consciousness and the testing of reality, among the great institutions of the ego and shall also find evidence elsewhere showing that it can become diseased independently. In the clinical picture of melancholia dissatisfaction with the self on moral grounds is far the most outstanding feature; the self-criticism much less frequently concerns itself with bodily infirmity, ugliness, weakness, social inferiority; among these latter ills that the patient dreads or asseverates the thought of poverty alone has a favoured position.

There is one observation, not at all difficult to make, which supplies an explanation of the contradiction mentioned above. If one listens patiently to the many and various self-accusations of the melancholiac, one cannot in the end avoid the impression that often the most violent of them are hardly at all applicable to the patient himself, but that with insignificant modifications they do fit someone else, some person whom the patient loves, has loved or ought to love. This conjecture is confirmed every time one examines the facts. So we get the key to the clinical picture—by perceiving that the self-reproaches are reproaches against a loved object which have been shifted on to the patient's own ego.

The woman who loudly pities her husband for being bound to such a poor creature as herself is really accusing her husband of being a poor creature in some sense or other. There is no need to be greatly surprised that among those transferred from him some genuine self-reproaches are mingled: they are allowed to obtrude themselves since they help to mask the others and make recognition of the true state of affairs impossible; indeed, they derive from the "for" and "against" contained in the conflict that has led to the loss of the loved object. The behaviour of the patients too becomes now much more comprehensible. Their complaints are really "plaints" in the legal sense of the word; it is because everything derogatory that they say of themselves at bottom relates to someone else that they are not ashamed and do not hide their heads. Moreover, they are far from evincing towards those around them the attitude of humility and submission that alone would befit such worthless persons; on the contrary, they give a great deal of trouble, perpetually taking offence and behaving as if they had been treated with great injustice. All this is possible only because the reactions expressed in their behaviour still proceed from an attitude of revolt, a mental constellation which by a certain process has become transformed into melancholic contrition.

Once this is recognized there is no difficulty in reconstructing this process. First there existed an object-choice, the libido had attached itself to a certain person; then, owing to a real injury or disappointment concerned with the loved person, this object-relationship was undermined. The result was not the normal one of withdrawal of the libido from this object and transference of it to a new one, but something different for which various conditions seem to be necessary. The object-cathexis proved to have little power of resistance, and was abandoned; but the free libido was withdrawn into the ego and not directed to another object. It did not find application there, however, in any one of several possible ways, but served simply to establish an *identification* of the ego with the abandoned object. Thus the shadow of the object fell upon the ego, so that the latter could henceforth be criticized by a special mental faculty like an object, like the forsaken object. In this way the loss of the object became transformed into a loss in the ego, and the conflict between the ego and the loved person transformed into a cleavage between the criticizing faculty of the ego and the ego as altered by the identification.

Certain things may be directly inferred with regard to the necessary conditions and effects of such a process. On the one hand, a strong fixation to the love-object must have been present; on the other hand, in contradiction to this, the object-cathexis can have had little power of resistance. As Otto Rank has aptly remarked, this contradiction seems to imply that the object-choice had been effected on a narcissistic basis, so that when obstacles arise in the way of the object-cathexis it can regress into narcissism. The narcissistic identification with the object then becomes a substitute for the erotic cathexis, the result of which is that in spite of the conflict with the loved person the love-relation need not be given up. This kind of substitution of identification for object-love is an important mechanism in the narcissistic affections; Karl Landauer has lately been able to point to it in the process of recovery in schizophrenia. It of course represents a regression from one type of object-choice to the primal narcissism. We have elsewhere described how object-choice develops from a preliminary stage of identification, the way in which the ego first adopts an object and the ambivalence in which this is expressed. The ego wishes to incorporate this object into itself, and the method by which it would do so, in this oral or cannibalistic stage, is by devouring it. Abraham is undoubtedly right in referring to this connection the refusal of nourishment met with in severe forms of melancholia.

The conclusion which our theory would require, namely, that the disposition to succumb to melancholia—or some part of it—lies in the narcissistic type of object-choice, unfortunately still lacks confirmation by investigation. In the opening remarks of this paper I admitted that the empirical material upon which this study is founded does not supply all we could wish. On the assumption that the results of observation would accord with our inferences, we should not hesitate to include among the special characteristics of melancholia a regression from object-cathexis to the still narcissistic oral phase of the libido. Identifications with the object are by no means rare in the transference-neuroses too; indeed, they are a well-known mechanism in symptom-formation, especially in hysteria. The difference, however, between narcissistic and hysterical identification may be perceived in the object-cathexis, which in the first is relinquished, whereas in the latter it persists and exercises an influence, usually confined to certain isolated actions and innervations. Nevertheless, even in the transference-neuroses identification is the expression of a community which may signify love. The narcissistic identification is the older, and it paves the way to comprehension of the hysterical form, which has been less thoroughly studied.

Some of the features of melancholia, therefore, are borrowed from grief, and the others from the process of regression from narcissistic object-choice to narcissism. On the one hand, like mourning, melancholia is the reaction to a real loss of a loved object; but, over and above this, it is bound to a condition which is absent in normal grief or which, if it supervenes, transforms the latter into a pathological variety. The loss of a love-object constitutes an excellent opportunity for the ambivalence in love-relationships to make itself felt and come to the fore. Consequently where there is a disposition to obsessional neurosis the conflict of ambivalence casts a pathological shade on the grief, forcing it to express itself in the form of self-reproaches, to the effect that the mourner himself is to blame for the loss of the loved one, *i.e.* desired it. These obsessional states of depression following upon the death of loved persons show us what the conflict of ambivalence by itself can achieve, when there is no regressive withdrawal of libido as well. The occasions giving rise to melancholia for the most part extend beyond the clear case of a loss by death, and include all those situations of being wounded, hurt, neglected, out of favour, or disappointed, which can import opposite feelings of love and hate into the relationship or reinforce an already existing ambivalence. This conflict of ambivalence, the origin of which lies now more in actual experience, now more in constitution, must not be neglected among the conditioning factors in melancholia. If the object-love, which cannot be given up, takes refuge in narcissistic identification, while the object itself is abandoned, then hate is expended upon this new substitute-object, railing at it, depreciating it, making it suffer and deriving sadistic gratification from its suffering. The self-torments of melancholiacs, which are without doubt pleasurable, signify, just like the corresponding phenomenon in the obsessional neurosis, a gratification of sadistic tendencies and of hate, both of which relate to an object and in this way have both been turned round upon the self. In both disorders the sufferers usually succeed in the end in taking revenge, by the circuitous path of self-punishment, on the original objects and in tormenting them by means of the illness, having developed the latter so as to avoid the necessity of openly expressing their hostility against the loved ones. After all, the person who has occasioned the injury to the patient's feelings, and against whom his illness is aimed, is usually to be found among those in his near neighbourhood. The melancholiac's erotic cathexis of his object thus undergoes a twofold fate: part of it regresses to identification, but the other part, under the influence of the conflict of ambivalence, is reduced to the stage of sadism, which is nearer to this conflict.

It is this sadism, and only this, that solves the riddle of the tendency to suicide which makes melancholia so interesting—and so dangerous. As the primal condition from which instinct-life proceeds we have come to recognize a self-love of the ego which is so immense, in the fear that rises up at the menace of death we see liberated a volume of narcissistic libido which is so vast, that we cannot conceive how this ego can connive at its own destruction. It is true we have long known that no neurotic harbours thoughts of suicide which are not murderous impulses against others re-directed upon himself, but we have never been able to explain what interplay of forces could carry such a purpose through to execution. Now the analysis of melancholia shows that the ego can kill itself only when, the object-cathexis having been withdrawn upon it, it can treat itself as an object, when it is able to launch against itself the animosity relating to an object—that primordial reaction on the part of the ego to all objects in the outer world. Thus in the regression from narcissistic object-choice the object is indeed abolished, but in spite of all it proves itself stronger than the ego's self. In the two contrasting situations of intense love and of suicide the ego is overwhelmed by the object, though in totally different ways.

We may expect to find the derivation of that one striking feature of melancholia, the manifestations of dread of poverty, in anal erotism, torn out of its context and altered by regression.

Melancholia confronts us with yet other problems, the answer to which in part eludes us. The way in which it passes off after a certain time has elapsed without leaving traces of any gross change is a feature it shares with grief. It appeared that in grief this period of time is necessary for detailed carrying out of the behest imposed by the testing of reality, and that by accomplishing this labour the ego succeeds in freeing its libido from the lost object. We may imagine that the ego is occupied with some analogous task during the course of a melancholia; in neither case have we any insight into the economic processes going forward. The sleeplessness characteristic of melancholia evidently testifies to the inflexibility of the condition, the impossibility of effecting the general withdrawal of cathexes necessary for sleep. The complex of melancholia behaves like an open wound, drawing to itself cathectic energy from all sides (which we have called in the transference-neuroses "anti-cathexes") and draining the ego until it is utterly depleted; it proves easily able to withstand the ego's wish to sleep. The amelioration in the condition that is regularly noticeable towards evening is probably due to a somatic factor and not explicable psychologically. These questions link up with the further one, whether a loss in the ego apart from any object (a purely narcissistic wound to the ego) would suffice to produce the clinical picture of melancholia and whether an impoverishment of ego-libido directly due to toxins would not result in certain forms of the disease.

The most remarkable peculiarity of melancholia, and one most in need of explanation, is the tendency it displays to turn into mania accompanied by a completely opposite symptomatology. Not every melancholia has this fate, as we know. Many cases run their course in intermittent periods, in the intervals of which signs of mania may be entirely absent or only very slight. Others show that regular alternation of melancholic and manic phases which has been classified as circular insanity. One would be tempted to exclude these cases from among those of psychogenic origin, if the psycho-analytic method had not succeeded in effecting an explanation and therapeutic improvement of several cases of the kind. It is not merely permissible, therefore, but incumbent upon us to extend the analytic explanation of melancholia to mania.

I cannot promise that this attempt will prove entirely satisfying; it is much more in the nature of a first sounding and hardly goes beyond that. There are two points from which one may start: the first is a psycho-analytic point of view, and the second one may probably call a matter of general observation in mental economics. The psycho-analytic point is one which several analytic investigators have already formulated in so many words, namely, that the content of mania is no different from that of melancholia, that both the disorders are wrestling with the same "complex," and that in melancholia the ego has succumbed to it, whereas in mania it has mastered the complex or thrust it aside. The other point of view is founded on the observation that all states such as joy, triumph, exultation, which form the normal counterparts of mania, are economically conditioned in the same way. First, there is always a long-sustained condition of great mental expenditure, or one established by long force of habit, upon which at last some influence supervenes making it superfluous, so that a volume of energy becomes available for manifold possible applications and ways of discharge,—for instance, when some poor devil, by winning a large sum of money, is suddenly relieved from perpetual anxiety about his daily bread, when any long and arduous struggle is finally crowned with success, when a man finds himself in a position to throw off at one blow some heavy burden, some false position he has long endured, and so on. All such situations are characterized by high spirits, by the signs of discharge of joyful emotion, and by increased readiness to all kinds of action, just like mania, and in complete contrast to the dejection and inhibition of melancholia. One may venture to assert that mania is nothing other than a triumph of this sort, only that here again what the ego has surmounted and is triumphing over remains hidden from it. Alcoholic intoxication, which belongs to the same group of conditions, may be explained in the same way—in so far as it consists in a state of elation; here there is probably a relaxation produced by toxins of the expenditure of energy in repression. The popular view readily takes for granted that a person in a maniacal state finds such delight in movement and action because he is so "cheery." This piece of false logic must of course be exploded. What has happened is that the economic condition described above has been fulfilled, and this is the reason why the maniac is in such high spirits on the one hand and is so uninhibited in action on the other.

If we put together the two suggestions reached, we have the following result. When mania supervenes, the ego must have surmounted the loss of the object (or the mourning over the loss, or perhaps the object itself), whereupon the whole amount of anti-cathexis which the painful suffering of melancholia drew from the ego and "bound" has become available. Besides this, the maniac plainly shows us that he has become free from the object by whom his suffering was caused, for he runs after new object-cathexes like a starving man after bread.

This explanation certainly sounds plausible, but in the first place it is too indefinite, and, secondly, it gives rise to more new problems and doubts than we can answer. We will not evade a discussion of them, even though we cannot expect it to lead us to clear understanding.

First, then: in normal grief too the loss of the object is undoubtedly surmounted, and this process too absorbs all the energies of the ego while it lasts. Why then does it not set up the economic condition for a phase of triumph after it has run its course or at least produce some slight indication of such a state? I find it impossible to answer this objection off-hand. It reminds us again that we do not even know by what economic measures the work of mourning is carried through; possibly, however, a conjecture may help us here. Reality passes its verdict—that the object no longer exists—upon each single one of the memories and hopes through which the libido was attached to the lost object, and the ego, confronted as it were with the decision whether it will share this fate, is persuaded by the sum of its narcissistic satisfactions in being alive to sever its attachment to the non-existent object. We may imagine that, because of the slowness and the gradual way in which this severance is achieved, the expenditure of energy necessary for it becomes somehow dissipated by the time the task is carried through.

It is tempting to essay a formulation of the work performed during melancholia on the lines of this conjecture concerning the work of mourning. Here we are met at the outset by an uncertainty. So far we have hardly considered the topographical situation in melancholia, nor put the question in what systems or between what systems in the mind the work of melancholia goes on. How much of the mental processes of the disease is still occupied with the unconscious object-cathexes that have been given up and how much with their substitute, by identification, in the ego?

Now, it is easy to say and to write that "the unconscious (thing-)presentation of the object has been abandoned by the libido." In reality, however, this presentation is made up of innumerable single impressions (unconscious traces of them), so that this withdrawal of libido is not a process that can be accomplished in a moment, but must certainly be, like grief, one in which progress is slow and gradual. Whether it begins simultaneously at several points or follows some sort of definite sequence is not at all easy to decide; in analyses it often becomes evident that first one, then another memory is activated and that the laments which are perpetually the same and wearisome in their monotony nevertheless each time take their rise in some different unconscious source. If the object had not this great significance, strengthened by a thousand links, to the ego, the loss of it would be no meet cause for either mourning or melancholia. This character of withdrawing the libido bit by bit is therefore to be ascribed alike to mourning and to melancholia; it is probably sustained by the same economic arrangements and serves the same purposes in both.

As we have seen, however, there is more in the content of melancholia than in that of normal grief. In melancholia the relation to the object is no simple one; it is complicated by the conflict of ambivalence. This latter is either constitutional, *i.e.* it is an element of every love-relation formed by this particular ego, or else it proceeds from precisely those experiences that involved a threat of losing the object. For this reason the exciting causes of melancholia are of a much wider range than those of grief, which is for the most part occasioned only by a real loss of the object, by its death. In melancholia, that is, countless single conflicts in which love and hate wrestle together are fought for the object; the one seeks to detach the libido from the object, the other to uphold this libido-position against assault. These single conflicts cannot be located in any system but the Ucs [Unconscious], the region of memory-traces of things (as contrasted with word-cathexes). The efforts to detach the libido are made in this system also during mourning; but in the latter nothing hinders these processes from proceeding in the normal way through the Pcs [Preconscious] to consciousness. For the work of melancholia this way is blocked, owing perhaps to a number of causes or to their combined operation. Constitutional ambivalence belongs by nature to what is repressed, while traumatic experiences with the object may have stirred to activity something else that has been repressed. Thus everything to do with these conflicts of ambivalence remains excluded from consciousness, until the outcome characteristic of melancholia sets in. This, as we know, consists in the libidinal cathexis that is being menaced at last abandoning the object, only, however, to resume its occupation of that place in the ego whence it came. So by taking flight into the ego love escapes annihilation. After this regression of the libido the process can become conscious; it appears in consciousness as a conflict between one part of the ego and its self-criticizing faculty.

That which consciousness is aware of in the work of melancholia is thus not the essential part of it, nor is it even the part which we may credit with an influence in bringing the suffering to an end. We see that the ego debases itself and rages against itself, and as little as the patient do we understand what this can lead to and how it can change. We can more readily credit such an achievement to the unconscious part of the work, because it is not difficult to perceive an essential analogy between the work performed in melancholia and in mourning. Just as the work of grief, by declaring the object to be dead and offering the ego the benefit of continuing to live, impels the ego to give up the object, so each single conflict of ambivalence, by disparaging the object, denigrating it, even as it were by slaying it, loosens the fixation of the libido to it. It is possible, therefore, for the process in the Ucs to come to an end, whether it be that the fury has spent itself or that the object is abandoned as no longer of value. We cannot tell which of these two possibilities is the regular or more usual one in bringing melancholia to an end, nor what influence this termination has on the future condition of the case. The ego may enjoy here the satisfaction of acknowledging itself as the better of the two, as superior to the object.

Even if we accept this view of the work of melancholia, it still does not supply an explanation of the one point upon which we hoped for light. By analogy with various other situations we expected to discover in the ambivalence prevailing in melancholia the economic condition for the appearance of mania when the melancholia has run its course. But there is one fact to which our expectations must bow. Of the three conditioning factors in melancholia—loss of the object, ambivalence, and regression of libido into the ego—the first two are found also in the obsessional reproaches arising after the death of loved persons. In these it is indubitably the ambivalence that motivates the conflict, and observation shows that after it has run its course nothing in the nature of a triumph or a manic state of mind is left. We are thus directed to the third factor as the only one that can have this effect. That accumulation of cathexis which is first of all "bound" and then, after termination of the work of melancholia, becomes free and makes mania possible must be connected with the regression of the libido into narcissism. The conflict in the ego, which in melancholia is substituted for the struggle surging round the object, must act like a painful wound which calls out unusually strong anti-cathexes. Here again, however, it will be well to call a halt and postpone further investigations into mania until we have gained some insight into the economic conditions, first, of bodily pain, and then of the mental pain which is its analogue. For we know already that, owing to the interdependence of the complicated problems of the mind, we are forced to break off every investigation at some point until such time as the results of another attempt elsewhere can come to its aid.

PART 2

After Freud

The Depressive Position

MELANIE KLEIN WAS BORN IN Vienna in 1882 and died in London in 1960. She was one of the most influential but also controversial thinkers to extend and expand Freudian insights. Her influence has been felt particularly in her adopted home of England, where she lived and practiced after 1926. Here, she inspired the British neo-Freudian school of object-relations psychology associated with W. R. D. Fairbairn and Donald Winnicott.

Klein's early years were spent in country towns outside of Vienna, where her Galatian father, learned but ineffectual, worked first as a theater doctor and later as a dentist. Her mother, from an enlightened Slovak Jewish family, supported the family's three children with help from her brother. Melanie was an outstanding student and was considered very beautiful. Her youthful plan to study medicine was interrupted by her marriage to her cousin, Arthur Klein, which was soon followed by the birth of three children. After the death of her mother, and a lingering depression that lasted for much of her youth and young motherhood, she entered into psychoanalysis with Freud's protégée, Sandor Ferenczi, in Budapest, where she then lived. Klein's experience as a mother directed her interest toward the earliest years of life. At Ferenczi's urging she began developing the method of child analysis, with a new emphasis on the interpretation of play, and it was from this that all her subsequent contributions to psychoanalysis stemmed. At first she analyzed her own children; later, she took on others. At the urging of her mentor and greatest influence, Karl Abraham, she moved to Berlin. There, although without formal medical training, she attracted attention within the psychoanalytic community through her innovative application of Freud's ideas and her written papers, delivered in the various psychoanalytical institutes in Europe and England. Her eventual move to London came in part because of the more hospitable attitude toward her ideas in England. Nevertheless, she continued to find her ideas challenged, and in 1927 acrimonious and public disagreement marked the split between her school of psychoanalytic thinking and that of Anna Freud.

Klein's interest lay in the relationships established by an infant during the first years of life. Reinterpreting Freud's account of the conflicts among instincts, Klein developed a theory about the interplay of attitudes, particularly of love and hate, felt in relation to the infant's first "objects," the mother and parts of the mother, such as her breasts, as both external objects and internal representations. The centrality accorded to these early feelings, particularly the intense, negative ones, is a distinguishing mark of Kleinian theory.

Klein first wrote of the depressive position in 1935 and continued to alter and develop her analysis for the rest of her life. In the excerpt that follows, from 1940, *depressive position* referred to the infant's inner turmoil and distress accompanying weaning; the first painful, frustrating, and alarming experience of separation and loss; and the recognition that a whole object is both loved and hated. Elaborating on the feelings of loss associated with early separation about which Freud had written in "Mourning and Melancholia," Klein postulated that this period of infancy involved in every case a kind of infantile neurosis, similar to melancholia. It was, as she put it, melancholia in *statu nascendi,* which she called the *depressive position,* a stage, she believed, that must be recognized as the central one in the child's development. The distress and sense of loss experienced by the infant in the depressive position is relived and reactivated with the occurrence of many adult neuroses, not only melancholia but also manic-depressive, obsessional, and paranoid conditions. Adult mourning also returns its sufferer to the depressive position, for adult mourning is itself a kind of neurosis. Not only do adult neruoses lead back to the depressive position: a failure to satisfactorily resolve the depressive position accounts for all adult adjustment problems. Such a satisfactory resolution, for Klein, requires introjecting the sense of love, goodness, and security provided by the "good" object. Klein employs the same concepts as Freud in describing the way the infant incorporates the mother or a fantasied idea of the mother, but she elaborates extensively on these ideas. From the start the infant feels ambivalence toward the object: bad as well as good aspects of the other are recognized and later incorporated; hatred and rage as well as love are directed toward the other.

In later writing Klein continued to see feelings as clustered around the two basic positions of depressive and paranoid-schizoid, but these two "positions" became affective structures reflecting differences in ego integration. More recent psychoanalytic theories have also cast the depressive position as a mode of relating to objects based on ego integration. Rather than an infantile stage to be overcome, the depressive position is a relatively mature psychic achievement. Fluctuation between the depressive and more primitive paranoid-schizoid modes, on this elaboration, is a central factor in psychic life (Bion, 1963).

Klein's emphasis on the early experiences of the infant and on the infant-mother dyad has powerfully influenced the later evolution of psychoanalytic thinking. Nonetheless, her attribution of these elaborate and attenuated feelings to infants has been the source of much subsequent criticism of her work.

•⤳ • ⌣•

From Melanie Klein, "Mourning and Its Relation to Manic-Depressive States" (1940)

. . . In my view there is a close connection between the testing of reality in normal mourning and early processes of the mind. My contention is that the child goes through states of mind comparable to the mourning of the adult, or rather, that this early mourning is revived whenever grief is experienced in later life. The most important of the methods by which the child overcomes his states of mourning, is, in my view, the testing of reality; this process, however, as Freud stresses, is part of the work of mourning.

In my paper "A Contribution to the Psychogenesis of Manic-Depressive States," I introduced the conception of the *infantile depressive position* and showed the connection between that position and manic-depressive states. Now in order to make clear the relation between the infantile depressive position and normal mourning I must first briefly refer to some statements I made in that paper, and shall then enlarge on them. In the course of this exposition I also hope to make a contribution to the further understanding of the connection between normal mourning, on the one hand, and abnormal mourning and manic-depressive states, on the other.

I said there that the baby experiences depressive feelings which reach a climax just before, during and after weaning. This is the state of mind in the baby which I termed the "depressive position," and I suggested that it is a melancholia in *statu nascendi*. The object which is being mourned is the mother's breast and all that the breast and the milk have come to stand for in the infant's mind: namely, love, goodness and security. All these are felt by the baby to be lost, and lost as a result of his own uncontrollable greedy and destructive phantasies and impulses against his mother's breasts. Further distress about impending loss (this time of both parents) arises out of the Oedipus situation, which sets in so early and in such close connection with breast frustrations that in its beginnings it is dominated by oral impulses and fears. The circle of loved objects who are attacked in phantasy, and whose loss is therefore feared, widens owing to the child's ambivalent relations to his brothers and sisters. The aggression against phantasied brothers and sisters, who are attacked inside the mother's body, also gives rise to feelings of guilt and loss. The sorrow and concern about the feared loss of the "good" objects, that is to say, the depressive position, is, in my experience, the deepest source of the painful conflicts in the Oedipus situation, as well as in the child's relations to people in general. In normal development these feelings of grief and fears are overcome by various methods.

Along with the child's relation, first to his mother and soon to his father and other people, go those processes of internalization on which I have laid so much stress in my work. The baby, having incorporated his parents, feels them to be live people inside his body in the concrete way in which deep unconscious phantasies are experienced—they are, in his mind, "internal" or "inner" objects, as I have termed them. Thus an inner world is being built up in the child's unconscious mind, corresponding to his actual experiences and the impressions he gains from people and the external world, and yet altered by his own phantasies and impulses. If it is a world of people predominantly at peace with each other and with the ego, inner harmony, security and integration ensue.

There is a constant interaction between anxieties relating to the "external" mother—as I will call her here in contrast to the "internal" one—and those relating to the "internal" mother, and the methods used by the ego for dealing with these two sets of anxieties are closely inter-related. In the baby's mind, the "internal" mother is bound up with the "external" one, of whom she is a "double," though one which at once undergoes alterations in his mind through the very process of internalization; that is to say, her image is influenced by his phantasies, and by internal stimuli and internal experiences of all kinds. When external situations which he lives through become internalized—and I hold that they do, from the earliest days onwards—they follow the same pattern: they also become "doubles" of real situations, and are again altered for the same reasons. The fact that by being internalized, people, things, situations and happenings—the whole inner world which is being built up—becomes inaccessible to the child's accurate observation and judgement, and cannot be verified by the means of perception which are available in connection with the tangible and palpable object-world, has an important bearing on the phantastic nature of this inner world. The ensuing doubts, uncertainties and anxieties act as a continuous incentive to the young child to observe and make sure about the external object-world, from which this inner world springs, and by these means to understand the internal one better. The visible mother thus provides continuous proofs of what the "internal" mother is like, whether she is loving or angry, helpful or revengeful. The extent to which external reality is able to disprove anxieties and sorrow relating to the internal reality varies with each individual, but could be taken as one of the criteria for normality. In children who are so much dominated by their internal world that their anxieties cannot be sufficiently disproved and counteracted even by the pleasant aspects of their relationships with people, severe mental difficulties are unavoidable. On the other hand, a certain amount even of unpleasant experiences is of value in this testing of reality by the child if, through overcoming them, he feels that he can retain his objects as well as their love for him and his love for them, and thus preserve or re-establish internal life and harmony in face of dangers.

All the enjoyments which the baby lives through in relation to his mother are so many proofs to him that the loved object *inside as well as outside* is not injured, is not turned into a vengeful person. The increase of love and trust, and the diminishing of fears through happy experiences, help the baby step by step to overcome his depression and feeling of loss (mourning). They enable him to test his inner reality by means of outer reality. Through being loved and through the enjoyment and comfort he has in relation to people his confidence in his own as well as in other people's goodness becomes strengthened, his hope that his "good" objects and his own ego can be saved and preserved increases, at the same time as his ambivalence and acute fears of internal destruction diminish.

Unpleasant experiences and the lack of enjoyable ones, in the young child, especially lack of happy and close contact with loved people, increase ambivalence, diminish trust and hope and confirm anxieties about inner annihilation and external persecution; moreover they slow down and perhaps permanently check the beneficial processes through which in the long run inner security is achieved.

In the process of acquiring knowledge, every new piece of experience has to be fitted into the patterns provided by the psychic reality which prevails at the time; whilst the psychic reality of the child is gradually influenced by every step in his progressive knowledge of external reality. Every such step goes along with his more and more firmly establishing his inner "good " objects, and is used by the ego as a means of overcoming the depressive position.

In other connections I have expressed the view that every infant experiences anxieties which are psychotic in content, and that the infantile neurosis[1] is the normal means of dealing with and modifying these anxieties. This conclusion I can now state more precisely, as a result of my work on the infantile depressive position, which has led me to believe that it is the central position in the child's development. In the infantile neurosis the early depressive position finds expression, is worked through and gradually overcome; and this is an important part of the process of organization and integration which, together with the sexual development, characterizes the first years of life. Normally the child passes through the infantile neurosis, and among other achievements arrives step by step at a good relation to people and to reality. I hold that this satisfactory relation to people depends upon his having succeeded in his struggles against the chaos inside him (the depressive position) and having securely established his "good" internal objects.

Let us now consider more closely the methods and mechanisms by which this development comes about.

In the baby, processes of introjection and projection, since they are dominated by aggression and anxieties which reinforce each other, lead to fears of persecution by terrifying objects. To such fears are added those of losing his loved objects; that is to say, the depressive position has arisen. When I first introduced the concept of the depressive position, I put forward the suggestion that the introjection of the whole loved object gives rise to concern and sorrow lest that object should be destroyed (by the "bad" objects and the id), and that these distressed feelings and fears, in addition to the paranoid set of fears and defences, constitute the depressive position. There are thus two sets of fears, feelings and defences, which, however varied in themselves and however intimately linked together, can, in my view, for purposes of theoretical clearness, be isolated from each other. The first set of feelings and phantasies are the persecutory ones, characterized by fears relating to the destruction of the ego by internal persecutors. The defences against these fears are predominantly the destruction of the persecutors by violent or secretive and cunning methods. With these fears and defences I have dealt in detail in other contexts. The second set of feelings which go to make up the depressive position I formerly described without suggesting a term for them. I now propose to use for these feelings of sorrow and concern for the loved objects, the fears of losing them and the longing to regain them, a simple word derived from everyday language—namely the "pining" for the loved object. In short— persecution (by "bad" objects) and the characteristic defences against it, on the one hand, and pining for the loved ("good") object, on the other, constitute the depressive position.

When the depressive position arises, the ego is forced (in addition to earlier defences) to develop methods of defence which are essentially directed against the "pining" for the loved object. These are fundamental to the whole ego-organization. I formerly termed some of these methods *manic defences,* or the *manic position,* because of their relationship to the manic-depressive illness.

The fluctuations between the depressive and the manic position are an essential part of normal development. The ego is driven by depressive anxieties (anxiety lest the loved objects as well as itself should be destroyed) to build up omnipotent and violent phantasies, partly for the purpose of controlling and mastering the "bad," dangerous objects, partly in order to save and restore the loved ones. From the very beginning these omnipotent phantasies, both the destructive and the reparative ones, stimulate and enter into all the activities, interests and sublimations of the child. In the infant the extreme character both of his sadistic and of his constructive phantasies is in line with the extreme frightfulness of his persecutors—and, at the other end of the scale, the extreme perfection of his "good" objects.[2] Idealization is an essential part of the manic position and is bound up with another important element of that position, namely denial. Without partial and temporary denial of psychic reality the ego cannot bear the disaster by which it feels itself threatened when the depressive position is at its height. Omnipotence, denial and idealization, closely bound up with ambivalence, enable the early ego to assert itself to a certain degree against its internal persecutors and against a slavish and perilous dependence upon its loved objects, and thus to make further advances in development. I will here quote a passage from my former paper:

". . . in the earliest phase the persecuting and the good objects (breasts) are kept wide apart in the child's mind. When, along with the introjection of the whole and real object, they come closer together, the ego has over and over again recourse to that mechanism—so important for the development of the relations to objects—namely, a splitting of its imagos into loved and hated, that is to say, into good and dangerous ones.

"One might think that it is actually at this point that ambivalence which, after all, refers to object-relations—that is to say, to whole and real objects—sets in. Ambivalence, carried out in a splitting of the imagos, enables the young child to gain more trust and belief in its real objects and thus in its internalized ones—to love them more and to carry out in an increasing degree its phantasies of restoration of the loved object. At the same time the paranoid anxieties and defences are directed towards the 'bad' objects. The support which the ego gets from a real 'good' object is increased by a flight-mechanism, which alternates between its external and internal good objects. [Idealization.]

"It seems that at this stage of development the unification of external and internal, loved and hated, real and imaginary objects is carried out in such a way that each step in the unification leads again to a renewed splitting of the imagos. But as the adaptation to the external world increases, this splitting is carried out on planes which gradually become increasingly nearer and nearer to reality. This goes on until love for the real and the internalized objects and trust in them are well established. Then ambivalence, which is partly a safeguard against one's own hate and against the hated and terrifying objects, will in normal development again diminish in varying degrees."

As has already been stated, omnipotence prevails in the early phantasies, both the destructive and the reparative ones, and influences sublimations as well as object relations. Omnipotence, however, is so closely bound up in the unconscious with the sadistic impulses with which it was first associated that the child feels again and again that his attempts at reparation have not succeeded, or will not succeed. His sadistic impulses, he feels, may easily get the better of him. The young child, who cannot sufficiently trust his reparative and constructive feelings, as we have seen, resorts to manic omnipotence. For this reason, in an early stage of development the ego has not adequate means at its disposal to deal efficiently with guilt and anxiety. All this leads to the need in the child—and for that matter to some extent in the adult also—to repeat certain actions obsessionally (this, in my view, is part of the repetition compulsion), or—the contrasting method—omnipotence and denial are resorted to. When the defences of a manic nature fail (defences in which dangers from various sources are in an omnipotent way denied or minimized) the ego is driven alternately or simultaneously to combat the fears of deterioration and disintegration by attempted reparations carried out in obsessional ways. I have described elsewhere my conclusion that the obsessional mechanisms are a defence against paranoid anxieties as well as a means of modifying them, and here I will only show briefly the connection between obsessional mechanisms and manic defences in relation to the depressive position in normal development.

The very fact that manic defences are operating in such close connection with the obsessional ones contributes to the ego's fear that the reparation attempted by obsessional means has also failed. The desire to control the object, the sadistic gratification of overcoming and humiliating it, of getting the better of it, the *triumph* over it, may enter so strongly into the act of reparation (carried out by thoughts, activities of sublimations) that the "benign" circle started by this act becomes broken. The objects which were to be restored change again into persecutors, and in turn paranoid fears are revived. These fears reinforce the paranoid defence mechanisms (of destroying the object) as well as the manic mechanisms (of controlling it or keeping it in suspended animation, and so on). The reparation which was in progress is thus disturbed or even nullified—according to the extent to which these mechanisms are activated. As a result of the failure of the act of reparation, the ego has to resort again and again to obsessional and manic defences.

When in the course of normal development a relative balance between love and hate is attained, and the various aspects of objects are more unified, then also a certain equilibrium between these contrasting and yet closely related methods is reached, and their intensity is diminished. In this connection I wish to stress the importance of *triumph,* closely bound up with contempt and omnipotence, as an element of the manic position. We know the part rivalry plays in the child's burning desire to equal the achievements of the grown-ups. In addition to rivalry, his wish, mingled with fears, to "grow out" of his deficiencies (ultimately to overcome his destructiveness and his bad inner objects and to be able to control them) is an incentive to achievements of all kinds. In my experience, the desire to reverse the child-parent relation, to get power over the parents and to triumph over them, is always to some extent associated with desires directed to the attainment of success. A time will come, the child phantasies, when he will be strong, tall and grown up, powerful, rich and potent, and father and mother will have changed into helpless children, or again, in other phantasies, will be very old, weak, poor and rejected. The triumph over the parents in such phantasies, through the guilt to which it gives rise, often cripples endeavours of all kinds. Some people are obliged to remain unsuccessful, because success always implies to them the humiliation or even the damage of somebody else, in the first place the triumph over parents, brothers and sisters. The efforts by which they seek to achieve something may be of a highly constructive nature, but the implicit triumph and the ensuing harm and injury done to the object may outweigh these purposes, in the subject's mind, and therefore prevent their fulfilment. The effect is that the reparation to the loved objects, which in the depths of the mind are the same as those over which he triumphs, is again thwarted, and therefore guilt remains unrelieved. The subject's triumph over his objects necessarily implies to him their wish to triumph over him, and therefore leads to distrust and feelings of persecution. Depression may follow, or an increase in manic defences and more violent control of his objects, since he has failed to reconcile, restore, or improve them, and therefore feelings of being persecuted by them again have the upper hand. All this has an important bearing on the infantile depressive position and the ego's success or failure in overcoming it. The triumph over his internal objects which the young child's ego controls, humiliates and tortures is a part of the destructive aspect of the manic position which disturbs the reparation and re-creating of his inner world and of internal peace and harmony; and thus triumph impedes the work of early mourning.

To illustrate these developmental processes let us consider some features which can be observed in hypomanic people. It is characteristic of the hypomanic person's attitude towards people, principles and events that he is inclined to exaggerated valuations: over-admiration (idealization) or contempt (devaluation). With this goes his tendency to conceive of everything on a large scale, to think in *large numbers,* all this in accordance with the greatness of his omnipotence, by which he defends himself against his fear of losing the one irreplaceable object, his mother, whom he still mourns at bottom. His tendency to minimize the importance of details and small numbers, and a frequent casualness about details and contempt of conscientiousness contrast sharply with the very meticulous methods, the concentration on the smallest things (Freud), which are part of the obsessional mechanisms.

This contempt, however, is also based to some extent on denial. He must deny his impulse to make extensive and detailed reparation because he has to deny the cause for the reparation; namely, the injury to the object and his consequent sorrow and guilt.

Returning to the course of early development, we may say that every step in emotional, intellectual and physical growth is used by the ego as a means of overcoming the depressive position. The child's growing skills, gifts and arts increase his belief in the psychic reality of his constructive tendencies, in his capacity to master and control his hostile impulses as well as his "bad" internal objects. Thus anxieties from various sources are relieved, and this results in a diminution of aggression and, in turn, of his suspicions of "bad" external and internal objects.

The strengthened ego, with its greater trust in people, can then make still further steps towards unification of its imagos—external, internal, loved and hated—and towards further mitigation of hatred by means of love, and thus to a general process of integration.

When the child's belief and trust in his capacity to love, in his reparative powers and in the integration and security of his good inner world increase as a result of the constant and manifold proofs and counter-proofs gained by the testing of external reality, manic omnipotence decreases and the obsessional nature of the impulses towards reparation diminishes, which means in general that the infantile neurosis has passed.

We have now to connect the infantile depressive position with normal mourning. The poignancy of the acutal loss of a loved person is, in my view, greatly increased by the mourner's unconscious phantasies of having lost his *internal* "good" objects as well. He then feels that his internal "bad" objects predominate and his inner world is in danger of disruption. We know that the loss of a loved person leads to an impulse in the mourner to reinstate the lost loved object in the ego (Freud and Abraham). In my view, however, he not only takes into himself (reincorporates) the person whom he has just lost, but also reinstates his internalized good objects (ultimately his loved parents), who became part of his inner world from the earliest stages of his development onwards. These too are felt to have gone under, to be destroyed, whenever the loss of a loved person is experienced. Thereupon the early depressive position, and with it anxieties, guilt and feelings of loss and grief derived from the breast situation, the Oedipus situation and from all other sources, are reactivated. Among all these emotions, the fears of being robbed and punished by both dreaded parents—that is to say, feelings of persecution—have also been revived in deep layers of the mind.

If, for instance, a woman loses her child through death, along with sorrow and pain her early dread of being robbed by a "bad" retaliating mother is reactivated and confirmed. Her own early aggressive phantasies of robbing her mother of babies gave rise to fears and feelings of being punished, which strengthened ambivalence and led to hatred and distrust of others. The reinforcement of feelings or persecution in the state of mourning is all the more painful because, as a result of an increase in ambivalence and distrust, friendly relations with people, which might at that time be so helpful, become impeded.

The pain experienced in the slow process of testing reality in the work of mourning thus seems to be partly due to the necessity, not only to renew the links to the external world and thus continuously to re-experience the loss, but at the same time and by means of this to rebuild with anguish the inner world, which is felt to be in danger of deteriorating and collapsing. Just as the young child passing through the depressive position is struggling, in his unconscious mind, with the task of establishing and intergrating his inner world, so the mourner goes through the pain of re-establishing and reintegrating it.

In normal mourning early psychotic anxieties are reactivated. The mourner is in fact ill, but because this state of mind is common and seems so natural to us, we do not call mourning an illness. (For similar reasons, until recent years, the infantile neurosis of the normal child was not recognized as such.) To put my conclusions more precisely: I should say that in mourning the subject goes through a modified and transitory manic-depressive state and overcomes it, thus repeating, though in different circumstances and with different manifestations, the processes which the child normally goes through in his early development.

The greatest danger for the mourner comes from the turning of his hatred against the lost loved person himself. One of the ways in which hatred expresses itself in the situation of mourning is in feelings of triumph over the dead person. I refer in an earlier part of this paper to triumph as part of the manic position in infantile development. Infantile death-wishes against parents, brothers and sisters are actually fulfilled whenever a loved person dies, because he is necessarily to some extent a representative of the earliest important figures, and therefore takes over some of the feelings pertaining to them. Thus his death, however shattering for other reasons, is to some extent also felt as a victory, and gives rise to triumph, and therefore all the more to guilt.

. . . Having described some of the processes which I have observed at work in mourning and in depressive states, I wish now to link up my contribution with the work of Freud and Abraham.

Based on Freud's and his own discoveries about the nature of the archaic processes at work in melancholia, Abraham found that such processes also operate in the work of normal mourning. He concluded that in this work the individual succeeds in establishing the lost loved person in his ego, while the melancholic has failed to do so. Abraham also described some of the fundamental factors upon which that success or failure depends.

My experience leads me to conclude that, while it is true that the characteristic feature of normal mourning is the individual's setting up the lost loved object inside himself, he is not doing so for the first time but, through the work of mourning, is reinstating that object as well as all his loved *internal* objects which he feels he has lost. He is therefore *recovering* what he had already attained in childhood.

In the course of his early development, as we know, he establishes his parents within his ego. (It was the understanding of the processes of introjection in melancholia and in normal mourning which, as we know, led Freud to recognize the existence of the super-ego in normal development.) But, as regards the nature of the super-ego and the history of its individual development, my conclusions differ from those of Freud. As I have often pointed out, the processes of introjection and projection from the beginning of life lead to the institution inside ourselves of loved and hated objects, who are felt to be "good" and "bad," and who are interrelated with each other and with the self: that is to say, they constitute an inner world. This assembly of internalized objects becomes organized, together with the organization of the ego, and in the higher strata of the mind it becomes discernible as the super-ego. Thus, the phenomenon which was recognized by Freud, broadly speaking, as the voices and the influence of the actual parents established in the ego, is according to my findings, a complex object-world, which is felt by the individual, in deep layers of the unconscious, to be concretely inside himself, and for which I and some of my colleagues therefore use the term "internalized objects" and an "inner world." This inner world consists of innumerable objects taken into the ego, corresponding partly to the multitude of varying aspects, good and bad, in which the parents (and other people) appeared to the child's unconscious mind throughout various stages of his development. Further, they also represent all the real people who are continually becoming internalized in a variety of situations provided by the multitude of ever-changing external experiences as well as phantasied ones. In addition, all these objects are in the inner world in an infinitely complex relation both with each other and with the self.

If I now apply this description of the super-ego organization, as compared with Freud's super-ego, to the process of mourning, the nature of my contribution to the understanding of this process becomes clear. In normal mourning the individual reintrojects and reinstates, as well as the actual lost person, his loved parents who are felt to be his "good" inner objects. His inner world, the one which he has built up from his earliest days onwards, in his phantasy was destroyed when the actual loss occurred. The rebuilding of this inner world characterizes the successful work of mourning.

. . . I have shown here and in my previous paper the deeper reasons for the individual's incapacity to overcome successfully the infantile depressive position. Failure to do so may result in depressive illness, mania or paranoia. I pointed out (op. cit.) one or two other methods by which the ego attempts to escape from the sufferings connected with the depressive position, namely either the flight to internal good objects (which may lead to severe psychosis) or the flight to external good objects (with the possible outcome of neurosis). There are, however, many ways, based on obsessional, manic and paranoid defences, varying from individual to individual in their relative proportion, which in my experience all serve the same purpose, that is, to enable the individual to escape from the sufferings connected with the depressive position. (All these methods, as I have pointed out, have a part in normal development also.) This can be clearly observed in the analyses of people who fail to experience mourning. Feeling incapable of saving and securely reinstating their loved objects inside themselves, they must turn away from them more than hitherto and therefore deny their love for them. This may mean that their emotions in general become more inhibited; in other cases it is mainly feelings of love which become stifled and hatred is increased. At the same time, the ego uses various ways of dealing with paranoid fears (which will be the stronger the more hatred is reinforced). For instance, the internal "bad" objects are manically subjugated, immobilized and at the same time denied, as well as strongly projected into the external world. Some people who fail to experience mourning may escape from an outbreak of manic-depressive illness or paranoia only by a severe restriction of their emotional life which impoverishes their whole personality.

Whether some measure of mental balance can be maintained in people of this type often depends on the ways in which these various methods interact, and on their capacity to keep alive in other directions some of the love which they deny to their lost objects. Relations to people who do not in their minds come too close to the lost object, and interest in things and activities, may absorb some of this love which belonged to the lost object. Though these relations and sublimations will have some manic and paranoid qualities, they may nevertheless offer some reassurance and relief from guilt, for through them the lost loved object which has been rejected and thus again destroyed is to some extent restored and retained in the unconscious mind.

If, in our patients, analysis diminishes the anxieties of destructive and persecuting internal parents, it follows that hate and thus in turn anxieties decrease, and the patients are enabled to revise their relation to their parents—whether they be dead or alive—and to rehabilitate them to some extent even if they have grounds for actual grievances. This greater tolerance makes it possible for them to set up "good" parent-figures more securely in their minds, alongside the "bad" internal objects, or rather to mitigate the fear of these "bad" objects by the trust in "good" objects. This means enabling them to experience emotions—sorrow, guilt and grief, as well as love and trust—to go through mourning, but to overcome it, and ultimately to overcome the infantile depressive position, which they have failed to do in childhood.

To conclude. In normal mourning, as well as in abnormal mourning and in manic-depressive states, the infantile depressive position is reactivated. The complex feelings, phantasies and anxieties included under this term are of a nature which justifies my contention that the child in his early development goes through a transitory manic-depressive state as well as a state of mourning, which become modified by the infantile neurosis. With the passing of the infantile neurosis, the infantile depressive position is overcome.

The fundamental difference between normal mourning on the one hand, and abnormal mourning and manic-depressive states on the other, is this: the manic-depressive and the person who fails in the work of mourning, though their defences may differ widely from each other, have this in common, that they have been unable in early childhood to establish their internal "good" objects and to feel secure in their inner world. They have never really overcome the infantile depressive position. In normal mourning, however, the early depressive position, which had become revived through the loss of the loved object, becomes modified again, and is overcome by methods similar to those used by the ego in childhood. The individual is reinstating his actually lost loved object; but he is also at the same time reestablishing inside himself his first loved objects—ultimately the "good" parents—whom, when the actual loss occurred, he felt in danger of losing as well. It is by reinstating inside himself the "good" parents as well as the recently lost person, and by rebuilding his inner world, which was disintegrated and in danger, that he overcomes his grief, regains security, and achieves true harmony and peace.

A Learned Helplessness Model of Depression

SELIGMAN

BORN IN 1942 IN ALBANY, New York, Martin Seligman is pro-fessor of psychology and director of clinical training at the University of Pennsylvania. He received his education at Princeton University and at the University of Pennsylvania, from which institution he was awarded a doctorate in psychology in 1967.

Best known for his experimentally based research on learned help-lessness, Seligman has published widely in experimental psychology, learning psychology, and clinical psychology. His publications include *Helplessness: On Depression, Development, and Death* published in 1975, with a second edition in 1991; a 1980 volume entitled *Human Helplessness: Theory and Application,* which he edited with J. Garber; and more recent work on optimism (*Learned Optimism* [1991] and *What You Can Change and What You Can't* [1993]).

Seligman's analysis of depression as learned helplessness grew out of his work on the effects of experimentally contrived helplessness in laboratory animals. Such induced helplessness, he discovered, shared several important traits with naturally occurring states of clinical depression. This enabled him to postulate a learned helplessness model of depression, out of which can be derived an etiological account of depression. Clinical depression results from a belief in one's own power-lessness, a belief, in its turn, engendered by life experiences.

Several points about this experimental approach deserve note. First, in offering this account of depression, Seligman means to explain both the so-called reactive or exogenous depression, whose social and psychological causes are identifiable, and the endogenous depression, without apparent or known triggers in the individual's life experience.

Second, Seligman recognizes that his definition of depression as learned helplessness diverges from customary accounts of depressive subjectivity, as we can see it does also from traditional accounts of melancholy and melancholia. Because subjective states like dejected mood, feelings of self-blame, suicidal thoughts, and loss of mirth are not susceptible to investigation through animal studies, as he points out, these no longer attach to the definition of depression. Nor, more-over, does generalized pessimism: Learned helplessness involves pessimism over one's own actions, not other states in the world. Many would insist such traits as these are essential to melancholic and depressive states; for them, Seligman's narrowed concept of depression scarcely deserves the title depression and cannot be regarded as making reference to what is loosely known as clinical depression.

Although Seligman's intention was not to explain the link between women and depression, his theory's appeal to a deprivation of opportunity as the cause of depression has been recognized to complement explanations of women's greater proneness to depression in terms of gender role.

Seligman's identification of the state of helplessness with loss also takes him from "loss" as understood in other theories of depression. Although it is trivially true that helplessness corresponds to a deprivation or loss of opportunities to act, the state of helplessness identified by Seligman implies neither loss of any personified object of the kind found in psychoanalytic loss theories, nor even conscious recognition of the state of helplessness on the part of its subject. Under these circumstances, Seligman's identificaion of his as a loss theory is rather confusing.

•ﾞ • ﾞ•

From Martin Seligman, "The Learned Helplessness
Model of Depression," in Helplessness: On Depression,
Development and Death (1975)

It has happened more than once that investigators have discovered striking maladaptive behaviors in their laboratories and suggested that the behaviors represented some form of naturally occurring psychopathology. Pavlov (1928) found that conditioned reflexes of dogs disintegrated when discrimination problems became very difficult. H. Liddell (1953) found that sheep gave up making conditioned flexion responses after very many trials of signals paired with shock. Both Pavlov and Liddell claimed they had demonstrated experimental neuroses. J. H. Masserman (1943) found that hungry cats stopped eating in compartments where they had been shocked; he claimed that he had brought phobias into the laboratory. The experimental analyses of such phenomena were reasonably thorough, but the claim that they analyzed real psychopathology was usually unconvincing. Worse, they usually employed "plausibility" arguments that are very hard to confirm. How, for example, would one ever *test* whether Pavlov's dogs had anxiety neuroses, rather than compulsions or psychoses? I believe that psychopathology in man, like physical pathology, can be captured and analyzed in the laboratory. To do this, however, a superficial validity argument of the form "this looks like a phobia" is insufficient. Therefore, I want to suggest some necessary ground rules for testing whether some laboratory phenomenon, either animal or human, is a model of a natural form of psychopathology in man.

Ground Rules

There are four relevant lines of evidence for asserting that two phenomena are similar: (1) behavioral and physiological symptoms, (2) etiology or cause, (3) cure, and (4) prevention. If two phenomena are similar on one or two of these criteria, we can then test the model by looking for similarities predicted on the other criteria. Suppose that learned helplessness has symptoms and etiology similar to reactive depression, and further, that we can cure learned helplessness in dogs by forcing them to respond in a way that produces relief. This makes a prediction about the cure of depression in man: the central issue in successful therapy should be the patient's recognition that his responding is effective. If this is tested and confirmed, the model is strengthened; if disconfirmed, the model is weakened. In this case, the laboratory phenomena suggest what to look for in real-life psychopathology, but it is also possible to strengthen the model empirically from the other direction: for example, if the drug imipramine helps reactive depression, it should also relieve learned helplessness in animals.

A suitable model not only improves testability, but helps to sharpen the definition of the clinical phenomenon, since the laboratory phenomenon is well defined, while the definition of the clinical phenomenon is almost always fuzzy. For example, consider whether learned helplessness and depression have similar symptoms. Because it is a laboratory phenomenon, helplessness has necessary behaviors that define its presence or absence. On the other hand, there is no one symptom that all depressives have, since depression is a convenient diagnostic label that embraces a family of symptoms, no one of which is necessary. Depressives often feel sad, but sadness need not be present to diagnose depression; if a patient doesn't feel sad, but is verbally and motorically retarded, cries a lot, has lost twenty pounds in the last month, and the onset of symptoms can be traced to his wife's death, then depression is the appropriate diagnosis. Motor retardation also is not necessary, for a depressive can be quite agitated.

A laboratory model does not have the open-endedness of the clinical phenomenon; it clips the clinical concept off at the edges by imposing necessary features on it. So if our model of depression is valid, some phenomena formerly called depressions will probably be excluded. The label "depression" applies to passive individuals who believe they cannot do anything to relieve their suffering, who become depressed when they lose an important source of nurture—the perfect case for learned helplessness to model; but it also applies to agitated patients who make many active responses, and who become depressed with no obvious external cause. Learned helplessness need not characterize the whole spectrum of depressions, but only those primarily in which the individual is slow to initiate responses, believes himself to be powerless and hopeless, and sees his future as bleak—which began as a reaction to having lost his control over gratification and relief from suffering.

The definition and categorization of illness is customarily refined by the verification of a theory about the illness. The presence of little poxes on the body was once the defining feature of smallpox. When a germ theory of smallpox was proposed and confirmed, the presence of the germ became part of the definition. As a result, some cases previously called smallpox were excluded, and others, previously ignored, were included. Ultimately, if the learned-helplessness model of depression proves adequate, the very concept of depression may be reshaped: if learned helplessness significantly illuminates some depressions, others, such as manic-depression, may eventually be seen as a different disorder, and still other problems, such as the disaster syndrome, that are not usually thought of as depression, may be called depression.

Symptoms of Depression and Learned Helplessness

. . . Six symptoms of learned helplessness have emerged; each of them has parallels in depression:

1. Lowered initiation of voluntary responses—animals and men who have experienced uncontrollability show reduced initiation of voluntary responses.
2. Negative cognitive set—helpless animals and men have difficulty learning that responses produce outcomes.
3. Time course—helplessness dissipates in time when induced by a single session of uncontrollable shock; after multiple sessions, helplessness persists.
4. Lowered aggression—helpless animals and men initiate fewer aggressive and competitive responses, and their dominance status may diminish.
5. Loss of appetite—helpless animals eat less, lose weight, and are sexually and socially deficient.
6. Physiological changes—helpless rats show norepinephrine depletion and helpless cats may be cholinergically over-active.

. . . There are also a number of features of depression that have been as yet insufficiently investigated in learned helplessness. Preeminent among these are the depressive symptoms that cannot be investigated in animals: dejected mood, feelings of self-blame and self-dislike, loss of mirth, suicidal thoughts, and crying. Now that learned helplessness has been reliably produced in man, it can be determined whether any or all of these states occur in helplessness. If such studies are undertaken, the investigators must take great care to undo any effects that the laboratory manipulation produces. . . .

Etiology of Depression and Learned Helplessness

Learned helplessness is caused by learning that responding is independent of reinforcement; so the model suggests that the cause of depression is the belief that action is futile. What kind of events set off reactive depressions? Failure at work and school, death of a loved one, rejection or separation from friends and loved ones, physical disease, financial difficulty, being faced with insoluble problems, and growing old.

There are many others, but this list captures the flavor.

I believe that what links these experiences and lies at the heart of depression is unitary: the depressed patient believes or has learned that he cannot control those elements of his life that relieve suffering, bring gratification, or provide nurture—in short, he believes that he is helpless. Consider a few of the precipitating events: What is the meaning of job failure or incompetence at school? Often it means that all of a person's efforts have been in vain, that his responses have failed to achieve his desires. When an individual is rejected by someone he loves, he can no longer control this significant source of gratification and support. When a parent or lover dies, the bereaved is powerless to elicit love from the dead person. Physical disease and growing old are helpless conditions par excellence; the person finds his own responses ineffective and is thrown upon the care of others.

Endogenous depressions, while not set off by an explicit helplessness-inducing event, also may involve the belief in helplessness. I suspect that a continuum of susceptibility to this belief may underlie the endogenous-reactive continuum. At the extreme endogenous end, the slightest obstacle will trigger in the depressive a vicious circle of beliefs in how ineffective he is. At the extreme reactive end, a sequence of disastrous events in which a person is actually helpless is necessary to force the belief that responding is useless. Consider, for example, premenstrual susceptibility to feelings of helplessness. Right before her period, a woman may find that just breaking a dish sets off a full-blown depression, along with feelings of helplessness. Breaking a dish wouldn't disturb her at other times of the month; it would take several successive major traumas for depression to set in.

Is depression a cognitive or an emotional disorder? Neither and both. Clearly, cognitions of helplessness lower mood, and a lowered mood, which may be brought about physiologically, increases susceptibility to cognitions of helplessness; indeed, this is the most insidious vicious circle in depression. In the end, I believe that the cognition-emotion distinction in depression will be untenable. Cognition and emotion need not be separable entities in nature simply because our language separates them. When depression is observed close up, the exquisite interdependence of feelings and thought is undeniable: one does not *feel* depressed without depressing thoughts, nor does one have depressing thoughts without feeling depressed. I suggest that it is a failure of language, not a failure of understanding, that has fostered the confusion about whether depression is a cognitive or an emotional disorder. . . .

Summary

I have reviewed the findings from two converging literatures, those of depression and learned helplessness. As summarized [below], the major symptoms of learned helplessness all have parallels in the symptoms of depression. This suggests that reactive depression, as well as learned helplessness, has its roots in the belief that valued outcomes are uncontrollable. The central goal of therapy for depression, therefore, is the patient's regaining his belief that he can control events important to him. Selected therapeutic findings lend some support to this proposition. Finally, I have speculated that early experience with uncontrollable events may predispose a person to depression, while early experience with mastery may immunize him.

Summary of Features Common to Learned Helplessness and Depression

	Learned Helplessness	Depression
Symptoms	Passivity	Passivity
	Difficulty learning that responses produce relief	Negative cognitive set
	Dissipates in time	Time course
	Lack of aggression	Introjected hostility
	Weight loss, appetite loss, social and sexual deficits	Weight loss, appetite loss, social and sexual deficits
	Norepinephrine depletion and cholinergic activity	Norepinephrine depletion and cholinergic activity
	Ulcers and stress	Ulcers (?) and stress
		Feelings of helplessness
Cause	Learning that responding and reinforcement are independent	Belief that responding is useless
Cure	Directive therapy: forced exposure to responses that produce reinforcement	Recovery of belief that responding produces reinforcement
	Electroconvulsive shock	Electroconvulsive shock
	Time	Time
	Anticholinergics; norepinephrine stimulants (?)	Norepinephrine stimulants; anticholinergics (?)
Prevention	Immunization by mastery over reinforcement	(?)

A Cognitivist Analysis of Depression

BECK

Aaron t. beck is University Professor at the University of Pennsylvania School of Medicine, a position he has held since 1983. Born in 1921, in Providence, Rhode Island, Beck attended Brown University as an undergraduate and received his medical degree from Yale University in 1946. He is the author of numerous books on depression, cognitive disorder, and cognitive therapy, including *Depression: Clinical, Experimental and Theoretical Aspects* (1967) and *Cognitive Therapy and the Emotional Disorders* (1976), and of a widely used diagnostic instrument, the Beck Depression Inventory. He is best known for his cognitivist theory of depression and his pioneering cognitivist approach to the treatment of depression.

Several aspects of Beck's cognitivist account of depression deserve particular attention. One is its causal emphasis; another is the role played by erroneous reasoning patterns that result in false and distorted beliefs; a third is his broad use of the concept of loss.

Beck's cognitivism is notable for its careful analysis of what he here calls the *chronology* of depression, the sequence of symptoms and attributes making up the complex *depressive constellation*. (These include beliefs, feelings, and wishes, as well as physiological responses such as loss of appetite and sleep.) Such a chronology is causal. First comes a precipitating event, characterized in Beck's analysis as some form of "loss" experience; the awareness of this experience causes cognitive states; these states, in turn, effect negative mood states; eventually, physiological reactions ensue. While each depression begins with a precipitating event in this way, the causal sequence is not simply linear. Beck describes a circular chain reaction whereby, as he says, the various symptoms such as sadness, decreased physical activity, and sleep disturbance feed back into the psychological system.

Although the force of Beck's theory is greatest where there is a clearcut precipitating factor, psychological awareness of which prompts the sufferers' first cognitive reactions, he insists that even depressions that are not "reactive" and are without such apparent external causes follow the same pattern.

In naming belief states as the initiating psychological causes of other aspects of depression, Beck differs from philosophical "cognitivists" who posit that the beliefs involved in emotions like depression are not causes but *constituents* of those conditions. A person's feeling of sadness is not merely *because of* but also *over or about* his or her loss, they insist. The belief states are intrinsic to the experience of depression, and part of how we identify it as an experience of that kind (see Griffiths, 1989).

Beck's cognitivism emphasizes the faulty reasoning found in depressive thought. He discerns distorted evaluations, hasty and inaccurate conclusions, and overgeneralization at the heart of much depressive thought. As errors of logic, these cognitive symptoms permit of remedy. By drawing his patients' attention to their errors in reasoning, Beck maintains he is able to cure the moods, motivations, and physiological reactions that are the sequelae of those patients' erroneous beliefs.

In its emphasis on the false and distorted beliefs involved in clinical depression, and on the preeminent place of cognitive states in this and indeed all mental disorder, Beck's theory is reminiscent of the analyses of Boerhaave and Kant from the eighteenth century. Each proposes that failures of reasoning and delusional beliefs lie at the heart of melancholic states; in addition, each relegates the noncognitive elements of the condition to a secondary and relatively insignificant place.

Beck portrays the event precipitating depression in terms of loss. In his broad use of this notion, he is notable among the depression theorists in adopting Freudian language without maintaining Freudian conceptions: loss, on Beck's interpretation, corresponds to the source of almost any imaginable disappointment.

·⤳ • ⤶·

From Aaron Beck, "The Paradoxes of Depression,"
in *Cognitive Therapy and Emotional Disorders* (1976)

Depression

The thought content of depressed patients centers on a significant loss. The patient perceives that he has lost something he considers essential to his happiness or tranquility; he anticipates negative outcomes from any important undertaking; and he regards himself as deficient in the attributes necessary for achieving important goals. This theme may be formulated in terms of the cognitive triad: a negative conception of the self, a negative interpretation of life experiences, and a nihilistic view of the future.

The sense of irreversible loss and negative expectation leads to the tyical emotions associated with depression: sadness, disappointment, and apathy. Furthermore, as the sense of being trapped in an unpleasant situation or of being enmeshed in insoluble problems increases, spontaneous constructive motivation dissipates. The patient, moreover, feels impelled to escape from the apparently intolerable condition via suicide.

. . . The complete reversal in the depressed patient's behavior seems, initially, to defy explanation. During his depression, the patient's manifest personality is far more like that of other depressives than his own previous personality. Feelings of pleasure and joy are replaced by sadness and apathy; the broad range of spontaneous desires and involvement in activities are eclipsed by passivity and desires to escape; hunger and sexual drive are replaced by revulsion toward food and sex; interest and involvement in usual activities are converted into avoidance and withdrawal. Finally, the desire to live is switched off and replaced by the wish to die.

As an initial step in understanding depression, we can attempt to arrange the various phenomena into some kind of understandable sequence. Various writers have assigned primacy to one of the following: intense sadness, wishes to "hibernate," self-destructive wishes, or physiological disturbance.

Is the painful emotion the catalytic agent? If depression is a primary affective disorder, it should be possible to account for the other symptoms on the basis of the emotional state. However, the unpleasant subjective state in itself does not appear to be an adequate stimulus for the other depressive symptoms. Other states of suffering such as physical pain, nausea, dizziness, shortness of breath, or anxiety rarely lead to symptoms typical of depression such as renunciation of major objectives in life, obliteration of affectionate feelings, or the wish to die. On the contrary, people suffering physical pain seem to treasure more than ever those aspects of life they have found meaningful. Moreover, the state of sadness does not have qualities we would expect to produce the self-castigation, distortions in thinking, and loss of drive for gratifications characteristic of depression.

Similar problems are raised in assigning primacy to other aspects of depression. Some writers have latched onto the passivity and withdrawal of attachments to other people to advance the notion that depression results from an atavistic wish to hibernate. If the goal of depression is to conserve energy, however, why is the patient driven to castigate himself and engage in continuous, aimless activities when agitated? Why does he seek to destroy himself—the source of energy?

Ascribing the primary role to the physiological symptoms such as disturbances in sleep, appetite, and sexuality also poses problems. It is difficult to understand the sequence by which these physiological disturbances lead to such varied phenomena as self-criticisms, the negative view of the world, and loss of the anger and mirth responses. Certainly, physiological responses such as loss of appetite and sleep resulting from an acute physical illness do not lead to other components of the depressive constellation.

The Clue: The Sense of Loss

The task of sorting the phenomena of depression into an understandable sequence may be simplified by asking the patient what he feels sad about and by encouraging him to express his repetitive ideas. Depressed patients generally provide essential information in spontaneous statements such as: I'm sad because I'm worthless"; "I have no future"; "I've lost everything"; "My family is gone"; "I have nobody"; "Life has nothing for me." It is relatively easy to detect the dominant theme in the statements of the moderately or severely depressed patient. *He regards himself as lacking some element or attribute that he considers essential for his happiness:* competence in attaining his goals, attractiveness to other people, closeness to family or friends, tangible possessions, good health, status or position. Such self-appraisals reflect the way the depressed patient perceives his life situation.

In exploring the theme of loss, we find that the psychological disorder revolves around a cognitive problem. The depressed patient shows specific distortions. He has a negative view of his world, a negative concept of himself, and a negative appraisal of his future: the *cognitive triad.*

The distorted evaluations concern shrinkage of his domain, and lead to sadness. The depressive's conception of his valued attributes, relationships, and achievements is saturated with the notion of loss— past, present, and future. When he considers his present position, he sees a barren world; he feels pressed to the wall by external demands that cheat him of his meager resources and keep him from attaining what he wants.

The term "loser" captures the flavor of the depressive's appraisal of himself and his experience. He agonizes over the notion that he has experienced significant losses, such as his friends, his health, his prized possessions. He also regards himself as a "loser" in the colloquial sense: He is a misfit—an inferior and an inadequate being who is unable to meet his responsibilities and attain his goals. If he undertakes a project or seeks some gratification, he expects to be defeated or disappointed. He finds no respite during sleep. He has repetitive dreams in which he is a misfit, a failure.

In considering the concept of loss, we should be sensitive to the crucial importance of meanings and connotations. What represents a painful loss for one person may be regarded as trivial by another. It is important to recognize that the depressed patient dwells on hypothetical losses and pseudo losses. When he thinks about a potential loss, he regards the possibility as though it were an accomplished fact. A depressed man, for example, characteristically reacted to his wife's tardiness in meeting him with the thought, "She might have died on the way." He then construed the hypothetical loss as an actual event and became forlorn. Pseudo loss refers to the incorrect labeling of any event as a loss; for example, a change in status that may in actuality be a gain. A depressed patient who sold some shares of stock at a large profit experienced a prolonged sense of deprivation over eliminating the securities from his portfolio; he ruminated over the notion that the sale had impoverished him.

Granted that the perception of loss produces feelings of sadness, how does this sense of loss engender other symptoms of depression: pessimism, self-criticism, escape-avoidance-giving up, suicidal wishes, and physiological disorders?

In order to answer this question, it would be useful to explore the chronology of depression, the onset and full development of symptoms. This sequence is most clearly demonstrated in cases of "reactive depression," that is, depression in which there is a clear-cut precipitating factor. Other cases of depression, in which the onset is more insidious, show similar (although more subtle) patterns.

Development of Depression

In the course of his development, the depression-prone person may become sensitized by certain unfavorable types of life situations, such as the loss of a parent or chronic rejection by his peers. Other unfavorable conditions of a less obvious nature may similarly produce vulnerability to depression. These traumatic experiences predispose the person to overreact to analogous conditions later in life. He has a tendency to make extreme, absolute judgments when such situations occur. A loss is viewed as irrevocable; indifference, as total rejection. Other depression-prone people set rigid, perfectionistic goals for themselves during childhood, so that their universe collapses when they confront inevitable disappointments later in life.

The stresses responsible for adult depressions impinge on the person's specific vulnerability. Numerous clinical and research reports agree on the following types of precipitating events: the disruption of a relationship with a person to whom the patient is attached; failure to attain an important goal; loss of a job; financial reverses; unexpected physical disability; and loss of social status or reputation. If such an event is appraised as a total, irreversible depletion of one's personal domain, it may trigger a depression.

To justify the label, "precipitating event," the experience of loss must have substantial significance to the patient. The precipitating factor, however, is not always a discrete event; insidious stresses such as the gradual withdrawal of affection by a spouse or a chronic discrepancy between goals and achievements may also erode the personal domain sufficiently to set the stage for a depression. The individual, for example, may be continually dissatisfied with his or her performance as a parent, housewife, income producer, student, or creative artist. Moreover, the repeated recognition of a gap between what a person expects and what he receives from an important interpersonal relationship, from his career, or from other activities may topple him into a depression. In brief, the sense of loss may be the result of unrealistically high goals and grandiose expectations.

Experiences just prior to the onset of depression are often no more severe than those reported by those who do not become depressed. The depression-prone differ in the way they construe a particular deprivation. They attach overgeneralized or extravagant meanings to the loss.

The manner in which traumatic circumstances involving a loss lead to the constellation of depression may be delineated by an illustrative case: a man whose wife has deserted him unexpectedly. The effect of the desertion on the husband may not be predictable. Obviously, not every person deserted by a spouse becomes depressed. Even though he may experience the desertion as a painful loss, he may have other sources of satisfaction—family members and friends—to help fill the void. If the problem were simply a new hiatus in his life, we would expect that, in the course of time, he would be able to sustain his loss without becoming clinically depressed. Nonetheless, we know that certain vulnerable individuals respond to such a loss with a profound psychological disturbance.

The impact of the loss depends, in part, on the kind and intensity of the meanings attached to the key person. The deserting wife has been the hub of shared experiences, fantasies, and expectations. The deserted husband in our example has built a network of positive ideas around his wife, such as "she is part of me"; "she is everything to me"; "I enjoy life because of her"; "she is my mainstay"; "she comforts me when I am down." These positive associations range from realistic to extremely unrealistic or imaginary. The more extreme and rigid these positive concepts, the greater the impact of the loss on the domain.

If the damage to the domain is great enough, it sets off a chain reaction. The positive assets represented by his wife are totally wiped out. The deprivation of such valued attributes as "the only person who can make me happy" or "the essence of my existence" magnifies the impact of the loss and generates further sadness. Consequently, the deserted husband draws extreme, negative conclusions that parallel the extreme positive associations to his wife. He interprets the consequences of the loss as: "I am nothing without her; I can never be happy again"; "I can't go on without her."

The further reverberations of the desertion lead the husband to question his worth: "If I had been a better person, she wouldn't have left me." Further, he foresees other negative consequences of the breakup of the marriage. "All of our friends will go over to her side"; "The children will want to live with her, not me"; "I will go broke trying to maintain two households."

As the chain reaction progresses to a full-blown depression, his self-doubts and gloomy predictions expand into negative generalizations about himself, his world, and his future. He starts to see himself as permanently impoverished in terms of emotional satisfactions, as well as financially. In addition, he exacerbates his suffering by overly dramatizing the event: "It is too much for a person to bear" or, "This is a terrible disaster." Such ideas undermine his ability and motivation to absorb the shock.

The husband divorces himself from activities and goals that formerly gave him satisfaction. He may withdraw his investment in his career goals ("because they are meaningless without my wife"). He is not motivated to work or even to take care of himself ("because it isn't worth the effort"). His distress is aggravated by the physiological concomitants of depression, such as loss of appetite and sleep disturbances. Finally, he thinks of suicide as an escape ("because life is too painful").

Since the chain reaction is circular, the depression becomes progressively worse. The various symptoms—sadness, decreased physical activity, sleep disturbance—feed back into the psychological system. Hence, as he experiences sadness, his pessimism leads him to conclude, "I shall always be sad." This ideation leads to more sadness, which is further interpreted in a negative way. Similarly, he thinks, "I shall never be able to eat again or to sleep again," and concludes that he is deteriorating physically. As he observes the various manifestations of his disorder (decreased productivity, avoidance of responsibility, withdrawal from other people), he becomes increasingly critical of himself. His self-criticisms lead to further sadness; thus, we see a continuing vicious cycle.

Affiliation, Cultural Roles, and Women's Depression

MILLER

J EAN BAKER MILLER EARNED her B.A. at Sarah Lawrence College and her M.D. at Columbia, University. Certified by the New York Medical College in 1958, she was for many years a practicing psychoanalyst and psychiatrist attached to the Department of Psychiatry at the Albert Einstein College of Medicine in New York. She is now director of the Jean Baker Miller Training Institute at Wellesley College and clinical professor of psychiatry at the Boston University Medical School. In addition to *Toward a New Psychology of Women,* she is author of numerous other influential publications. She is coauthor, with Judith Jordan, of *Women's Growth in Connection* and is editor of a volume entitled *Psychoanalysis and Women.*

First published in 1976, Miller's *Toward a New Psychology of Women,* from which the following excerpt is taken, was a key text for the feminist of the 1970s. It ushered in what has come to be distinguished as one of several separate strands of feminist thought, that which is sometimes called *cultural feminism.* Cultural feminism focuses on women's traits and seeks to acknowledge and value hitherto undervalued differences distinguishing women's psychology, responses, and capabilities from men's. The cultural feminist school is associated with the notion of relational individualism and with the work of later thinkers such as Carol Gilligan.

Subsequent writing both by Miller and by other cultural feminists has expanded and refined the analysis of women's depression sketched in these pages. Moreover, some of Miller's empirical observations seem to us today blessedly outmoded. Nonetheless, her remarks here introduce several themes that have become influential in attempts over the last two decades to understand women's depression.

First, this analysis is innovative in offering an explanation of depression that points not to psychological trauma or some form of loss but to cultural roles. Responding in conformity with these gendered social roles, Miller makes clear, may not even be entirely conscious and intentional on the part of the person subject to them. If women are more prone to depression than men, the roles assigned to women in our culture may explain why. Here, then, is a new style of explanation, in which depression is not a function of biology, nor of conscious beliefs and responses, but of cultural patterns that impose gender roles.

These roles are to be understood, moreover, not merely in terms of social expectations but also in terms of the different self-identity experienced, and sought, by women and men. Women's sense of self is built around attachment to and affiliation with others. This pull toward affiliation, which makes women feel capable and complete in relationship, and leaves them prone to depression when their attachments and affiliations are threatened or devalued, is something to be both recognized and honored. As Miller puts it: "The pull toward affiliation that women feel in themselves is not wrong or backward" (1976:95). These ideas in Miller's work inaugurated the "relational individualism" associated with much subsequent feminist theory, which rejects the male ideal of the autonomous individual as not only unrealistic but also undesirable.

Miller offers no more than a few passing comments on the way women's depression occurs; nonetheless, her theory is a powerful and subtle one that has found support in subsequent empirical study (see, for instance, the work of Jack, 1991). She makes clear that women's affiliative roles are dysfunctional not in themselves but within a certain cultural context, one in which males deny their own affiliative needs and satisfactions, thus requiring women to be, as she says, "the 'carriers' of the basic necessity for human communion" (Miller, 1976:86), and at the same time denigrate women's more relational selves.

· ∽ ● ∾ ·

From Jean Baker Miller, "Ties to Others," in *Toward a New Psychology of Women* (1976)

Male society, by depriving women of the right to its major "bounty"— that is, development according to the male model—overlooks the fact that women's development *is* proceeding, but on another basis. One central feature is that women stay with, build on, and develop in a context of attachment and affiliation with others. Indeed, women's sense of self becomes very much organized around being able to make and then to maintain affiliations and relationships. Eventually, for many women the threat of disruption of an affiliation is perceived not as just a loss of a relationship but as something closer to a total loss of self.

Such psychic structuring can lay the groundwork for many problems. Depression, for example, which is related to one's sense of the loss of affiliation with another(s), is much more common in women, although it certainly occurs in men.

What has not been recognized is that this psychic starting point contains the possibilities for an entirely different (and more advanced) approach to living and functioning—very different, that is, from the approach fostered by the dominant culture. In it, affiliation is valued as highly as, or more highly than, self-enhancement. Moreover, it allows for the emergence of the truth: that for everyone—men as well as women—individual development proceeds *only* by means of affiliation. At the present time, men are not as prepared to *know* this. This proposition requires further explanation. Let us start with some common observations and examples and then return to unravel this complex, but basic, issue. . . .

How Affiliation Works

. . . Problems . . . result when all affiliations, as we have so far known them, grow out of the basic domination-subordination model.

According to psychological theory, [some] women . . . might be described as "dependent" (needing others "too much") or immature in several ways (not developed past a certain early stage of separation and individuation or not having attained autonomy). I would suggest instead that while these women do face a problem, one that troubles them greatly, the problem arises from the dominant role that affiliations have been made to play in women's lives. Women are, in fact, being "punished" for making affiliations central in their lives.

We all begin life deeply attached to the people around us. Men, or boys, are encouraged to move out of this state of existence—in which they and their fate are intimately intertwined in the lives and fate of other people. Women are encouraged to remain in this stage but, as they grow, to transfer their attachment to a male figure.

Boys are rewarded for developing other aspects of themselves. These other factors—power or skills—gradually begin to displace some of the importance of affiliations and eventually to supersede them. There is no question that women develop and change too. In an inner way, however, the development does not displace the value accorded attachments to others. The suggestion here is that the parameters of the female's development are not the same as the male's and that the same terms do not apply. Women can be highly developed and still give great weight to affiliations.

Here again, women are geared all their lives to be the "carriers" of the basic necessity for human communion. Men can go a long distance away from fully recognizing this need because women are so groomed to "fill it in" for them. But there is another side: women are also more thoroughly prepared to move toward more advanced, more affiliative ways of living—and less wedded to the dangerous ways of the present. For example, aggression will get you somewhere in this society if you are a man; it may get you quite far indeed if you are one of the few lucky people. But if you continue to be directly aggressive, let us say in pursuit of what seem to be your rights or needs as a man, you will at some time find that it will get you into trouble too. (Other inequalities such as class and race play an important part in this picture.) However, you will probably find this out somewhat later, *after* you have already built up a belief in the efficacy of aggression; you already believe it is important to your sense of self. By then it is hard to give up the push toward aggression and the belief in its necessity. Moreover, it is still rewarded in some measure: you can find places to get some small satisfaction and applause for it, even if it is only from friends in the local bar, by identifying with the Sunday football players, or by pushing women around. To give it up altogether can seem like the final degradation and loss—loss especially of manhood, sexual identification. In fact, if events do not go your way you may be inclined to increase the aggression in the hope that you can force situations. This attempt can and often does enlarge aggression into violence, either individual or group. It is even the underlying basis of national policy, extending to the threat of war and war itself.

Instead, one can, and ultimately must, place one's faith in others, in the context of being a social being, related to other human beings, in their hands as well as one's own. Women learn very young that they must rest primarily on this faith. They cannot depend on their own individual development, achievement, or power. If they try, they are doomed to failure; they find this out early.

Men's only hope lies in affiliation, too, *but* for them it can *seem* an impediment, a loss, a danger, or at least second best. By contrast, affiliations, relationships, make women feel deeply satisfied, fulfilled, "successful," free to go on to other things.

It is not that men are not concerned about relationships, or that men do not have deep yearnings for affiliation. Indeed, this is exactly what people in the field of psychodynamics are constantly finding—evidence of these needs in men as well as in women, deep *under the surface* of social appearance. This has been said in many different ways. One common formulation states, for example, that men search all their lives for their mothers. I do not think that is *a* mother *per se* that they seek. I do think men are longing for an affiliative mode of living—one that would not have to mean going back to mother if one could find a way to go on to greater human communion. Men have deprived themselves of this mode, left it with women. Most important, they have made themselves unable to really *believe* in it. It is true that the time with their mothers was the time when they could really believe in and rely on affiliation. As soon as they start to grow in the male mold, they are supposed to give up this belief and even this desire. Men are led to cast out this faith, even to condemn it in themselves, and build their lives on something else. *And they are rewarded for doing so.*

Practically everyone now bemoans Western man's sense of alienation, lack of community, and inability to find ways of organizing society for human ends. We have reached the end of the road that is built on the set of traits held out for male identity—advance at any cost, pay any price, drive out all competitors, and kill them if necessary. The opportunity for the full exercise of such manly virtues was always available only to the very few, but they were held out as goals and guidelines for all men. As men strove to define themselves by these ideas, they built their psychic organizations around this striving.

It may be that we had to arrive at a certain stage of "mastery" over the physical environment or a certain level of technology, to see not only the limits but the absolute danger of this kind of social organization. On the other hand, it may be that we need never have come this long route in the first place; perhaps it has been a vast, unnecessary detour. It now seems clear we have arrived at a point from which we must return to a basis of faith in affiliation—and not only faith but recognition that it is a requirement for the existence of human beings. The basis for what seem the absolutely essential next steps in Western history if we are to survive is already available.

A most basic social advance can emerge through women's outlook, through women putting forward women's concerns. Women have already begun to do so. Here, again, it is not a question of innate biological characteristics. It is a question of the kind of psychological structuring that is encompassed differentially by each sex at this time in our development as a society of human beings—and a question of who can offer the motivation and direction for moving on from here.

The central point here is that women's great desire for affiliation is both a fundamental strength, essential for social advance and at the same time the inevitable source of many of women's current problems. That is, while women have reached for and already found a psychic basis for a more advanced social existence, they are not able to act fully and directly on this valuable basis in a way that would allow it to flourish. Accordingly, they have not been able to cherish or even recognize this valuable strength. On the contrary, when women act on the basis of this underlying psychological motive, they are usually led into subservience. That is, the only forms of affiliation that have been available to women are subservient affiliations. In many instances, the search for affiliation can lead women to a situation that creates serious emotional problems. Many of these are then labeled neuroses and other such names.

But what is most important is to see that even so-called neuroses can, and most often do, contain within them the starting points, the searching for a more advanced form of existence. The problem has been that women have been seeking affiliations that are impossible to attain under the present arrangements, but in order to conduct the search women have been willing to sacrifice whole parts of themselves. And so women have concluded, as we so readily do, that we must be wrong or, in modern parlance, "sick."

The Search for Attachment—"Neuroses"

We have raised two related topics: one is social and political, the other more psychological. One is the question of how women can evolve forms of affiliation which will advance women's development and help women to build on this strength to effect real change in the real world? Secondly, until we accomplish this task—and along the way—can we understand more about the psychological events of our lives? Can we better understand why we suffer? At the very least, we may be able to stop undermining ourselves by condemning our strengths.

In the attempt to understand the situation further we can return to some of the women [seen in therapy by the author—Ed.]. They all expressed a common theme: the lack of ability to really value and credit their own thoughts, feelings, and actions. It is as if they have lost a full sense of satisfaction in the use of themselves and all of their own resources—or rather, never had the full right to do so in the first place. As [one] put it, there is the sense "that there has to be that other person there." Alone, her being and her doing do not have their full meaning; she becomes dry, empty, devoid of good feeling. It is not that [this woman] needs someone else to reflect herself back to her. (She knew she was, in fact, an excellent and accurate judge herself.) Her need seems even more basic than that. Unless there is another person present, the entire event—the thought, the feeling, the accomplishment, or whatever it may be—lacks pleasure and significance. It is not simply that she feels like half a person, but still able to take some satisfaction and wanting another person, but still able to take some satisfaction from her own half. It is like being no person at all—at least no person that matters. As soon as she can believe she is using herself *with* someone else and *for* someone else, her own self moves into action and seems satisfying and worthwhile.

The women referred to [here] are not so-called "symbiotic" or other immature types of personalities. (Such terms, incidentally, may well require re-examination in relation to women.) In fact, they are very highly developed and able people who could not possibly be categorized in such a way. Nor, on a more superficial level, do phrases like "seeking approval" or "being afraid of disapproval," really cover the situation, although these factors play a part.

Their shared belief that one needs another person in a very particular way manifests itself in different ways for different people. In one form it leads readily into depression. The experiences of the women described here may thus provide some further clues to depression, may help us understand some aspects of it. . . .

All forms of oppression encourage people to enlist in their own enslavement. For women, especially, this enlistment inevitably takes psychological forms and often ends in being called neuroses and other such things. (Men, too, suffer psychological troubles, as we all know; and the dynamic for them is related, but it *does* take a different path.)

In this sense, psychological problems are not so much caused by the unconscious as by deprivations of full consciousness. If we had paths to more valid consciousness all along through life, if we had more accurate terms in which to conceptualize (at each age level) what was happening, if we had more access to the emotions produced, and if we had ways of knowing our own true options—if we had all these things, we could make better programs for action. Lacking full consciousness, we create out of what is available. For women only distorted conceptions about what is happening and what a person can and should be have been provided. (The conceptions available for men may be judged as even more distorted. The possible programs for action and the subsequent dynamic are, however, different.)

Even the very words, the terms in which we conceptualize, reflect the prevailing consciousness—not necessarily the truth about what is happening. This is true in the culture at large and in psychological theory too. We need a terminology that is not based on inappropriate carryovers from men's situation. Even a word like *autonomy,* which many of us have used and liked, may need revamping for women. It carries the implication—and for women therefore the threat—that one should be able to pay the price of giving up affiliations in order to become a separate and self-directed individual. In reality, when women have struggled through to develop themselves as strong, independent individuals they did, and do, threaten many relationships, relationships in which the other person will not tolerate a self-directed woman. But, when men are autonomous, there is no reason to think that their relationships will be threatened. On the contrary, there is reason to believe that self-development will win them relationships. Others—usually women—will rally to them and support them in their efforts, and other men will respect and admire them. Since women have to face very different consequences, the word *autonomy* seems possibly dangerous; it is a word derived from men's development, not women's.

There is a further sense in which the automatic transfer of a concept like autonomy as a goal for women can cause problems. Women are quite validly seeking something more complete than autonomy as it is defined for men, a fuller not a lesser ability to encompass relationships to others, simultaneous with the fullest development of oneself. Thus, many of our terms need re-examination.

Many women have now moved on to determine the nature of their affiliations, and to decide for themselves with whom they will affiliate. As soon as they attempt this step, they find the societal forms standing in opposition. In fact, they are already outside the old social forms looking for new ones. But, they do not feel like misfits, wrong again, but like seekers. To be in this unfamiliar position is not always comfortable, but it is not wholly uncomfortable either—and indeed it begins to bring its own *new* and different rewards. Here, even on the most immediate level, women now find a community of other seekers, others who are engaged in this pursuit. No one can undertake this formidable task alone. (Therapy, even if we knew how to do it in some near perfect way—which we do not—is not enough.)

It is extremely important to recognize that the pull toward affiliation that women feel in themselves is not wrong or backward; women need not add to the condemnation of themselves. On the contrary, we can recognize this pull as the basic strength it is. We can also begin to choose relationships that foster mutual growth. . . .

Other questions are equally hard. How do we conceive of a society organized so that it permits both the development and the mutuality of all people? And how do we get there? How do women move from a powerless and devalued position to fully valued effectiveness? How do we get the power to do this, even if we do not want or need power to control or submerge others? It would be difficult enough if we started from zero, but we do not. We start from a position in which others have power and do not hesitate to use it. Even if they do not consciously use it against women, all they have to do is remain in the position of dominance, keep doing what they are doing, and nothing will change. The women's qualities that I believe are ultimately, and at all times, valuable and essential are not the ones that make for power in the world as it is now. How then can we use these strengths to enhance our effectiveness rather than let them divert us from action?

One part of the answer seems clear already. Women will not advance except by joining together in cooperative action. What has not been as clear is that no other group, so far, has had the benefit of women's leadership, the advantage of women's deep and special strengths. Most of these strengths have been hidden in this culture, and hidden from women themselves. I have been emphasizing one of these strengths—*the* very strength that is most important for concerted group action. Unlike other groups, women do not *need* to set affiliation and strength in opposition one against the other. We can readily integrate the two, search for more and better ways to use affiliation to enhance strength—and strength to enhance affiliation.

For women to derive strength from relationships, then, clearly requires a transformation and restructuring of the nature of relationships. The first essential new ingredients in this process are self-determination and the power to make the self-determination a reality. But even before getting to this major issue, there are questions facing many women: "If I want self-determination, what is it I really want to determine? What do I want? Who am I anyhow?" The difficulty of answering these questions has sometimes served to discourage women. The discouragement occurs even in women who are convinced that there is something deeply wrong with the old way. Given the history that women's lives have been so totally focused on others, it is easy to see that such questions bear a special cogency and come from a particularly hidden place in women. . . .

It is important here to note that this discussion of the importance of affiliations for women is by no means exhaustive. Nor is it a full discussion of any of the related, complicated problems, such as depression. Rather, it is an attempt to unravel a topic that requires much new examination. I hope that it will give rise to further discussion.

Mourning the Lost Mother and the Lost Self

KRISTEVA

BORN IN 1941, Julia Kristeva is professor of linguistics at the University of Paris. She is also a practicing psychoanalyst and the author of many books and articles on feminism, psychoanalysis, semiotics, and aesthetics. Widespread interest in Kristeva's writing developed in the United States as her articles began to appear in translation through the 1970s. Her books include *Desire in Language* (1980), *Powers of Horror: An Essay in Abjection* (1982), *Revolution in Poetic Language* (1984), and *Strangers to Ourselves* (1989). Although her work is commonly identified as "French feminism," Kristeva has herself explicitly repudiated the title of "feminist," disparaging feminists as merely wanting to acquire "phallic" power. Nor, in fact, is she French. Born and raised in Bulgaria, she came to France to further her education but stayed on as a refugee from Bulgarian-Soviet communism.

Kristeva is a prolific writer and an evolving and complex thinker working within the psychoanalytic tradition. A full appreciation of her work on melancholia and depression would require further background than is possible to provide here, both on her own theories and on the Freudian and Lacanian traditions to which she responds. I can merely draw attention to a few salient points in the passages taken from her work *Black Sun: Depression and Melancholy* (1989).

Kristeva's primary analysis proposes a loss theory of melancholia in the tradition of Freud's "Mourning and Melancholia." Like Freud and Klein before her, she asserts that early development results in a separation of the infant-mother dyad, and she identifies the sadness of depression with a mourning for the lost other (mother, breast) relinquished at weaning. In addition to such "objectal" depression, Kristeva adapts Freud's theory of the death wish to introduce the notion of a kind of depression that is "narcissistic." Thus, as well as a form of mourning for the lost mother, melancholia is a mourning for the lost self. This object, however, represents an undifferentiated, unsymbolized item at this early stage in the infant's conceptual development. The mourned self is ineffable, a "preobject" or "Thing." (In this regard, Kristeva reflects the influence of Lacanian thinking.) Only through literary and artistic expression, she stresses, can we approach such unsymbolized aspects of psychic life.

Confusingly, Kristeva adds to her adoption of the idea of the attack on the introjected other within oneself, a universal matricidal impulse. For a girl the experiences of both this matricidal impulse and of loss will be different from that experienced by a boy, because the Thing hated and lost, respectively, is the same sex as the girl herself. This alters and complicates the course of the female's development more generally, and also transforms, and worsens, the subsequent depressive states she experiences.

Male development in a heterosexist culture reflects the easier adaptation: The boy eventually replaces the mourned maternal object with an opposite-sex (female) substitute. But were the girl to seek such a replacement, it would be a homosexual love choice. Freud's response to this particular developmental disparity between the sexes was not linked to his theory of melancholia. He insisted that a mature woman *changed* her love object from female to male. Not accepting this solution, Kristeva's analysis proposes that women maintain the original love object as female but with the risk of depression and of homosexuality. The matricidal impulse also invites depression in women. Through introjection, the melancholic's rage is already inverted. But due to her "spectacular identification" with the mother, a woman's matricidal impulse is doubly inverted: "The hatred I bear her is not oriented toward the outside but locked up within myself" (Kristeva, 1989:29).

Left uncertain in this text, and in other writing, is the extent to which melancholia and depression are the inevitable lot of women, and homosexuality women's unfailing disposition. Several of her critics have accused Kristeva of homophobia in this analysis and have portrayed her women as "melancholy heterosexuals longing for lost love" (Butler, 1993:111).

Difficult and unresolved as Kristeva's account appears to be, it is nonetheless an important contribution to the study of melancholy and depression in terms of loss. Whatever its similarities to earlier loss theories like Freud's and Klein's, the central and differentiating role attributed to gender in Kristeva's analysis distinguishes it and forces a reconsideration of those earlier theories.

·◡ • ◠·

From Julia Kristeva, "A Counterdepressant," in
Black Sun: Depression and Melancholy (1987)

Melancholia/Depression

I shall call *melancholia* the institutional symptomatology of inhibition and asymbolia that becomes established now and then or chronically in a person, alternating more often than not with the so-called manic phase of exaltation. When the two phenomena, despondency and exhilaration, are of lesser intensity and frequency, it is then possible to speak of neurotic depression. While acknowledging the difference between melancholia and depression, Freudian theory detects everywhere the same *impossible mourning for the maternal object*. Question: impossible on account of what paternal weakness? Or what biological frailty? Melancholia—we again encounter the generic term after having demarcated psychotic and neurotic symptomatologies—admits of the fearsome privilege of situating the analyst's question at the intersection of the biological and the symbolical. Parallel series? Consecutive sequences? A dangerous crossing that needs to be clarified, another relationship that needs to be thought up?

The terms melancholia and depression refer to a composite that might be called melancholy/depressive, whose borders are in fact blurred, and within which psychiatrists ascribe the concept of "melancholia" to the illness that is irreversible on its own (that responds only to the administration of antidepressants). . . . I shall examine matters from a *Freudian point of view*. On that basis, I shall try to bring out, from the core of the melancholy/depressive composite, blurred as its borders may be, what pertains to a common experience of *object loss* and of a *modification of signifying bonds*. These bonds, language in particular, prove to be unable to insure, within the melancholy/depressive composite, the autostimulation that is required in order to initiate given responses. Instead of functioning as a "rewards system," language, on the contrary, hyperactivates the "anxiety-punishment" pair, and thus inserts itself in the slowing down of thinking and decrease in psychomotor activity characteristic of depression. If temporary sadness of mourning on the one hand, and melancholy stupor on the other are clinically and nosologically different, they are nevertheless supported by *intolerance for object loss* and *the signifier's failure* to insure a compensating way out of the states of withdrawal in which the subject takes refuge to the point of inaction (pretending to be dead) or even suicide. Thus I shall speak of depression and melancholia without always distinguishing the particularities of the two ailments but keeping in mind their common structure.

The Depressive Person: Full of Hatred or Wounded, Mourned "Object" and Mourned "Thing"

According to classic psychoanalytic theory (Abraham, Freud, and Melanie Klein), depression, like mourning, conceals an aggressiveness toward the lost object, thus revealing the ambivalence of the depressed person with respect to the object of mourning. . . . the analysis of depression involves bringing to the fore the realization that the complaint against oneself is a hatred for the other, which is without doubt the substratum of an unsuspected sexual desire. Clearly such an advent of hatred within transference entails risk for the analysand as well as the analyst, and the therapy of depression (even the one called neurotic) verges on schizoid fragmentation.

Melancholy cannibalism, which was emphasized by Freud and Abraham and appears in many dreams and fantasies of depressed persons accounts for this passion for holding within the mouth (but vagina and anus also lend themselves to this control) the intolerable other that I crave to destroy so as to better possess it alive. Better fragmented, torn, cut up, swallowed, digested . . . than lost. The melancholy cannibalistic imagination is a repudiation of the loss's reality and of death as well. It manifests the anguish of losing the other through the survival of self, surely a deserted self but not separated from what still and ever nourishes it and becomes transformed into the self—which also resuscitates—through such a devouring.

Nevertheless, the treatment of narcissistic individuals has led modern analysts to understand another form of depression. Far from being a hidden attack on an other who is thought to be hostile because he is frustrating, sadness would point to a primitive self—wounded, incomplete, empty. Persons thus affected do not consider themselves wronged but afflicted with a fundamental flaw, a congenital deficiency. Their sorrow doesn't conceal the guilt or the sin felt because of having secretly plotted revenge on the ambivalent object. Their sadness would be rather the most archaic expression of an unsymbolizable, unnameable narcissistic wound, so precocious that no outside agent (subject or agent) can be used as referent. For such narcissistic depressed persons, sadness is really the sole object; more precisely it is a substitute object they become attached to, an object they tame and cherish for lack of another. In such a case, suicide is not a disguised act of war but a merging with sadness and, beyond it, with that impossible love, never reached, always elsewhere, such as the promises of nothingness, of death.

Thing and Object

The depressed narcissist mourns not an Object but the Thing. Let me posit the "Thing" as the real that does not lend itself to signification, the center of attraction and repulsion, seat of the sexuality from which the object of desire will become separated. . . .

Ever since that archaic attachment the depressed person has the impression of having been deprived of an unnameable, supreme good, of something unrepresentable, that perhaps only devouring might represent, or an *invocation* might point out, but no word could signify. Consequently, for such a person, no erotic object could replace the irreplaceable perception of a place or preobject confining the libido or severing the bonds of desire. Knowingly disinherited of the Thing, the depressed person wanders in pursuit of continuously disappointing adventures and loves; or else retreats, disconsolate and aphasic, alone with the unnamed Thing. The "primary identification" with the "father in individual prehistory" would be the means, the link that might enable one to become reconciled with the loss of the Thing. Primary identification initiates a compensation for the Thing and at the same time secures the subject to another dimension, that of imaginary adherence, reminding one of the bond of faith, which is just what disintegrates in the depressed person.

With those affected by melancholia, primary identification proves to be fragile, insufficient to secure other identifications, which are symbolic this time, on the basis of which the *erotic Thing* might become a captivating *Object of desire* insuring continuity in a metonymy of pleasure. The melancholy Thing interrupts desiring metonymy, just as it prevents working out the loss within the psyche. How can one approach the place I have referred to? Sublimation is an attempt to do so: through melody, rhythm, semantic polyvalency, the so-called poetic form, which decomposes and recomposes signs, is the sole "container" seemingly able to secure an uncertain but adequate hold over the Thing. . . .

The Thing is inscribed within us without memory, the buried accomplice of our unspeakable anguishes. One can imagine the delights of reunion that a regressive daydream promises itself through the nuptials of suicide.

The looming of the Thing summons up the subject's life force as that subject is in the process of being set up; the premature being that we all are can survive only if it clings to an other, perceived as supplement, artificial extension, protective wrapping. Nevertheless, such a life drive is fully the one that, *at the same time,* rejects me, isolates me, rejects him (or her). Never is the ambivalence of drive more fearsome than in this beginning of otherness where, lacking the filter of language, I cannot inscribe my violence in "no," nor in any other sign. I can expel it only by means of gestures, spasms, or shouts. I impel it, I project it. My necessary Thing is also and absolutely my enemy, my foil, the delightful focus of my hatred. The Thing falls from me along the outposts of significance where the Word is not yet my Being. A mere nothing, which is a cause, but at the same time a fall, before being an Other, the Thing is the recipient that contains my dejecta and everything that results from *cadere* [Latin: to fall]—it is a waste with which, in my sadness, I merge. It is Job's ashpit in the Bible.

Anality is summoned during the process of setting up this Thing, one that is our own and proper Thing as much as it is improper, unclean. The melancholy person who extols that boundary where the self emerges, but also collapses in deprecation, fails to summon the anality that could establish separations and frontiers as it does normally or as a bonus with obsessive persons. On the contrary, the entire ego of those who are depressed sinks into a diseroticized and yet jubilatory anality, as the latter becomes the bearer of a jouissance fused with the archaic Thing, perceived not as a significant object but as the self's borderline element. For those who are depressed, the Thing like the self is a downfall that carries them along into the invisible and unnameable. *Cadere.* Waste and cadavers all. . . .

The Death Drive as Primary Inscription of Discontinuity (Trauma or Loss)

Freud's postulate of a *primary masochism* is consonant with aspects of narcissistic melancholia in which the dying out of all libidinal bonds appears not to be a simple matter of turning aggressiveness toward the object back into animosity against the self but is asserted as previous to any possibility of object positioning. . . .

Is Mood a Language?

Sadness is the fundamental mood of depression, and even if manic euphoria alternates with it in the bipolar forms of that ailment, sorrow is the major outward sign that gives away the desperate person. Sadness leads us into the enigmatic realm of *affects*—anguish, fear, or joy. Irreducible to its verbal or semiological expressions, sadness (like all affect) is the *psychic representation of energy displacements* caused by external or internal traumas. The exact status of such psychic representations of energy displacements remains, in the present state of psychoanalytic and semiological theories, very vague. No conceptual framework in the relevant sciences (particularly linguistics) has proven adequate to account for this apparently very rudimentary representation, presign and prelanguage. The "sadness" mood triggered by a stimulation, tension, or energy conflict within a psychosomatic organism is not a *specific* answer to a release mechanism (I am not sad as a response to or sign for X and only X). Mood is a "generalized transference" (E. Jacobson) that stamps the *entire* behavior and all the sign systems (from motor functions to speech production and idealization) without either identifying with them or disorganizing them. We are justified in believing that an archaic *energy signal* is involved, a phylogenetic inheritance, which, within the psychic space of the human being, is *immediately* assumed by verbal representation and consciousness. Nevertheless, such an "assumption" is not related to what occurs when the energies that Freud calls "bonded" lend themselves to verbalization, association, and judgment. Let us say that representations germane to affects, notably sadness, are *fluctuating* energy cathexes: insufficiently stabilized to coalesce as verbal or other signs, acted upon by primary processes of displacement and condensation, dependent just the same on the agency of the ego, they record through its intermediary the threats, orders, and injunctions of the superego. Thus moods are *inscriptions,* energy disruptions, and not simply raw energies. They lead us toward a modality of significance that, on the threshold of bioenergetic stability, insures the preconditions for (or manifests the disintegration of) the imaginary and the symbolic. On the frontier between animality and symbol formation, moods—and particularly sadness—are the ultimate reactions to our traumas, they are our basic homeostatic recourses. For if it is true that those who are slaves to their moods, beings drowned in their sorrows, reveal a number of psychic or cognitive frailties, it is equally true that a diversification of moods, variety in sadness, refinement in sorrow or mourning are the imprint of a humankind that is surely not triumphant but subtle, ready to fight, and creative. . . .

Literary creation is that adventure of the body and signs that bears witness to the affect—to sadness as imprint of separation and beginning of the symbol's sway; to joy as imprint of the triumph that settles me in the universe of artifice and symbol, which I try to harmonize in the best possible way with my experience of reality. But that testimony is produced by literary creation in a material that is totally different from what constitutes mood. It transposes affect into rhythms, signs, forms. The "semiotic" and the "symbolic" become the communicable imprints of an affective reality, perceptible to the reader (I like this book because it conveys sadness, anguish, or joy) and yet dominated, set aside, vanquished.

. . . At the outset we have objectal depression (implicitly aggressive), and narcissistic depression (logically previous to the libidinal object relation)—an affectivity struggling with signs, going beyond, threatening, or modifying them. Starting from such a setting, the line of questioning that I shall pursue could be summed up as follows: aesthetic and particularly literary creation, and also religious discourse in its imaginary, fictional essence, set forth a device whose prosodic economy, interaction of characters, and implicit symbolism constitute a very faithful semiological representation of the subject's battle with symbolic collapse. Such a literary representation is not an *elaboration* in the sense of "becoming aware" of the inter- and intrapsychic causes of moral suffering; that is where it diverges from the psychoanalytic course, which aims at dissolving this symptom. Nevertheless, the literary (and religious) representation possesses a real and imaginary effectiveness that comes closer to catharsis than to elaboration; it is a therapeutic device used in all societies throughout the ages. If psychoanalysts think they are more efficacious, notably through strengthening the subject's cognitive possibilities, they also owe it to themselves to enrich their practice by paying greater attention to these sublimatory solutions to our crises, in order to be lucid counterdepressants rather than neutralizing antidepressants. . . .

Death-Bearing Woman

For man and for woman the loss of the mother is a biological and psychic necessity, the first step on the way to becoming autonomous. Matricide is our vital necessity, the sine-qua-non condition of our individuation, provided that it takes place under optimal circumstances and can be eroticized—whether the lost object is recovered as erotic object (as is the case for male heterosexuality or female homosexuality), or it is transposed by means of an unbelievable symbolic effort, the advent of which one can only admire, which eroticizes the *other* (the other sex, in the case of the heterosexual woman) or transforms cultural constructs into a "sublime" erotic object (one thinks of the cathexes, by men and women, in social bonds, intellectual and aesthetic productions, etc.). The lesser or greater violence of matricidal drive, depending on individuals and the milieu's tolerance, entails, when it is hindered, its inversion on the self; the maternal object having been introjected, the depressive or melancholic putting to death of the self is what follows, instead of matricide. In order to protect mother I kill myself while knowing—phantasmatic and protective knowledge—that it comes from her, the death-bearing she-Gehenna. . . . Thus my hatred is safe and my matricidal guilt erased. I make of Her an image of Death so as not to be shattered through the hatred I bear against myself when I identify with Her, for that aversion is in principle meant for her as it is an individuating dam against confusional love. Thus the feminine as image of death is not only a screen for my fear of castration, but also an imaginary safety catch for the matricidal drive that, without such a representation, would pulverize me into melancholia if it did not drive me to crime. No, it is She who is death-bearing, therefore I do not kill myself in order to kill her but I attack her, harass her, represent her. . . .

For a woman, whose specular identification with the mother as well as the introjection of the maternal body and self are more immediate, such an inversion of matricidal drive into a death-bearing maternal image is more difficult, if not impossible. Indeed, how can She be that bloodthirsty Fury, since I am She (sexually and narcissistically), She is I? Consequently, the hatred I bear her is not oriented toward the outside but is locked up within myself. There is no hatred, only an implosive mood that walls itself in and kills me secretly, very slowly, through permanent bitterness, bouts of sadness, or even lethal sleeping pills that I take in smaller or greater quantities in the dark hope of meeting . . . no one, unless it be my imaginary wholeness, increased with my death that accomplishes me. The homosexual shares the same depressive economy: he is a delightful melancholy person when he does not indulge in sadistic passion with another man. . . .

In its climax, ["negative narcissism"] weakens the aggressive (matricidal) affect toward the other as well as the despondent affect within oneself and substitutes what one might call an "oceanic void." It is a feeling and fantasy of pain, but anestheticized, of jouissance, but in suspense, of an expectation and a silence as empty as they are fulfilled. In the midst of its lethal ocean, the melancholy woman is the dead one that has always been abandoned within herself and can never kill outside herself. Modest, silent, without verbal or desiring bonds with others, she wastes away by striking moral and physic blows against herself, which, nevertheless, do not give her sufficient pleasures. Until the fatal blow—the definitive nuptials of the Dead Woman with the Same, whom she did not kill.

One cannot overemphasize the tremendous psychic, intellectual, and affective effort a woman must make in order to find the other sex as erotic object. In his philogenetic musings, Freud often admires the intellectual accomplishment of the man who has been (or when he is) deprived of women (through glaciation or tyranny on the part of the father of the primal horde, etc.). If the discovery of her invisible vagina already imposes upon woman a tremendous sensory, speculative, and intellectual effort, shifting to the symbolic order *at the same time* as to a sexual object of a sex other than that of the primary maternal object represents a gigantic elaboration in which a woman cathexes a psychic potential greater than what is demanded of the male sex. When this process is favorably carried out, it is evidenced by the precocious awakening of girls, their intellectual performances often more brilliant during the school years, and their continuing female maturity. Nevertheless, it has its price in the constant tendency to extol the problematic mourning for the lost object . . . not so fully lost, and it remains, throbbing, in the "crypt" of feminine ease and maturity. Unless a massive introjection of the ideal succeeds, at the same time, in satisfying narcissism with its negative side *and* the longing to be present in the arena where the world's power is at stake.

31
•

Biomedical Analyses of Depression

GOODWIN AND JAMISON

FREDERICK GOODWIN obtained his undergraduate education at Georgetown University, graduating in 1958, and earned his medical degree from Saint Louis University in 1963. He practices medicine, specializing in psychiatry, in Bethesda, Maryland, and has had numerous appointments at the National Institute of Mental Health, where for many years he worked in the Alcohol, Drug Abuse and Mental Health Administration, and where, in 1992, he was appointed director. He has published extensively on biomedical aspects of mood disorder. He is currently on the faculty at the George Washington School of Medicine and has held appointments at the University of California at Irvine, the University of Wisconsin, Boston University, and Duke University.

Kay Redfield Jamison attended the University of California at Los Angeles and Saint Andrews University in Scotland, receiving her doctorate in clinical psychology from UCLA in 1971. Her first appointment was on the faculty at UCLA. Currently professor of psychiatry at the Johns Hopkins University School of Medicine, Jamison is the author of numerous publications on manic-depressive disorder, including *Touched with Fire: Manic-Depressive Illness and the Artistic Temperament* (1993), and her autobiographical best-seller, *An Unquiet Mind* (1995), which describes her own lifelong struggles with manic-depressive disorder.

The work from which the following passages are taken, Goodwin and Jamison's 900-page *Manic-Depressive Illness,* published in 1990, is regarded by some as the definitive volume, from a biomedical perspective, on every aspect of clinical treatment, theory, and research relating to unipolar and bipolar affective disorder. Diverging from nosological trends to be found in recent editions of the *Diagnostic and Statistic Manual,* the authors adhere to Kraepelin's category of *manic-depressive illness* to denote the range of recurrent affective disorders, including unipolar depression and unipolar mania as well as bipolar manic-depressive conditions. In emphasizing the breadth of this category, these authors note what they regard as two "knowledge gaps among clinicians" (70). First, the failure to emphasize longitudinal "course" of illness, as opposed to cross-sequential symptoms, particularly in the

United States, has led to a tendency to underdiagnose recurrence in unipolar disorders, yet recurrence is "fundamental to the major affective disorders." Second, there is a tendency to underdiagnose bipolarity. Acknowledgement of these tendencies explains the authors' use of the Kraepelinian nosological convention.

In the summary included here from their chapter on biochemical models, Goodwin and Jamison trace thirty years of increasingly sophisticated, though, as they note, also increasingly inaccessible, attempts to explain the interaction among neurotransmitters, neuromodulators, receptors, and other parts of the central nervous system apparently implicated in the several forms of affective disorder.

Animal models have been at the center of efforts to understand mental disorder and its treatment in humans. By reproducing in other species the behavioral signs of human disorders, and then reversing these signs through the application of the same pharmacological agents used to control symptoms in humans, researchers have been able to discover not only what but also where, and even how, such agents work. Because of the cross-species links provided by such psychopharmacological agents, these efforts illustrate what is known as a *pharmacological bridge,* allowing a two-way interaction between clinical care of humans at the bedside and basic research on animals at the laboratory bench.

Goodwin and Jamison here discuss three systems that have been implicated in human manic-depressive disorders: monoamine neurotransmitters, neuropeptides, and electrolytes. Specific neuronal systems in which monoamines (norepinephrine, serotonin, and dopamine) are the principle neurotransmitters have been the subject of special interest for mood disorder researchers since the 1960s. Such systems have the characteristics we would expect of the seat of affective disorder. They are complex, widely distributed throughout the brain, and serve an integrative function. Moreover, these neurotransmitters in animals are affected by drugs known to produce changes in mood or cognition in humans.

The second area of research summarized here is that in which simpler neurotransmitters known as *neuropeptides* are the subject of focus. These agents, such as glutamate and glycole, constitute a new class of neurotransmitters, other than the monoamines, that have effects on mood and cognition. Dysfunction of neuropeptides may also play a role in the etiology and/or pathogenesis of mood disorders.

Finally, these authors note that simple electrolytes such as water, sodium, potassium, calcium, and magnesium also play an important role in neuronal function, and abnormalities of these electrolytes in the brain may produce mood-altering effects.

Despite enormous progress in understanding both the neurobiology of the brain and the effects of psychopharmacological agents, Goodwin and Jamison acknowledge the limitations of such findings. We cannot yet say whether the neurobiological changes associated with these new psychopharmacological agents are specific to, or necessary for, the clinical effects (Goodwin and Jamison, 1990:584). An equally serious problem results from shifts in the precision of diagnostic boundaries. New problems of epistemology and methodology have been created by "a conceptual drift . . . in the name of diagnostic reliability," whereby the diagnostic criteria "are being used *in practice* as sufficient, and not merely as necessary for the diagnosis of depression." This drift, they conclude, "threatens to retard the field by increasing the variance present in clinical populations and by obscuring historical insights that helped us construct the amine paradigm 20 years ago. . . . How is a theory of depression to be developed, how is it to be tested, and how is an antidepressant drug effect to be recognized if the clinical entity (or independent variable) no longer corresponds to the original?" (582).

·◡ • ◠·

From Frederick Goodwin and Kay Redfield Jamison,
"Biomedical Models," in *Manic-Depressive Illness* (1990)

. . . Attempts to comprehend the brain's role in mania and depression—a quest the ancients could undertake only in rhetorical flight—began in earnest as clinically effective mood-altering drugs began to appear in the late 1950s and early 1960s. The psychopharmacological revolution fortuitously coincided with the arrival of new techniques that were making it possible to characterize neurotransmitter function in the central nervous system. Over the next three decades, a vast literature grew from research into the biochemistry and pharmacology of affective illness. Studies were, by and large, designed to detect relative excess or deficiency associated with pathological states. This too much/too little premise was an understandable supposition, given the profound changes wrought by the new medications. As experience with the drugs refined knowledge of their actions and limitations and as research results accumulated, the implicit assumptions of the early work were refined to account for interactions among neurotransmitter systems, neuromodulators, receptors, and other components of the central nervous system. More sophisticated, if less accessible, models are now emerging. . . .

Amine Neurotransmitter Systems

Originally formulated in the early 1960s to explain the actions of mood-altering drugs, the amine hypotheses both stimulated and emerged in parallel with basic animal studies that were characterizing specific neuronal systems in which monoamines are the principal neurotransmitters. The cell bodies of these systems are distributed predominantly in midbrain structures making up the limbic system (Papez, 1937; MacLean, 1952), a diffuse yet highly integrated set of structures characterized by multiple feedback loops. . . . The limbic system is implicated in the regulation of sleep, appetite, arousal, sexual function, and emotional states such as fear and rage. It has also been shown to be involved in various self-stimulation behaviors (Kupfermann, 1985).

Many groups of monoamine neurons, although originating from a small number of cell bodies, are distributed widely throughout the central nervous system. . . . A single norepinephrine neuron projecting from the locus coeruleus to the cortex can, for example, synapse with many thousands of other nerve cells. The monoaminergic systems, by and large, do not provide the principal drive for critical life-sustaining functions. Rather, they subserve much more subtle and complex modulatory and integrative functions.

It seemed reasonable to assume that the biological substrate of a syndrome as complex as manic-depressive illness, with its interrelated cognitive, emotional, psychomotor, appetitive, and autonomic manifestations, would be found in just such systems: complex, widely distributed throughout the brain, and essentially integrative in function. Such a biological substrate would also have to be affected by drugs known to produce changes in mood or cognition. The monoamine neurotransmitter systems meet these qualifications.

The most cohesive of the early amine hypotheses was the catecholamine hypothesis (Prange, 1964; Schildkraut, 1965; Bunney and Davis, 1965), which posits that depression is associated with a functional deficiency of catecholamines and mania an excess. The neurotransmitter serotonin was hypothesized to be low in both states. . . .

For years, the study of drug effects in animals was limited to acute administration, despite occasional pleas by a few clinical investigators who pointed out that the therapeutic effects of these drugs in patients occurred only after chronic administration, usually for 2 weeks or more, whereas the presynaptic effects of tricyclics, MAOIs [monoamine oxidase inhibitors], and (in part) lithium occurred immediately (reviewed in Goodwin and Sack, 1973). Chronic administration research paradigms allowed investigators to explore drug effects that develop more slowly over time, that is, more in parallel with their clinical effects. In addition, animal behavioral models of antidepressant effects, such as the enhancement of self-stimulation behavior, have been observed more consistently using chronic drug administration paradigms.

The emphasis on chronic drug studies gave impetus to one of the most productive and exciting developments in neurobiology over the past 10 years: the discovery and characterization of neurotransmitter and drug receptors in the brain and various peripheral tissues. Receptors, which represent specific recognition sites (usually proteins) for the binding of a given neurohumoral substance, provide the selectivity by which a target tissue (or cell) responds to a biological signal. Once a neurotransmitter or hormone binds to its receptor (i.e., becomes a receptor ligand), a series of intracellular events occurs (e.g., increases in cyclic nucleotide levels and protein kinase activity, hydrolysis of phosphoinositide, . . . ion permeability changes). This results ultimately in a physiological event. Substances that produce or contribute to the activation of a receptor-mediated event are referred to as *agonists* for that receptor, whereas substances that bind to the receptor and block or interfere with its natural agonist are called *antagonists*. A given receptor is defined by its response to a series of agonists or antagonists (Nutt and Linnoila, 1988).

Since one neurotransmitter can activate more than one receptor (e.g., norepinephrine is the physiological agonist at both α- and β-adrenergic receptors) and since a given receptor can be linked or coupled to more than one second messenger system (e.g., cyclic nucleotides or PI hydrolysis), the possible consequences of receptor activation are quite complex, and in most cases, the neurophysiological and behavioral effects of such stimulation are unknown. Nevertheless, techniques for measuring both the number and functional activity of neurotransmitter or drug receptors are now readily available, and several have been used in studies of possible receptor alterations in manic-depressive illness.

Important to receptor techniques is the ability to distinguish nonspecific binding from true receptor activation by a neurotransmitter or drug. If the binding affinities could be shown to have a high correlation with the physiological or pharmacological effect produced, a particular recognition site could be designated as a physiologically significant receptor. Studies of chronic drug effects also can assess the biochemical consequences of receptor activation by following the generation of second messengers. Effects of chronic drug administration on presynaptic autoreceptors (which, in most instances, serve to regulate the release of transmitter) add to this increasingly complex picture. Studies of chronic effects of drugs on the firing rates of single neurons have provided a physiological confirmation of the receptor-mediated effects of these drugs.

Phasic alterations in receptor sensitivity have been hypothesized to underlie one aspect of the illness—the sudden switch from depression to mania (Bunney et al., 1972 a,b,c). Given the evidence that postsynaptic receptor sensitivity tends to adapt to the level of presynaptic output of transmitter, the theory goes on to posit that the timing of this adaptation can get out of phase. Thus, a state of decreased presynaptic transmitter output would, after a while, result in an adaptive increase in the number of postsynaptic receptors (hypersensitivity). Later, if the presynaptic output were to again increase, the now greater amount of transmitter would interact with a supersensitive receptor complex, resulting in an exaggerated behavioral response, that is, mania. The reverse of this would explain the subsequent onset of depression as the excess neurotransmitter begins to down-regulate the receptor.

Neuroendocrine Systems and Neuropeptides

The hypothesis that altered endocrine function might explain or contribute to pathological mood states largely grew out of clinical observations of patients with thyroid or Cushing's disease and antedated the discovery of biogenic amine neurotransmitters. One reason that this field has evolved rapidly is the potential that neuroendocrine substances may serve as a window into the brain's neurotransmitter systems. Current explorations of pathophysiology using neuroendocrine strategies have tended to develop research tools into diagnostic tests (e.g., the dexamethasone suppression test) prematurely. But tests of this kind are most useful for research into mechanisms of illness when the illness itself remains the independent variable, an approach that allows exploration of its clinical, pharmacological, genetic, and other biological correlates independent of predetermined diagnostic boundaries.

The primary components of the neuroendocrine systems are neuropeptides, and thus the distinction between endocrine and peptide studies is somewhat artificial. New peptide neurotransmitter or neuromodulator candidates emerge with increasing frequency as methods for their isolation, characterization, and synthesis become more and more sophisticated and efficient. It is likely that we are about to experience a surge of new, as yet undreamed of peptides in the central nervous system, discoveries that will come very rapidly from application of the tools of molecular genetics (Bloom, 1987).

Electrolyte-Based and Membrane Hypotheses

Studies of total body water and electrolyte balance (principally sodium) grew out of classic observations of such state-related fluctuations in manic-depressive illness as urine volume and body weight. They also were prompted by a growing appreciation of the importance of sodium, potassium, calcium, and magnesium in nerve cell excitation, synaptic transmission, and, possibly, the mechanism of action of lithium. Although relatively prominent in the 1960s, studies in this area inexplicably died out in succeeding decades but may now be experiencing a resurgence in the emerging literature in the chemistry and biophysics of membrane function. For example, a deficiency in the membrane-bound sodium pump was initially hypothesized to explain reported excessive cellular sodium retention but later became important in its own right. Later the lithium-sodium counterflow mechanism in the red cell was characterized, and biophysical studies revealed protein structural differences between patients and controls.

Membrane studies in manic-depressive illness occupy a special place, not only because they provide a biological handle on genetic vulnerability but also because of the vital role of membrane transport mechanisms in transmitter function at the synaptic level. Indeed, it would not be unreasonable to anticipate that all of the biological findings in manic-depressive illness ultimately may be explained on the basis of some membrane abnormality, either localized or generalized. An implicit assumption of membrane studies is that a genetically transmitted abnormality found in an available peripheral tissue, such as the red cell or platelet, will also be expressed in other tissues, including the central nervous system.

The Pharmacological Bridge

The pharmacological bridge between biochemical pharmacology in animals and the clinical actions of drugs supported the growth of the major biochemical hypotheses of manic-depressive illness. . . .

Historically, the potential of the amine-depleting antihypertensive reserpine to induce depression was the first pharmacological bridge, one that led to formulation of the amine hypothesis. The most reasonable interpretation of reserpine's clinical effect was that it activated a preexisting vulnerability. It is not clear, however, whether a bipolar or a unipolar history confers a different degree of vulnerability to this drug or whether, continuously administered, reserpine could precipitate recurrent depressive or manic-depressive illness.[1] Reserpine's effects appear to be associated primarily with depletion of catecholamines (rather than indoleamines) because they are reversed by catecholamine and not indoleamine agonists. The relative involvement of the two catecholamines (norepinephrine and dopamine) in the behavioral effects of reserpine is not settled. Propranolol, the peripheral and centrally active β-receptor antagonist, may occasionally produce depressive episodes in standard therapeutic doses and, in high doses, appears to have interesting effects on cycle length in some manic-depressive patients.

Drugs that act as stimulants in normal individuals are not generally found to be therapeutic in patients suffering from major depressive illness (Klein and Davis, 1969). Conversely, drugs that have antidepressant activity do not tend to be stimulants in normals (Oswald et al., 1972). L-Dopa, a precursor of both dopamine and norepinephrine, which at least acutely increases their output, is not an effective antidepressant. Nevertheless, it does produce some activation with increases in anger and psychosis ratings in some patients and hypomanic episodes superimposed on the depression in many bipolar patients (Goodwin et al., 1970; Murphy et al., 1971).

Early findings on lithium were interpreted as indicating a drug-induced decreases of functional amines,[2] although the picture is now considerably more complex, giving more emphasis to the ion's effects on postsynaptic second messenger mechanisms involving cyclic nucleotides, PI, and G proteins. All neuroleptics block the action of dopamine at its postsynaptic receptor (at least in certain regions), although they do not have uniform effects on norepinephrine. α-Methyl-paratyrosine, a relatively specific inhibitor of dopamine and norepinephrine synthesis, depletes the amount of transmitter available for release. Piribedil and bromocriptine are both partial dopamine receptor agonists. Both have antidepressant and possibly mania-inducing effects, although in different doses, the latter actually has antimanic effects.

The most consistent pharmacological bridge is built on the findings that direct or indirect dopamine or norepinephrine agonists can precipitate episodes of mania or hypomania in patients with manic-depressive illness.

Many of the so-called classic biochemical effects comprising one end of the pharmacological bridge are based on the ability of drugs to alter acutely the turnover of the neurotransmitter, that is, the combined rate of synthesis, release, and elimination of a particular substance. High turnover traditionally implies a higher level of function, and low turnover implies the reverse, although by itself this does not take receptor adaptation (e.g., down-regulation) into account. For the pharmacological bridge, the net action of a drug on the output of the amine system is the focus, rather than the complexities of drug effects on different components of these systems. . . .

Beyond the effects of a drug on the state of depression or mania are effects on the cycle length. Tricyclic antidepressants can increase the frequency of cycles in some patients. MAO inhibitors, like other antidepressants, can precipitate mania, but their long-term effect on cycles has not been studied extensively. This effect may depend on the inhibition of type-B MAO, since a selective MAO-A inhibition appears not to increase cycling. ECT apparently can both precipitate and terminate manias in bipolar patients and either increase or decrease cycle frequency depending on the phase of illness in which it is administered. Tricyclic or heterocyclic antidepressants can reverse depression, precipitate mania, and increase cycle frequency in at least a subgroup of bipolar patients. MAOIs can reverse depression, precipitate mania, and, in the case of the MAO type-A inhibitors, decrease cycle frequency, although the nonspecific (mixed A and B) MAOIs may, like TCAs, increase cycle frequency. Lithium can reverse mania, reverse depression, and decrease cycle frequency. Carbamazepine, less extensively evaluated biochemically than the others, also may have at least three classes of action. It is partially antidepressant, certainly antimanic, and anticycling. Finally, there are a growing number of antidepressants termed *second generation and third generation* or *heterocyclic* (because of different cyclic structures than the tricyclics); these have not been used long enough to assess whether they affect cycle frequency. Some, especially those that are primarily serotonin uptake inhibitors, may be less likely than standard antidepressants to precipitate mania.

Notes

PREFACE

1. This lore is found in the *Caraka Samhita,* a compilation written by the physician Caraka in the first century C.E.

2. The most influential text for Chinese medicine, composed during the second and first centuries B.C.C., was the *Huangdi neijing* (*The Yellow Emperor's Manual of Corporeal Medicine*), a work on acupuncture.

INTRODUCTION

1. Samuel Johnson and others spoke of a *depression* of spirits, using the term as a modifier, but the word does not occur to name a disorder until the very end of the nineteenth century, and only begins to eclipse *melancholia* to refer to a disorder category in our present century.

2. For a fuller discussion of the notion of partial insanity, see Jackson, 1983, 1986. This sense of melancholia as partial insanity functioned—the way the category of "neurotic" has done during parts of the twentieth century—to mark off non-psychotic and less disabling disorders.

3. Bennett Simon has developed a similar theory to account for the power of the associations of melancholy with blackness and with bile. Simon portrays a form of magical thinking: "primordial, subjective, psychosomatic fantasy based on the blending of mental and somatic sensations" by which "there is a nexus of associations among anger, darkness or blackness surging up with . . . anger, and blackness as poisonous (for example, *Iliad* 17.591—'a black cloud of distress'). Thus cholos, anger and chole, bile, often overlap in poetic and literary usage and we . . . see that the associations of blackness, bile, and dejection arise from common (perhaps universal) subjective experiences and associations involved in becoming and feeling depressed" (Simon, 1978:235).

4. Saturn also provided redemption in Ficino's system: the gifted melancholic who suffered under Saturn, might save himself by adopting the activity of creative contemplation—that activity "which is the particular domain of the sublime star of speculation" (Klibansky, Panofsky, and Saxl, 1964:271).

5. The theme of the mad artist had acquired the status of a truism in the nineteenth century, as Gilman puts it 1988:221–22). Not only did creative people suffer melancholy, but the melancholy, and more generally the mad, were poets and painters. A late nineteenth-century fascination with the additional creativity of the deranged, exemplified in the 1864 publication of Cesare Lombroso's *Genius and Madness,* has been documented by Wittkower and Wittkower (1963), Becker (1978), and Gilman (1988), for example.

6. For a discussion challenging this classificatory convention, see Goodwin and Jamison, 1990: chapter 3.

7. As director of a large asylum, Kraepelin had the resources and meticulous records of an inpatient hospital at his disposal, and a large, long-term patient population as his empirical "database." His *Memoirs* provide a portrait of this setting (Kraepelin, 1987).

8. The conception of a lesion was quite elastic at this time (Gosling, 1987). Nonetheless, the position identifying mental disorder with brain lesions had its serious detractors in the first years of the new century, who believed it to impede the progress of the new science of psychiatry. For an account of this controversy see Lunbeck (1994:118).

9. Recent empirical evidence has challenged the presumption that these represent either discrete or notable categories in nature, that they are "natural kinds." (Kendell and Gourlay, 1970; Brockington and Kendell, 1979; Crow, 1986, 1987; Angst, 1993).

10. It reemerged even in the twentieth century, as a recent historical review has shown (Berrios and Beer, 1994).

11. For contemporary philosophical work with these presuppositions, see Sartre, 1948, 1977; Calhoun, 1984; Griffiths, 1989; and Turski, 1994. But see also Descartes and Spinoza.

12. In some behaviorist traditions, verbal behavior was included; in others, it was excluded, as unreliable evidence.

13. One symptom must be included in the criteria for depression, noted Levitt, Lubin, and Brooks. "It would be entirely unreasonable, even ridiculous, to exclude the symptom of expressed mood of unhappiness from the eventual pattern. Otherwise why use a word like depression at all?" (Levitt, Lubin, and Brooks, 1983:57).

14. For a discussion of early twentieth-century resistance to the perceived vacuity of the "descriptive" approach to nosology, see Lunbeck, 1994: chapter 5. On the other hand, the antipsychiatry writing of the 1950s through the 1970s has shown the danger associated with embracing etiological models. A nuanced discussion of the limitations of causal explanation in psychiatry is to be found in Slavney and McHugh's *Psychiatric Polarities* (1987).

15. Kleinman recognizes the methodological dilemma raised here, and in a progression since his earlier remark that a purely cultural perspective "cannot be maintained" in the face of clinical and psychophysiological evidence (Kleinman and Good, 1985:493), he more recently declared apparent allegiance to such a purely cultural perspective in his insistence that clinical depression must be placed (descriptively) "within a broader array of social suffering" (1995:11).

16. The phenomenological analysis of moods to be found in Heidegger's writing is not to be confused with this analytic tradition.

17. Writing in *The Origin of German Tragic Drama,* Walter Benjamin has pointed to the vagueness and lack of unitary meaning attached to melancholy in explaining this persistent gender association: if, he says "according to the Western medical and philosophical tradition, the physiological state of disease is stubbornly linked with the figure of woman (whether as its cause or its icon), the often vague and contradictory symptomatology of melancholia is also what allows it to be manipulated . . . in the creation of an elite psychological condition implicitly or explicitly associated with the genius of 'great *men*'" (1977:151).

18. Charts reproduced by Lunbeck reveal both points noted here. More women than men are diagnosed with these two major mental illnesses by a ratio of 226 : 179; and women are diagnosed with manic-depressive illness almost twice as often as are men (women=241 : men=142) (Lunbeck, 1994:148).

19. By way of confirmation of this generalization, let me quote first from Sir Aubrey Lewis, who remarks of self-reproach and self-accusation in melancholia, "These are among the most striking of melancholic symptoms" (1934:312). Then note Hamilton, writing nearly fifty years later. When depressive illness is severe, he remarks, three features are clearly present: "depressed mood, *feelings of guilt* and

suicidal thoughts," and these are "generally regarded as the central features of the illness" (Hamilton, 1982:4).

20. Twentieth-century references to "melancholic" symptoms (of depression or other disorders) have sometimes cast them as a form of anhedonic mood state characterized by the inability to find or take pleasure in the activities or events that would be expected to give pleasure. But, in contrast, see Parker and Hadzi-Pavlovic's sign-based, experimental definition of melancholia (1996).

21. For a careful discussion of the confusions and conflicts involved in the long debate over endogenous depression that raged through the middle of the twentieth century, see Hill, 1968. A sophisticated attempt to reconstruct the categories is found in Donald Klein's work on "endogenomorphic" depression (1974), and a recent "binarian" analysis in Parker and Hadzi-Pavlovic, 1996.

22. Alternative typologies to mine also suggest themselves. Thus, for example, Akiskal and McKinney distinguish four models of depression that, while encompassing the same range of theories, separate them by slightly different criteria: (1) the model that sees depression as *"hostility turned inward* upon the loss of an ambivalently loved person"; (2) the *"object loss"* model, which includes "traumatic separation from a loved person—that is, the disruption of an attachment bond"; (3) the *"reinforcement"* model, which "postulates that depression is the name given to behaviors that result from the loss of major sources of reinforcement"; and, finally, (4) the *"biogenic amine"* model (Akiskal and McKinney, 1973).

CHAPTER 1

This selection is from book XXX of *Aristotle: Problems,* vol. 16, translated by W. S. Hett (Cambridge, Mass.: Harvard University Press, 1957). Reprinted with the permission of the publisher and the Loeb Classical Library.

CHAPTER 2

This selection is from book III, chapter 10, of *Galen: On the Affected Parts,* translated by Rudolph E. Siegel (Basel: S. Karger, 1976). Reprinted with the permission of the publisher.

CHAPTER 3

This selection is from book X, chapters 1–4, of *The Foundations of the Cenobitic Life and the Eight Capital Sins* (Grand Rapids, Mich.: W. B. Eerdmans, 1955).

CHAPTER 4

This selection is from the unpublished translation of *Avicenna: Canon of Medicine,* book 3: *On Black Bile and Melancholia* by Martin Eisner (1999). Printed with permission.

Translator's Note: Since there is no modern critical edition of Avicenna's *Canon of Medicine,* I have translated from two manuscript copies. The first is Gerard of Cremona's version (Venice, 1507; facsimile, Hildesheim, 1964). The second is the Gerard version with corrections and annotations by the physician Andrea Alpagus (first published, Venice, 1527; Basil, 1556). Despite the text's extraordinary popularity throughout the Middle Ages, Gerard's translation is anything but transparent. As Nancy Siraisi notes in her book *Avicenna in Renaissance Italy,* the translation is "characterized by a high proportion of both errors and obscurely rendered passages. It also retains numerous transliterated Arabic words, especially . . . for anatomical terms" (Siraisi, 1987:20). Even with Andrea's corrections, the text continues to be obscure in places. Gerard uses normal Latin words in a new, technical way. He also adopts wholesale Arabic words, further obstructing our access to an accurate reading—M. E.

CHAPTER 5

This selection is from *St. Hildegard of Bingen: Holistic Healing*, translated by Palmquist and Kulas (Collegeville, Minn.: The Liturgical Press, 1994). Reprinted with the permission of the publisher.

CHAPTER 6

This selection is from book I, chapters 3–5, of *Marcilio Ficino: Three Books on Life*, translated by Carol Kaske and John Clark (Binghampton, N.Y.: Center of Medieval and Renaissance Studies, 1989). Reprinted with the permission of the publisher.

CHAPTER 7

This selection is from book III, chapters 5–7 and 16; book IV, chapter 25; and book VI, chapter 23, of *Johann Weyer: Witches, Devils and Doctors in The Renaissance* (*De Praestigiis Daemonum*), translated by John Shea (Binghampton, N.Y.: Center of Medieval and Renaissance Studies, 1991). Reprinted with the permission of the publisher.

CHAPTER 8

This selection is (a) from VI:1 (6, 7, 8, 9, 10); VI:2 (3, 4, 5, 6, 7); VI:3 (2, 3, 4, 5, 7), *The Collected Works of St. Teresa of Avila*, vol. 2, translated by Kieran Kavanaugh and Otilio Rodriguez. Copyright © 1976 by Washington Province of Discalced Carmelites, ICS Publications, 2131 Lincoln Road, N.E., Washington, D.C. 20002, USA. Reprinted with the permission of the publisher. This selection is (b) from chapter 7 (1, 2, 3, 4, 6, 7, 8, 9, 10), *The Collected Works of St. Teresa of Avila*, vol. 3, translated by Kieran Kavanaugh and Otilio Rodriguez. Copyright © 1976 by Washington Province of Discalced Carmelites, ICS Publications, 2131 Lincoln Road, N.E., Washington, D.C. 20002, USA. Reprinted with the permission of the publisher.

CHAPTER 9

This selection is from chapters 1, 17, and 34, of *A Treatise of Melancholy* (London: John Windet, 1586).

CHAPTER 10

This selection is from part 1, sections 1, numbers 1.5, 2.1, 2.2, and 3.2; part I, sections 2, numbers 2.6, 2.7; 3.1, and 3.15; and part 1, sections 3, numbers 1.1–1.3, of *Robert Burton: The Anatomy of Melancholy* (Oxford: Oxford University Press, 1989). Reprinted with the permission of the publisher.

CHAPTER 11

This selection is from *Characters*, edited with an introduction and notes by Charles W. Daves (Cleveland: Press of Case Western Reserve University, 1970).

CHAPTER 12

This selection is from the facsimile edition of *The Angel of Bethesda,* edited with an introduction by Gordon Jones (Barre, Mass.: American Antiquarian Society and Barre Publishers, 1972).

CHAPTER 13

This selection is from *Miscellany of Poems Written by a Lady,* edited by Gildon (London, 1701).

CHAPTER 14

This selection is from *Aphorisms: Concerning the Knowledge and Cure of Diseases* (London: W. Innys, 1735).

CHAPTER 15

This selection is from *The Sorrows of Young Werther* anon. trans. (Boston, Mass.: Dana Estes, 1892).

CHAPTER 16

This selection is from the "Anthropological Didactic on the Cognitive Faculty," (a) number 45, (c) number 50, *Immanuel Kant: Anthropology from a Practical Point of View,* translated by Victor Lyle Dowdell, revised and edited by Hans H. Rudnick (Carbondale, Ill.: Southern Illinois University Press, 1978). Copyright © (1978) by the Board of Trustees, Southern Illinois University. Reprinted with the permission of the publisher.

CHAPTER 17

This selection is from the "First Species of Mental Derangement," sections 54–59, in *A Treatise on Insanity, in Which are Contained the Principles of New and More Practical Nosology of Maniacal Disorders Than Has Yet Been Offered to the Public,* translated by D. D. Davis (Sheffield: W. Todd, 1806).

CHAPTER 18

This selection is from chapter 3 of *Medical Inquiries and Observations upon the Diseases of the Mind* (Philadelphia: Kimber & Richardson, 1812).

CHAPTER 19

From *The Poems of John Keats* (London: J. M. Dent, 1906). For a modern critical edition, readers can turn to *The Poems of John Keats,* edited by Jack Stillinger (Cambridge, Mass.: Belknap Press of Harvard University Press, 1978).

CHAPTER 20

This selection is from chapter 1, number 3, section II:16, of *Mental Pathology and Therapeutics,* translated by C. Lockhart Robertson and James Rutherford (London: The New Sydenham Society, 1867). For a modern critical edition, readers can turn to a facsimile of the 1867 edition (New York: Hafner, 1965).

CHAPTER 21

This selection is from the unpublished translations of Baudelaire's "Spleen" and "Autumn Song," by Nina Seidenman (1999). Printed with permission.

CHAPTER 22

This selection is from *Self-help: Character, Conduct and Perseverance* (New York: A. L. Burt, 1862).

CHAPTER 23

This selection is from chapter 3 of *The Physiology and Pathology of the Mind* (New York: Appleton, 1867).

CHAPTER 24

This selection is from chapter 5 of *Manic Depressive Illness*, translated by Mary Barclay and edited by George Robinson from the 8th edition of *Textbook of Psychiatry* (1909–1915) (Edingurgh: E&S Livingstone, 1920). The 1920 edition reproduces part of the *Textbook of Psychiatry*.

CHAPTER 25

This selection is from *The Standard Edition of the Complete Psychological Works of Sigmund Freud,* translated and edited by James Strachey (London: Random House, 1950). Acknowledgment is made to Sigmund Freud © Copyrights, The Institute of Psycho-Analysis and The Hogarth Press for permission to quote.

1. "Abraham, to whom we owe the most important of the few analytic studies on this subject, also took this comparison to his starting point. (*Zentralblatt*, Bd. II., 1912.)"
2. "The words 'painful' and 'pain' in this paragraph represent the German *Schmerz* (i.e., the ordinary connotation of *pain* in English) and not *Unlust,* the mental antithesis of pleasure, also technically translated as 'pain'.—Trans."
3. "The German here is *Schmerzunlust,* a combination of the two words for *pain.*—Trans."

CHAPTER 26

This selection is from *Melanie Klein: Love, Guilt and Reparation and Other Works, 1921–1945* (London: The Hogarth Press, 1975). Reprinted with the permission of the publisher.

1. "In the same book (*Writings,* 2, pp. 100–01, fn), referring to my view that every child passes through a neurosis differing only in degree from one individual to another, I added: 'This view, which I have maintained for a number of years now, has lately received valuable support. In his book, *The Question of Lay Analysis* (S.E. 20), Freud writes "since we have learnt how to look more sharply, we are tempted to say that neurosis in children is not the exception but the rule, as though it could scarcely be avoided on the path from the innate disposition of infancy to civilized society" (p. 215).'"
2. "I have pointed out in various connections (first of all in 'Early Stages of the Oedipus Complex,' p. 186) that the fear of phantastically 'bad' persecutors and the belief in phantastically 'good' objects are bound up with each other. Idealization is

an essential process in the young child's mind, since he cannot yet cope in any other way with his fears of persecution (a result of his own hatred). Not until early anxieties have been sufficiently relieved owing to experiences which increase love and trust, is it possible to establish the all-important process of bringing together more closely the various aspects of objects (extenal, internal, 'good' and 'bad', loved and hated), and thus for hatred to become actually mitigated by love—which means a decrease of ambivalence. While the separation of these contrasting *aspects*—felt in the unconscious as contrasting *objects*—operates strongly, feelings of hatred and love are also so much divorced from each other that love cannot mitigate hatred."

CHAPTER 27

This selection is from *Helplessness: On Depression, Development, and Death* (New York: W. H. Freeman, 1975). Copyright © 1992 by Martin E. P. Seligman. Used with permission of W. H. Freeman and Company.

In this selection, the author cites the following works:

Liddell, H. S. *Emotional hazards in animals and man.* Springfield, Illinois: The Free Press of Glencoe, 1953.
Masserman, J. H. *Behavior and neurosis.* Chicago: University of Chicago Press, 1943.
Pavlov, I. P. *Conditioned reflexes.* New York: Dover, 1927.

CHAPTER 28

This selection is from *Aaron T. Beck: Cognitive Therapy and Emotional Disorders* (Madison, Ct.: International University Press, 1975), pp. 103–111. Reprinted with the permission of the publisher.

CHAPTER 29

This selection is from chapter 8 of *Toward a New Psychology of Women* (Boston: Beacon Press, 1976). Copyright © 1976 by Jeanne Baker Miller. Reprinted with the permission of the Beacon Press, Boston.

CHAPTER 30

This selection is from chapter 1 of *Black Sun: Depression and Melancholy,* translated by Leon Roudiez (New York: Columbia University Press, 1989). Copyright © 1992 Columbia University Press. Reprinted with the permission of the publisher.

CHAPTER 31

This selection is from chapter 16 of *Goodwin and Jamison: Manic-Depressive Illness* (New York: Oxford University Press, 1990). Reprinted with permission of the publisher.

In this selection, the authors cite the following works:

Bloom, F. E. 1987. Future directions and goals in basic pharmacology and neurobiology. In H. Y. Meltzer (Ed.), *Psychopharmacology: The third generation of progress* (pp. 1685–1689). New York: Raven Press.
Bunney, W. E., Jr, & Davis, J. 1965. Norepinephrine in depressive reactions. *Arch Gen Psychiatry, 13,* 483–494.

Bunney, W. E., Jr., Murphy, D., Goodwin, F. K., & Borge, G. F. 1972a. The "switch process" in manic-depressive illness: I. A systematic study of sequential behavior change. *Arch Gen Psychiatry, 27,* 295–302.

Bunney, W. E., Jr., Goodwin, F. K., Murphy, D. L., House, K. M., & Gordon, E. K. 1972b. The "switch process" in manic-depressive illness: II. Relationship to catecholamines, REM sleep, and drugs. *Arch Gen Psychiatry, 27,* 304–309.

Bunney, W. E., Jr., Goodwin, F. K., & Murphy, D. L. 1972c. The "switch process" in manic-depressive illness: III. Theoretical implications. *Arch Gen Psychiatry, 27,* 312–317.

Goodwin, F. K., Murphy, D. L., Brodie, H. K., & Bunney, W. E., Jr. 1970. L-dopa, catecholamines, and behavior: A clinical and biochemical study in depressed patients. *Biol Psychiatry, 2,* 341–366.

Goodwin, F. K., & Sack, R. L. 1973. Affective disorders: The catecholamine hypothesis revisited. In E. Usdin & S. Snyder (Eds.), *Frontiers in catecholamine research* (pp. 1157–1164). New York: Pergamon Press.

Klein, D. F., & Davis, J. M. 1969. *Diagnosis and treatment of psychiatric disorders.* Baltimore: Williams & Wilkins.

Kupferman, I. 1985. Hypothalamus and limbic system II: Motivation. In E. R. Kandel & J. H. Schwartz (Eds.), *Principles of neural science* (2nd ed., pp. 626–635). New York: Elsevier.

Maclean, P. D. 1952. Some psychiatric implications of physiological studies on frontotemporal portion of limbic systems (visceral brain). *Electroencephalogr Clin Neurophysiol, 4,* 407–418.

Murphy, D. L., Brodie, H. K., Goodwin, F. K., & Bunney, W. E., Jr. 1971. Regular induction of hypomania by L-dopa in "bipolar" manic-depressive patients. *Nature, 229,* 135–136.

Nutt, D. J., & Linnoila, M. 1988. Neuroreceptor science: A clarification of terms. *J. Clin Psycopharm, 8,* 387–389.

Oswald, I., Brezinova, V., & Dunleavy, D. L. F. 1972. On the slowness of action of tricyclic antidepressant drugs. *Br J Psychiatry, 120,* 673–677.

Papez, J. W. 1937. A proposed mechanism of emotion. *Arch Neurol Psychiatry, 38,* 725–743.

Prange, A. J., Jr. 1964. The pharmacology and biochemistry of depression. *Dis Nerv Syst, 25,* 217–221.

Schildkraut, J. 1965. The catecholamine hypothesis of affective disorder: A review of supporting evidence. *American Journal of Psychiatry, 122,* 509–522.

1. "Methyldopa, believed to act by stimulating presynaptic receptors that inhibit norepinephrine release in the central nervous system, also can precipitate depression."

2. "The term *functional,* although somewhat imprecise, has been used to signify the level of amine in the synapse and, therefore, available to activate its postsynaptic receptors."

Bibliography

Akiskal and McKinney. 1973. "Depressive Disorder: Toward a Unified Hypothesis." *Science* 5 (October):20–29.

Al-Issa, Ihsan. 1995. *Handbook of Culture and Mental Illness.* Madison, Conn.: International Universities Press.

American Psychiatric Association. 1980. *Diagnostic and Statistical Manual of Mental Disorders.* 3rd ed. Washington, D.C.: American Psychiatric Association.

American Psychiatric Association. 1994. *Diagnostic and Statistical Manual of Mental Disorders.* 4th ed. Washington, D.C.: American Psychiatric Association.

Andreason, Nancy. 1982. "Concepts, Diagnosis, and Classification." In *Handbook of Affective Disorders,* edited by E. S. Paykel, 24–44. New York: Guilford Press.

Angst, J. 1993. "Today's Perspectives on Kraepelin's Nosology of Endogenous Psychoses." *European Archives of Psychiatry and Clinical Neuroscience* 2243:164–70.

Aretaeus of Cappadocia. 1856. "On The Causes and Symptoms of Chronic Diseases." In *The Extant Works of Aretaeus, the Cappadocian,* edited and translated by Francis Adams. London: Sydenham Society.

Aristotle. 1957. *Problems* II, Book XXX. Translated by W. S. Hett London and Cambridge, Mass.: Heinemann with Harvard University Press.

Avicenna. 1966. *Canon of Medicine.* Translated by Mazhar Shah. Karachi, Pakistan: Naveed Clinic Press.

Avicenna. 1999. "On the Signs of Melancholy's Appearance." In *On Black Bile and Melancholy,* book III of *Canon of Medicine.* Translated by Martin Eisner. Unpublished.

Babb, Lawrence. 1943. "Love Melancholy in the Elizabethan and Early Stuart Drama." *Bulletin of the History of Medicine* 13, no. 2: 117–32.

———. 1951. *Elizabethan Malady: A Study of Melancholia in English Literature from 1580 to 1642.* East Lansing: Michigan State University Press.

Baillarger, Jules. 1854. "Note sur un genre de folie dont les acces sont caracterises par deux periodes regulieres, l'une de depression et l'autre d'excitation." *Bulletin de l'Academie Imperiale de Medicine* 19:340–52.

Baudelaire, C. [1857] 1958. *The Flowers of Evil.* Translated by Jacques Leclerq. Mt. Vernon, N.Y.: Peter Pauper Press.

———. [1857] 1999. "Autumn Song" and "Spleen." Translated by Nina Seidenman. Unpublished.

———. [1887] 1920. *Journaux Intimes.* Edited by A. Van Bever. Paris: Cres.

Beck, A. 1967. *Depression: Clinical, Experimental, and Theoretical Aspects.* New York: Hoeber.

———. 1976. *Cognitive Therapy and the Emotional Disorders* New York: International Universities Press.

———. 1978. *Cognitive Theories of Depression.* Philadelphia: University of Pennsylvania, Press.

Becker, G. 1978. *The Mad Genius Controversy: A Study in the Sociology of Deviance.* Beverly Hills, Calif.: Sage.

Benjamin, W. 1977. *The Origin of German Tragic Drama.* Translated by John Osborne. London: New Left Books.

Berrios, G. E., and G. Beer. 1994. "The Notion of Unitary Psychosis: A Conceptual History." *History of Psychiatry* 5:13–36.

Berrios, G. E., and Roy Porter, eds. 1995. *A History of Clinical Psychiatry: The Origin and History of Psychiatric Disorders.* New York: New York University Press.

Bhagavad Gita. 1964. Translated and interpreted by Franklin Edgarton. New York: Harper and Row.

Bion, W. 1963. *Elements in Psycho-analysis.* London: Maresfield Reprints.

Blandford, G. Fielding. 1871. *Insanity and Its Treatment.* Philadelphia: Henry C. Lea.

Boerhaave, H. 1735. *Aphorisms: Concerning the Knowledge and Cure of Diseases.* Translated from the last Latin edition with useful observations and explanations. London: W. Innys.

———. [1703] 1983. "Oration on the Usefulness of the Mechanical Method in Medicine." In *Orations,* translated with an introduction by E. Kegel-Brinkgreve and A. M. Luyendijk-Elshout. Leiden: E. J. Brill/Leiden University Press.

Bright, Timothie. 1586. *A Treatise of Melancholy.* London: John Windet.

Brockington, I. F., and R. E. Kendell. 1979. "The Distinction between the Affective Psychoses and Schizophrenia." *British Journal of Psychiatry* 135:243–84.

Bucknill, J., and D. H. Tuke. 1858. *A Manual of Psychological Medicine.* Philadelphia: Blanchard and Lea.

Burton, R. [1621] 1979. *The Anatomy of Melancholy.* Edited by John Peters. New York: Frederick Ungar.

Burton, R. [1621] 1989. *The Anatomy of Melancholy.* Edited by Thomas Faulkner, Nicolas Kiessling, and Rhonda Blair. Oxford: Clarendon Press.

Busfield, J. 1996. *Men, Women, and Madness: Understanding Gender and Mental Disorder.* New York: New York University Press.

Bush, Douglas. 1962. "English Literature in the Earlier Seventeenth Century." In *Oxford History of English Literature.* Oxford: Oxford University Press.

Butler, Judith. 1990. *Gender Trouble: Feminism and the Subversive Identity.* New York: Routledge.

———. 1997. *The Psychic Life of Power: Theories in Subjection.* Stanford, Calif.: Stanford University Press.

———. 1993. *Bodies That Matter.* New York: Routledge.

Butler, Samuel. [1759] 1970. *Characters.* Edited with an introduction and notes by Charles W. Daves. Cleveland: Press of Case Western Reserve University.

Byron, George Gordon. [1806] 1980. "Hours of Idleness." In *The Complete Poetical Works,* edited by Jerome McGann. Oxford: Clarendon Press.

Calhoun, C. 1984. "Cognitive Emotions?" In *What Is an Emotion?* edited by C. Calhoun and R. Solomon, Oxford: Oxford University Press.

Caraka, 1997. *Caraka Samhita.* 2nd ed. Delhi: Sri Satguru Publications.

Carter, Robert Brudenell. 1853. *On the Pathology and Treatment of Hysteria.* London.

Cassian, J. 1955. *The Foundations of the Cenobitic Life and the Eight Capital Sins.* Grand Rapids, Mich.: W. B. Eerdmans.

Chambers, Ross. 1987. *The Writing of Melancholy.* Translated by Mary Seidman Trouille. Chicago: University of Chicago Press.

Chessler, P. 1972. *Women and Madness.* New York: Doubleday.

Conolly, J. [1858] 1976. *The Faces of Madness: Hugh W. Diamond and the Origin of Psychiatric Photography.* Edited by Sandor Gilman. New York: Brunner/Mazel.

Corob, Alison. 1987. *Working with Depressed Women: A Feminist Approach.* Aldershott: Gower.

Crow, T. J. 1986. "The Continuum of Psychosis and Its Implication for the Structure of the Gene." *British Journal of Psychiatry* 144:419–29.

———. 1987. "Psychosis as a Continuum and the Virogene Concept." *British Medical Bulletin* 43: 754–67.

Descartes, R. 1961. "The Passions of the Soul." in *Essential Works of Descartes.* Translated by Lowell Bair, with an introduction by Daniel Bronstein, 109–210. New York: Bantam Books.

Enterline, Lynn. 1995. *The Tears of Narcissus: Melancholia and Masculinity in Early Modern Writing.* Stanford, Calif.: Stanford University Press.

Esquirol. E. 1845. *Mental Maladies: A Treatise on Insanity.* Translated by E. K. Hunt. Philadelphia: Mathew Carey.

Falret, Jean Pierre. 1854. "Memoire sur la folie circulaire, forme de maladie mental caracterisee par la reproduction successive et reguliere de l'etat maniaque, de l'etat melancholique, et d'un intervalle lucide plus ou moins prolonge." *Bulletin de l'Academie Imperiale de Medecine* 19:382–400.

Feder, Lillian. 1980. *Madness in Literature.* Princeton, N.J.: Princeton University Press.

Ficino, Marsilio. [1482] 1989. *Three Books on Life.* A critical edition and translation with introduction and notes by Carol Kaske and John Clark. Medieval and Renaissance Texts and Studies, in conjunction with the Renaissance Society of America, Binghamton, New York.

Finch, Anne, Countess of Winchilsea. 1701. *Miscellany of Poems. Written by a Lady.* Edited by Gildon. London.

Foucault, Michel. [1961] 1973. *Madness and Civilization: A History of Madness in the Age of Reason.* New York: Vintage.

Freud, Sigmund. [1917] 1967. "Mourning and Melancholia." In *Collected Papers* Vol. 4. London: Hogarth Press.

Freud, Sigmund, and Wilhelm Fliess. 1985. *The Complete Letters of Freud to Wilhelm Fliess.* Translated and edited by Jeffrey Moussaieff. Cambridge, Mass.: Belknap Press of Harvard University Press.

Galen. 1916. *On The Natural Faculties.* Translated by Arthur John Brock. London: Heinemann and Harvard University Press.

———. 1976. *On The Affected Parts.* Translated from the Greek text by Rudolph E. Seigel. Basel: Karger.

Gibson, G. 1916. "The Relationship between Pelvic Disease and Manic Depressive Insanity." *American Journal of Obstetrics and Diseases of Women and Children* 74:439–44.

Gilman, Charlotte Perkins. [1913] 1980. "Why I Wrote 'The Yellow Wallpaper.'" In *The Charlotte Perkins Gilman Reader,* edited by Ann J. Lane. New York: Pantheon Books.

Gilman, Richard. 1979. *Decadence: The Strange Life of an Epithet.* New York: Farrar, Straus and Giroux.

Gilman, Sander, ed. 1976. *The Faces of Madness: Hugh W. Diamond and the Origin of Psychiatric Photography.* New York: Brunner/Mazel.

———. 1982. *Seeing the Insane.* Lincoln: University of Nebraska Press.

———. 1985. *Difference and Pathology.* Ithaca, N.Y.: Cornell University Press.

———. 1988. *Disease and Representation: Images of Illness from Madness to AIDS.* Ithaca, N.Y.: Cornell University Press.

———. 1995. *Picturing Health and Illness: Images of Identity and Difference.* Baltimore: Johns Hopkins University Press.

Gittings, R. 1968. *Keats.* London: Penguin.

Goethe, J. W. von [1774] 1892. *The Sorrows of Young Werther.* Trans. anon. Boston, Mass.: Dana Estes.

———. [1774] 1984. *The Sorrows of Young Werther and Novella.* Translated by Elizabeth Mayer and Louise Bogan. With a foreword by W. H. Auden. New York: Modern Library.

————. [1774] 1988. *The Sorrows of Werther: Elective Affinities: Travels in Italy.* Translated by Victor Lange and Judith Ryan. With an introduction by David Wellbery. New York: Suhrkamp.

Goodwin, F. K., and Kay Redfield Jamison. 1990. *Manic-Depressive Illness.* New York: Oxford University Press.

Gosling, F. G. 1987. *Before Freud: Neurasthenia and the American Medical Community, 1870–1910.* Urbana: University of Illinois Press.

Gosse, E. 1891. *Gossip in the Library.* London: William Heinemann.

Griesinger, W. 1867. *Mental Pathology and Therapeutics.* Translated by C. Lockhart Robertson and James Rutherford. London: The New Sydenham Society.

————. [1867] 1965. *Mental Pathology and Therapeutics.* Facsimile of the English edition of 1867, translated by C. Lockhart Robertson and James Rutherford. New York: Hafner.

Griffiths, P. E. 1989. "The Degeneration of the Cognitive Theory of Emotions." *Philosophical Psychology* 2:227–313.

Hamilton, M. 1982. "Symptoms and Assessment of Depression." In *Handbook of Affective Disorders,* edited by E. S. Paykel, 3–11. New York: Guilford Press.

Hartung, C., and T. Widiger. 1998–99. "Gender Differences in the Diagnosis of Mental Disorders: Conclusions and Controversies of DSM-IV." *Psychological Bulletin,* in press.

Hildegard of Bingen, Saint. 1994. *Book of Holistic Healing.* Edited by M. Palmquist and J. Kulas. Collegeville, Minn.: Liturgical Press.

Hill, D. 1968. "Depression: Disease, Reaction, or Posture?" *American Journal of Psychiatry* 125:445–57.

Hippocrates. 1923. *Works of Hippocrates.* 4 vols. Translated and edited by W. H. S. Jones and E. T. Withington. Cambridge, Mass.: Harvard University Press.

Howell, Elizabeth, Marjorie Bayes, eds. 1981. *Women and Mental Health.* New York: Basic Books.

Hunter, R., and I. Macalpine. 1970 *Three Hundred Years of Psychiatry, 1535–1860.* New York: Oxford University Press.

Irigaray, Luce. 1991. *The Irigaray Reader.* Edited with an introduction by Margaret Whitford. Oxford: Blackwell.

Jack, Dana. 1991. *Silencing the Self: Women and Depression.* Cambridge, Mass.: Harvard University Press.

Jackson, Stanley. 1983. "Melancholia and Partial Insanity." *Journal of the History of Behavioral Science* 19: 173–84.

————. 1986. *Melancholia and Depression.* New Haven, Conn.: Yale University Press.

James, William. 1902. *The Varieties of Religious Experience: A Study in Human Nature.* New York: Modern Library.

Jamison, Kay Redfield. 1993. *Touched with Fire: Manic-Depressive Illness and the Artistic Temperament.* New York: Simon and Schuster.

————. 1995. *An Unquiet Mind: A Memoir of Moods and Madness.* New York: Alfred A. Knopf.

Johnson, Samuel. [1755] 1805. *Dictionary of the English Language in Which the Words Are Deduced from their Originals, and Illustrated in Their Different Significations by Examples from the Best Writers.* 9th ed., 4 vols. London: Longman, Hurst, Rees, and Orme.

Kandel, E. R. 1998. "A New Intellectual Framework for Psychiatry." *American Journal of Psychiatry,* 155, no. 4:457–69.

Kant, I. [1793] 1978. *Anthropology from a Pragmatic Point of View.* Translated by Victor Lyle Dowdell, revised and edited by Hans H. Rudnick. Carbondale: Southern Illinois University Press.

Keats, John. 1904. *The Poems of John Keats.* London: J. M. Dent.

————. [1819] 1978. "Ode on Melancholy." In *The Poems of John Keats,* edited by Jack Stillinger. Cambridge, Mass.: Belknap Press of Harvard University Press.

————. [1818] 1979. "Sonnet on Darkness," or "What the Thrush Said." In *The Poems of John Keats,* edited by Jack Stillinger. Cambridge, Mass.: Belnap Press, Harvard University Press.

Kendell, R. E., and J. F. Brockington. 1980. "The Identification of Disease Entities and the Relationship between Schizophrenic and Affective Psychoses." *British Journal of Psychiatry* 135:324–31.

Kendell, R. E., and J. Gourley. 1970. "The Distinction between the Affective Psychoses and Schizophrenia." *British Journal of Psychiatry* 117:261–70.

Klein, D. F. 1974. "Endogenomorphic Depression." *Archives of General Psychiatry* 31:447–54.

Klein, Melanie. 1940/1975. *Love, Guilt, and Reparation and Other Works.* London: Hogarth.

Kleinman, Arthur. 1988. *Rethinking Psychiatry: From Cultural Category to Personal Experience.* New York: Free Press.

————. 1995. *Writing in the Margin.* Cambridge, Mass.: Harvard University Press.

Kleinman, A., and B. Good, eds. 1985. *Culture and Depression: Studies in the Anthropology and Cross-Cultural Psychiatry of Affect and Disorder.* Berkeley: University of California Press.

Klerman, G., and M. Weissman. 1989. "Increasing Rates of Depression." *Journal of the American Medical Association* 261:2229–35.

Klibansky, Raymond, Erwin Panofsky and Fritz, Saxl. 1964. *Saturn and Melancholy: Studies in the History of Natural Philosophy, History, and Art.* New York: Basic Books.

Kraepelin, E. 1883. *Compendium der Psychiatrie.* Leipzig: Abel. [First edition of what later became *Lehruch der Psychiatrie.*]

————. 1887. *Textbook of Psychiatry,* 6th ed. Leipzig: Abel.

————. 1904. *Lectures on Clinical Psychiatry.* Authorized translation. New York: Hafner.

————. 1920. *Manic-Depressive Illness.* Translated by Mary Barclay and edited by George Robinson from the 8th edition of the *Textbook of Psychiatry* (1909–15). Edinburgh: E&S Livingstone.

————. *Memoirs.* Berlin: Springer-Verlag.

Kristeva, Julia. 1982. *Powers of Horror: An Essay in Abjection.* Translated by Leon Roudiez. New York: Columbia University Press.

————. 1989. *Black Sun: Depression and Melancholy.* Translated by Leon Roudiez. New York: Columbia University Press.

Kuhn, Reinhard. 1987. *The Demon of Noontide: Ennui in Western Literature.* Princeton, N.J.: Princeton University Press.

Laycock, Thomas. 1840. *A Treatise on Nervous Diseases of Women.* London: Longman, Orme, Brown, Green and Longmans.

Lepenies, Wolf. 1992. *Melancholy and Society.* Translated by Jeremy Gaines and Doris Jones. Cambridge, Mass.: Harvard University Press.

Levitt, E. E., B. Lubin, and J. Brooks. 1983. *Depression: Concepts, Controversies, and Some New Facts.* 2d ed. Hillsdale, N.J.: Laurence Erlbaum.

Lewis, Aubrey. 1934. "Melancholia: A Critical Survey of Depressive States." *Journal of Mental Science* 80:277–378.

Lloyd, G. 1984. *The Man of Reason: "Male" and "Female" in Western Philosophy.* Minneapolis: University of Minnesota Press.

Lombroso, Cesare. 1864. *Genio e Follia.* Milan: Chiusi.

Lunbeck, E. 1994. *The Psychiatric Persuasion: Knowledge, Gender, and Power in Modern America.* Princeton, N.J.: Princeton University Press.

Lutz, C. 1985. "Depression and the Translation of Emotional Worlds." In *Culture and Depression: Studies in the Anthropology and Cross-Cultural Psychiatry of Affect* and Disorder, edited by A. Kleinman and B. Good, 63–100. Berkeley: University of California Press.

———. 1986. "Emotion, Thought, and Estrangement: Emotion as Cultural Category." *Cultural Anthropology* 1:287–309.

Maser, Edward A., ed. 1971. *Cesare Ripa: Baroque and Rococo Pictorial Imagery: The 1758–60 Hertel Edition of Ripa's "Iconologia" with Two Hundred Engraved Illustrations*. Translated by Edward A. Maser. New York: Dover.

Mather, Cotton. 1972. *The Angel of Bethesda*. Edited with an introduction by Gordon Jones. Barre, Mass.: American Antiquarian Society and Barre Publishers.

Maudsley, H. 1867. *The Physiology and Pathology of the Mind*. New York: Appleton.

McDonald, M. 1981. *Mystical Bedlam: Madness, Anxiety, and Healing in Seventeenth-Century England*. Cambridge: Cambridge University Press.

Mercier, C. 1982. A *Dictionary of Psychological Medicine in Two Volumes*. Edited by D. Hack Tuke. Philadelphia: P. Blackiston.

Miller, Jean Baker. 1976. *Toward a New Psychology of Women*. Boston: Beacon Press.

Milton, John. [1631] 1965. *The Complete Poetical Works of John Milton*. Edited by Douglas Bush. Boston: Houghton Mifflin.

Nguyen, Van Nghi. 1991. *Huangdi neijing*. Marseille: Ed. N.V.N.

Parker, G., and Dusan Hadzi-Pavlovic, eds. 1996. *Melancholia: A Disorder of Movement and Mood*. Cambridge: Cambridge University Press.

Paykel, E. S. 1991. "Depression in Women." *British Journal of Psychiatry* 1958:22–29.

Petrarch [1342] 1911. *Secretum*. Translated by William Draper. London: Chatto and Windrush.

Pinel, Philippe. 1806. *A Treatise on Insanity, in Which are Contained the Principles of New and More Practical Nosology of Maniacal Disorders Than Has Yet Been Offered to the Public*. Translated by D. D. Davis. Sheffield: W. Todd.

Pope, Alexander. [1714] 1963. "The Rape of the Lock." In *Pope*. The Laurel Poetry Series, edited by Richard Wilbur. New York: Dell.

Praz, Mario. 1968. *The Romantic Agony*. Translated from the Italian by Angus Davidson. New York: Meridian Books.

Radden, Jennifer. 1987. "Melancholy and Melancholia." In *Pathologies of the Modern Self: Postmodern Studies in Narcissism, Schizophrenia, and Depression*, edited by David Michael Levin, 231–50. New York: New York University Press.

———. 1996a. *Divided Minds and Successive Selves: Ethical Issues in Disorders of Identity and Personality*. Cambridge, Mass.: MIT Press.

———. 1996b. "Lumps and Bumps: Kantian Faculty Psychology, Phrenology, and Twentieth-Century Psychiatric Classification." *Philosophy, Psychiatry and Psychology* 3, no. 1:1–14.

Real, Terrence. 1997. *I Don't Want to Talk about It*. Cambridge, Mass.: Harvard University Press.

Ribot, T. 1881. *Maladies de la Memoire*. Paris.

———. 1883. *Maladies de la Volonte*. Paris.

———. 1885. *Maladies de la Personnalite*. Paris.

Ripa, C. 1971. *Baroque and Rococo Pictorial Imagery*. New York: Dover.

Rush, Benjamin. 1812. *Medical Inquiries and Observations upon the Diseases of the Mind*. Philadelphia: Kimber & Richardson.

Russell, Denise. 1995. *Women, Madness and Medicine*. Cambridge, England: Polity Press.

Sartre, Jean-Paul. 1948. *The Emotions: Outline of a Theory*. Translated by B. Frechtman. New York: Philosophical Library.

Schiesari, Juliana. 1992. *The Gendering of Melancholia: Feminism, Psychoanalysis, and the Symbolics of Loss in Renaissance Literature*. Ithaca, N.Y.: Cornell University Press.

Screech, M. A. 1983. *Montaigne and Melancholy*. Selinsgrove, Pa.: Susquehanna University Press.

Scull, Andrew. 1979. *Museums of Madness: The Social Organization of Insanity in Nineteenth-Century England*. New York: St. Martin's.

———. 1998. Interview by Emily Eakin for the article "Who's Afraid of Elaine Showalter? The MLA President Incites Mass Hysteria." *Lingua Franca*, September, 28–36.

Scull, Andrew, Charlotte MacKenzie, and Nicholas Hervey. 1996. *Masters of Bedlam: The Transformation of the Mad-Doctoring Trade*. Princeton, N.J.: Princeton University Press.

Seligman, M. 1975. *Helplessness: On Depression, Development, and Death*. New York: W. H. Freeman.

Sena, John. 1980. *A Bibliography of Melancholy*. London: Nether Press.

Shah, Mazhar. 1966. "Life and Work of Avicenna." In *The General Principles of Avicenna's Canon of Medicine*. Karachi, Pakistan: Naveed Clinic Press.

Showalter, Elaine. 1985. *The Female Malady*. New York: Random House.

Shweder, Richard. 1985. "Menstrual Pollution, Soul Loss, and the Comparative Study of Emotions." In *Culture and Depression: Studies in Anthropology and Cross-cultural Psychiatry of Affect and Disorder*, edited by Arthur Kleinman and Byron Good, 182–215. Berkeley: University of California Press.

Simon, Bennett. 1978. *Mind and Madness in Ancient Greece: The Classical Roots of Modern Psychiatry*. Ithaca, N.Y.: Cornell University Press.

Siraisi, N. 1987. *Avicenna in Renaissance Italy: The Canon and Medical Teaching in Italian Universities after 1500*. Princeton, N.J.: Princeton University Press.

Skultans, V. 1979. *English Madness: Ideas on Insanity, 1580–1890*. London: Routledge and Kegan Paul.

Slavney, P. R., and P. R. McHugh. 1987. *Psychiatric Polarities*. Baltimore: Johns Hopkins University Press.

Smiles. S. [1859] 1862. *Self-help: Character, Conduct and Perseverance*. New York: A. L. Burt.

Solomon, R. 1977. *The Passions*. New York: Doubleday Anchor.

Spinoza, B. 1992. *Ethics*. Translated by Samuel Shirley and edited by Seymour Feldman. Indianapolis: Hackett.

Sprenger, J. and H. Kramer. [1487] 1928. *Malleus Maleficarum*. Translated by Montague Summers. Reprint, New York: Benjamin Blom, 1970.

Taylor, G. 1996. "Deadly Vices?" In *How Should One Live? Essays on the Virtues*, edited by Roger Crisp. Oxford: Clarendon Press.

Teresa of Avila, Saint. [1577] 1985. *The Interior Castle*. Translated by Kieran Kavanaugh, O.C.D., and Otilio Rodriguez, O.C.D. In *The Collected Works of St. Teresa of Avila*. Washington, D.C.: Institute of Carmelite Studies.

———. [1610] 1985. *The Book of Foundations*. Translated by Kieran Kavanaugh, O.C.D., and Otilio Rodriguez, O.C.D. In *The Collected Works of St. Teresa of Avila*. Washington, D.C.: Institute of Carmelite Studies.

Turski, G. 1994. *Toward a Rationality of the Emotions*. Athens, Ohio University Press.

Virchow, R. [1858] 1971. *Cellular Pathology as Based upon Physiological and Pathological Histology*. Translated by Frank Chance. New York: Dover.

Weir Mitchell, S. 1877. *Fat and Blood and How to Make Them*. Philadelphia: Lippincott.

Weyer, Johann. [1562] 1991. *Of Deceiving Demons*. Translated by John Shea in the series Witches, Devils and Doctors in the Renaissance, edited by George Mora. With an Introduction by John Weber. Binghampton, N.Y.: Medieval and Renaissance Texts and Studies.

Willis, Thomas. 1672. *Two Discourses Concerning the Souls of Brutes*. Translated by S. Pordage. London: T. Dring, C. Harper and J. Leigh.

Wittkower, R., and M. Wittkower. 1963. *Born under Saturn: The Character and Conduct of Artists: A Documented History from Antiquity to the French Revolution*. London: Weidenfeld and Nicholson.

Wollstonecraft, M. [1792] 1988. *A Vindication of the Rights of Women.* 2d ed. Edited by Carol Poston. New York: W. W. Norton.

World Health Organization. 1991. *International Classification of Disease.* 10th edition. New York: World Health Organization.

Wyman, Rufus. 1830. "A Discourse on Mental Philosophy as Connected with Mental Disease, Delivered before the Massachusetts Medical Society, Boston." Reprinted in R. Hunter and I. Macalpine, *Three Hundred Years of Psychiatry, 1535–1860,* 810–11. London: Oxford University Press, 1970.

Zilboorg, G., and G. W. Henry. 1941. *A History of Medical Psychology.* New York: W. W. Norton.

Credits

Chapter 25. Acknowledgment is made to Sigmund Freud © Copyrights, The Institute of Psycho-Analysis and the Hogarth Press for permission to quote from *The Standard Edition of the Complete Psychological Works of Sigmund Freud*. Translated and edited by James Strachey. London: Random House, 1950.

Chapter 26. Reprinted with the permission of the publisher from *Melanie Klein: Love, Guilt and Reparation and Other Works, 1921–1945*. London: The Hogarth Press, 1975.

Chapter 27. From *Helplessness: On Depression, Development, and Death* by Martin E. P. Seligmen. Copyright © 1992 by Martin E. P. Seligman. Used with permission of W. H. Freeman and Company.

Chapter 28. Reprinted with the permission of the publisher from *Aaron T. Beck: Cognitive Therapy and Emotional Disorders*. Pages 103–111. Madison, Ct.: International Universities Press, 1975.

Chapter 29. Reprinted with the permission of the Beacon Press, Boston, from *Toward a New Psychology of Women* by Jeanne Baker Miller. Copyright © 1976 by Jeanne Baker Miller.

Chapter 30. From *Black Sun: Depression and Melancholy* by Julia Kristeva. Copyright © 1992 Columbia University Press. Reprinted with the permission of the publisher.

Chapter 31. Reprinted with permission of the publisher from *Goodwin and Jamison: Manic-Depressive Illness*. New York: Oxford University Press, 1990.

FIGURES

Figure 1. William Hogarth's engraving *Bedlam,* the eighth plate from *A Rake's Progress* (1735/1763), is reproduced with permission from The Royal Collection. Copyright © Her Majesty Queen Elizabeth II.

Figure 2. Augsburg Calender, Rar. 498 (*Melancholics*), is reproduced with permission from the Bayerische Staatsbibliothek, Munich.

Figure 3. Lucas Cranach the Elder's *Melancholy, An Allegory* (oil, 1532), photographed by Hans Petersen, is reproduced with permission from Statens Museum for Kunst, Copenhagen.

Figure 5. Eugène Delacroix's Tasso in the House of the Insane (oil, 1839) is reproduced with permission from the Oskar Reinhart Collection, "Am Romerholz," Winterhur, Switzerland.

Figure 6. Permission is granted to reproduce Albrecht Dürer's *Melencholia I* (1514). Engraving #57.122. Bequest of William P. Chapman Jr., Class of 1895. The Herbert F. Johnson Museum of Art, Cornell University.

Fihure 7. Pieter Breughel's *Desidia* (drawing, 1557) is reproduced with permission from the Graphische Sammlung Albertina, Vienna.

Figure 10. Hugh Diamond's *Portrait of a Woman Suffering Suicidal Melancholy* (photograph, 1856) is reproduced with permission from The Royal Society, London.

Figure 11. C. D. Friedrich's *The Monk by the Sea* (oil, 1809–10) is reproduced with permission of Bildarchiv Preussischer Kulturbesitz, Berlin.

Figure 12. Permission is granted to reproduce Edvard Munch's *Melancholy* (*Evening*) (woodcut, 1896). Munch Museum, Oslo. Photograph copyright © Munch Museum (Svein Andersen/Sidsel de Jong).

Figure 13. Permission is granted by artist to reproduce Sue Miller's *Tree* (1997).

Figure 14. Permission is granted to reproduced Théodore Géricault's *Insane Woman* (*Envy*) (oil, 1821–24). Musée des Beaux-Arts de Lyon

Figure 16. Permission is granted to reproduce Cesare Ripa's *Malinconia* (637.g.26) (1603). The British Library, London.

Figure 17. Alain Chartier's *Melancholy and Reason* (1565) is reproduced with permission from The Peirpont Morgan Library, New York (MS.M.438.f.1).

Index

neurasthenia, 43

nosology. *See* classification of mental disorders

objects
    internal and external, 300–301, 303, 304, 306–10
    loved and hated, 300–304, 306–10

partial insanity, 5, 22, 39, 204–205, 211, 213, 246, 249, 252, 255, 258

partial intellectual derangement. *See* partial insanity

periodic insanity. *See* circular insanity

Petrarch, 71

phlegm. *See* humors

phrenology, 25–26

post-partum depression, 43

preobject. *See* Thing

Prichard, James C., 241

Primary Verrucktheit, 224

psychiatric classification. *See* classification of mental disorders

psychicists, 223

psychopharmacological bridge, 346, 351–52

puerperal insanity. *See* post-partum depression

relational idividualism, 326

Romanticism, 15, 30, 32–33, 47, 181–82, 219–20, 235–36, 232

sacred disease. *See* epilepsy

sadness. *See* fear and sadness

Saturn. *See* astrology

sauda, 76. *See also* smoky vapor

self-hatred. *See* self-loathing

self-help movement, 235–36

self-loathing, 44–46, 48–49

self-murder. *See* suicide

sloth, 19, 20, 70–71

smoky vapor, 67, 76, 88, 90, 121–22, 124, 125, 158

social constructionism. *See* cultural constructionism

somaticists, 25, 223

somatism. *See* somatists

spleen, x, 12, 16, 62–63, 66, 78, 92, 122, 126, 140, 143, 151, 158, 168, 171, 172, 178

suicide, 59, 195–96, 162, 164, 195, 196, 201, 209, 210, 253, 254, 257, 270, 278, 289, 290, 323

symbolic unity, 9, 10

Symbolism, viii, 231

tædium vitæ, 114, 144–45, 210, 217

Thing, 335, 337–39

Tri-guna (three inherent qualities of nature), x

tristimania, 5, 39, 212–15

tristitia (dejection, sadness, sorrow), 19, 71

"unitary psychosis" hypothesis, 28, 224

"unreason," 21, 198

vapors, the, 168, 170

vegetative signs. *See* signs

volitional disorders, 275

Wertherism, 42, 235–37

Willis, Thomas, 162

wine, analogies with, 59, 92, 176

witches/witchcraft, viii, 95–96, 101, 104–105, 161, 162–63, 253

yellow bile. *See* humors